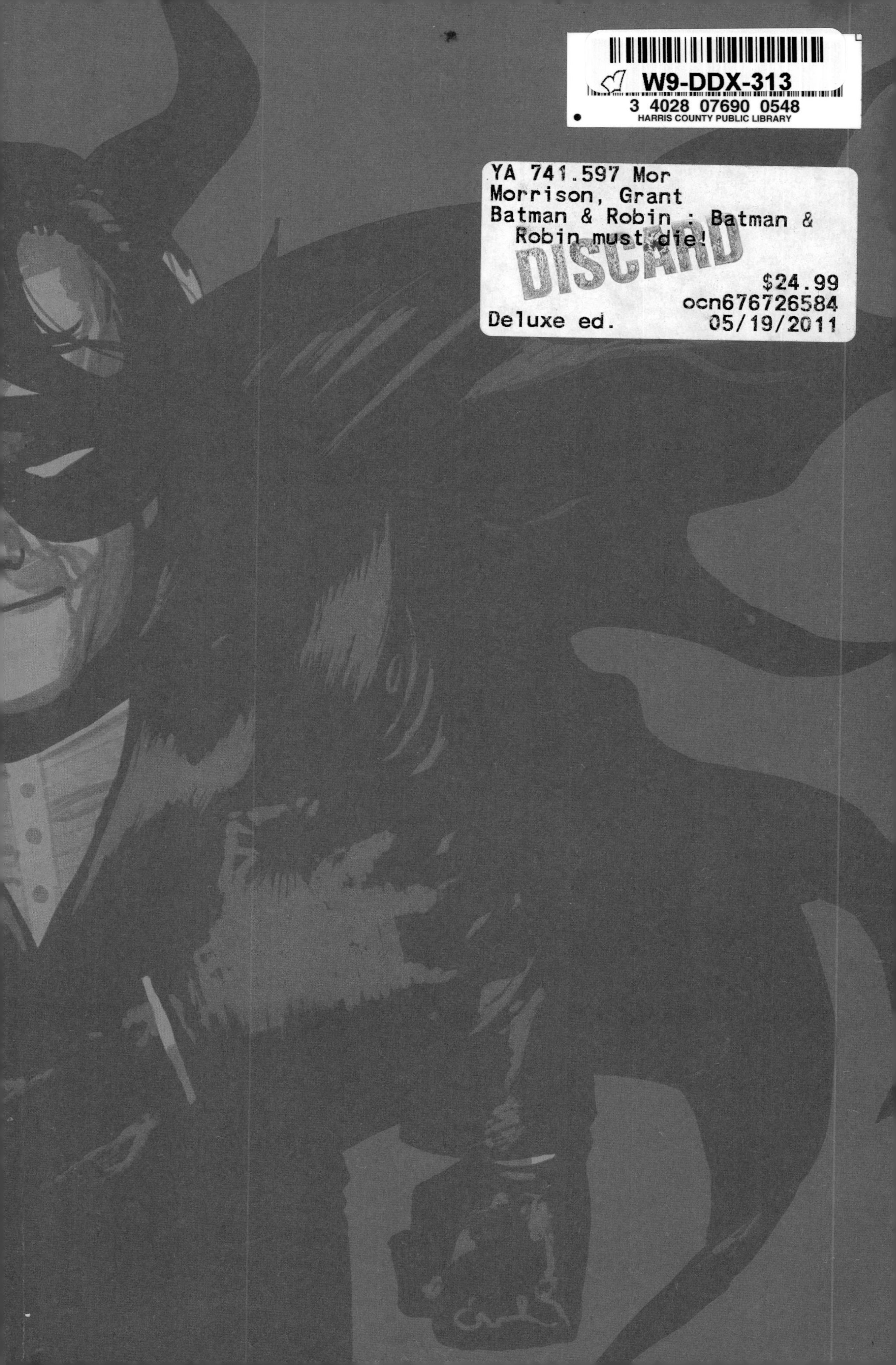

BATMAN & ROBIN

THE DELUXE EDITION

BATMAN & ROBIN MUST DIE!

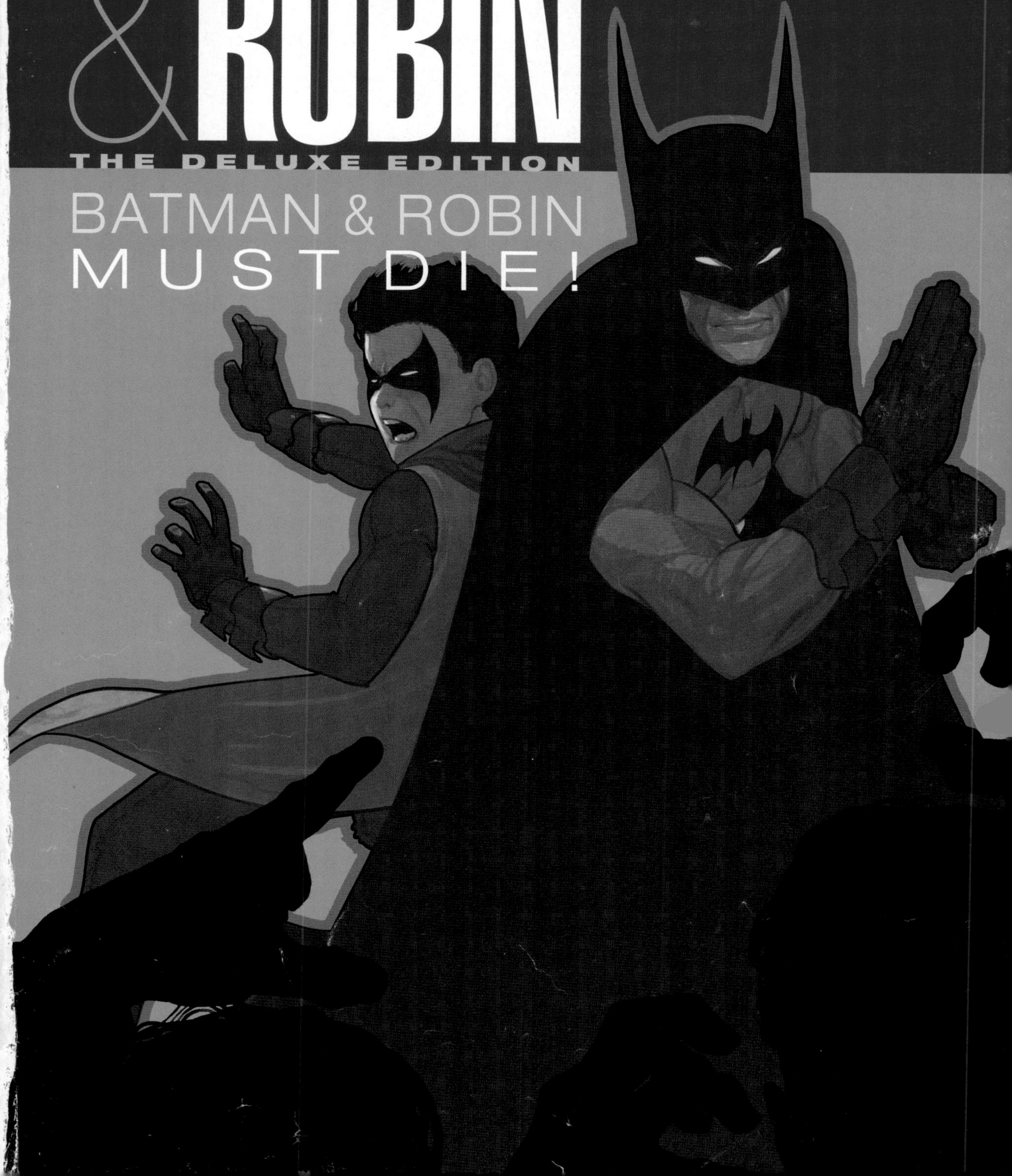

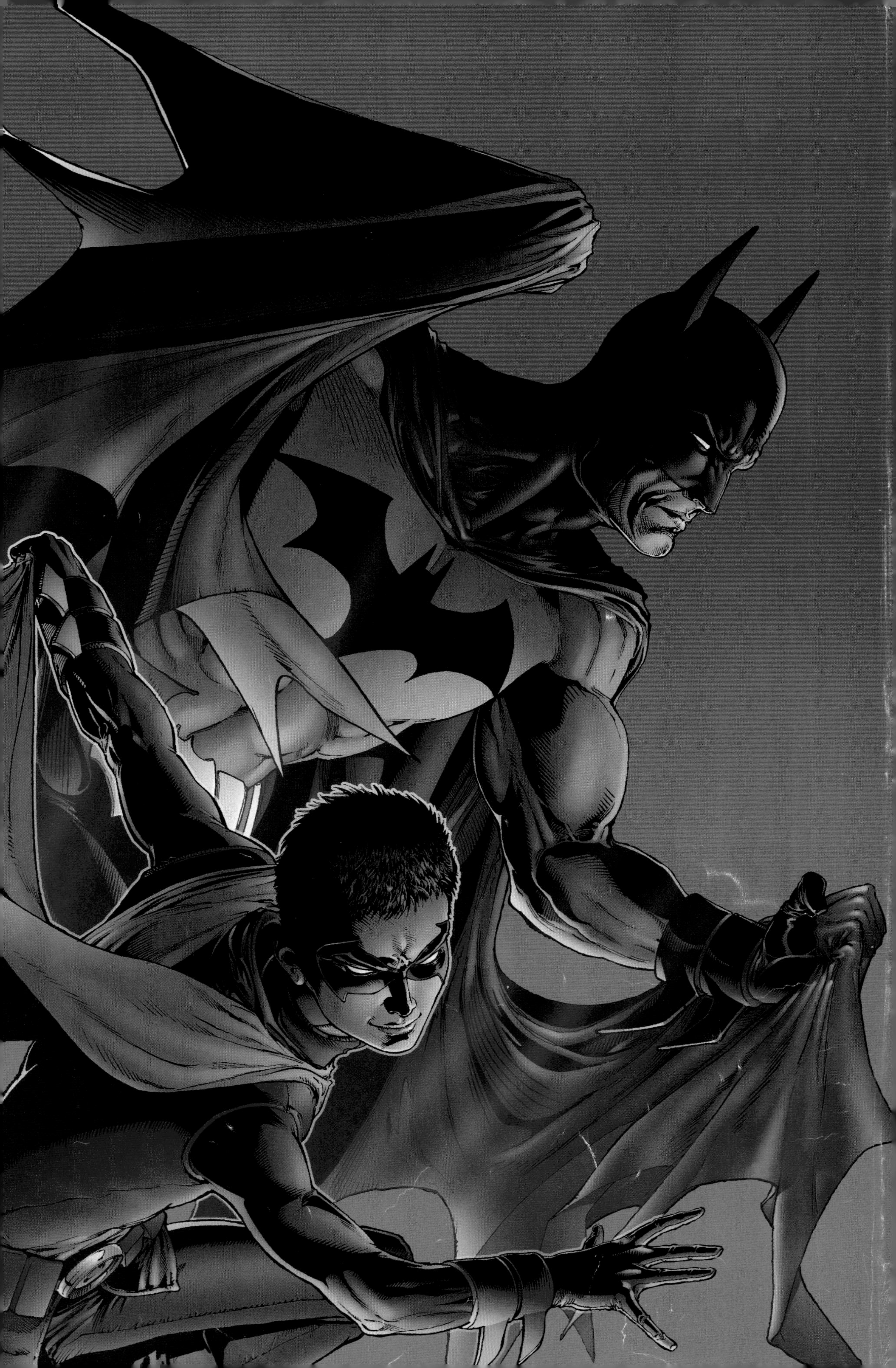

BATMAN & ROBIN

THE DELUXE EDITION

BATMAN & ROBIN MUST DIE!

written by
grant morrison

art by
frazer irving
david finch
cameron stewart
chris burnham
batt
ryan wynn

colored by
alex sinclair
peter steigerwald

lettered by
patrick brosseau
dave sharpe

cover art by
frank quitely

original series cover art by
frank quitely
frazer irving
ethan van sciver
david finch
scott williams
gene ha

batman created by **bob kane**

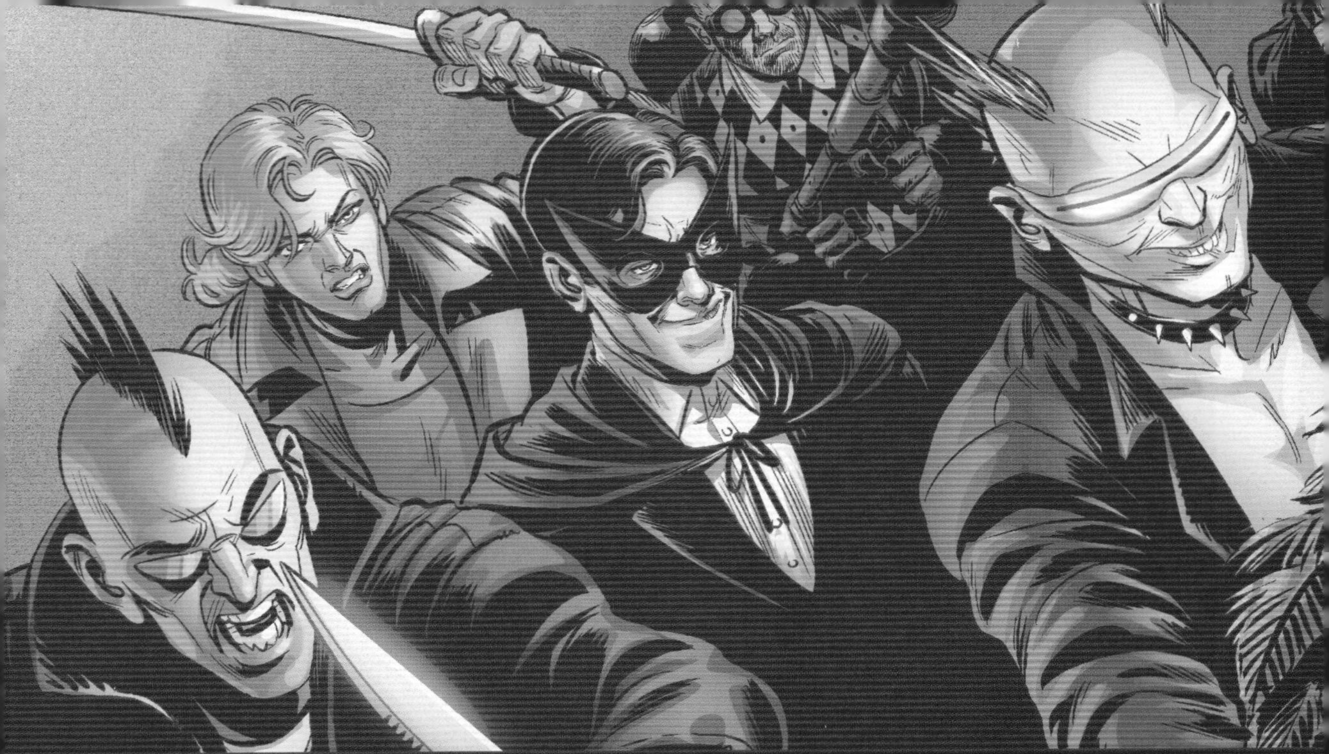

MIKE MARTS Editor - Original Series
JANELLE SIEGEL Assistant Editor - Original Series
BOB HARRAS Group Editor - Collected Editions
SCOTT NYBAKKEN Editor
ROBBIN BROSTERMAN Design Director - Books
CURTIS KING JR. Senior Art Director

DC COMICS
DIANE NELSON President
DAN DiDIO and JIM LEE Co-Publishers
GEOFF JOHNS Chief Creative Officer
PATRICK CALDON EVP – Finance and Administration
JOHN ROOD EVP – Sales, Marketing and Business Development
AMY GENKINS SVP - Business & Legal Affairs
STEVE ROTTERDAM SVP - Sales & Marketing
JOHN CUNNINGHAM VP - Marketing
TERRI CUNNINGHAM VP – Managing Editor
ALISON GILL VP – Manufacturing
DAVID HYDE VP – Publicity
SUE POHJA VP – Book Trade Sales
ALYSSE SOLL VP – Advertising and Custom Publishing
BOB WAYNE VP – Sales
MARK CHIARELLO Art Director

Cover color by Alex Sinclair.

BATMAN AND ROBIN: BATMAN AND ROBIN MUST DIE!—THE DELUXE EDITION

DC Comics, 1700 Broadway, New York, NY 10019.
A Warner Bros. Entertainment Company.
Printed by RR Donnelley,
Salem, VA, USA 4/8/11. First Printing.
ISBN: 978-1-4012-3091-3

SUSTAINABLE FORESTRY INITIATIVE
Certified Chain of Custody
Promoting Sustainable Forest Management
www.sfiprogram.org
Fiber used in this product line meets the sourcing requirements of the SFI program.
www.sfiprogram.org SGS-SFI/COC-US10/81072

CONTENTS

BATMAN & ROBIN

THE DELUXE EDITION

BATMAN & ROBIN MUST DIE!

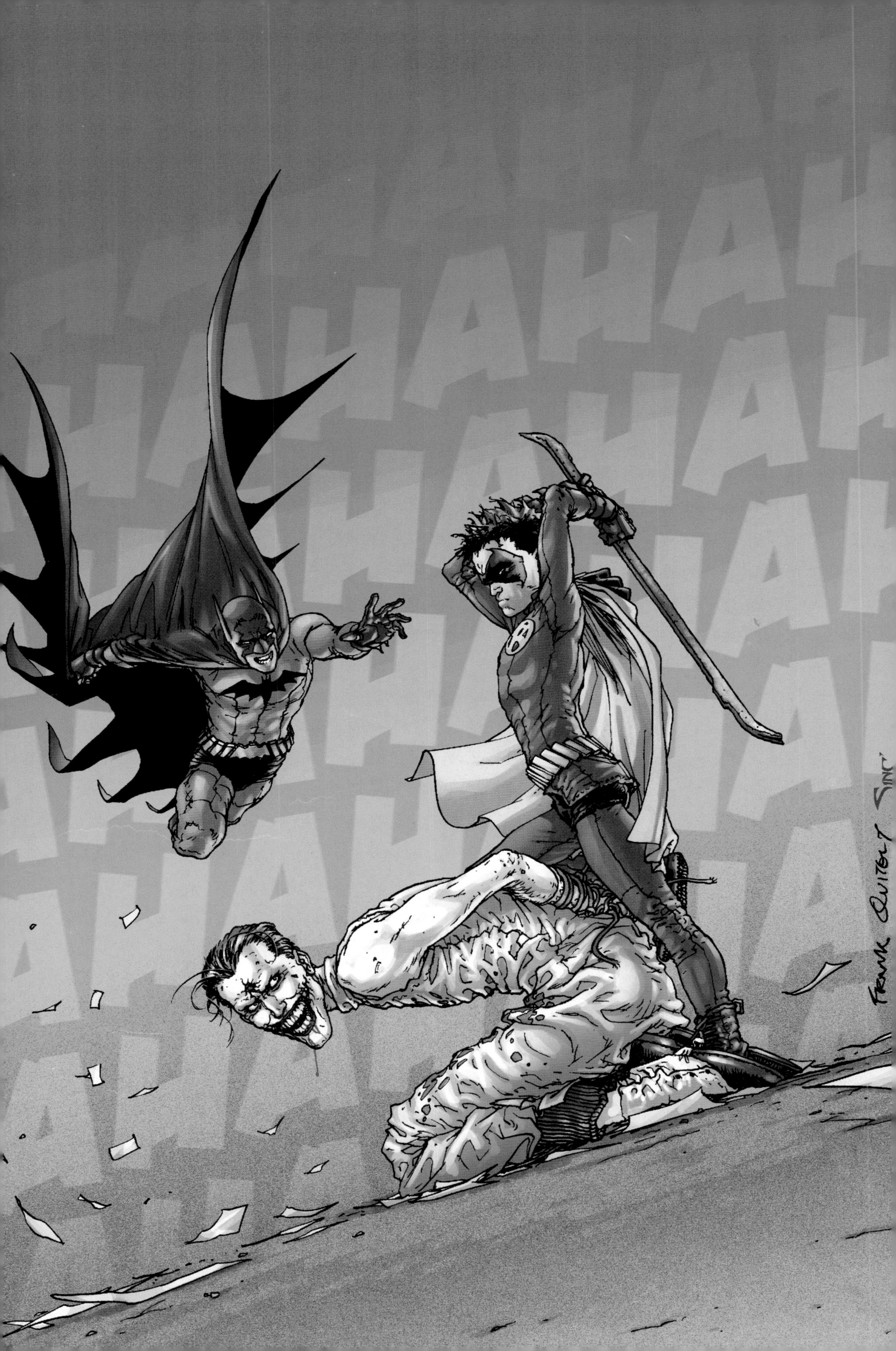

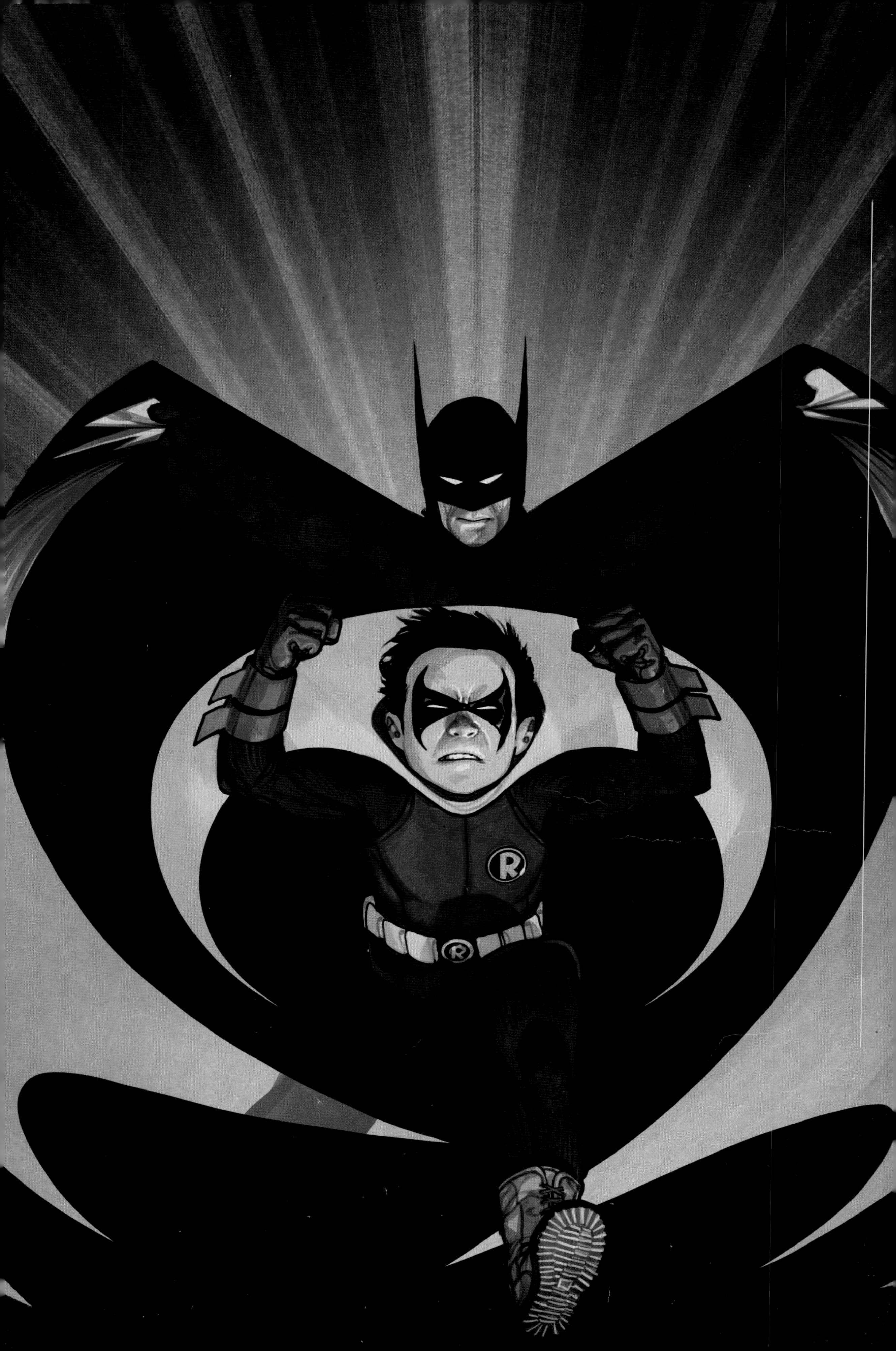

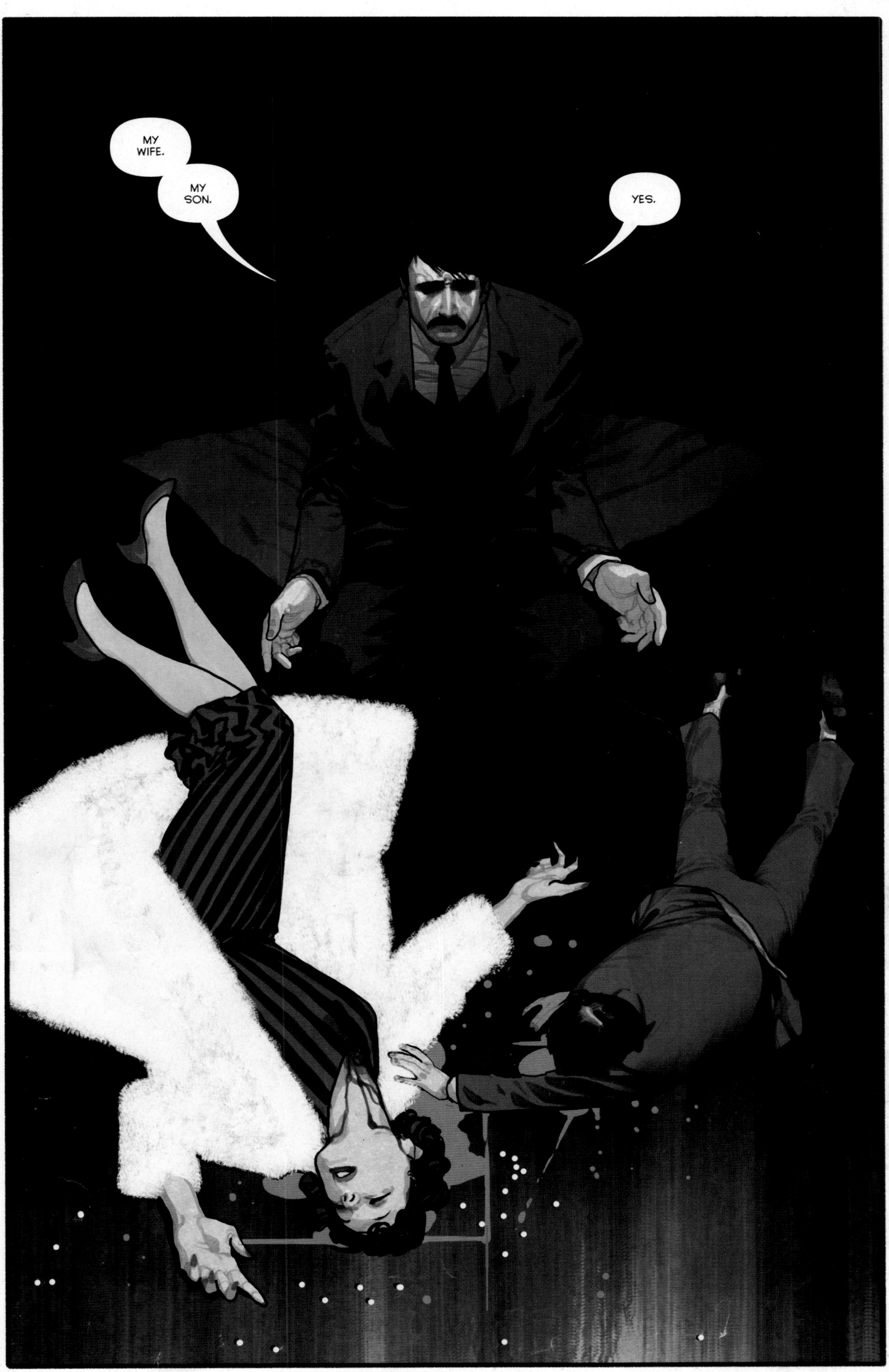
MY WIFE.
MY SON.
YES.

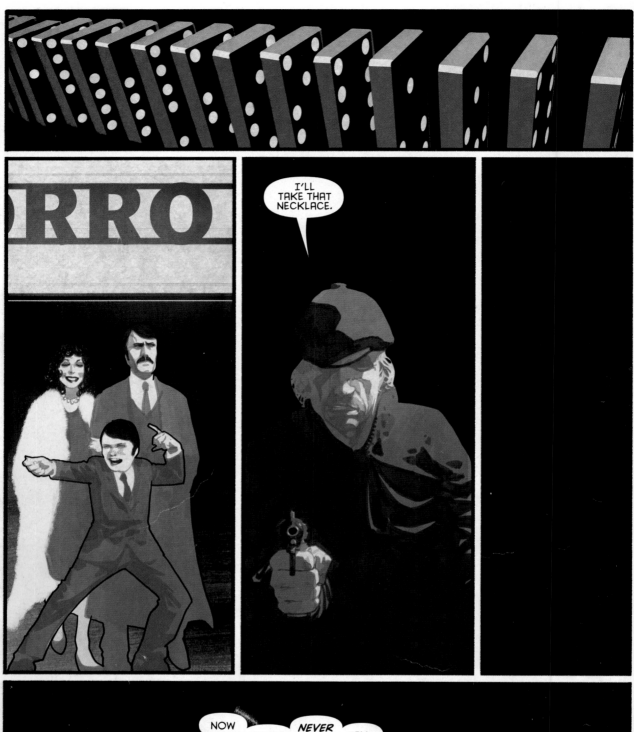

I'LL TAKE THAT NECKLACE.

NOW YOU'LL *NEVER* TELL.

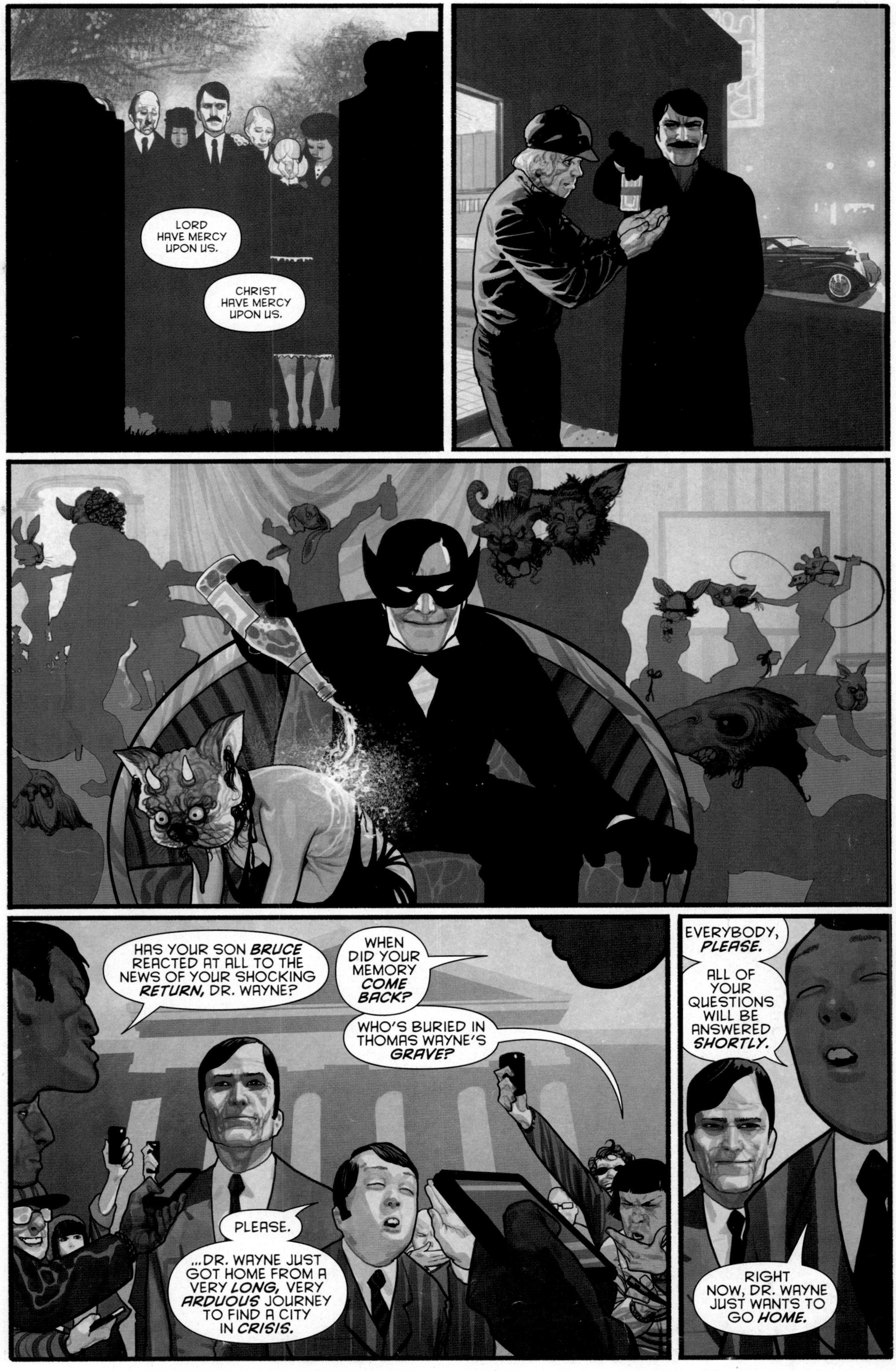
LORD HAVE MERCY UPON US.
CHRIST HAVE MERCY UPON US.
HAS YOUR SON BRUCE REACTED AT ALL TO THE NEWS OF YOUR SHOCKING RETURN, DR. WAYNE?
WHEN DID YOUR MEMORY COME BACK?
WHO'S BURIED IN THOMAS WAYNE'S GRAVE?
PLEASE.
...DR. WAYNE JUST GOT HOME FROM A VERY LONG, VERY ARDUOUS JOURNEY TO FIND A CITY IN CRISIS.
EVERYBODY, PLEASE.
ALL OF YOUR QUESTIONS WILL BE ANSWERED SHORTLY.
RIGHT NOW, DR. WAYNE JUST WANTS TO GO HOME.

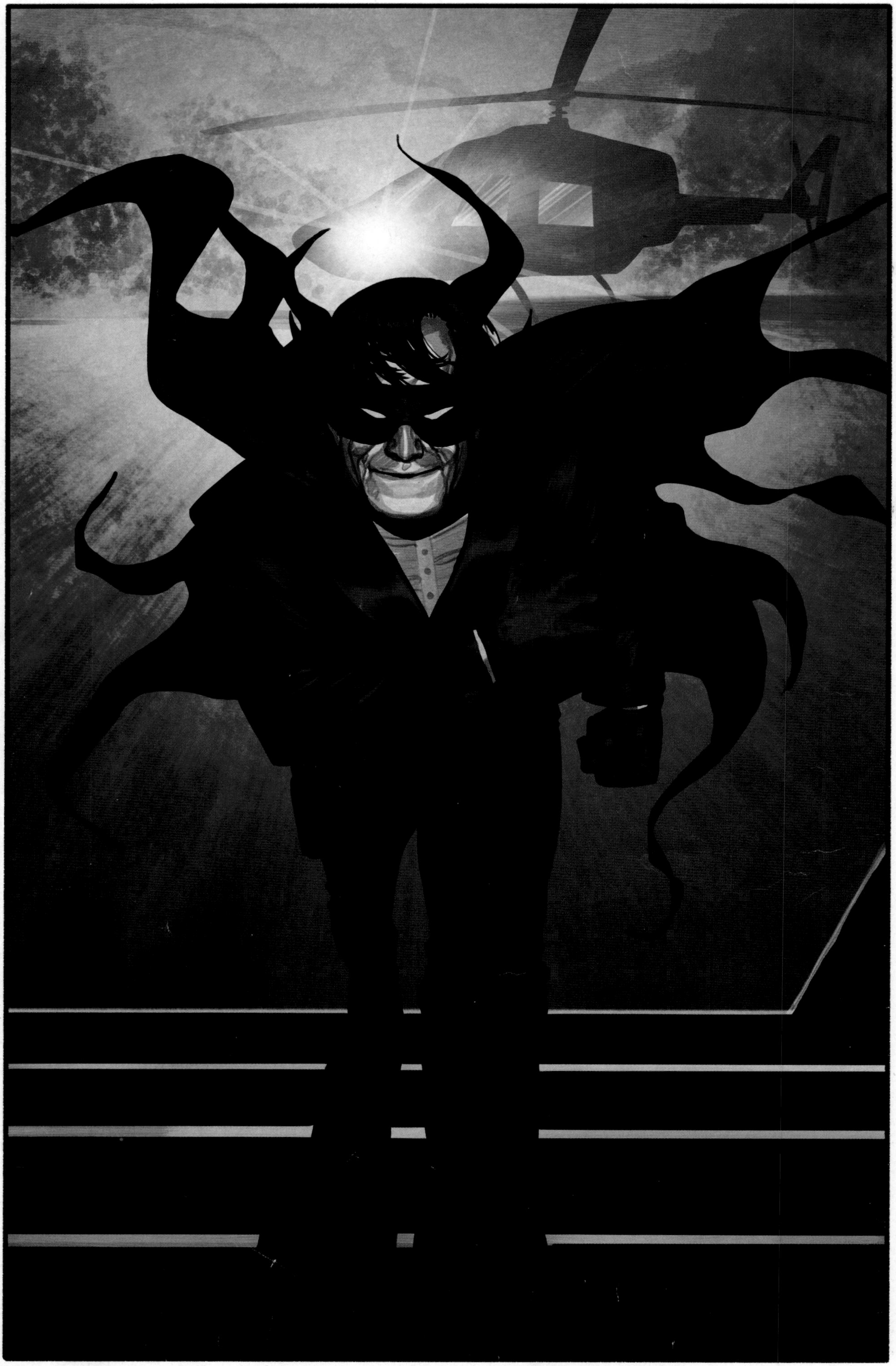

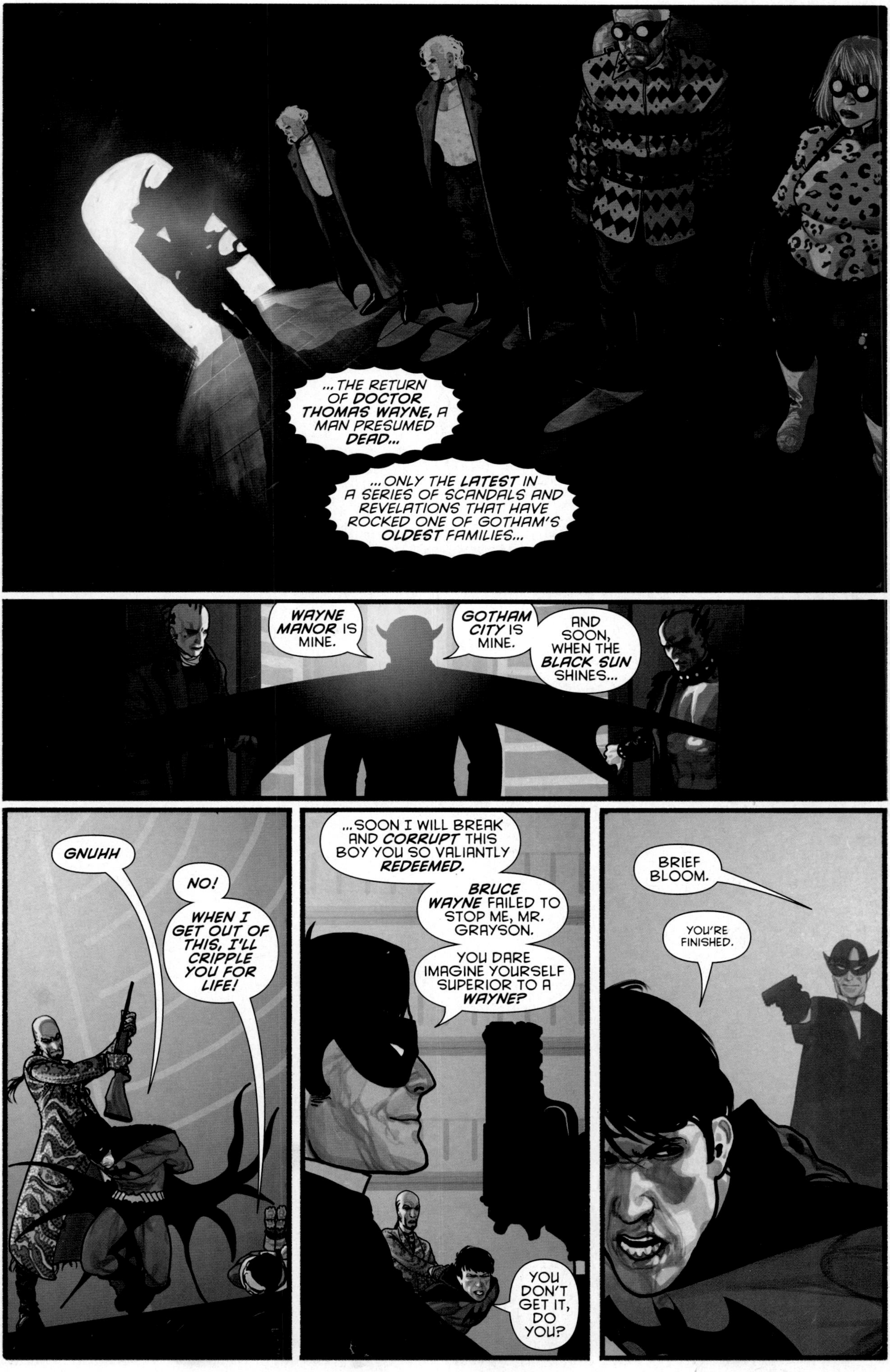
...THE RETURN OF DOCTOR THOMAS WAYNE, A MAN PRESUMED DEAD...
...ONLY THE LATEST IN A SERIES OF SCANDALS AND REVELATIONS THAT HAVE ROCKED ONE OF GOTHAM'S OLDEST FAMILIES...
WAYNE MANOR IS MINE.
GOTHAM CITY IS MINE.
AND SOON, WHEN THE BLACK SUN SHINES...
GNUHH
NO!
WHEN I GET OUT OF THIS, I'LL CRIPPLE YOU FOR LIFE!
...SOON I WILL BREAK AND CORRUPT THIS BOY YOU SO VALIANTLY REDEEMED.
BRUCE WAYNE FAILED TO STOP ME, MR. GRAYSON.
YOU DARE IMAGINE YOURSELF SUPERIOR TO A WAYNE?
YOU DON'T GET IT, DO YOU?
BRIEF BLOOM.
YOU'RE FINISHED.

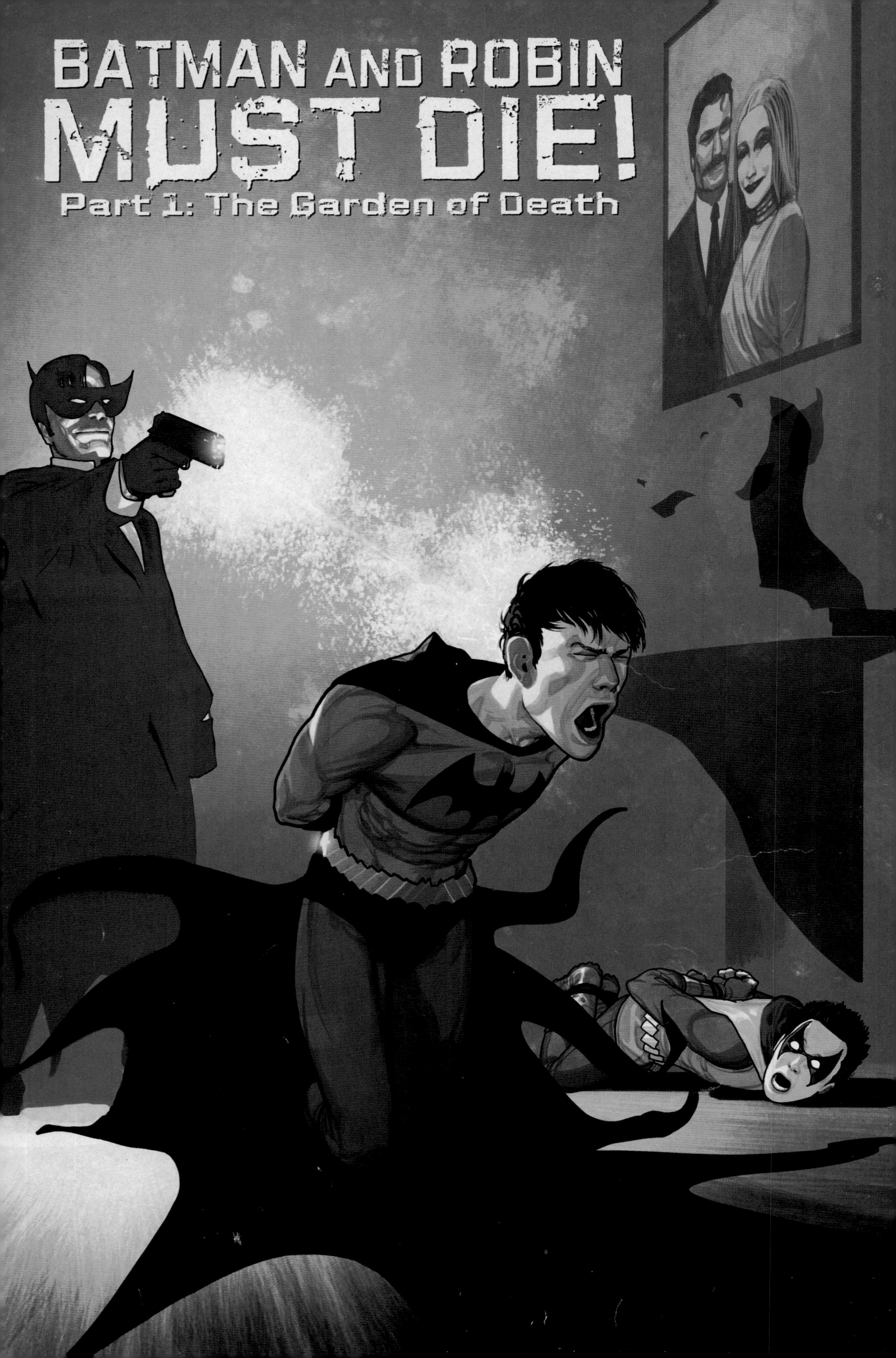
BATMAN AND ROBIN
MUST DIE!
Part 1: The Garden of Death

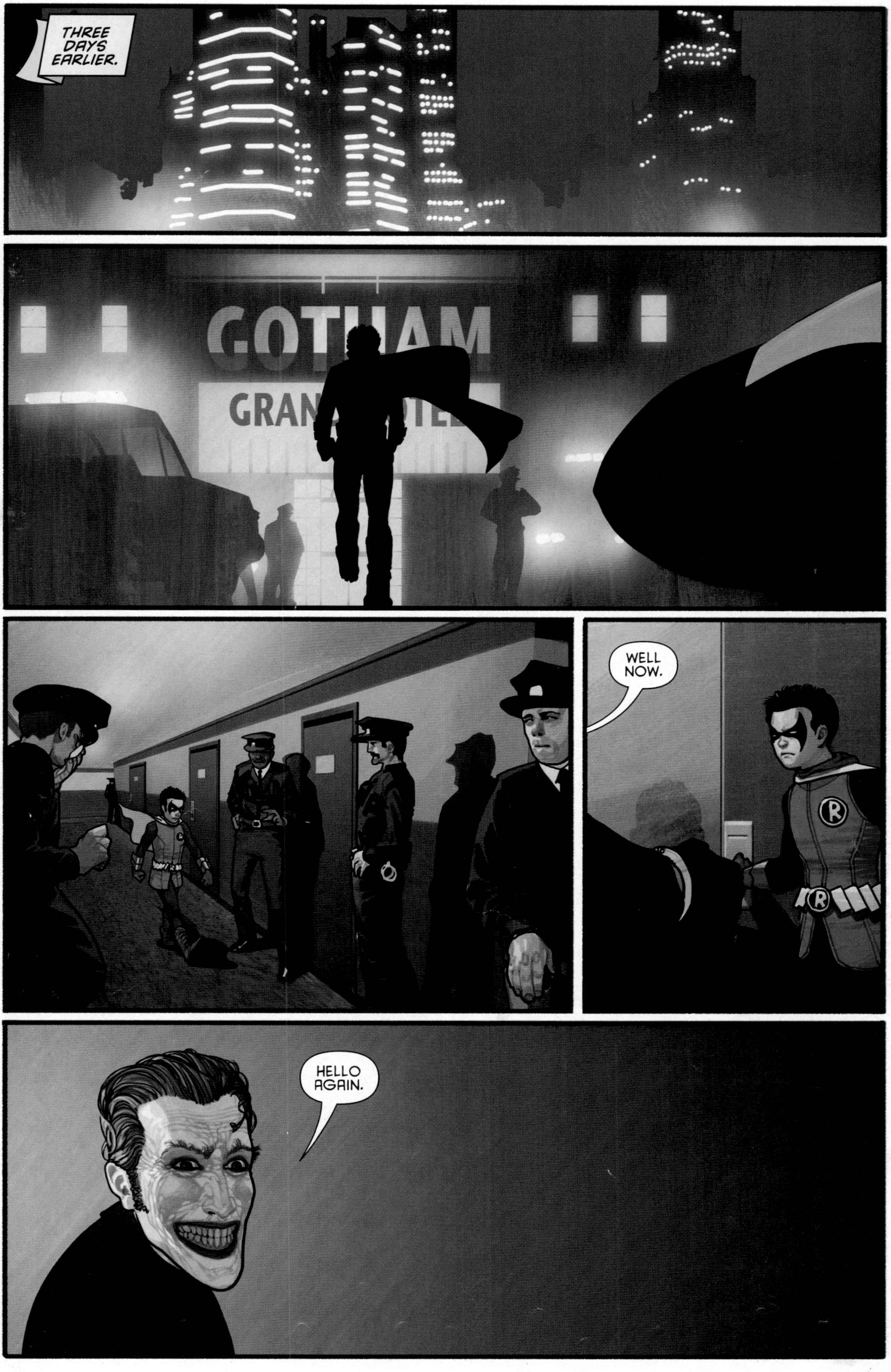
THREE DAYS EARLIER.
GOTHAM
GRAN
WELL NOW.
HELLO AGAIN.

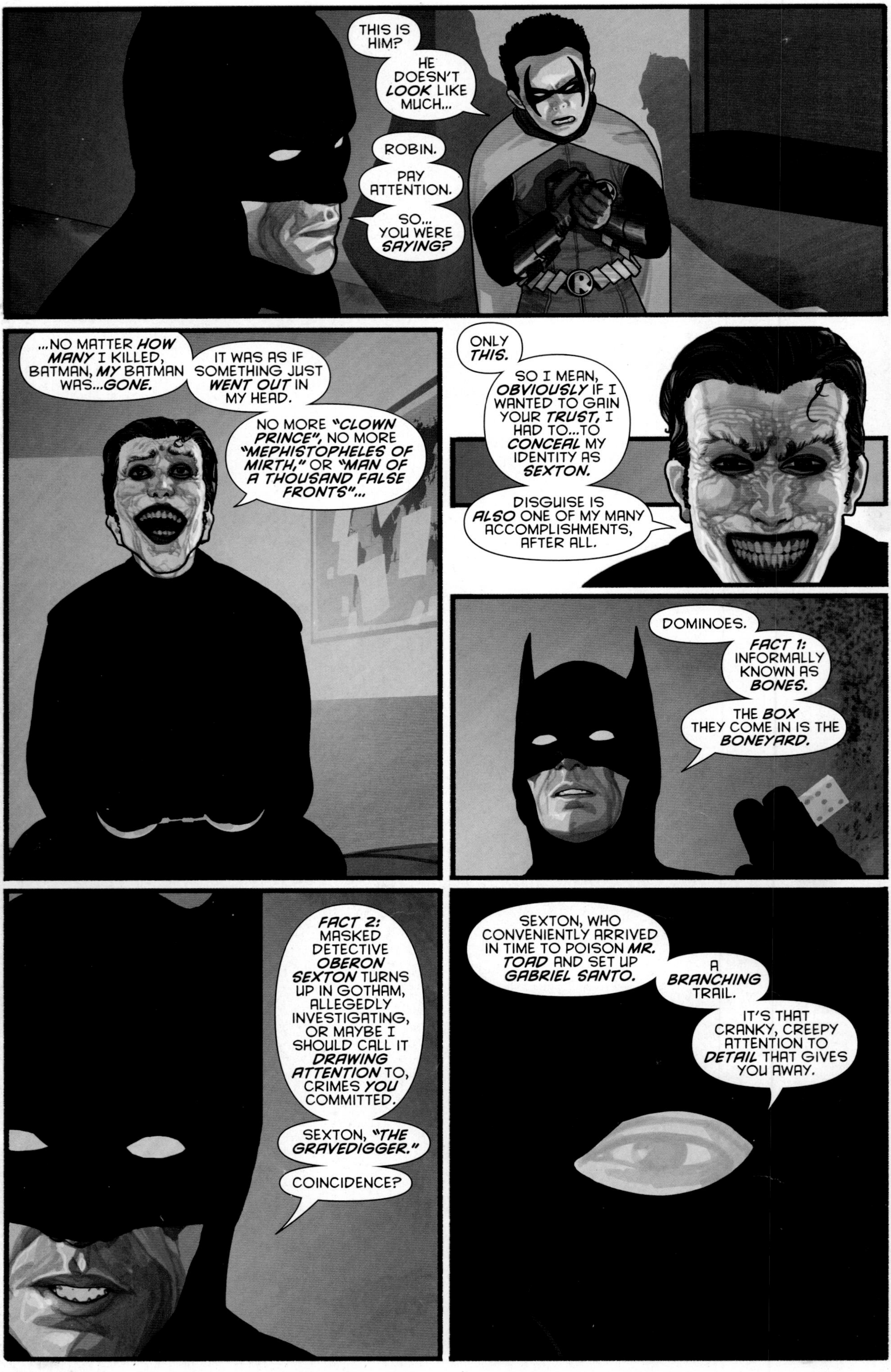
THIS IS HIM?
HE DOESN'T LOOK LIKE MUCH...
ROBIN.
PAY ATTENTION.
SO... YOU WERE SAYING?
...NO MATTER HOW MANY I KILLED, BATMAN, MY BATMAN WAS...GONE.
IT WAS AS IF SOMETHING JUST WENT OUT IN MY HEAD.
NO MORE "CLOWN PRINCE", NO MORE "MEPHISTOPHELES OF MIRTH," OR "MAN OF A THOUSAND FALSE FRONTS"...
ONLY THIS.
SO I MEAN, OBVIOUSLY IF I WANTED TO GAIN YOUR TRUST, I HAD TO...TO CONCEAL MY IDENTITY AS SEXTON.
DISGUISE IS ALSO ONE OF MY MANY ACCOMPLISHMENTS, AFTER ALL.
DOMINOES.
FACT 1: INFORMALLY KNOWN AS BONES.
THE BOX THEY COME IN IS THE BONEYARD.
FACT 2: MASKED DETECTIVE OBERON SEXTON TURNS UP IN GOTHAM, ALLEGEDLY INVESTIGATING, OR MAYBE I SHOULD CALL IT DRAWING ATTENTION TO, CRIMES YOU COMMITTED.
SEXTON, "THE GRAVEDIGGER."
COINCIDENCE?
SEXTON, WHO CONVENIENTLY ARRIVED IN TIME TO POISON MR. TOAD AND SET UP GABRIEL SANTO.
A BRANCHING TRAIL.
IT'S THAT CRANKY, CREEPY ATTENTION TO DETAIL THAT GIVES YOU AWAY.

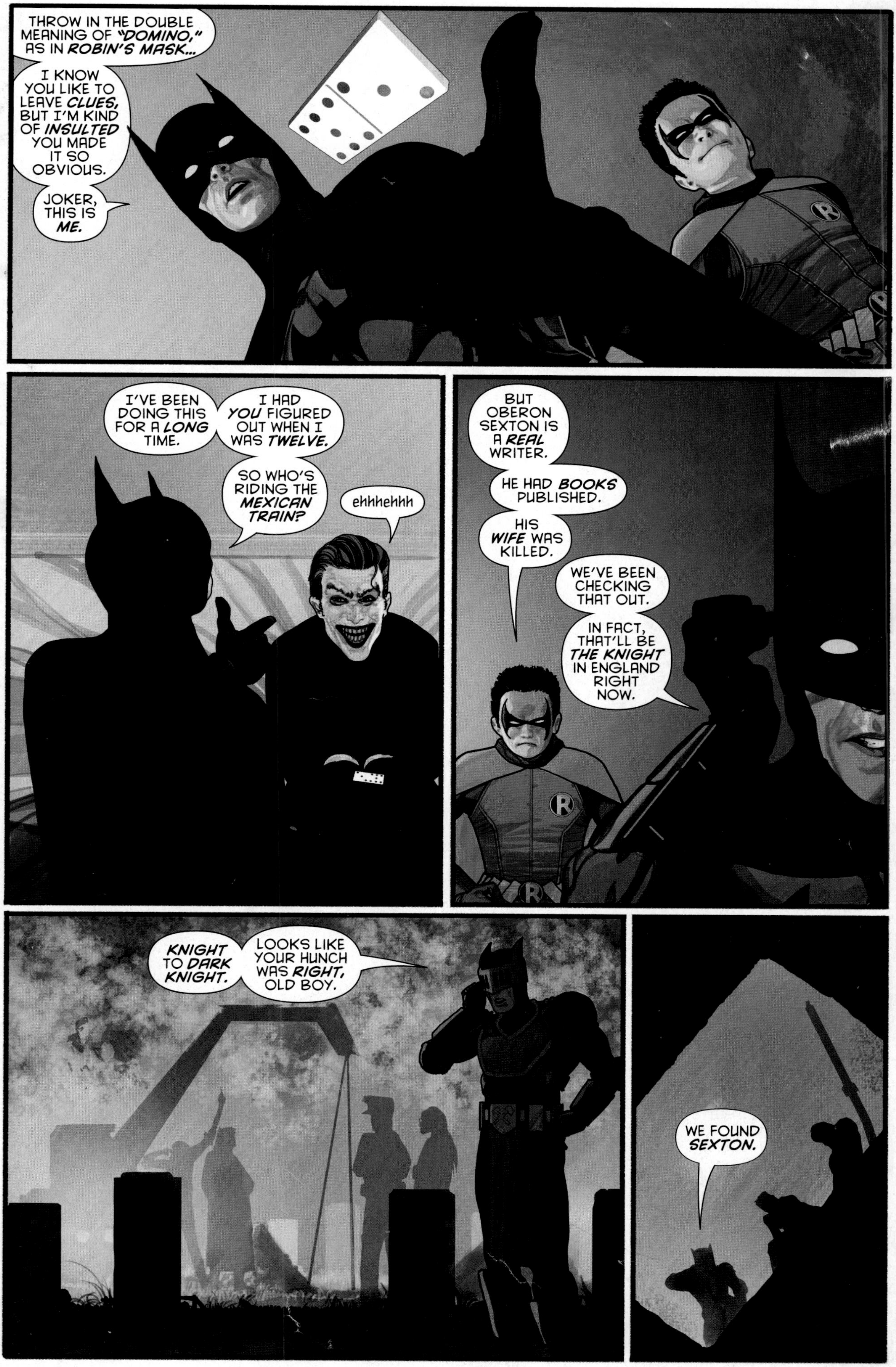
THROW IN THE DOUBLE MEANING OF "DOMINO," AS IN ROBIN'S MASK...
I KNOW YOU LIKE TO LEAVE CLUES, BUT I'M KIND OF INSULTED YOU MADE IT SO OBVIOUS.
JOKER, THIS IS ME.
I'VE BEEN DOING THIS FOR A LONG TIME.
I HAD YOU FIGURED OUT WHEN I WAS TWELVE.
SO WHO'S RIDING THE MEXICAN TRAIN?
ehhhehhh
BUT OBERON SEXTON IS A REAL WRITER.
HE HAD BOOKS PUBLISHED.
HIS WIFE WAS KILLED.
WE'VE BEEN CHECKING THAT OUT.
IN FACT, THAT'LL BE THE KNIGHT IN ENGLAND RIGHT NOW.
KNIGHT TO DARK KNIGHT.
LOOKS LIKE YOUR HUNCH WAS RIGHT, OLD BOY.
WE FOUND SEXTON.

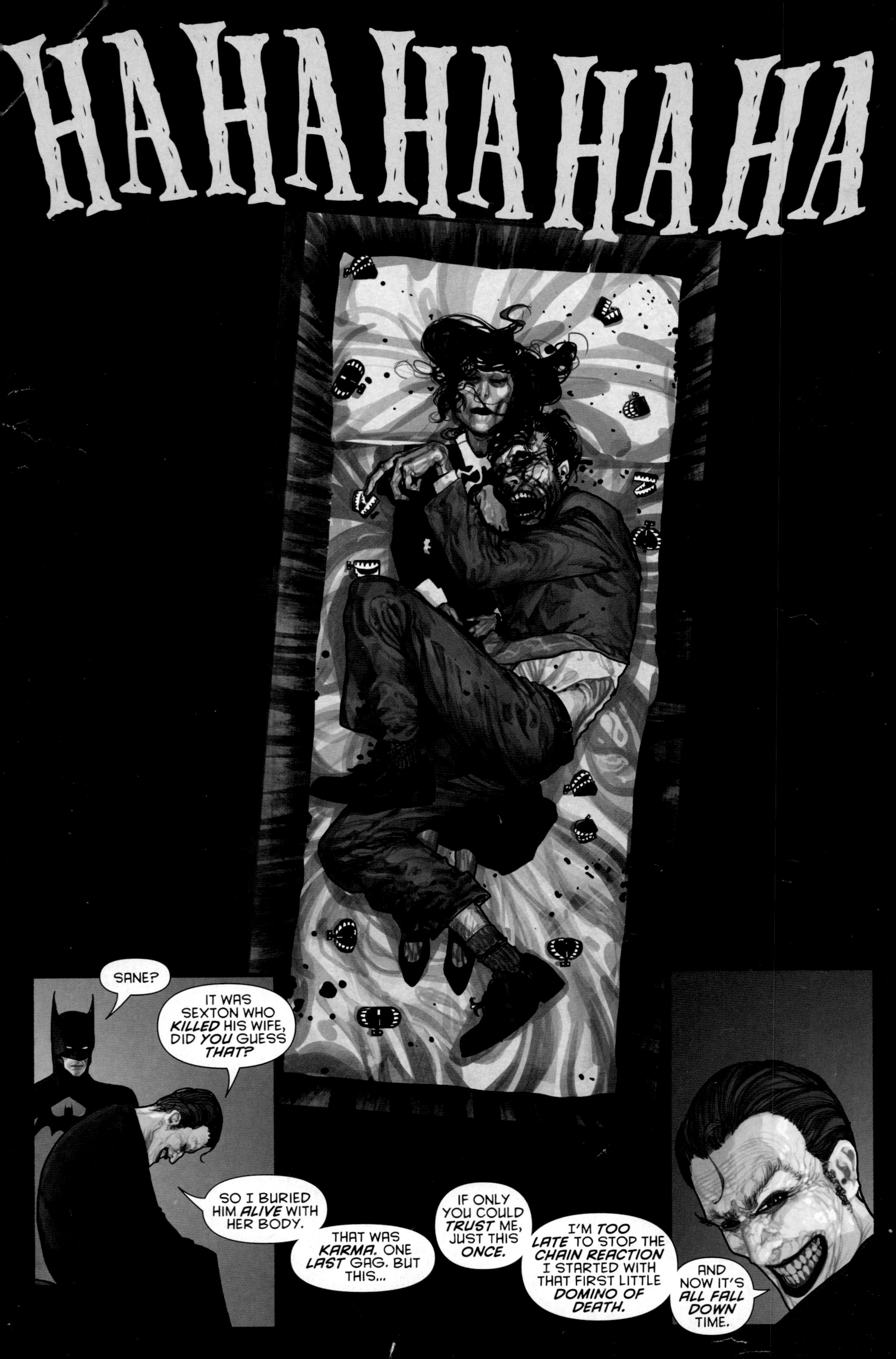
HAHAHAHAHAHAHA
SANE?
IT WAS SEXTON WHO KILLED HIS WIFE, DID YOU GUESS THAT?
SO I BURIED HIM ALIVE WITH HER BODY.
THAT WAS KARMA. ONE LAST GAG. BUT THIS...
IF ONLY YOU COULD TRUST ME, JUST THIS ONCE.
I'M TOO LATE TO STOP THE CHAIN REACTION I STARTED WITH THAT FIRST LITTLE DOMINO OF DEATH.
AND NOW IT'S ALL FALL DOWN TIME.

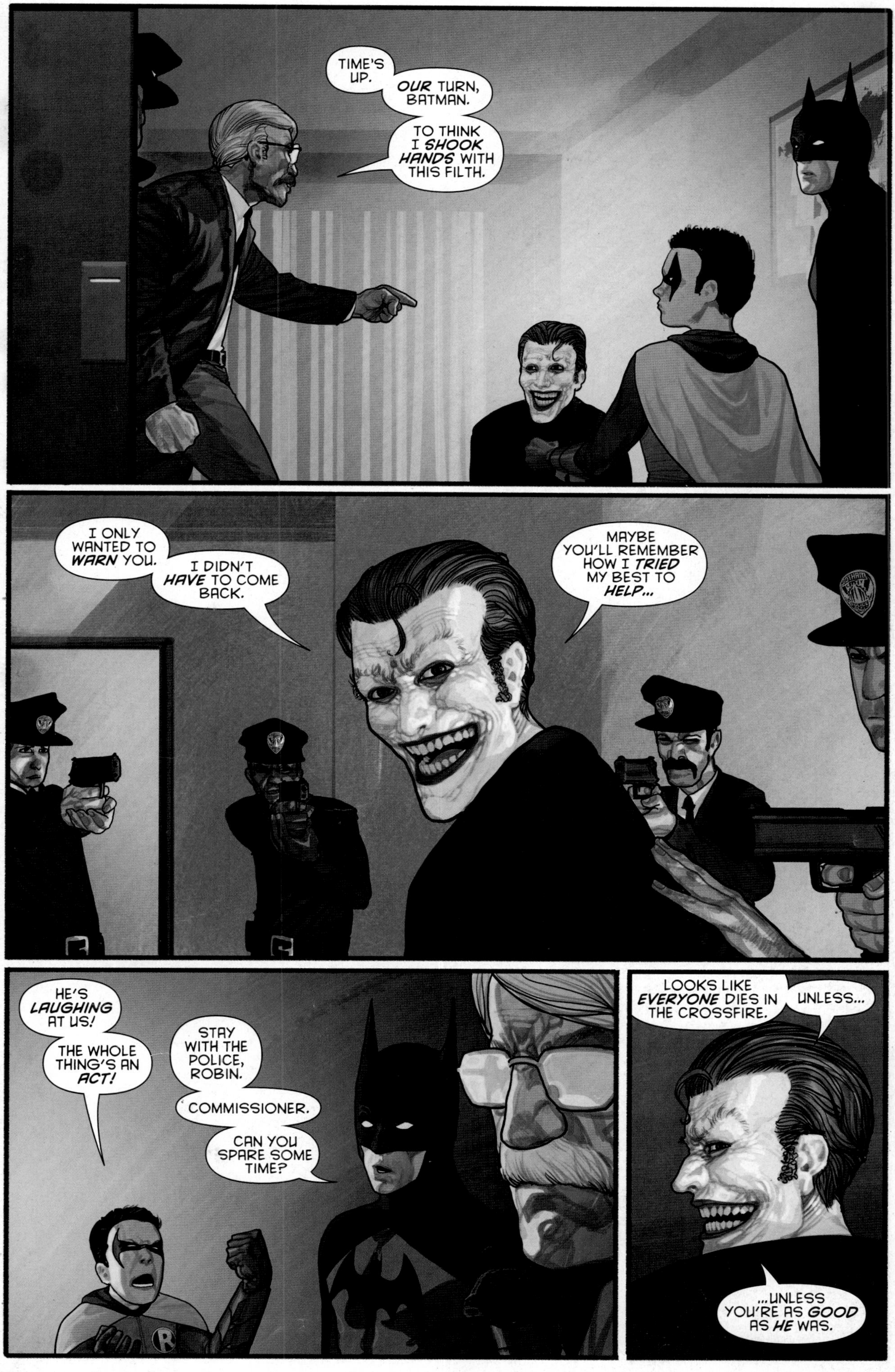

TIME'S UP.
OUR TURN, BATMAN.
TO THINK I SHOOK HANDS WITH THIS FILTH.
I ONLY WANTED TO WARN YOU.
I DIDN'T HAVE TO COME BACK.
MAYBE YOU'LL REMEMBER HOW I TRIED MY BEST TO HELP...
HE'S LAUGHING AT US!
THE WHOLE THING'S AN ACT!
STAY WITH THE POLICE, ROBIN.
COMMISSIONER.
CAN YOU SPARE SOME TIME?
LOOKS LIKE EVERYONE DIES IN THE CROSSFIRE.
UNLESS...
...UNLESS YOU'RE AS GOOD AS HE WAS.

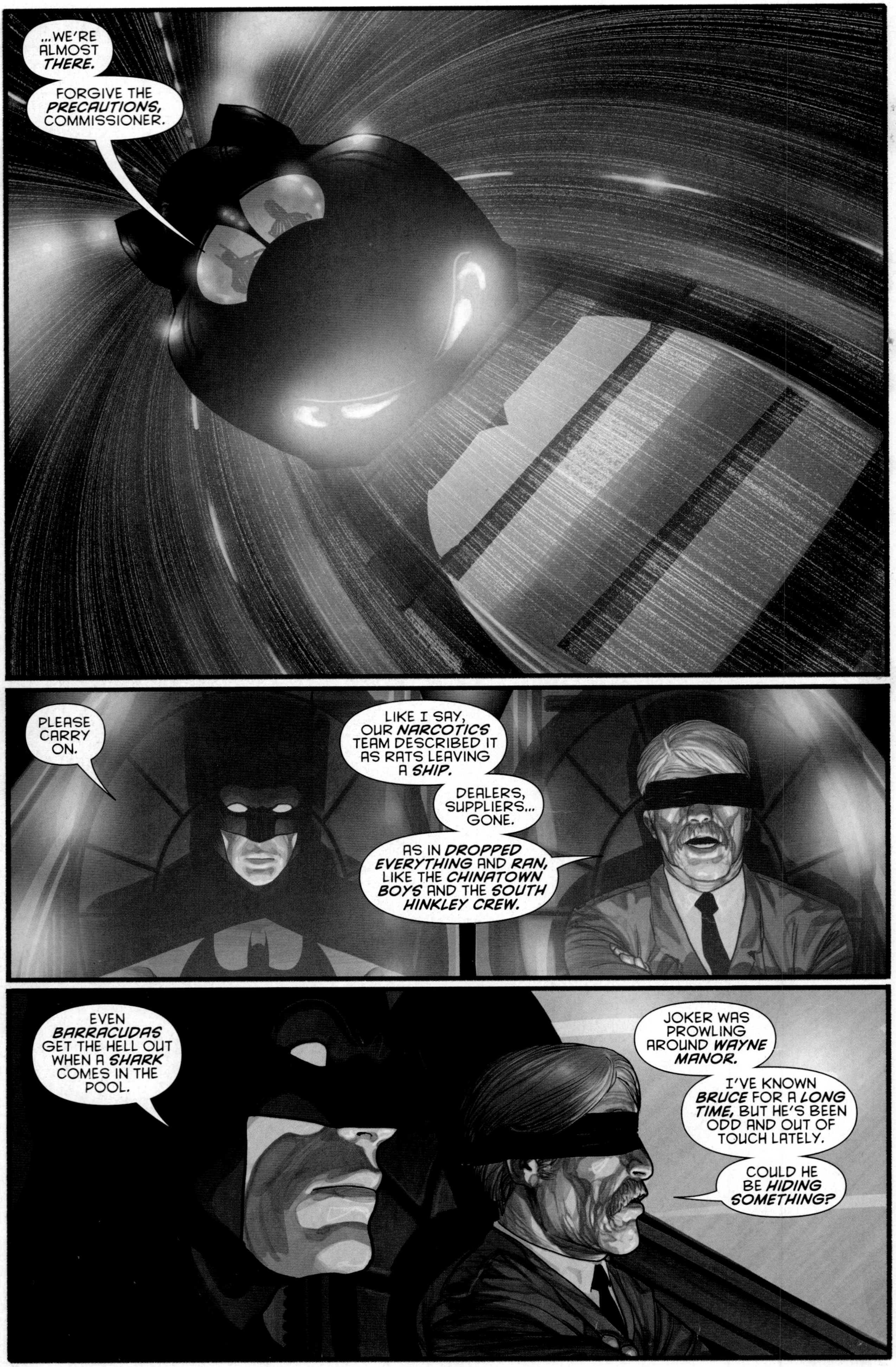
...WE'RE ALMOST THERE.
FORGIVE THE PRECAUTIONS, COMMISSIONER.
PLEASE CARRY ON.
LIKE I SAY, OUR NARCOTICS TEAM DESCRIBED IT AS RATS LEAVING A SHIP.
DEALERS, SUPPLIERS... GONE.
AS IN DROPPED EVERYTHING AND RAN, LIKE THE CHINATOWN BOYS AND THE SOUTH HINKLEY CREW.
EVEN BARRACUDAS GET THE HELL OUT WHEN A SHARK COMES IN THE POOL.
JOKER WAS PROWLING AROUND WAYNE MANOR.
I'VE KNOWN BRUCE FOR A LONG TIME, BUT HE'S BEEN ODD AND OUT OF TOUCH LATELY.
COULD HE BE HIDING SOMETHING?

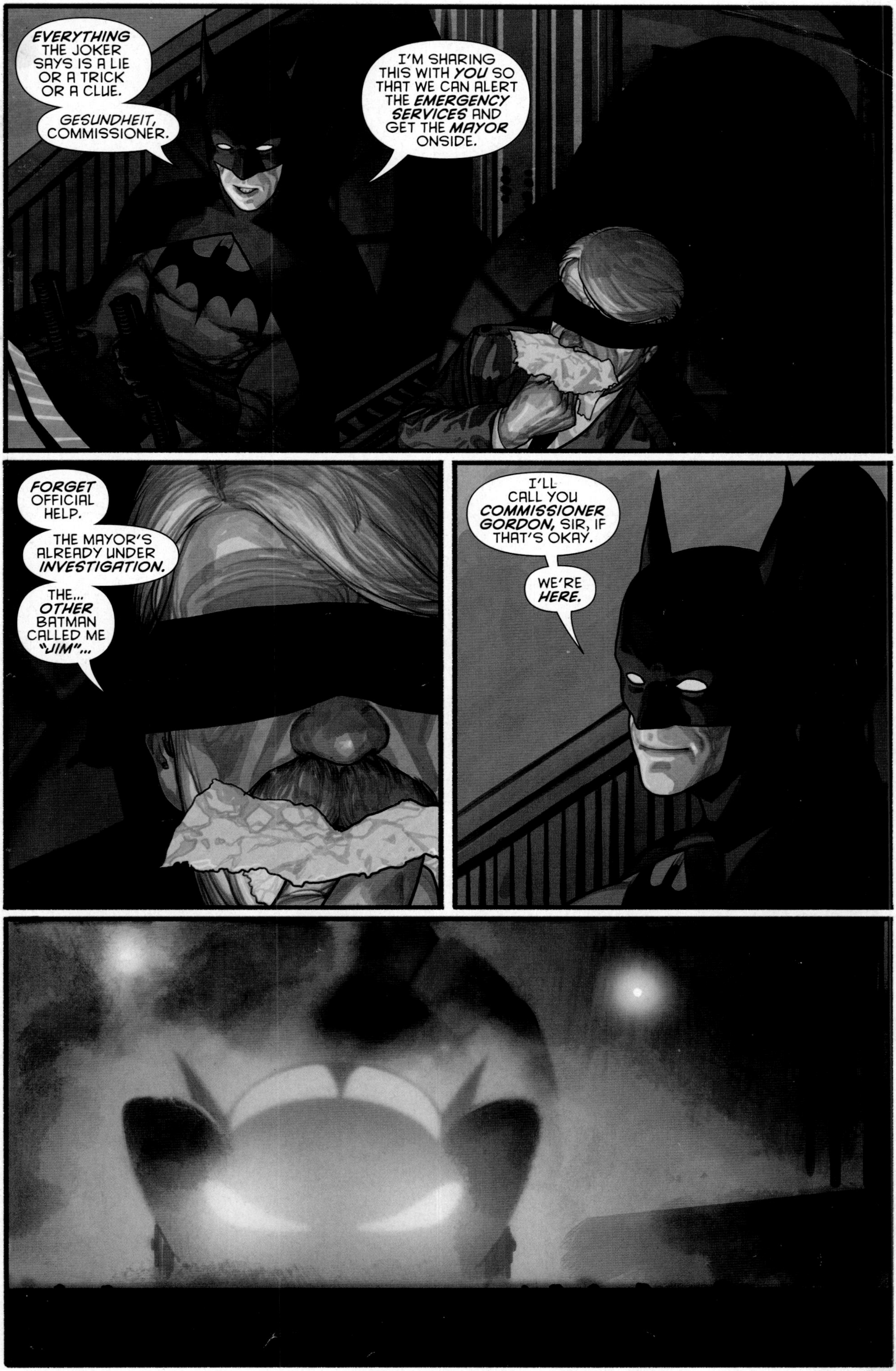
EVERYTHING THE JOKER SAYS IS A LIE OR A TRICK OR A CLUE.
GESUNDHEIT, COMMISSIONER.
I'M SHARING THIS WITH YOU SO THAT WE CAN ALERT THE EMERGENCY SERVICES AND GET THE MAYOR ONSIDE.
FORGET OFFICIAL HELP.
THE MAYOR'S ALREADY UNDER INVESTIGATION.
THE... OTHER BATMAN CALLED ME "JIM"...
I'LL CALL YOU COMMISSIONER GORDON, SIR, IF THAT'S OKAY.
WE'RE HERE.

WELCOME TO THE *BAT-BUNKER*.

NO ONE CAN SEE OR HEAR US.

YOU HAVE YOUR OWN *SUBWAY STATION?*

OF *COURSE* YOU DO.

IT'S BEEN A LONG TIME SINCE GOTHAM CITY BELONGED TO ANYONE BUT THE *BATMAN*, RIGHT?

I LIKE TO THINK I'M JUST KEEPING THE COSTUME *WARM*.

BUT THE *JOKER'S* ONLY THE *BEGINNING* OF SOMETHING MUCH *BIGGER*.

I STILL HAVEN'T MADE ALL THE *CONNECTIONS*.

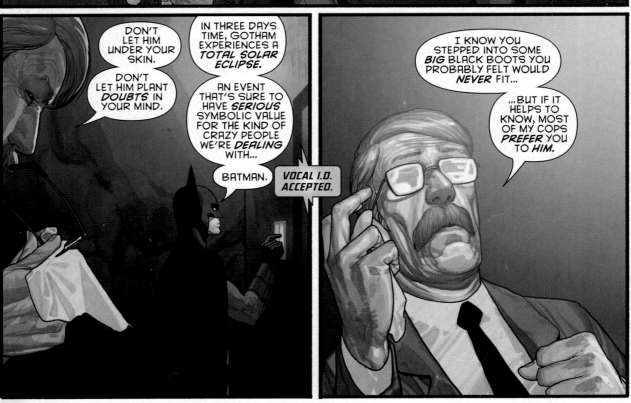

DON'T LET HIM UNDER YOUR SKIN.

DON'T LET HIM PLANT *DOUBTS* IN YOUR MIND.

IN THREE DAYS TIME, GOTHAM EXPERIENCES A *TOTAL SOLAR ECLIPSE*.

AN EVENT THAT'S SURE TO HAVE *SERIOUS* SYMBOLIC VALUE FOR THE KIND OF CRAZY PEOPLE WE'RE *DEALING* WITH...

BATMAN.

VOCAL I.D. ACCEPTED.

I KNOW YOU STEPPED INTO SOME *BIG* BLACK BOOTS YOU PROBABLY FELT WOULD *NEVER* FIT...

...BUT IF IT HELPS TO KNOW, MOST OF MY COPS *PREFER* YOU TO *HIM*.

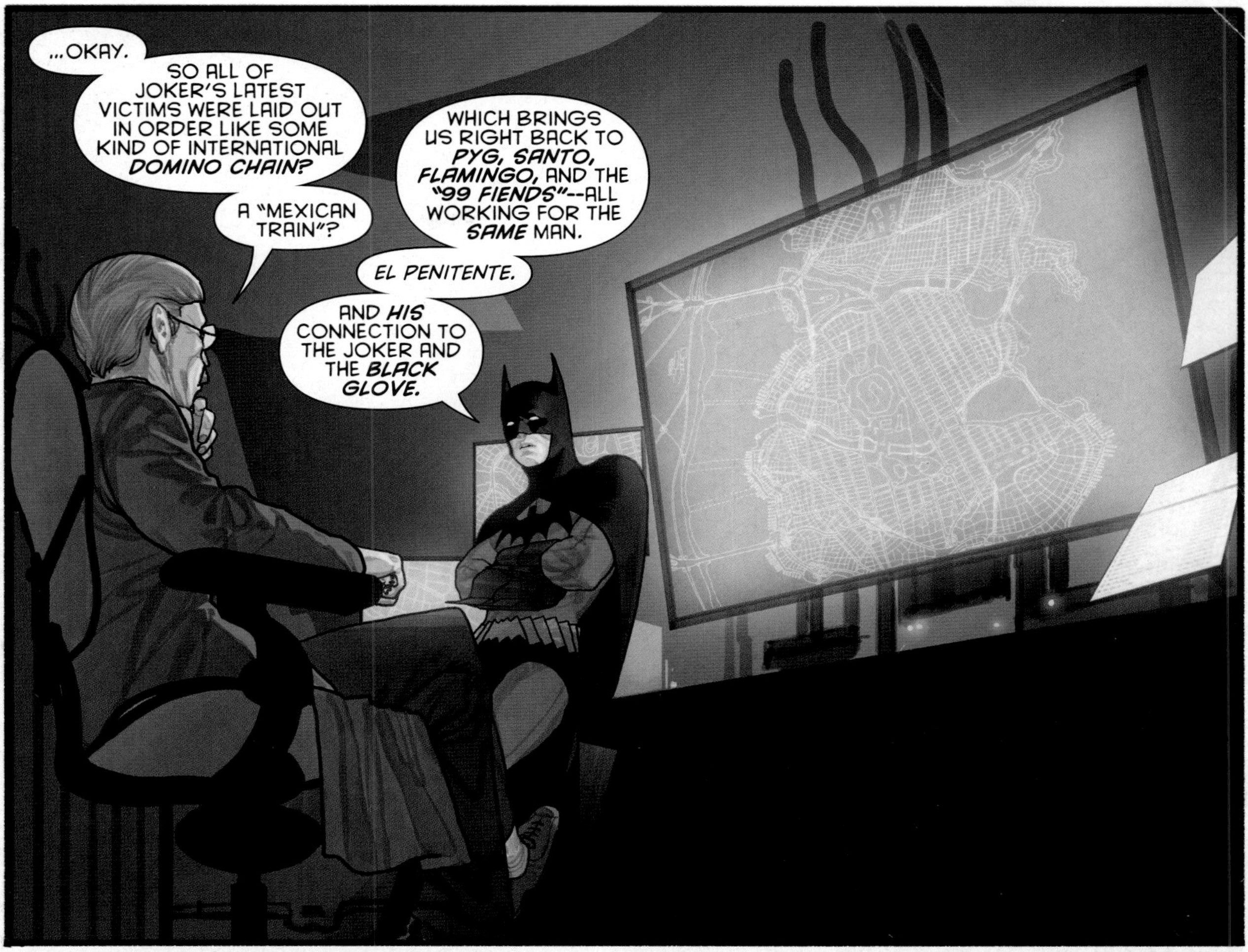
...OKAY.
SO ALL OF JOKER'S LATEST VICTIMS WERE LAID OUT IN ORDER LIKE SOME KIND OF INTERNATIONAL DOMINO CHAIN?
A "MEXICAN TRAIN"?
WHICH BRINGS US RIGHT BACK TO PYG, SANTO, FLAMINGO, AND THE "99 FIENDS"--ALL WORKING FOR THE SAME MAN.
EL PENITENTE.
AND HIS CONNECTION TO THE JOKER AND THE BLACK GLOVE.
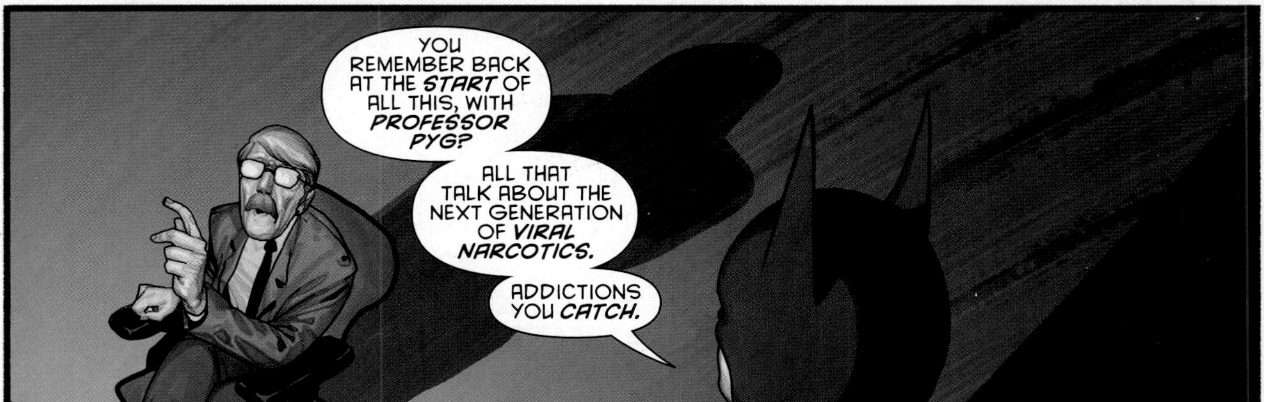
YOU REMEMBER BACK AT THE START OF ALL THIS, WITH PROFESSOR PYG?
ALL THAT TALK ABOUT THE NEXT GENERATION OF VIRAL NARCOTICS.
ADDICTIONS YOU CATCH.
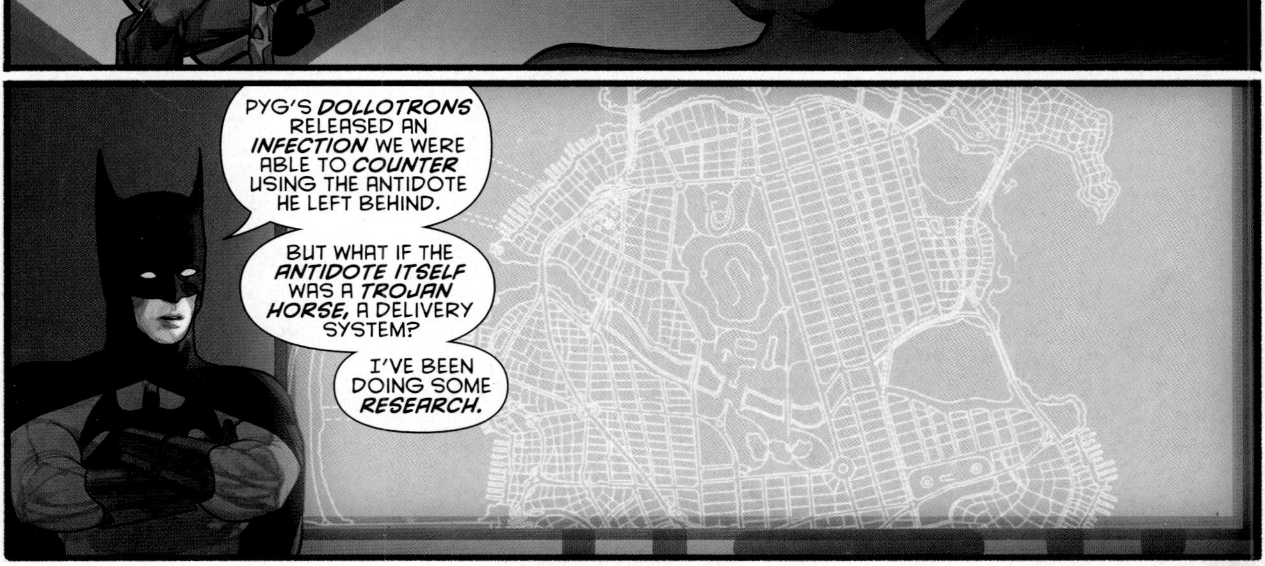
PYG'S DOLLOTRONS RELEASED AN INFECTION WE WERE ABLE TO COUNTER USING THE ANTIDOTE HE LEFT BEHIND.
BUT WHAT IF THE ANTIDOTE ITSELF WAS A TROJAN HORSE, A DELIVERY SYSTEM?
I'VE BEEN DOING SOME RESEARCH.

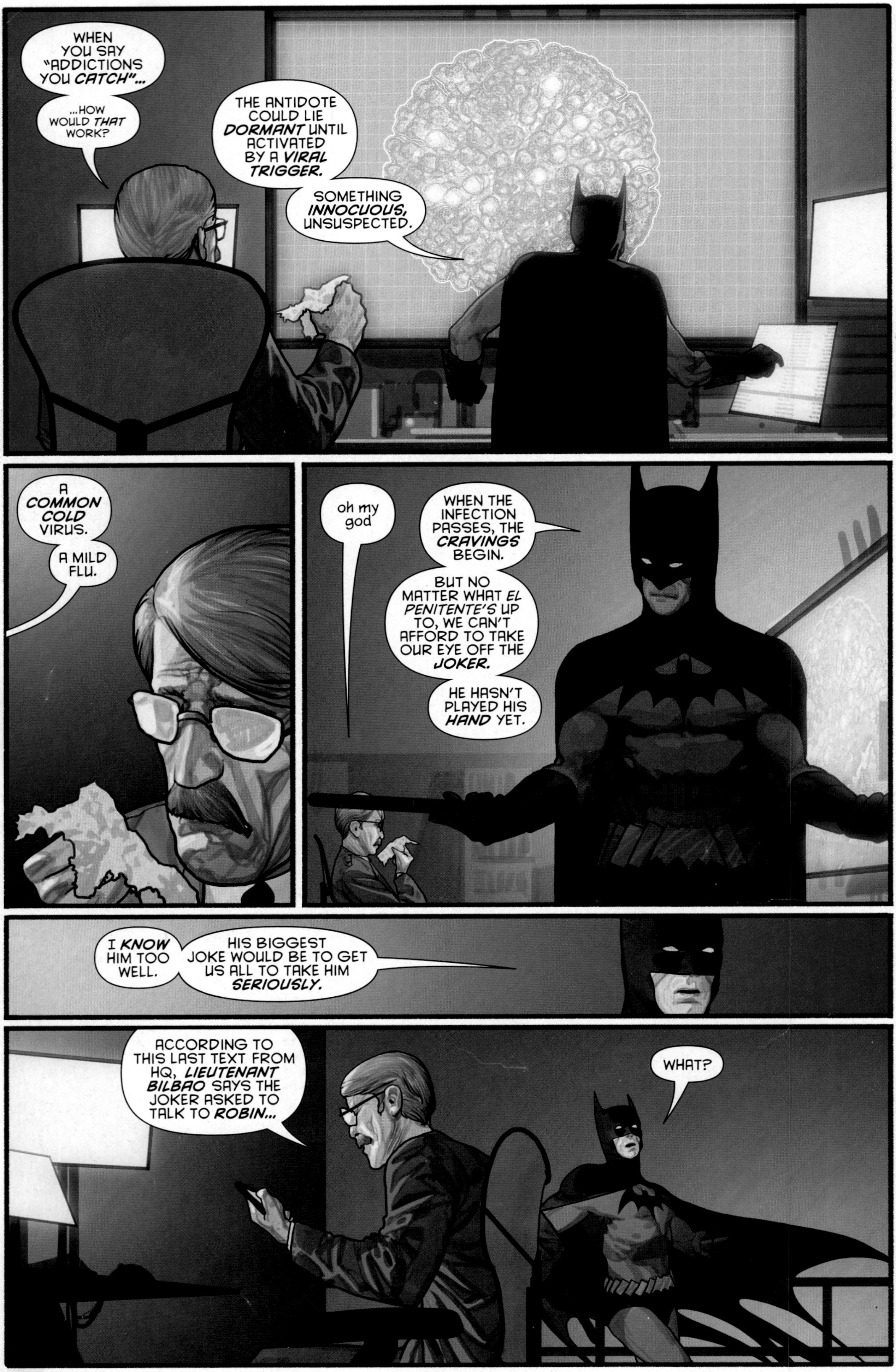
WHEN YOU SAY "ADDICTIONS YOU CATCH"...
...HOW WOULD THAT WORK?
THE ANTIDOTE COULD LIE DORMANT UNTIL ACTIVATED BY A VIRAL TRIGGER.
SOMETHING INNOCUOUS, UNSUSPECTED.
A COMMON COLD VIRUS.
A MILD FLU.
oh my god
WHEN THE INFECTION PASSES, THE CRAVINGS BEGIN.
BUT NO MATTER WHAT EL PENITENTE'S UP TO, WE CAN'T AFFORD TO TAKE OUR EYE OFF THE JOKER.
HE HASN'T PLAYED HIS HAND YET.
I KNOW HIM TOO WELL.
HIS BIGGEST JOKE WOULD BE TO GET US ALL TO TAKE HIM SERIOUSLY.
ACCORDING TO THIS LAST TEXT FROM HQ, LIEUTENANT BILBAO SAYS THE JOKER ASKED TO TALK TO ROBIN...
WHAT?

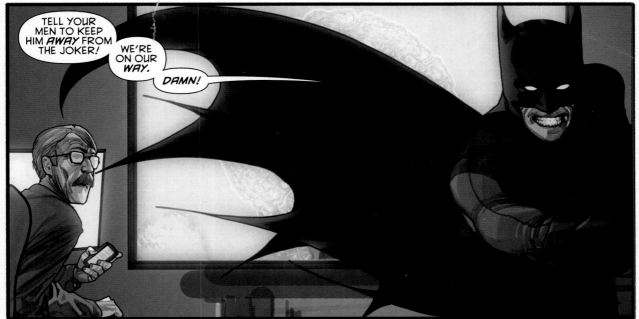

TELL YOUR MEN TO KEEP HIM *AWAY* FROM THE JOKER!

WE'RE ON OUR *WAY.*

DAMN!

HE COULD KILL HIM!

MY GOD.

DOES THAT POOR KID HAVE ANY IDEA WHAT HE'S *DEALING* WITH?

IT'S NOT *HIM.*

IT'S THE *JOKER* I'M WORRIED ABOUT.

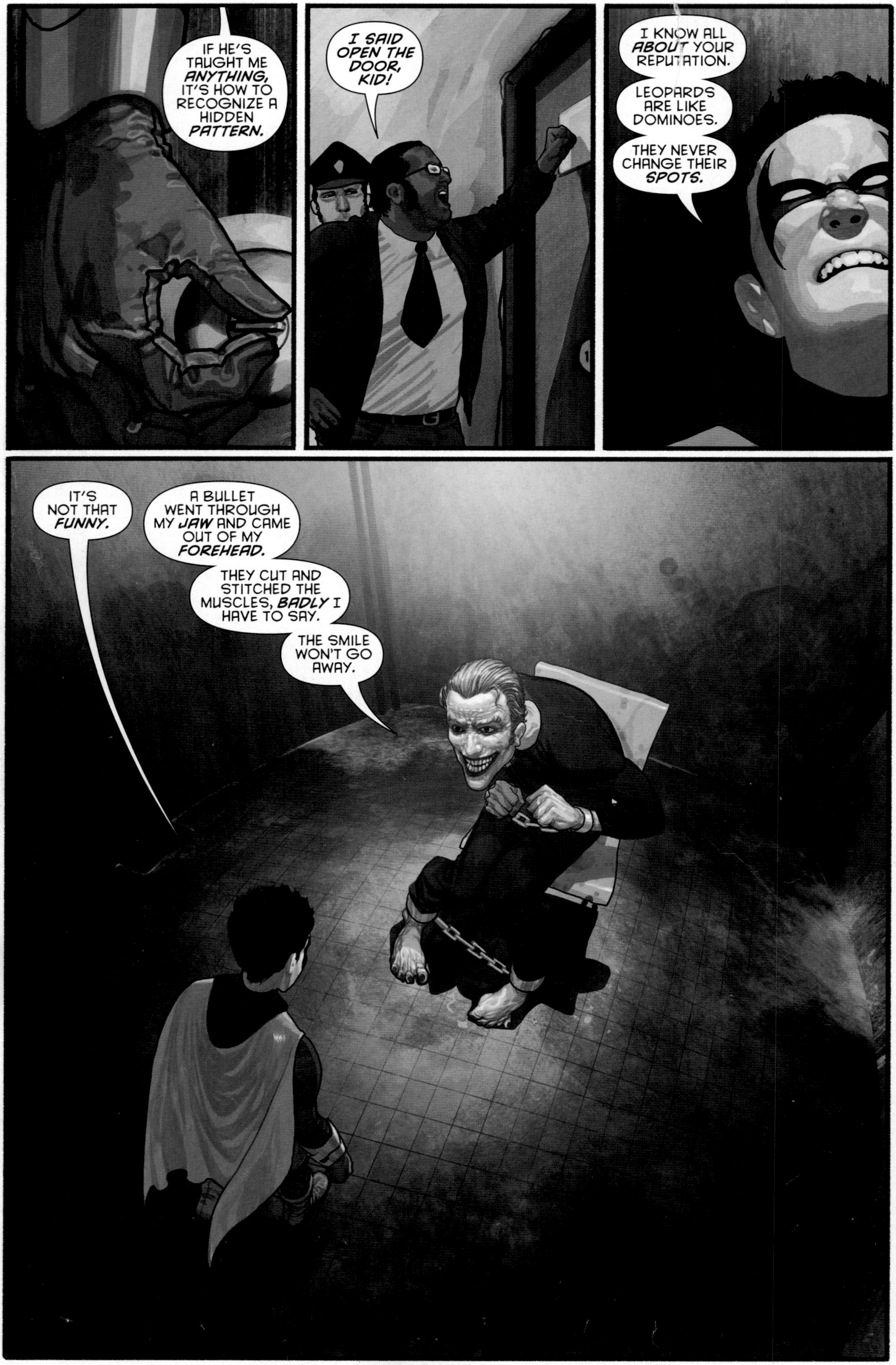
IF HE'S TAUGHT ME ANYTHING, IT'S HOW TO RECOGNIZE A HIDDEN PATTERN.
I SAID OPEN THE DOOR, KID!
I KNOW ALL ABOUT YOUR REPUTATION.
LEOPARDS ARE LIKE DOMINOES.
THEY NEVER CHANGE THEIR SPOTS.
IT'S NOT THAT FUNNY.
A BULLET WENT THROUGH MY JAW AND CAME OUT OF MY FOREHEAD.
THEY CUT AND STITCHED THE MUSCLES, BADLY I HAVE TO SAY.
THE SMILE WON'T GO AWAY.

LOOK WHAT THEY DID TO ME!

IN THE NAME OF GOD, EVEN *YOU* HAVE TO *UNDERSTAND* HOW *SORRY* I AM FOR WHAT I'VE DONE!

BEHIND THIS TERRIBLE, *TERRIBLE* FACE I'M JUST...I'M JUST...

HAUU-HAUUU

I WAS A *LITTLE BOY WONDER* ONCE, TOO.

I DIDN'T SET OUT TO BE THIS.

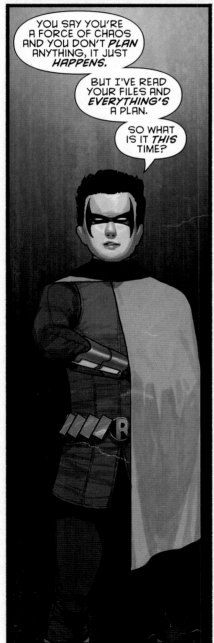

YOU SAY YOU'RE A FORCE OF CHAOS AND YOU DON'T *PLAN* ANYTHING, IT JUST *HAPPENS.*

BUT I'VE READ YOUR FILES AND *EVERYTHING'S* A PLAN.

SO WHAT IS IT *THIS* TIME?

BECAUSE I DON'T THINK YOU KNOW WHAT CHAOS *IS.*

CHAOS IS NEEDING SOMEONE TO CHANGE YOUR *FEEDING TUBE.*

CHAOS IS NOT BEING ABLE TO GO TO THE *TOILET* WITHOUT *HELP.*

YOU SOUND JUST LIKE...

LIKE HIM...

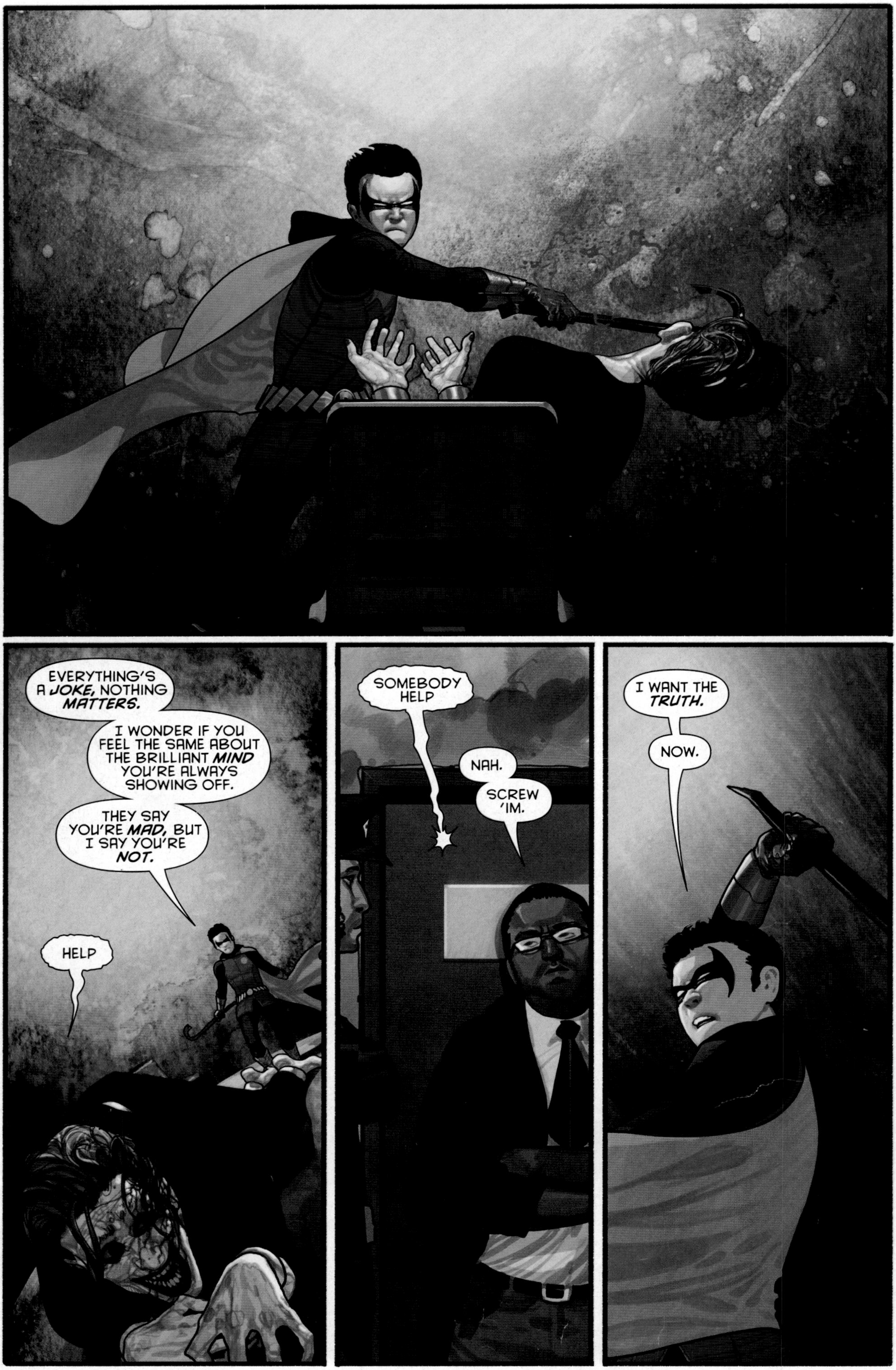
EVERYTHING'S A JOKE, NOTHING MATTERS.
I WONDER IF YOU FEEL THE SAME ABOUT THE BRILLIANT MIND YOU'RE ALWAYS SHOWING OFF.
THEY SAY YOU'RE MAD, BUT I SAY YOU'RE NOT.
HELP
SOMEBODY HELP
NAH.
SCREW 'IM.
I WANT THE TRUTH.
NOW.

IF I'M *RIGHT*, THEY COULD ADDICT THE ENTIRE *CITY* OVERNIGHT.

THEY COULD HOLD THE WHOLE *POPULATION* TO RANSOM.

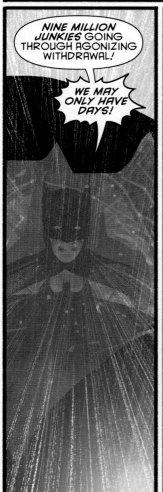

NINE MILLION *JUNKIES* GOING THROUGH AGONIZING WITHDRAWAL!

WE MAY ONLY HAVE *DAYS!*

BRACE FOR IMPACT!

WHAT THE HELL?!

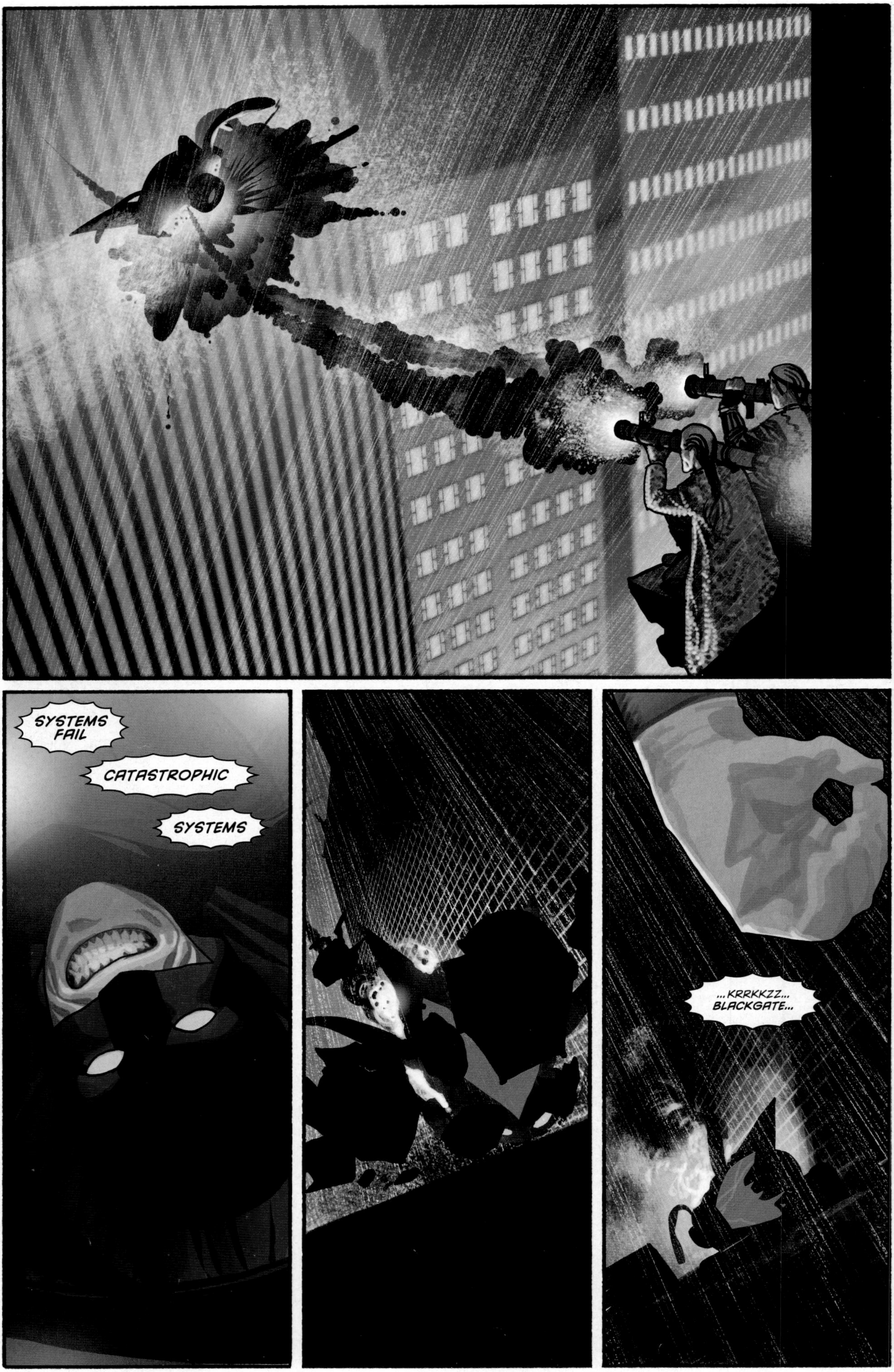
SYSTEMS FAIL
CATASTROPHIC
SYSTEMS
...KRRKKZZ... BLACKGATE...

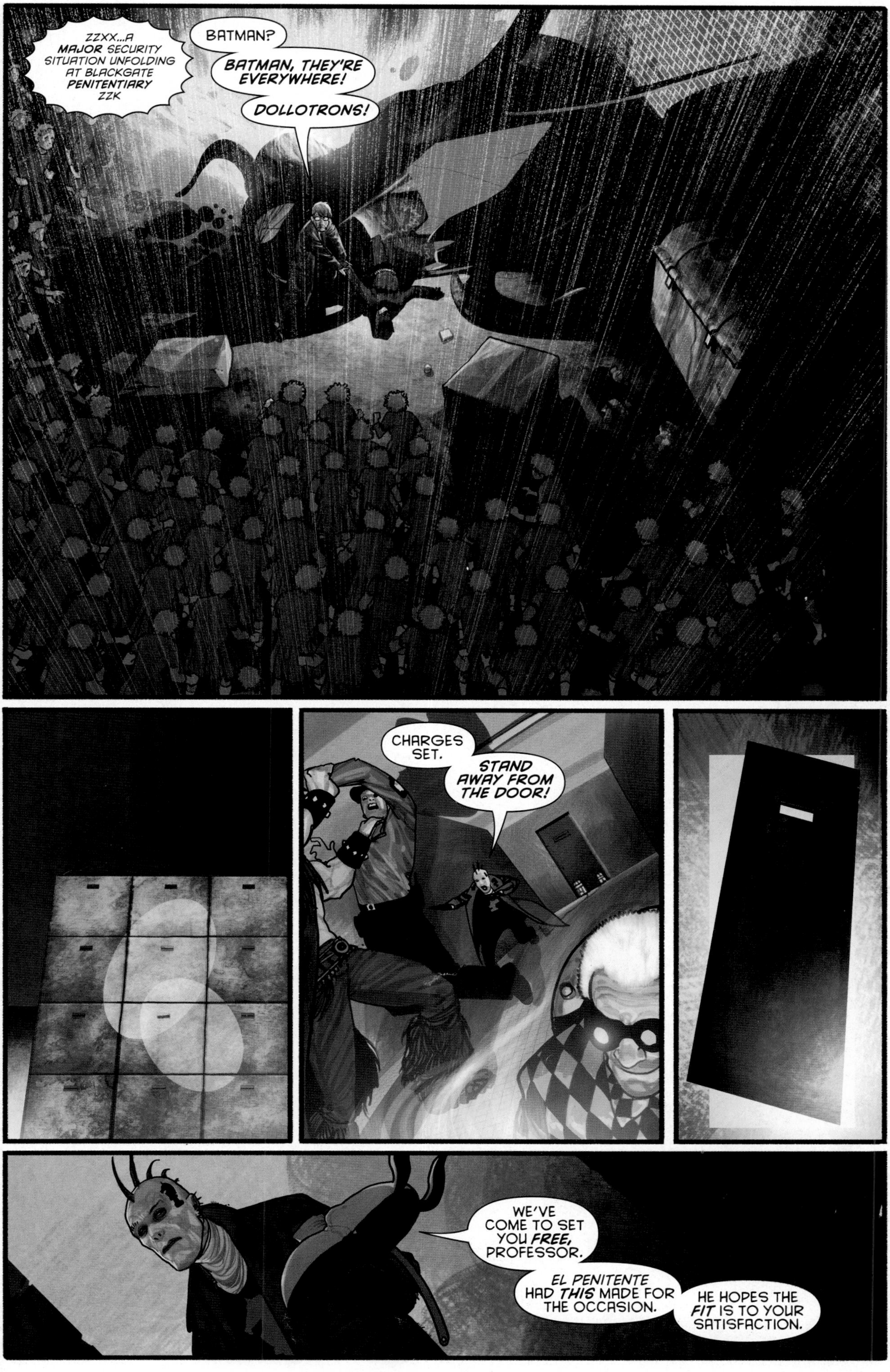
ZZXX...A MAJOR SECURITY SITUATION UNFOLDING AT BLACKGATE PENITENTIARY ZZK
BATMAN?
BATMAN, THEY'RE EVERYWHERE!
DOLLOTRONS!
CHARGES SET.
STAND AWAY FROM THE DOOR!
WE'VE COME TO SET YOU FREE, PROFESSOR.
EL PENITENTE HAD THIS MADE FOR THE OCCASION.
HE HOPES THE FIT IS TO YOUR SATISFACTION.

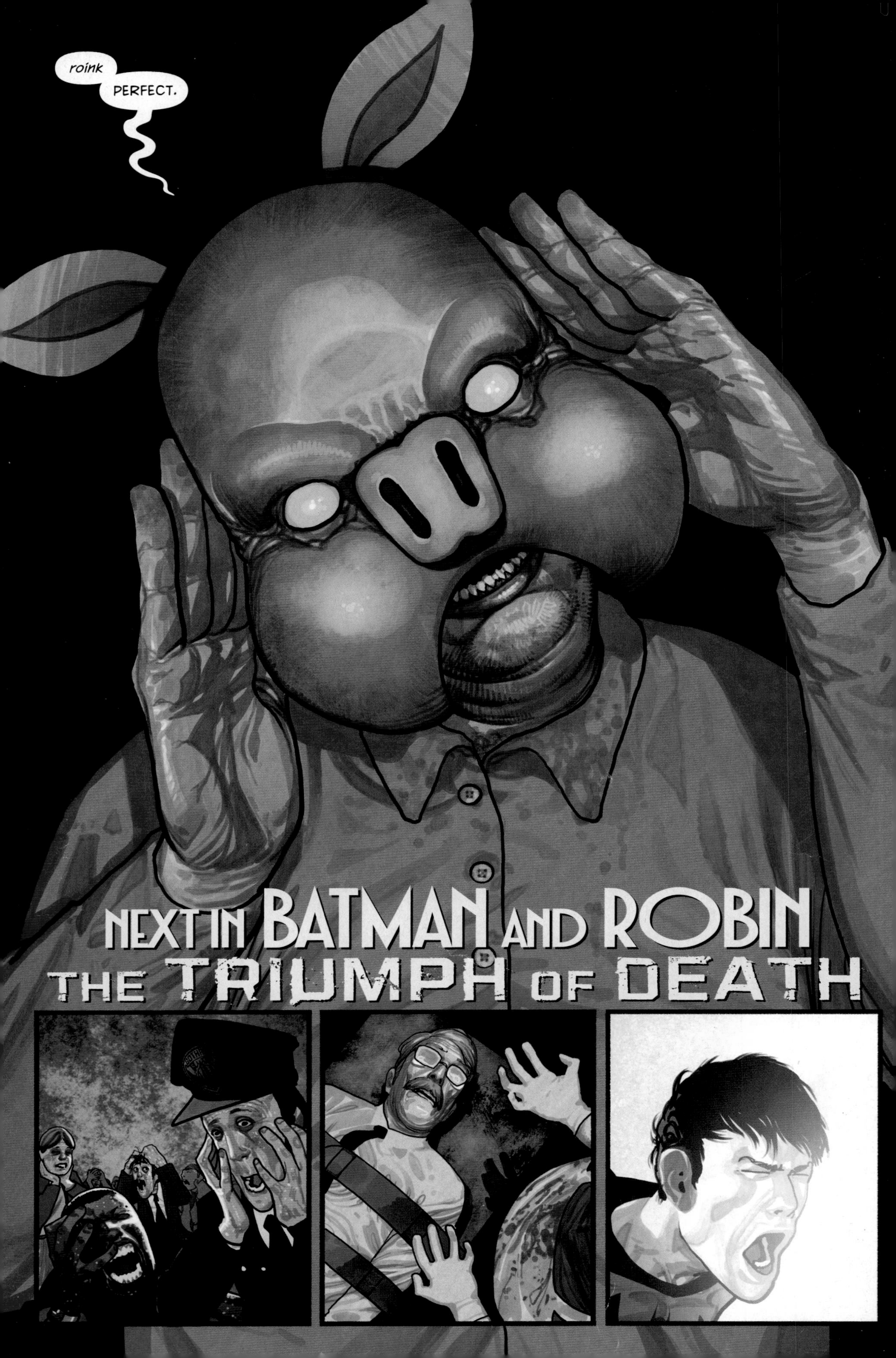
roink
PERFECT.
NEXT IN BATMAN AND ROBIN
THE TRIUMPH OF DEATH

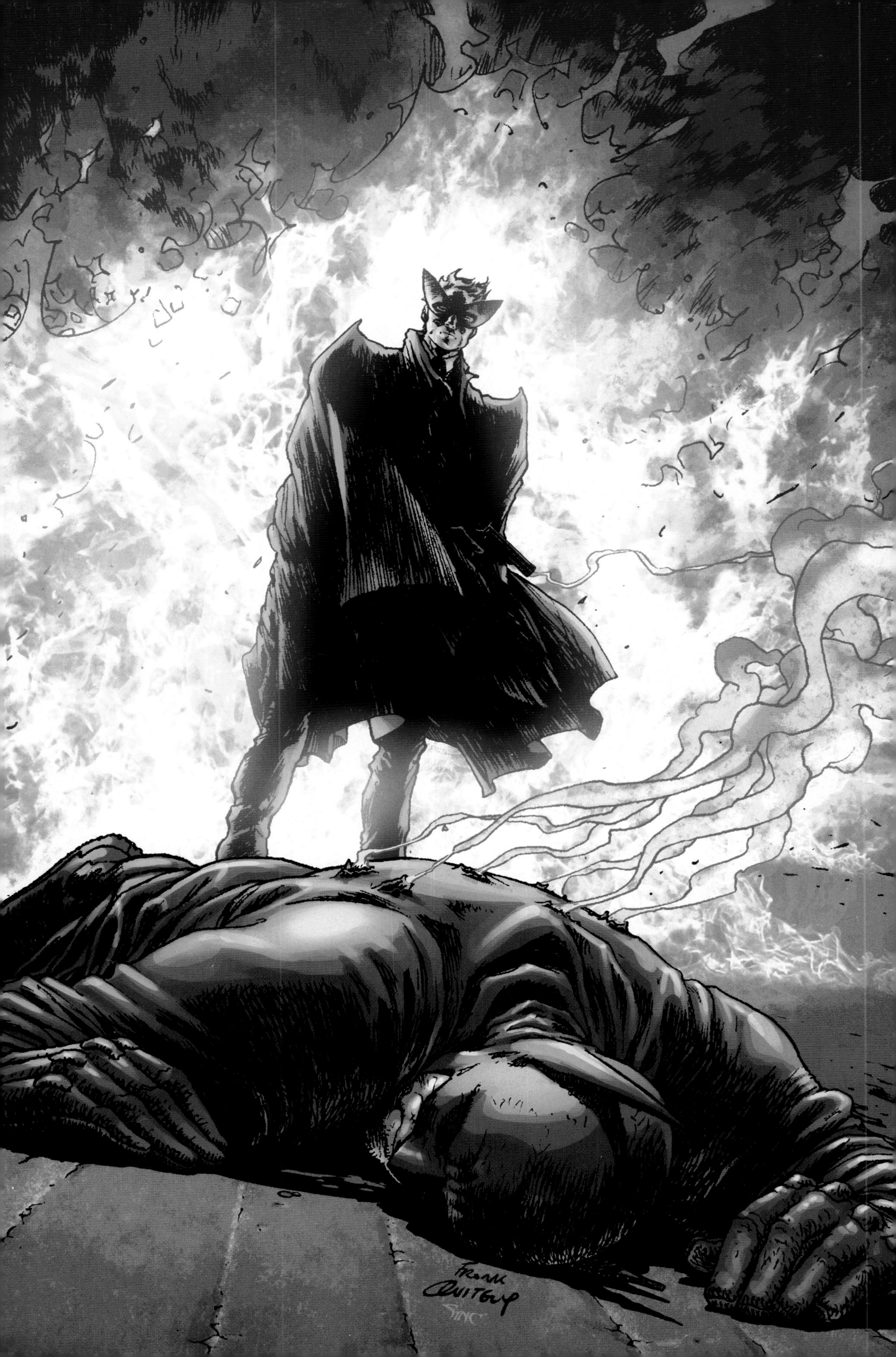
FRANK QUITELY

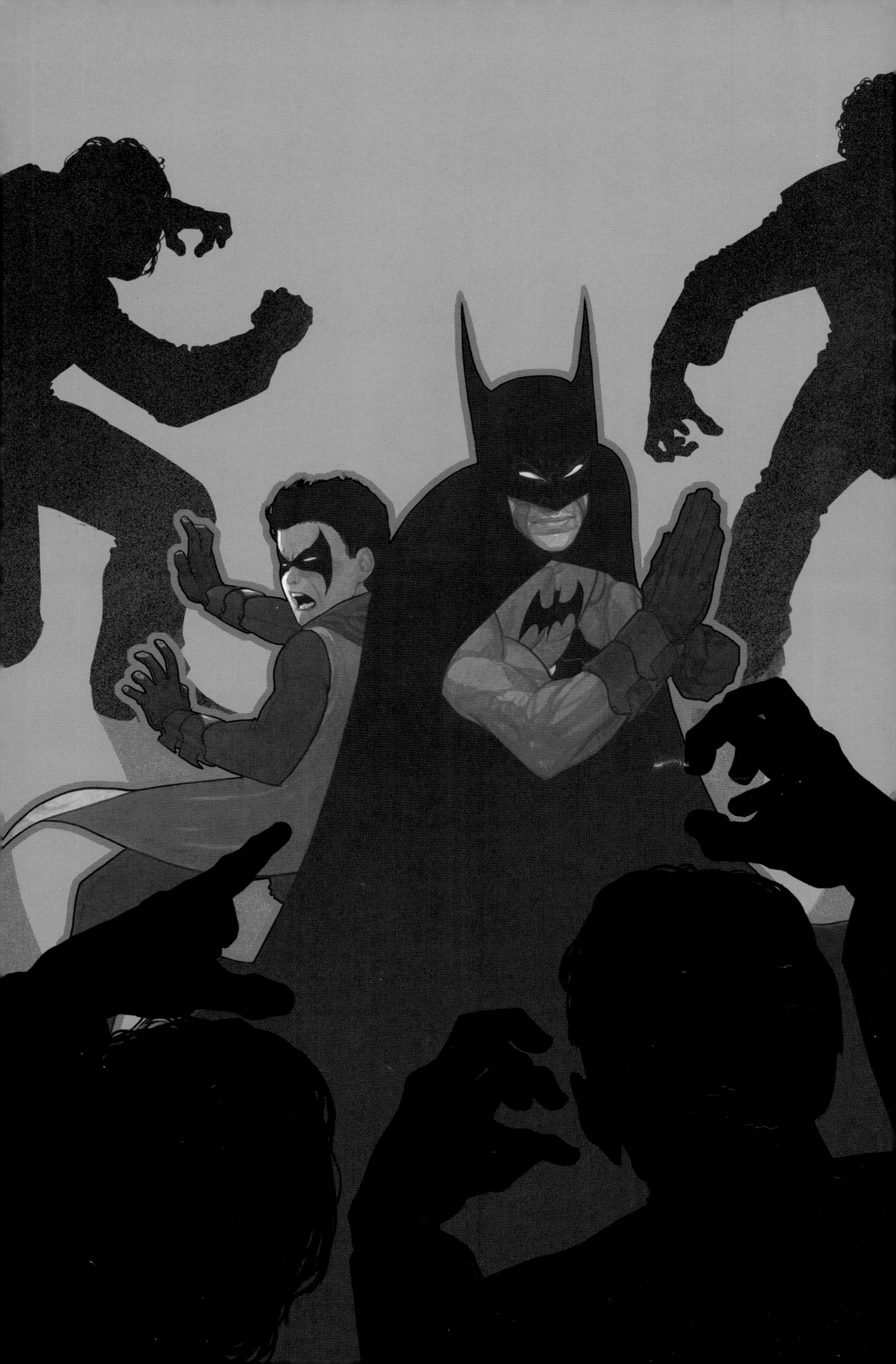

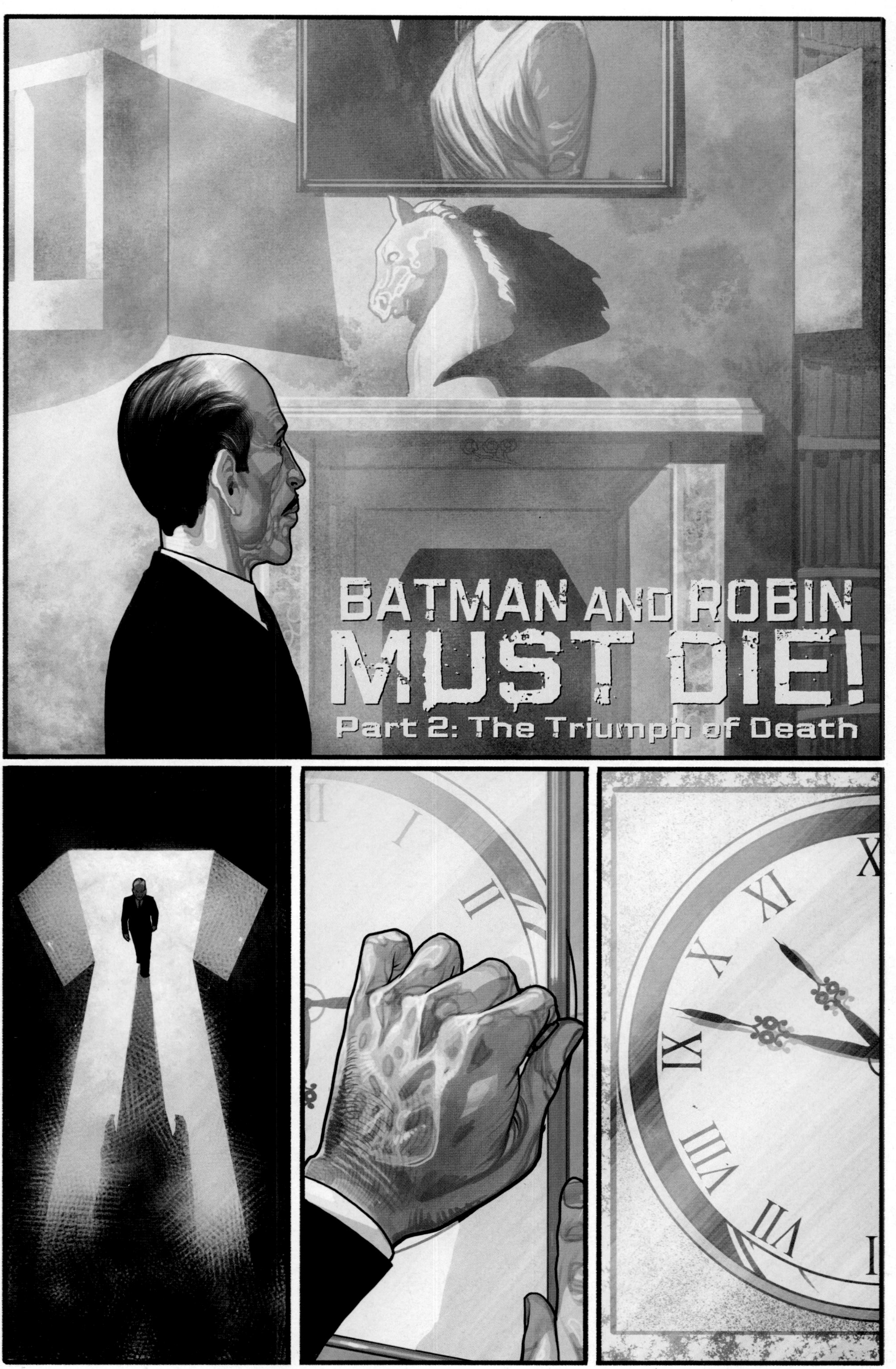
BATMAN AND ROBIN
MUST DIE!
Part 2: The Triumph of Death

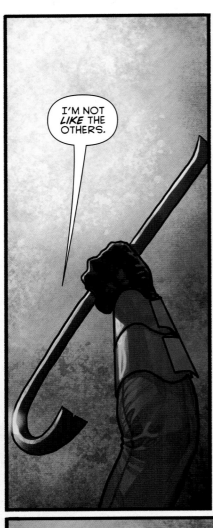

I'M NOT *LIKE* THE OTHERS.

I WAS RAISED BY *ASSASSINS* WHO TAUGHT ME HOW TO KILL *WITHOUT MERCY.*

IF YOU THINK FOR EVEN *ONE SECOND* THAT I WOULD *HESITATE* TO INFLICT SEVERE BRAIN DAMAGE...

WAIT.

...THE TRUTH...

...YOU SAID YOU WANTED THE TRUTH...

ANY TIME YOU'RE READY.

...THE *TRUTH* IS..

...THE TRUTH *IS*...

...I'M *USING* YOU...

I'M USING *ALL* OF YOU.

MY FIGHT'S WITH *HIM*, NOT YOU.

WITH THE *DOCTOR*, THE *BLACK GLOVE.*

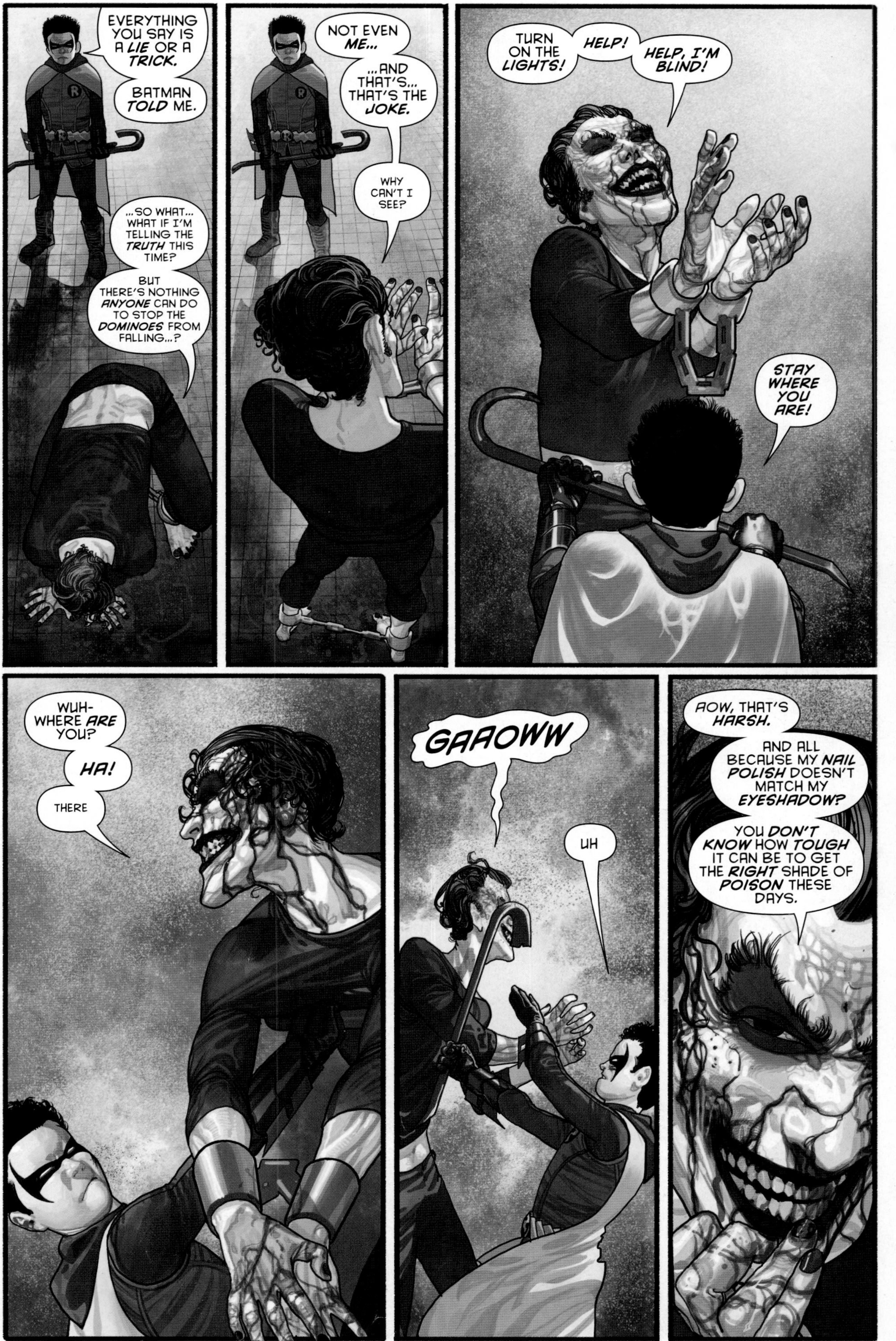
EVERYTHING YOU SAY IS A LIE OR A TRICK.
BATMAN TOLD ME.
...SO WHAT... WHAT IF I'M TELLING THE TRUTH THIS TIME?
BUT THERE'S NOTHING ANYONE CAN DO TO STOP THE DOMINOES FROM FALLING...?
NOT EVEN ME...
...AND THAT'S... THAT'S THE JOKE.
WHY CAN'T I SEE?
TURN ON THE LIGHTS!
HELP!
HELP, I'M BLIND!
STAY WHERE YOU ARE!
WUH-WHERE ARE YOU?
HA!
THERE
GAAOWW
UH
AOW, THAT'S HARSH.
AND ALL BECAUSE MY NAIL POLISH DOESN'T MATCH MY EYESHADOW?
YOU DON'T KNOW HOW TOUGH IT CAN BE TO GET THE RIGHT SHADE OF POISON THESE DAYS.

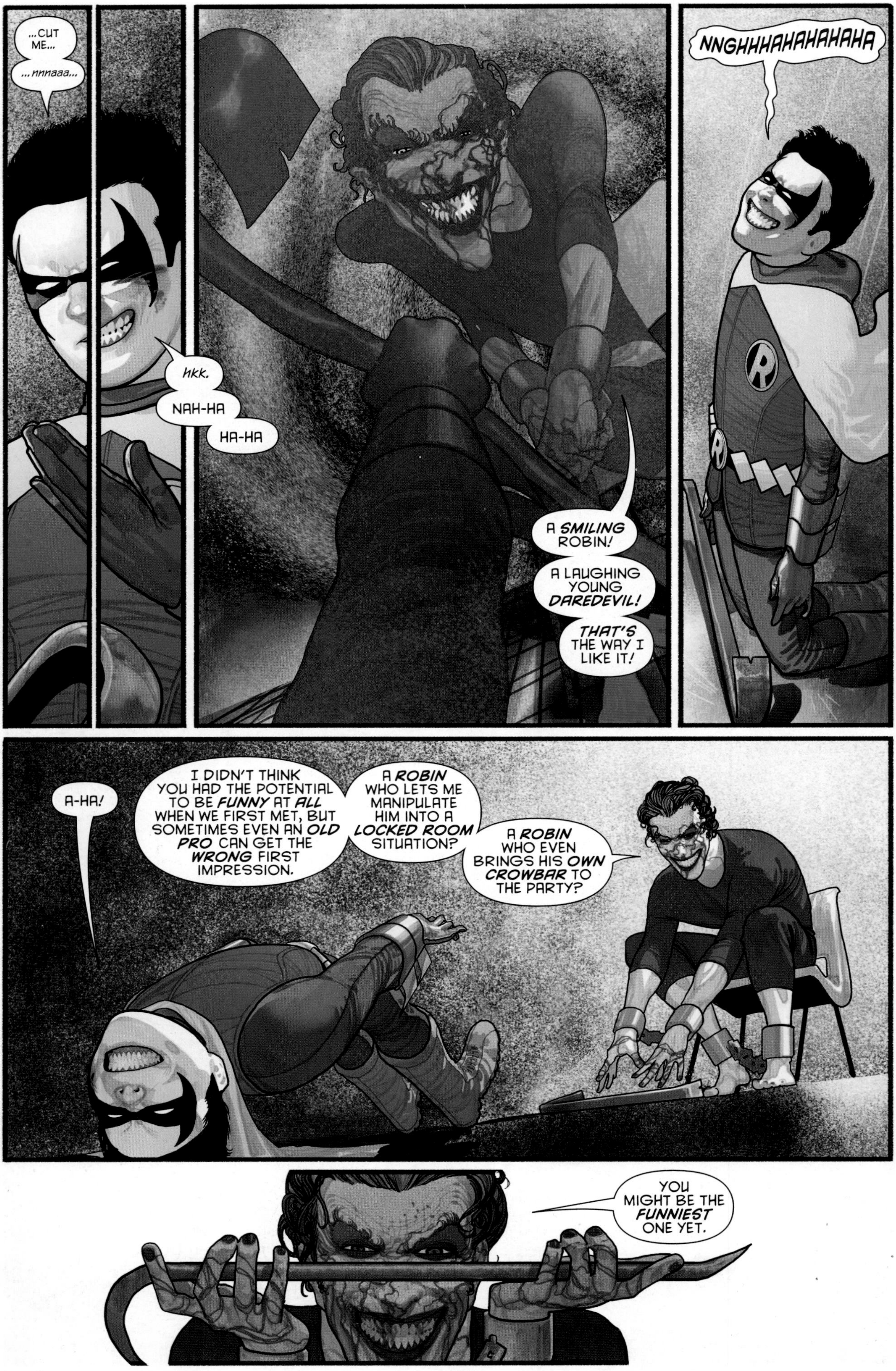
...CUT ME...
...nnnaaa...
hkk.
NAH-HA
HA-HA
A SMILING ROBIN!
A LAUGHING YOUNG DAREDEVIL!
THAT'S THE WAY I LIKE IT!
NNGHHHAHAHAHAHA
A-HA!
I DIDN'T THINK YOU HAD THE POTENTIAL TO BE FUNNY AT ALL WHEN WE FIRST MET, BUT SOMETIMES EVEN AN OLD PRO CAN GET THE WRONG FIRST IMPRESSION.
A ROBIN WHO LETS ME MANIPULATE HIM INTO A LOCKED ROOM SITUATION?
A ROBIN WHO EVEN BRINGS HIS OWN CROWBAR TO THE PARTY?
YOU MIGHT BE THE FUNNIEST ONE YET.

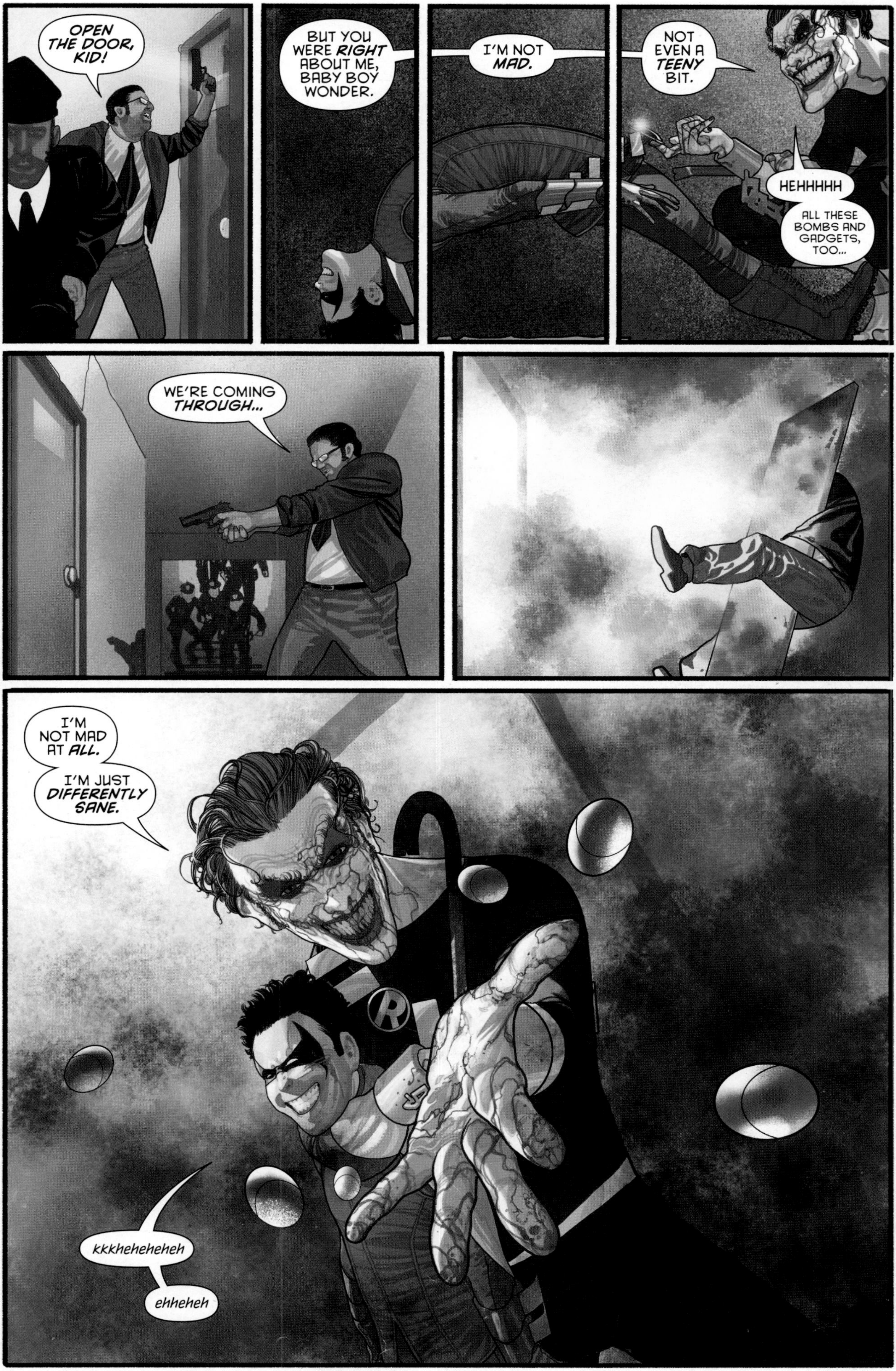
OPEN THE DOOR, KID!
BUT YOU WERE RIGHT ABOUT ME, BABY BOY WONDER.
I'M NOT MAD.
NOT EVEN A TEENY BIT.
HEHHHHH
ALL THESE BOMBS AND GADGETS, TOO...
WE'RE COMING THROUGH...
I'M NOT MAD AT ALL.
I'M JUST DIFFERENTLY SANE.
kkkheheheheh
ehheheh

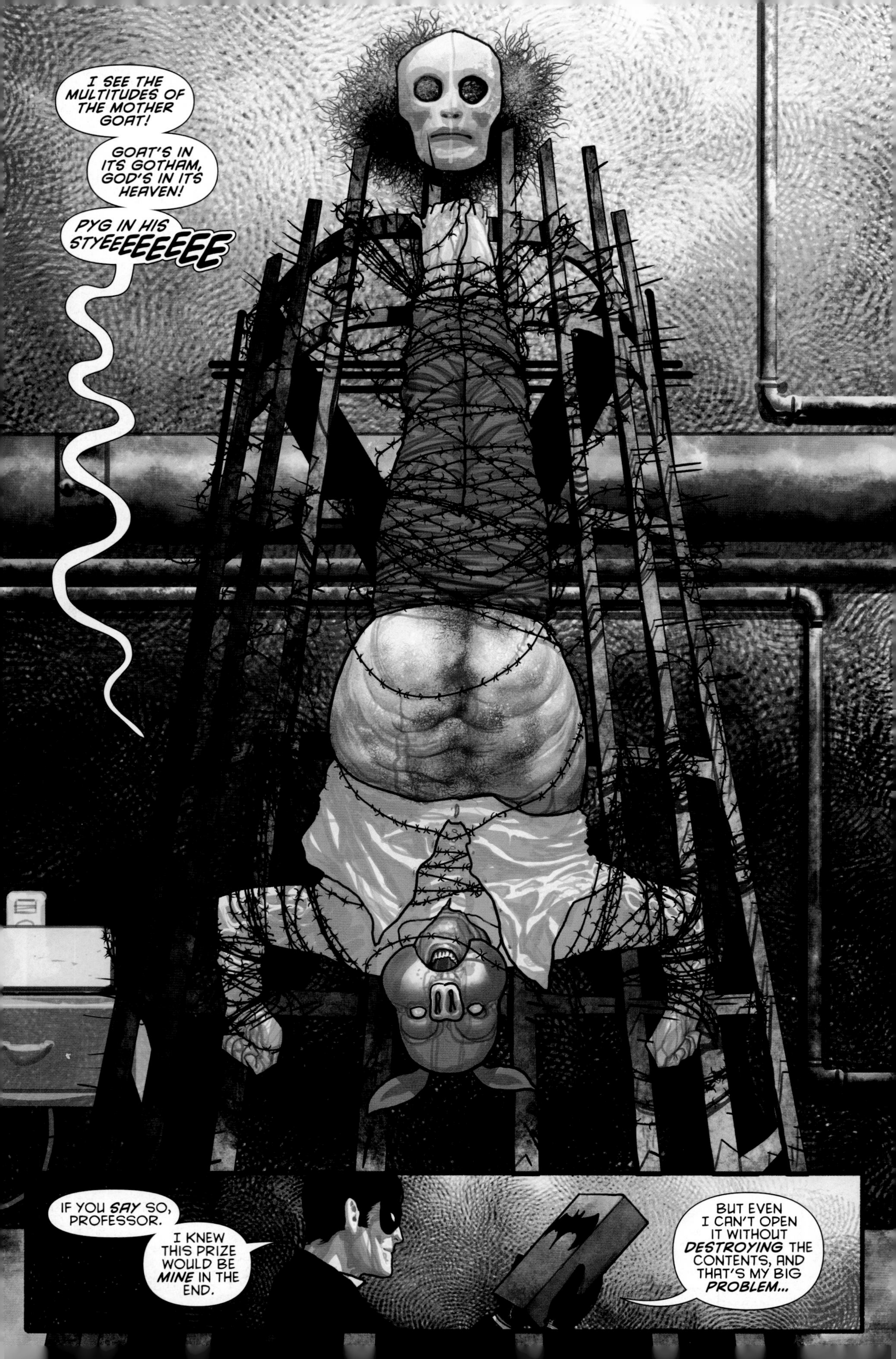
I SEE THE MULTITUDES OF THE MOTHER GOAT!
GOAT'S IN ITS GOTHAM, GOD'S IN ITS HEAVEN!
PYG IN HIS STYEEEEEEEEE
IF YOU SAY SO, PROFESSOR.
I KNEW THIS PRIZE WOULD BE MINE IN THE END.
BUT EVEN I CAN'T OPEN IT WITHOUT DESTROYING THE CONTENTS, AND THAT'S MY BIG PROBLEM...

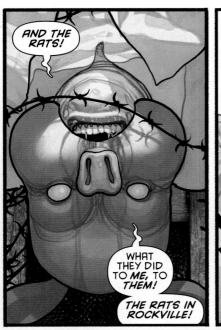

AND THE **RATS!**

WHAT THEY DID TO **ME,** TO **THEM!**

THE RATS IN ROCKVILLE!

LAZLO WAS A SPECIES OF **CIRCUS PERFORMER** WHO **ATE LIGHTBULBS** AND **NAILED** HIS PRIVATE PARTS TO MAHOGANY PLANKS, SENATOR VINE.

I CHALLENGED HIM TO OUTLINE HIS PERSONAL **VISION** FOR GOTHAM...

YOU **TOLD** ME YOU'D KEEP ME **OUTTA HARM'S WAY.**

THIS WHOLE THING STINKS OF SOME LOW RENT TORTURE PORNO.

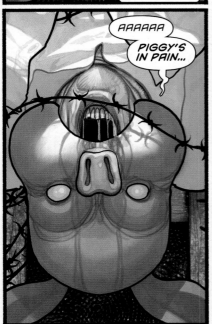

AAAAAA

PIGGY'S IN PAIN...

AH!

HH-HHRLLM

SLLTH

IT'S ALL **THEATER,** SENATOR.

BE SICK IN **THIS** BUCKET, PYG.

WHO **HURT** YOU? WHO BROKE YOUR PRECIOUS **MASK?**

AAUUUHHH

BATTTTMMMANNN

HOLY GOD.

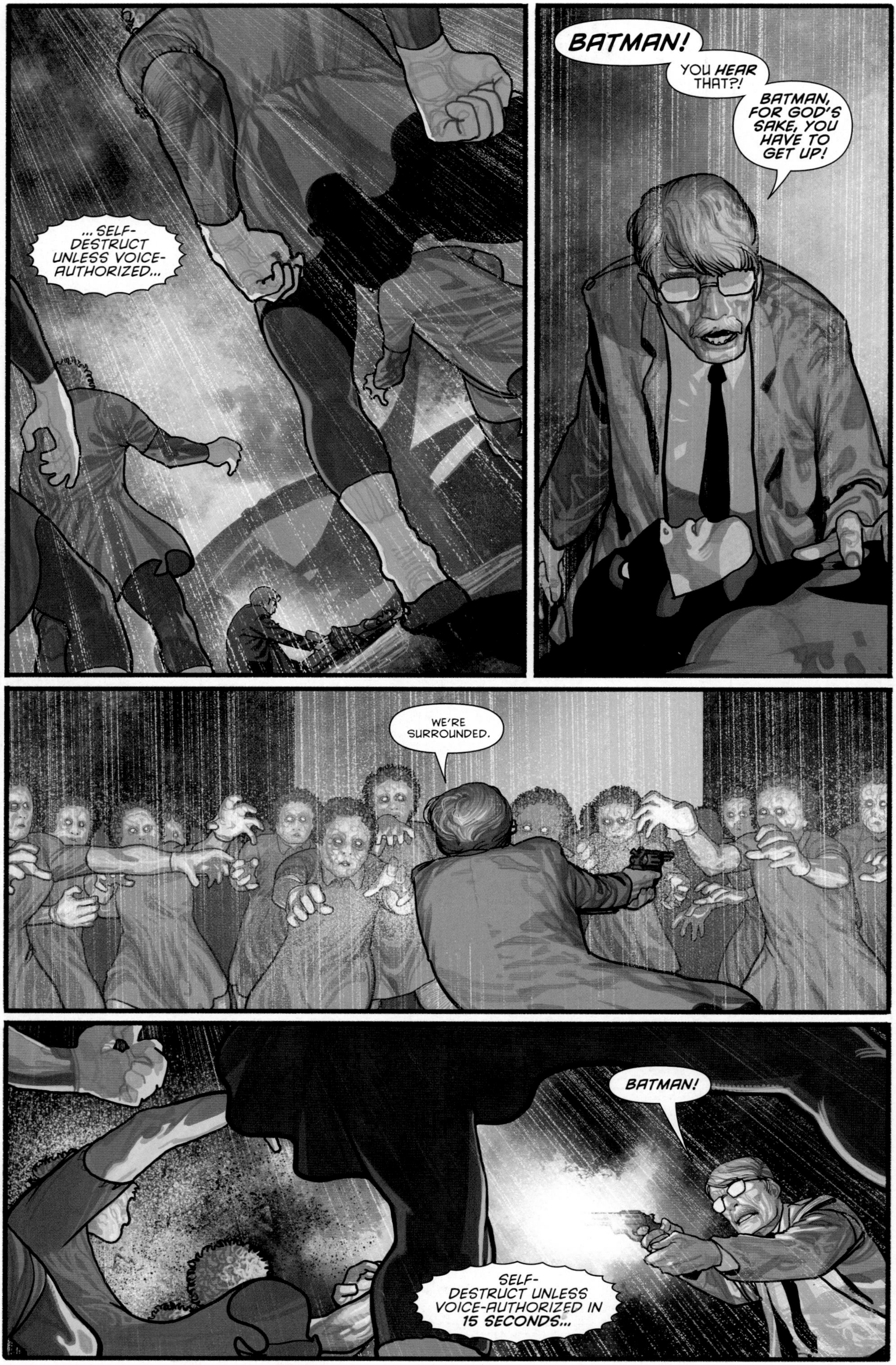
...SELF-DESTRUCT UNLESS VOICE-AUTHORIZED...
BATMAN!
YOU HEAR THAT?!
BATMAN, FOR GOD'S SAKE, YOU HAVE TO GET UP!
WE'RE SURROUNDED.
BATMAN!
SELF-DESTRUCT UNLESS VOICE-AUTHORIZED IN 15 SECONDS...

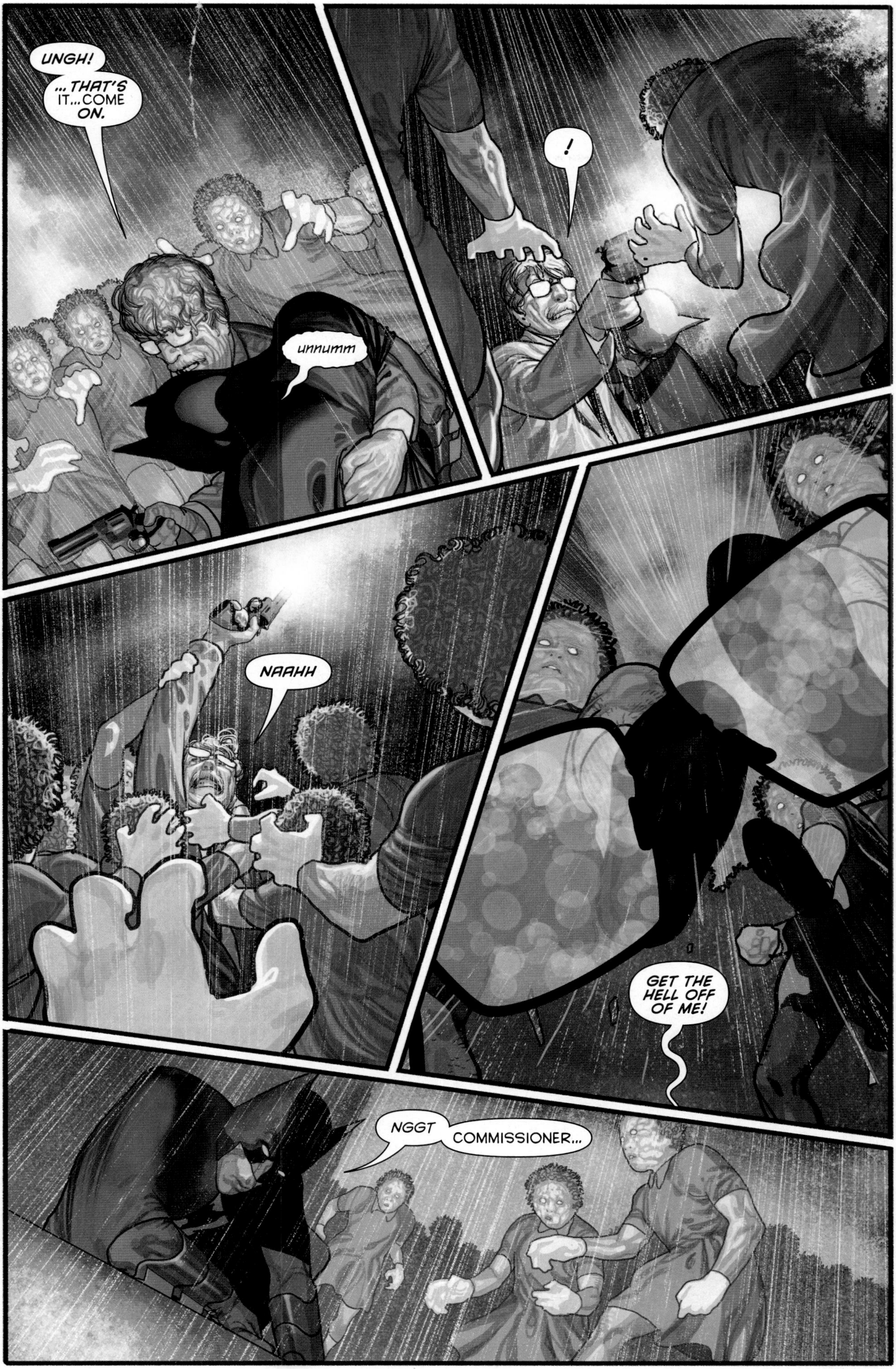
UNGH!
...THAT'S IT...COME ON.
unnumm
!
NAAHH
GET THE HELL OFF OF ME!
NGGT
COMMISSIONER...

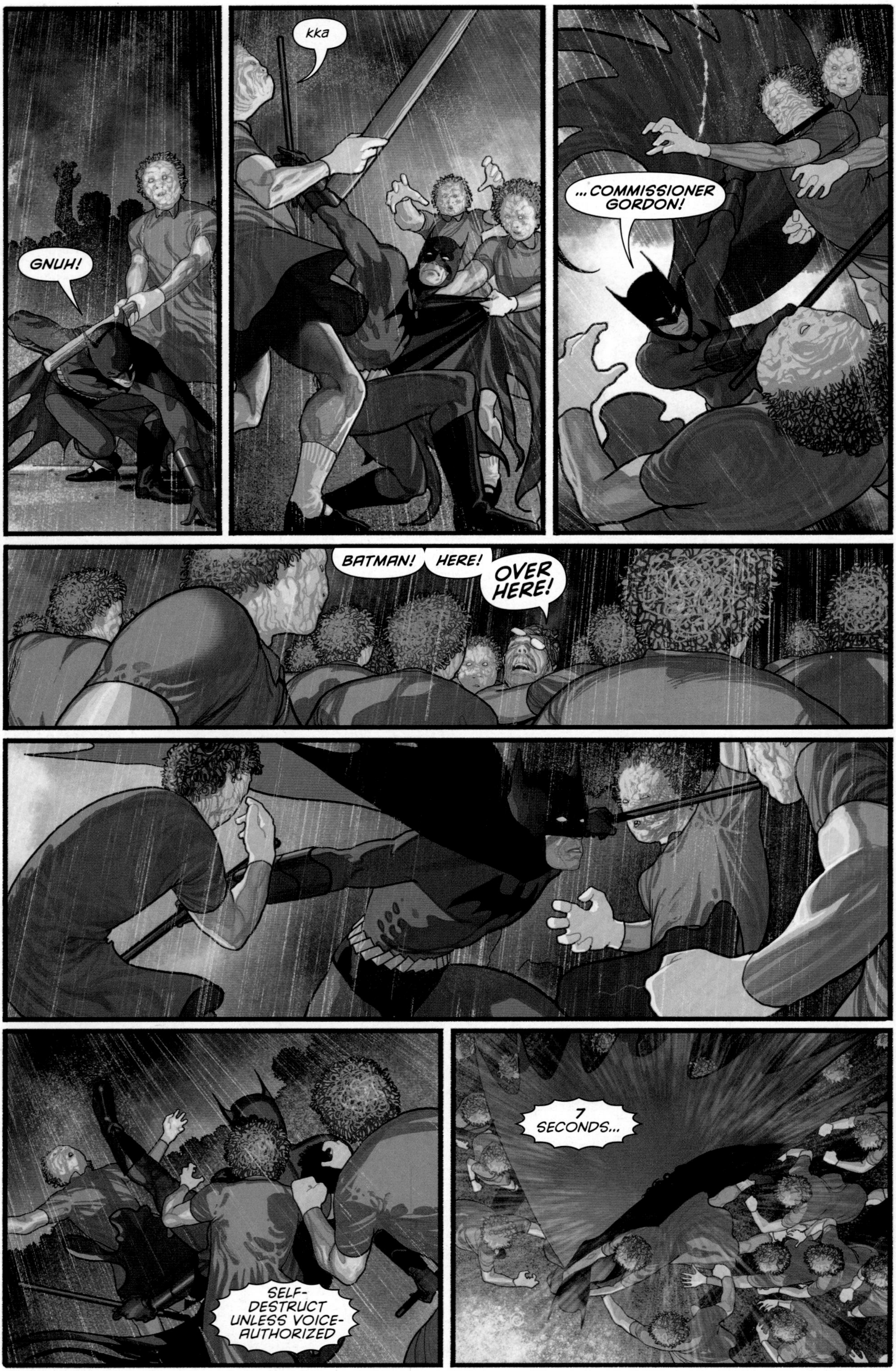
GNUH!
kka
...COMMISSIONER GORDON!
BATMAN!
HERE!
OVER HERE!
SELF-DESTRUCT UNLESS VOICE-AUTHORIZED
7 SECONDS...

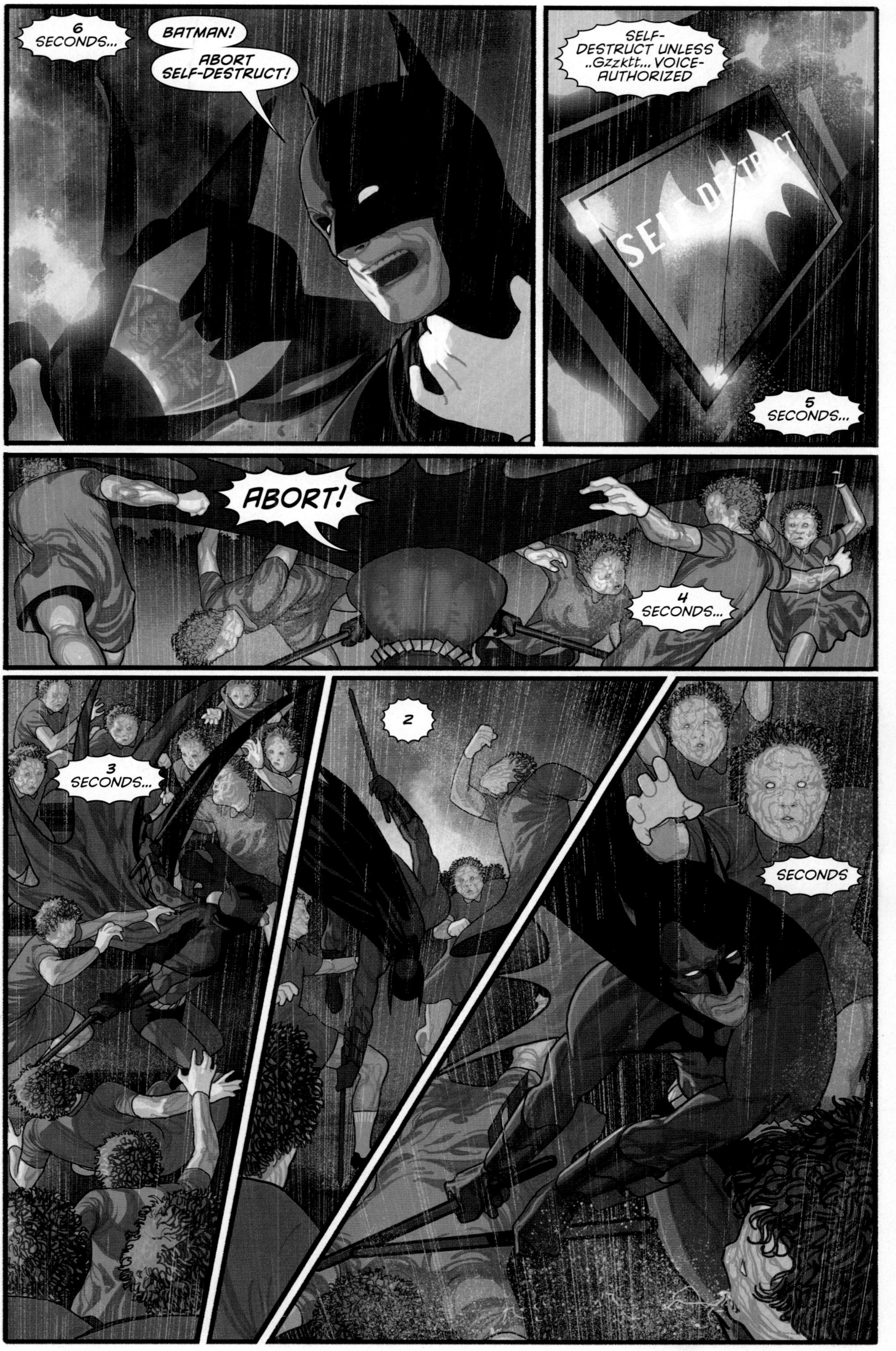

6 SECONDS...
BATMAN!
ABORT SELF-DESTRUCT!
SELF-DESTRUCT UNLESS ..Gzzktt... VOICE-AUTHORIZED
SELF DESTRUCT
5 SECONDS...
ABORT!
4 SECONDS...
3 SECONDS...
2
SECONDS

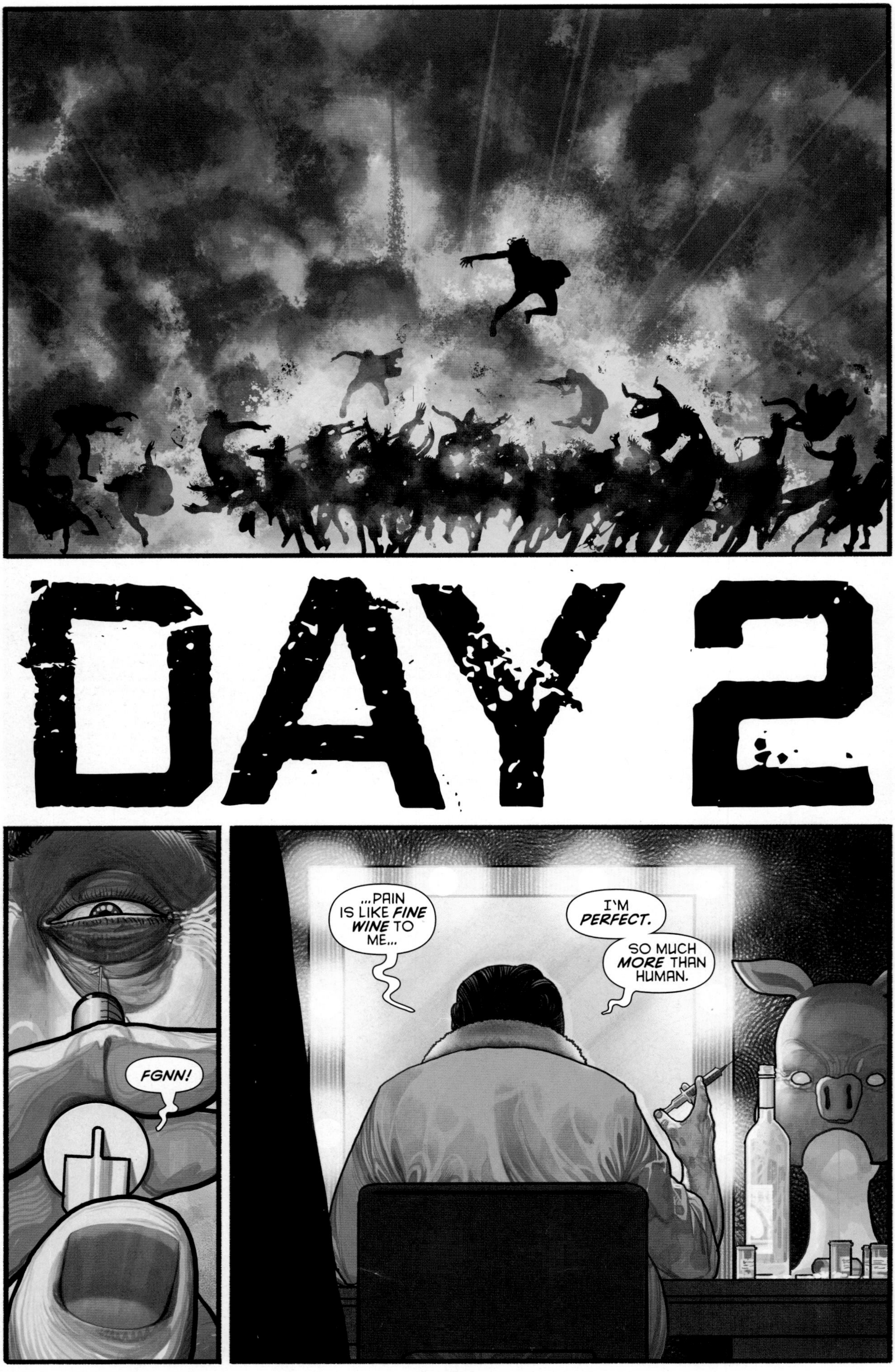
DAY 2
FGNN!
...PAIN IS LIKE FINE WINE TO ME...
I'M PERFECT.
SO MUCH MORE THAN HUMAN.

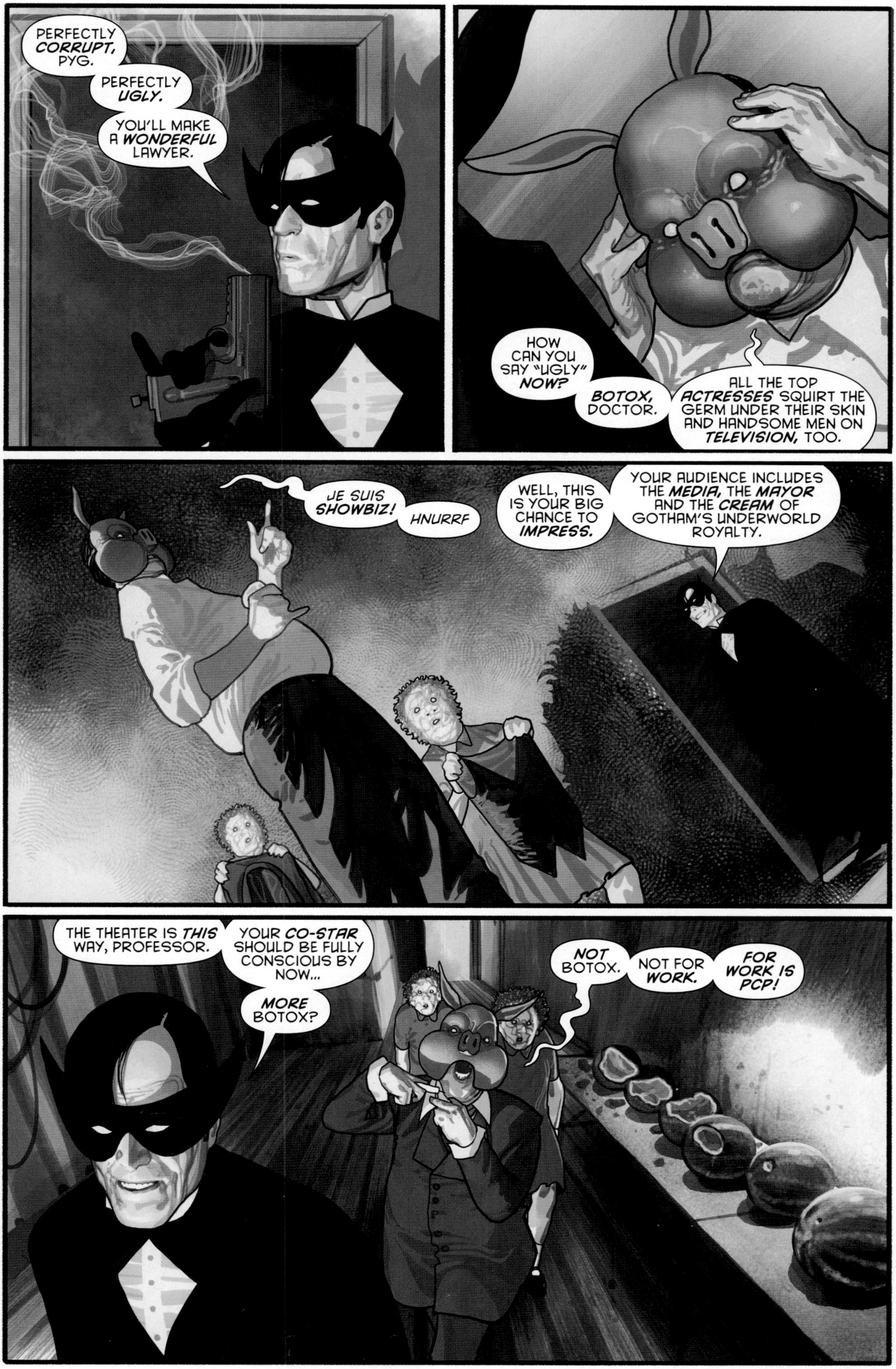
PERFECTLY CORRUPT, PYG.
PERFECTLY UGLY.
YOU'LL MAKE A WONDERFUL LAWYER.
HOW CAN YOU SAY "UGLY" NOW?
BOTOX, DOCTOR.
ALL THE TOP ACTRESSES SQUIRT THE GERM UNDER THEIR SKIN AND HANDSOME MEN ON TELEVISION, TOO.
JE SUIS SHOWBIZ!
HNURRF
WELL, THIS IS YOUR BIG CHANCE TO IMPRESS.
YOUR AUDIENCE INCLUDES THE MEDIA, THE MAYOR AND THE CREAM OF GOTHAM'S UNDERWORLD ROYALTY.
THE THEATER IS THIS WAY, PROFESSOR.
YOUR CO-STAR SHOULD BE FULLY CONSCIOUS BY NOW...
MORE BOTOX?
NOT BOTOX.
NOT FOR WORK.
FOR WORK IS PCP!

ARE YOU *KIDDING* ME?

HOW LONG HAVE I BEEN OUT?

UNNHHH

ALFRED.

TELL ME WHAT HAPPENED TO *COMMISSIONER GORDON.*

YOU'VE BEEN UNDER SEDATION FOR *SEVERAL* HOURS, SIR.

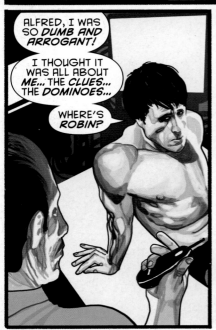

ALFRED, I WAS SO *DUMB AND ARROGANT!*

I THOUGHT IT WAS ALL ABOUT *ME...* THE *CLUES...* THE *DOMINOES...*

WHERE'S *ROBIN?*

THE WHOLE CITY'S IN SOMETHING OF AN *UPROAR.*

BUT PERHAPS YOU'LL HAVE BETTER LUCK THAN I...

ROBIN! RESPOND!

CZZZKK

THERE YOU ARE.

AT *LAST.*

HEHHHH

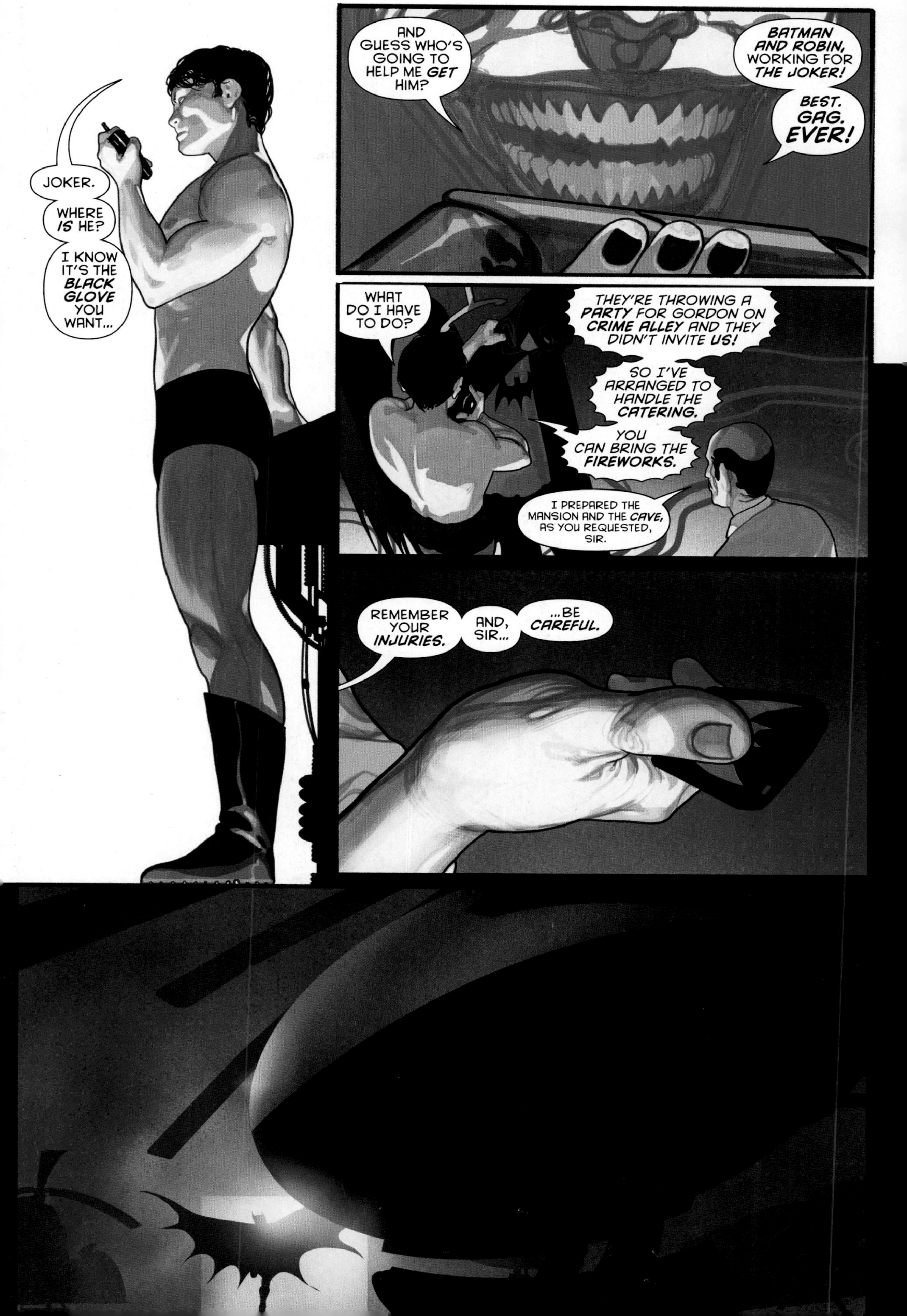
JOKER.
WHERE *IS* HE?
I KNOW IT'S THE *BLACK GLOVE* YOU WANT...
AND GUESS WHO'S GOING TO HELP ME *GET* HIM?
BATMAN AND ROBIN, WORKING FOR *THE JOKER!*
BEST. GAG. **EVER!**
WHAT DO I HAVE TO DO?
THEY'RE THROWING A **PARTY** FOR GORDON ON **CRIME ALLEY** AND THEY DIDN'T INVITE **US!**
SO I'VE ARRANGED TO HANDLE THE **CATERING.**
YOU CAN BRING THE **FIREWORKS.**
I PREPARED THE MANSION AND THE *CAVE,* AS YOU REQUESTED, SIR.
REMEMBER YOUR *INJURIES.*
AND, SIR...
...BE *CAREFUL.*

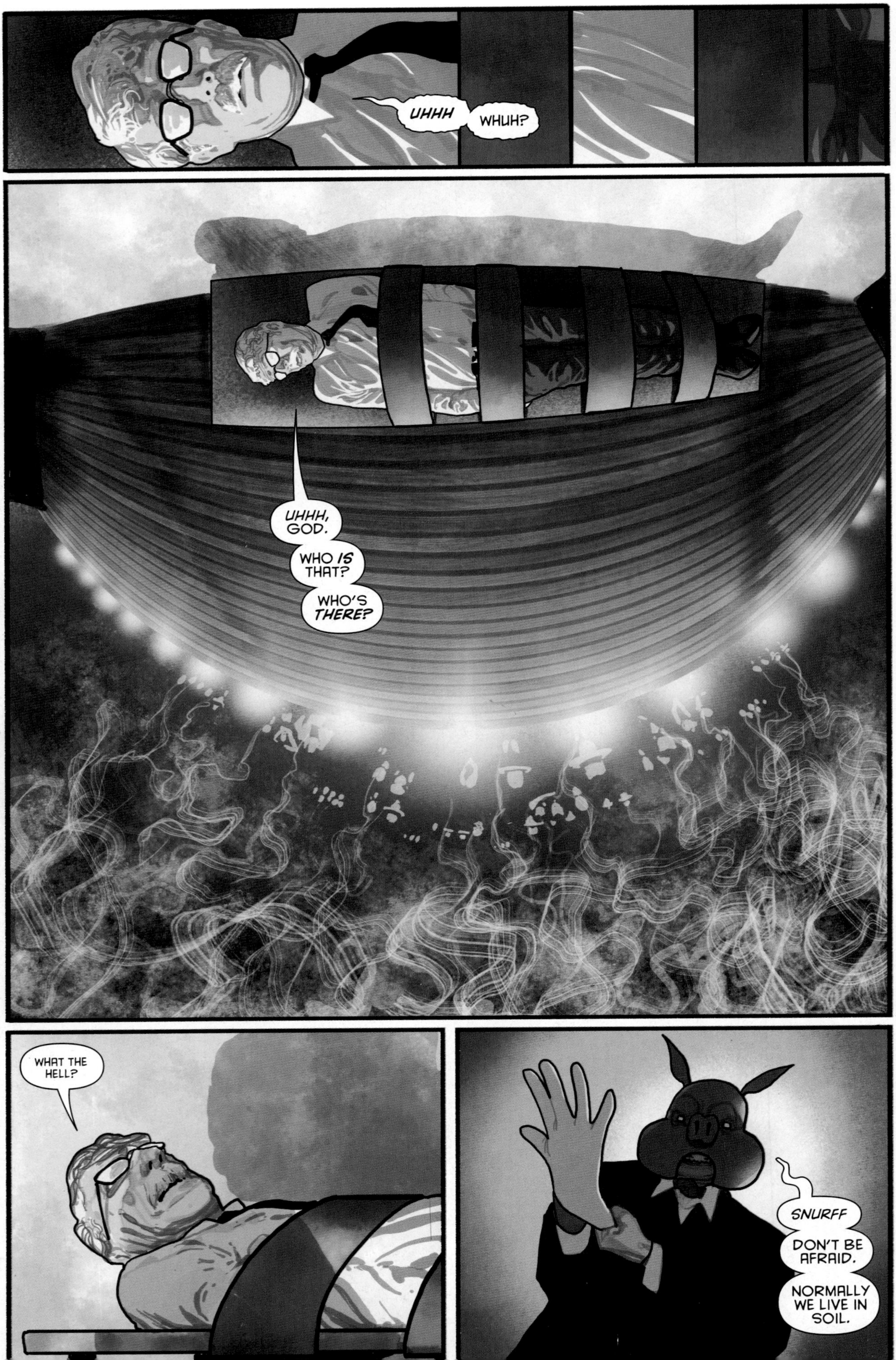
UHHH
WHUH?
UHHH, GOD.
WHO IS THAT?
WHO'S THERE?
WHAT THE HELL?
SNURFF
DON'T BE AFRAID.
NORMALLY WE LIVE IN SOIL.

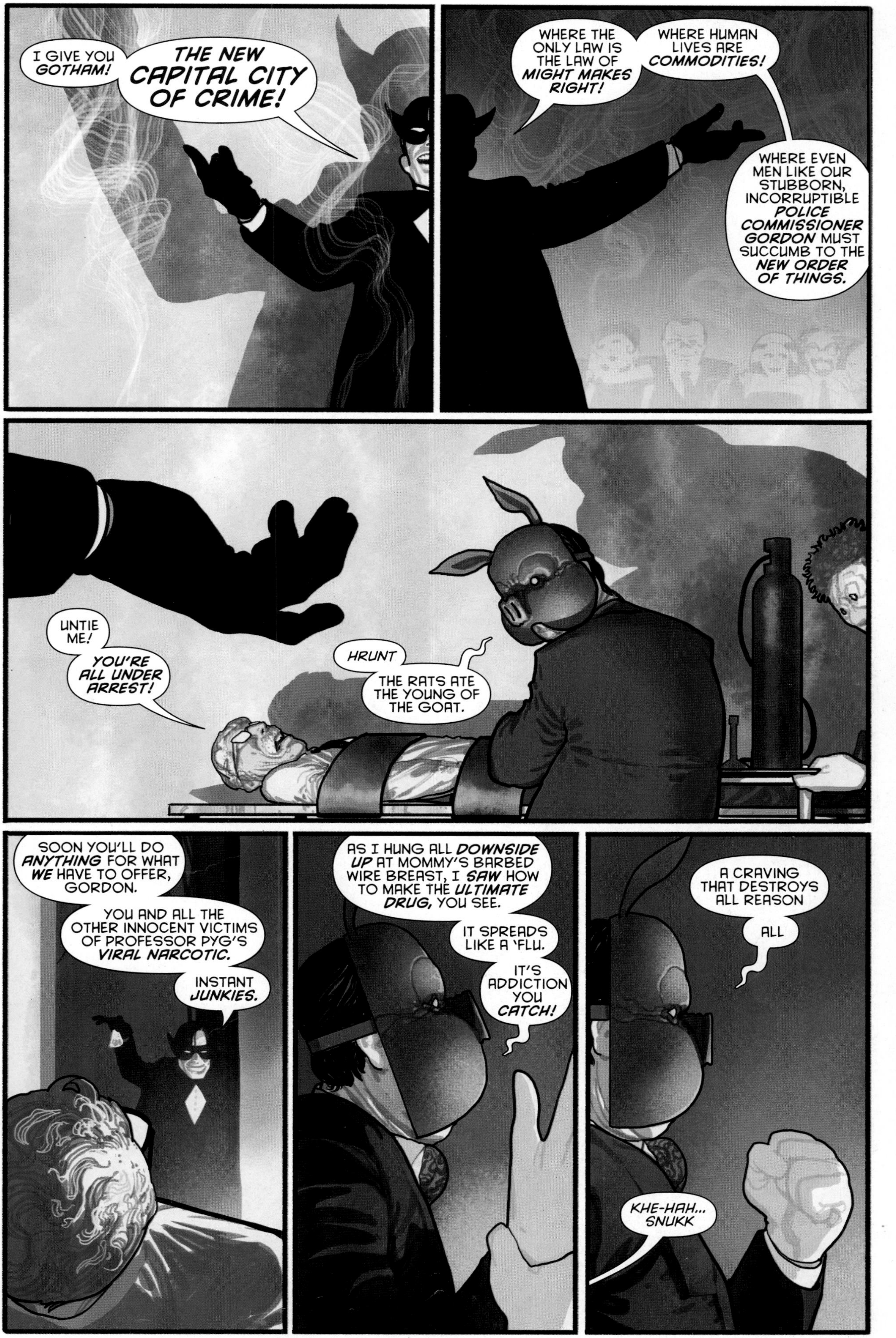
I GIVE YOU *GOTHAM!*
THE NEW CAPITAL CITY OF CRIME!
WHERE THE ONLY LAW IS THE LAW OF *MIGHT MAKES RIGHT!*
WHERE HUMAN LIVES ARE *COMMODITIES!*
WHERE EVEN MEN LIKE OUR STUBBORN, INCORRUPTIBLE *POLICE COMMISSIONER GORDON* MUST SUCCUMB TO THE *NEW ORDER OF THINGS.*
UNTIE ME!
YOU'RE ALL UNDER ARREST!
HRUNT
THE RATS ATE THE YOUNG OF THE GOAT.
SOON YOU'LL DO *ANYTHING* FOR WHAT *WE* HAVE TO OFFER, GORDON.
YOU AND ALL THE OTHER INNOCENT VICTIMS OF PROFESSOR PYG'S *VIRAL NARCOTIC.*
INSTANT *JUNKIES.*
AS I HUNG ALL *DOWNSIDE UP* AT MOMMY'S BARBED WIRE BREAST, I *SAW* HOW TO MAKE THE *ULTIMATE DRUG,* YOU SEE.
IT SPREADS LIKE A 'FLU.
IT'S ADDICTION YOU *CATCH!*
A CRAVING THAT DESTROYS ALL REASON
ALL
KHE-HAH... SNUKK

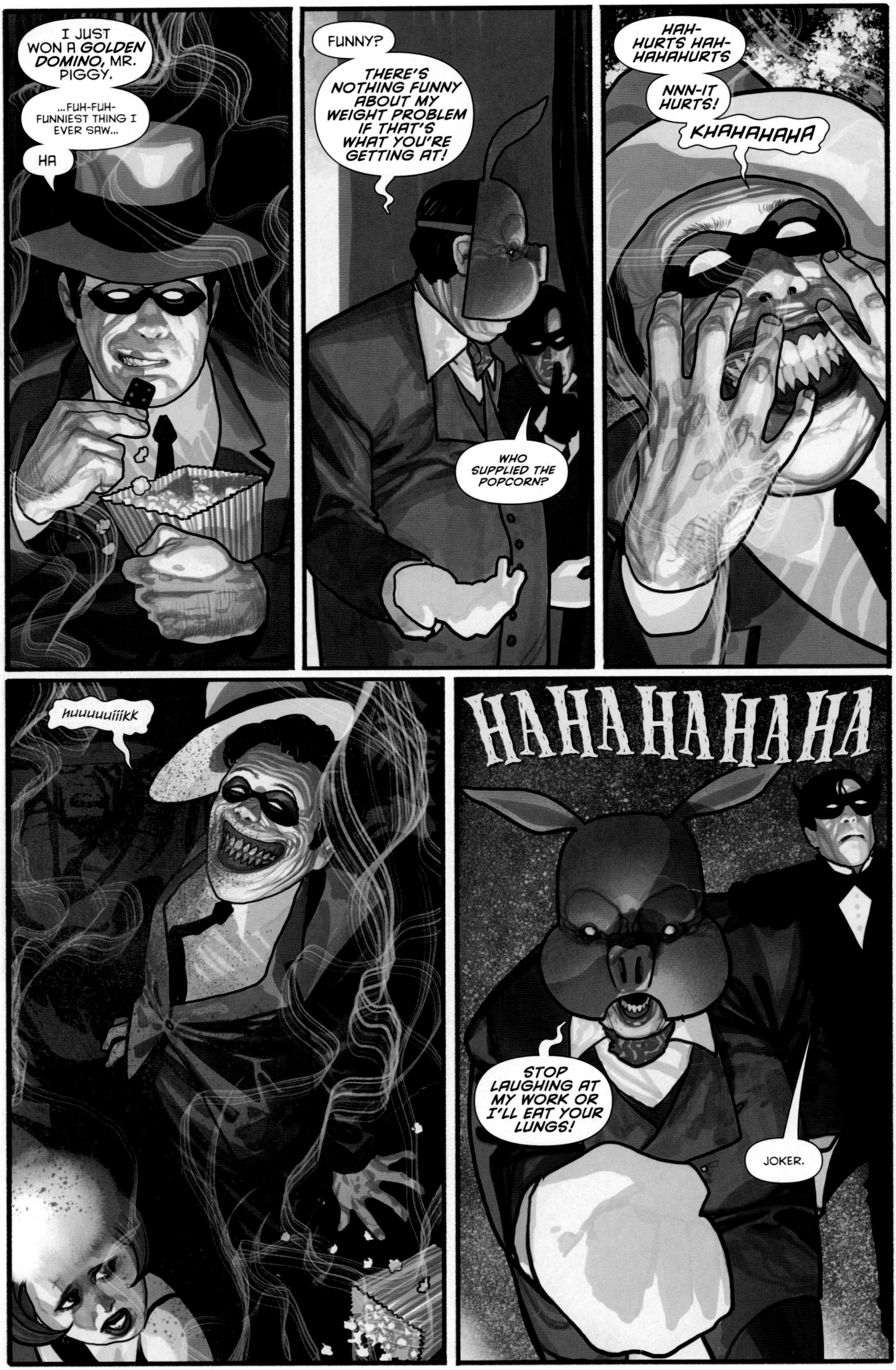

I JUST WON A *GOLDEN DOMINO*, MR. PIGGY.
...FUH-FUH-FUNNIEST THING I EVER SAW...
HA
FUNNY?
THERE'S NOTHING FUNNY ABOUT MY WEIGHT PROBLEM IF THAT'S WHAT YOU'RE GETTING AT!
WHO SUPPLIED THE POPCORN?
HAH-HURTS HAH-HAHAHURTS
NNN-IT HURTS!
KHAHAHAHA
huuuuuiiikk
HAHAHAHAHAHA
STOP LAUGHING AT MY WORK OR I'LL EAT YOUR LUNGS!
JOKER.

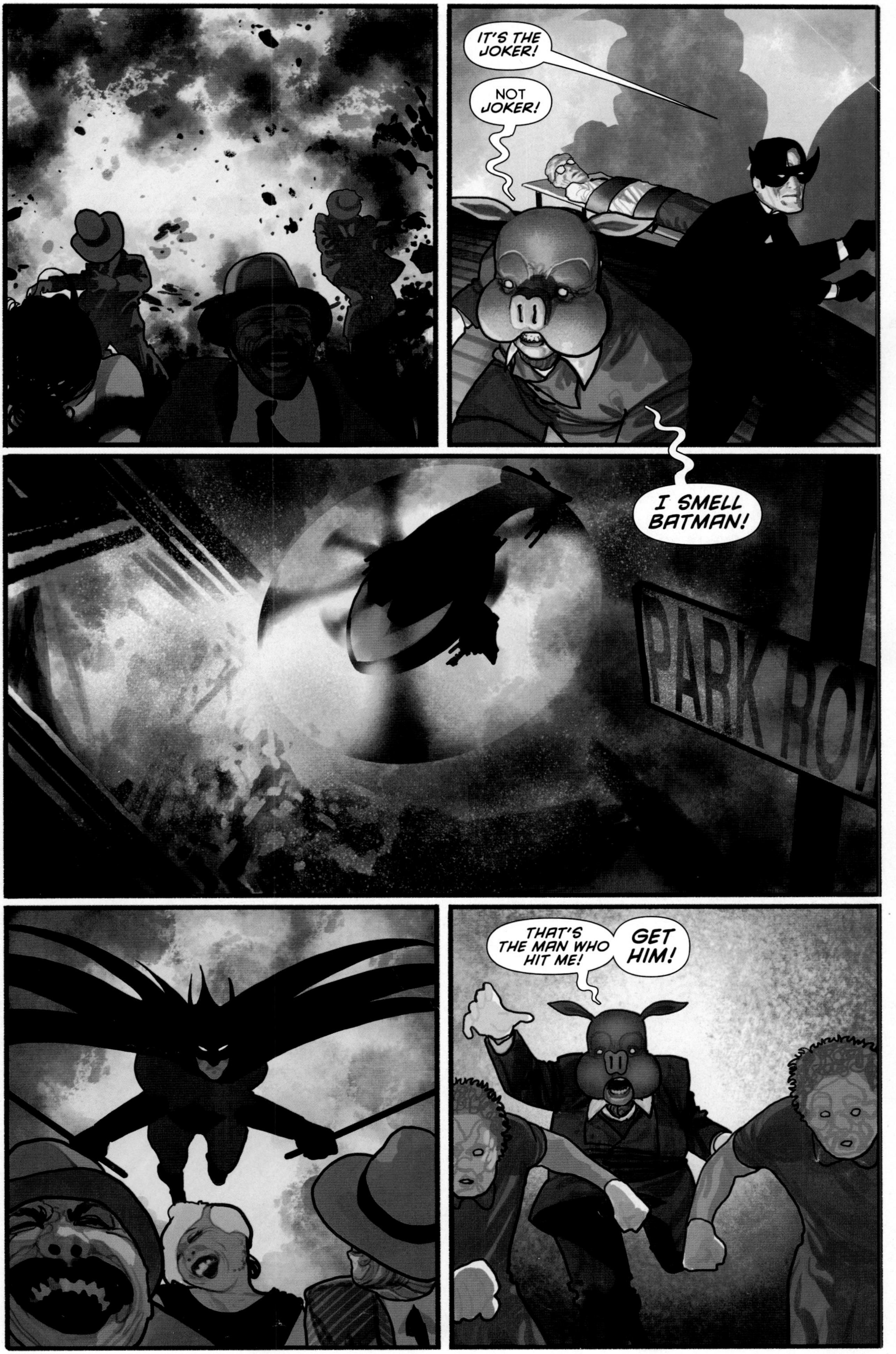
IT'S THE JOKER!
NOT JOKER!
I SMELL BATMAN!
PARK ROW
THAT'S THE MAN WHO HIT ME!
GET HIM!

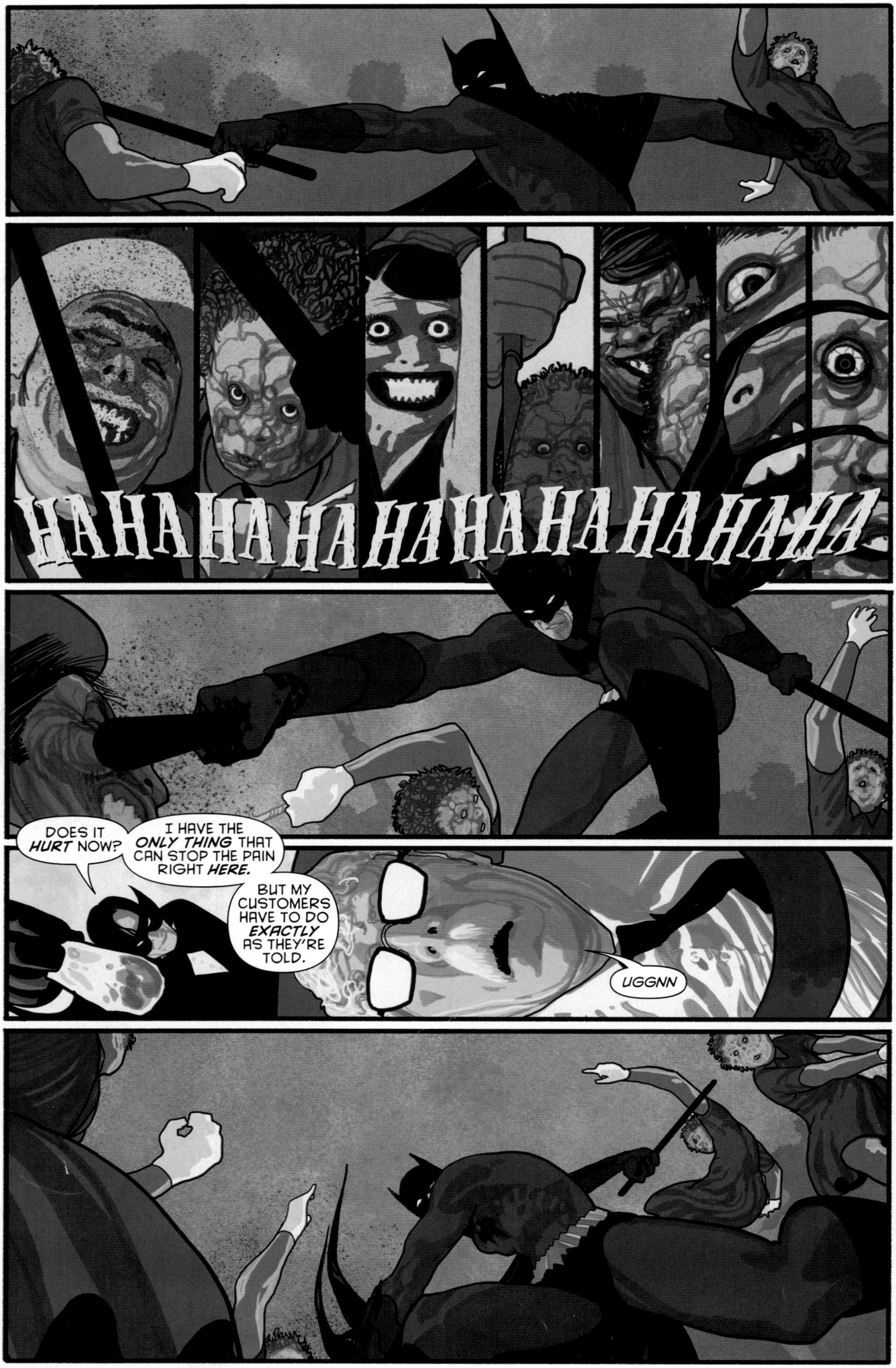
HAHAHAHAHAHAHAHAHAHAHAHA
DOES IT HURT NOW?
I HAVE THE ONLY THING THAT CAN STOP THE PAIN RIGHT HERE.
BUT MY CUSTOMERS HAVE TO DO EXACTLY AS THEY'RE TOLD.
UGGNN

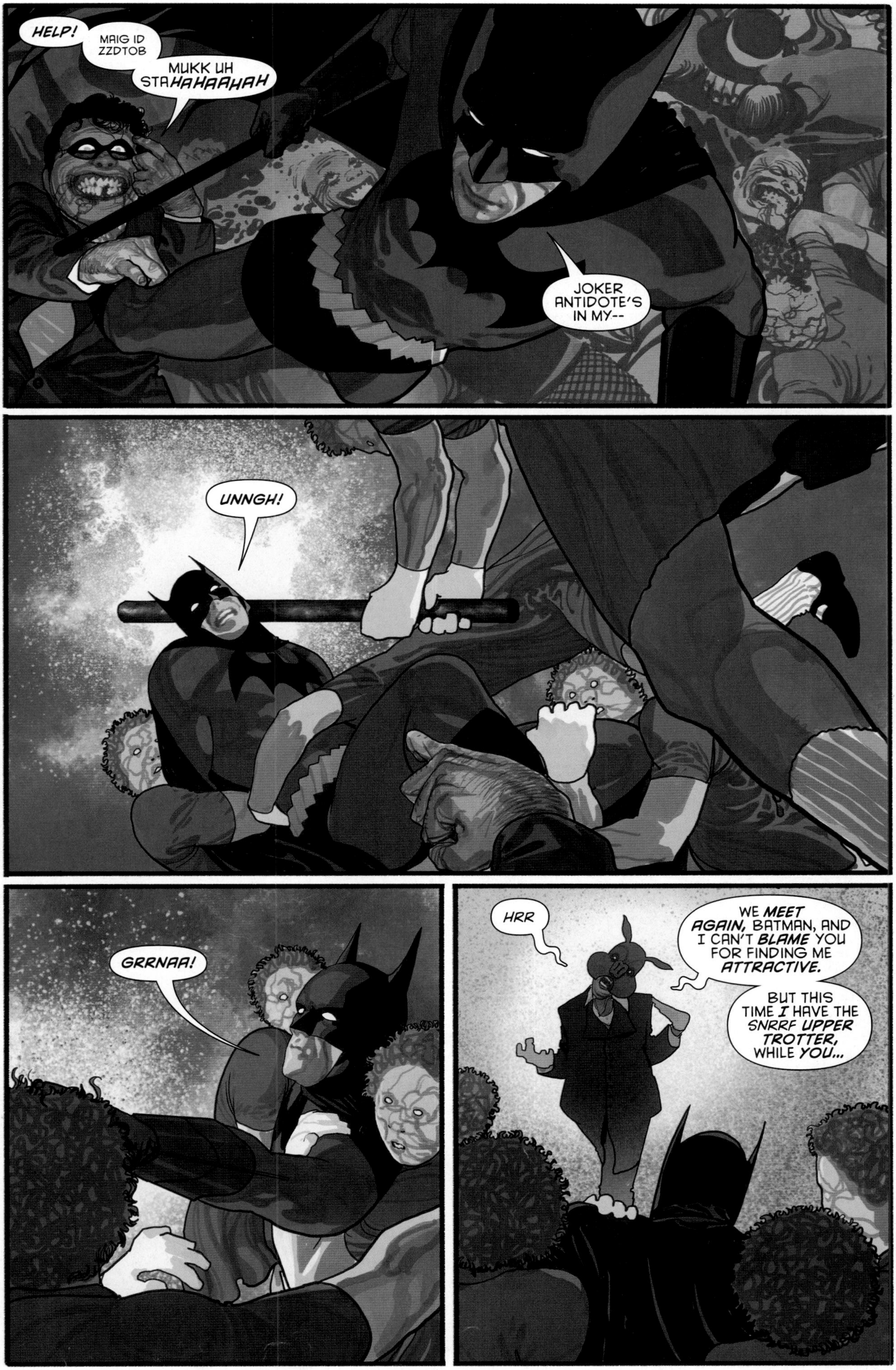
HELP!
MAIG ID ZZDTOB
MUKK UH STAHAHAAHAH
JOKER ANTIDOTE'S IN MY--
UNNGH!
GRRNAA!
HRR
WE MEET AGAIN, BATMAN, AND I CAN'T BLAME YOU FOR FINDING ME ATTRACTIVE.
BUT THIS TIME I HAVE THE SNRRF UPPER TROTTER, WHILE YOU...

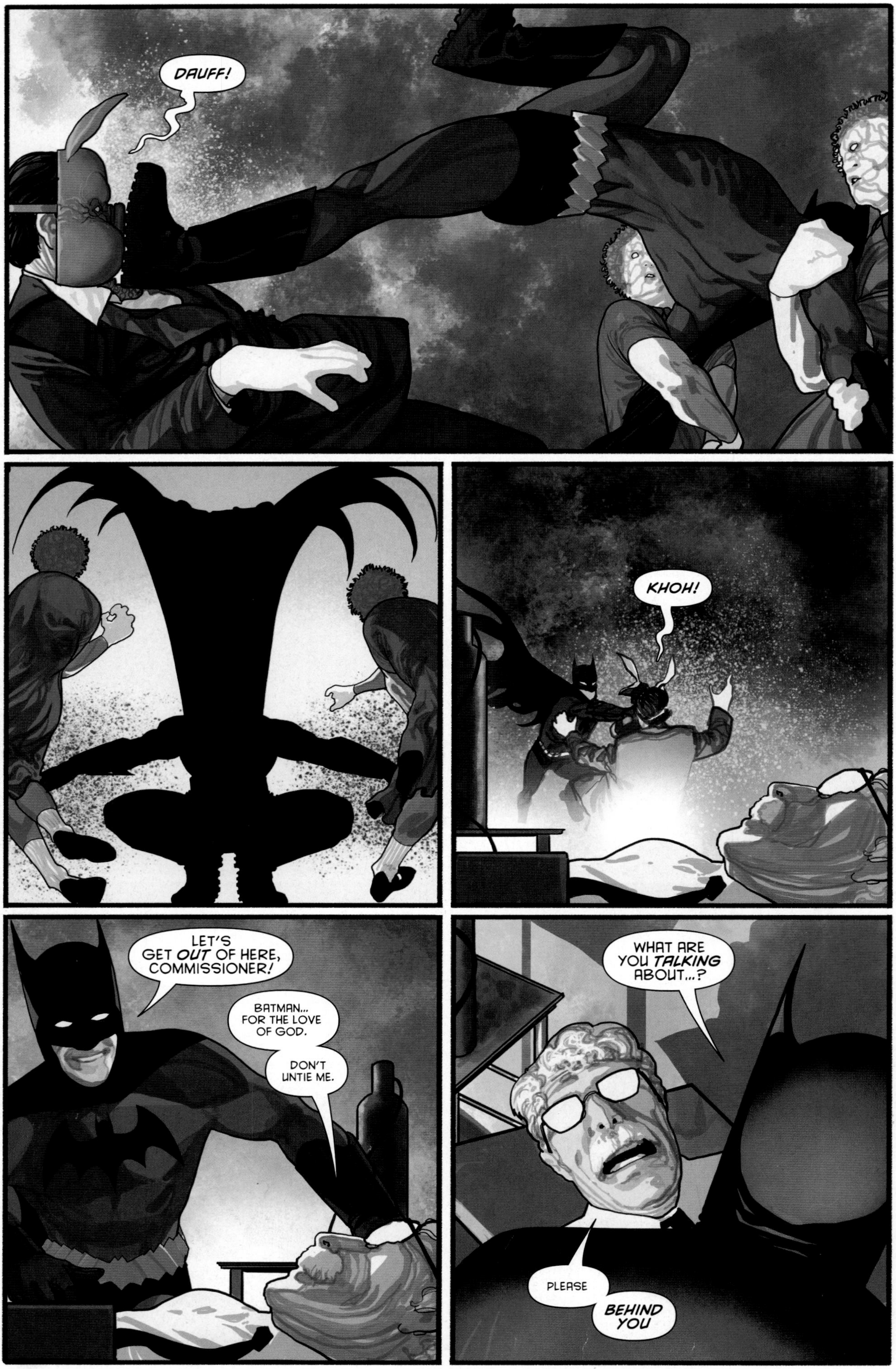
DAUFF!
KHOH!
LET'S GET OUT OF HERE, COMMISSIONER!
BATMAN... FOR THE LOVE OF GOD.
DON'T UNTIE ME.
WHAT ARE YOU TALKING ABOUT...?
PLEASE
BEHIND YOU

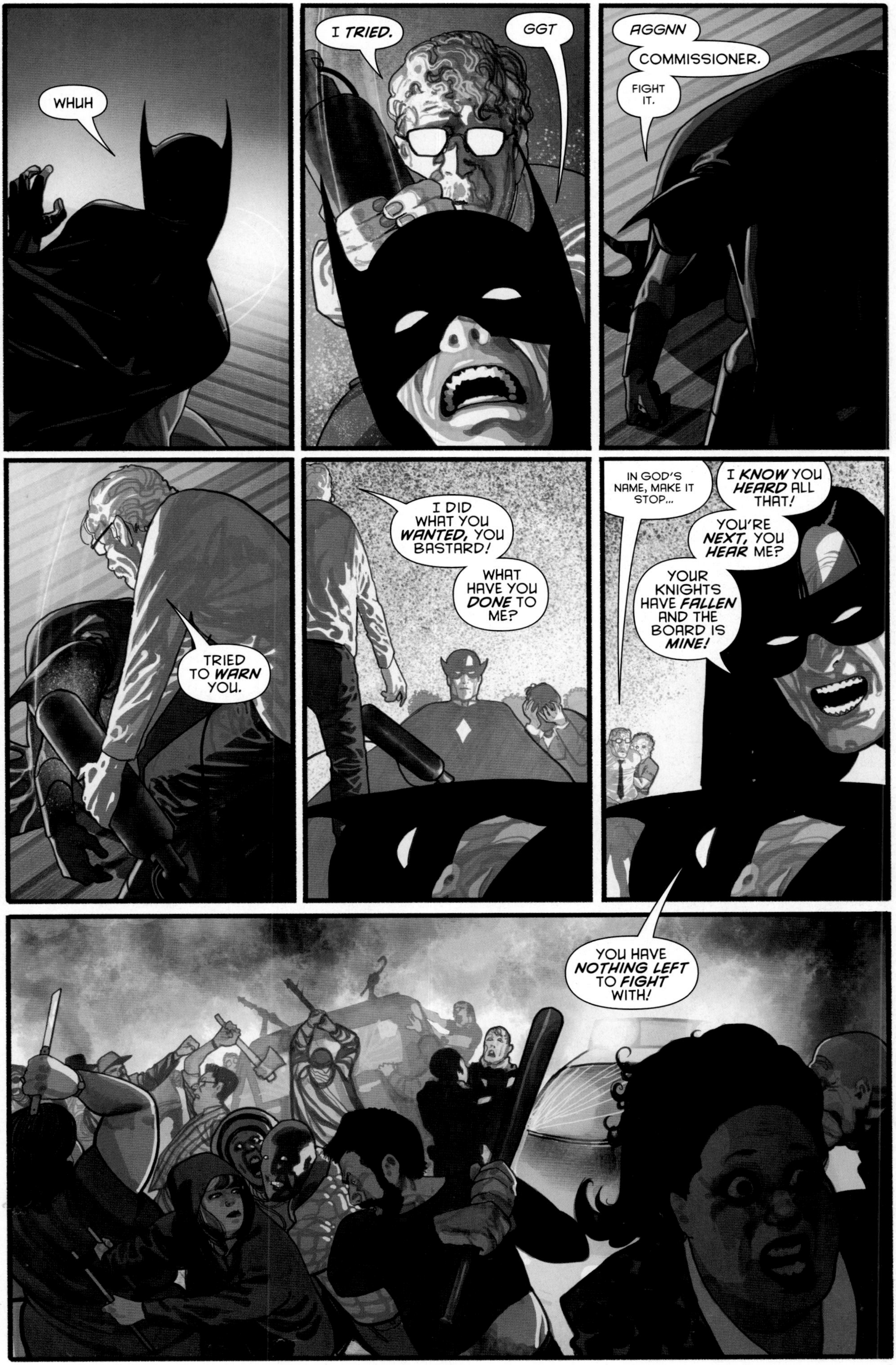
WHUH
I *TRIED.*
GGT
AGGNN
COMMISSIONER.
FIGHT IT.
TRIED TO *WARN* YOU.
I DID WHAT YOU *WANTED,* YOU BASTARD!
WHAT HAVE YOU *DONE* TO ME?
IN GOD'S NAME, MAKE IT STOP...
I *KNOW* YOU *HEARD* ALL THAT!
YOU'RE *NEXT,* YOU *HEAR* ME?
YOUR KNIGHTS HAVE *FALLEN* AND THE BOARD IS *MINE!*
YOU HAVE *NOTHING LEFT* TO *FIGHT* WITH!

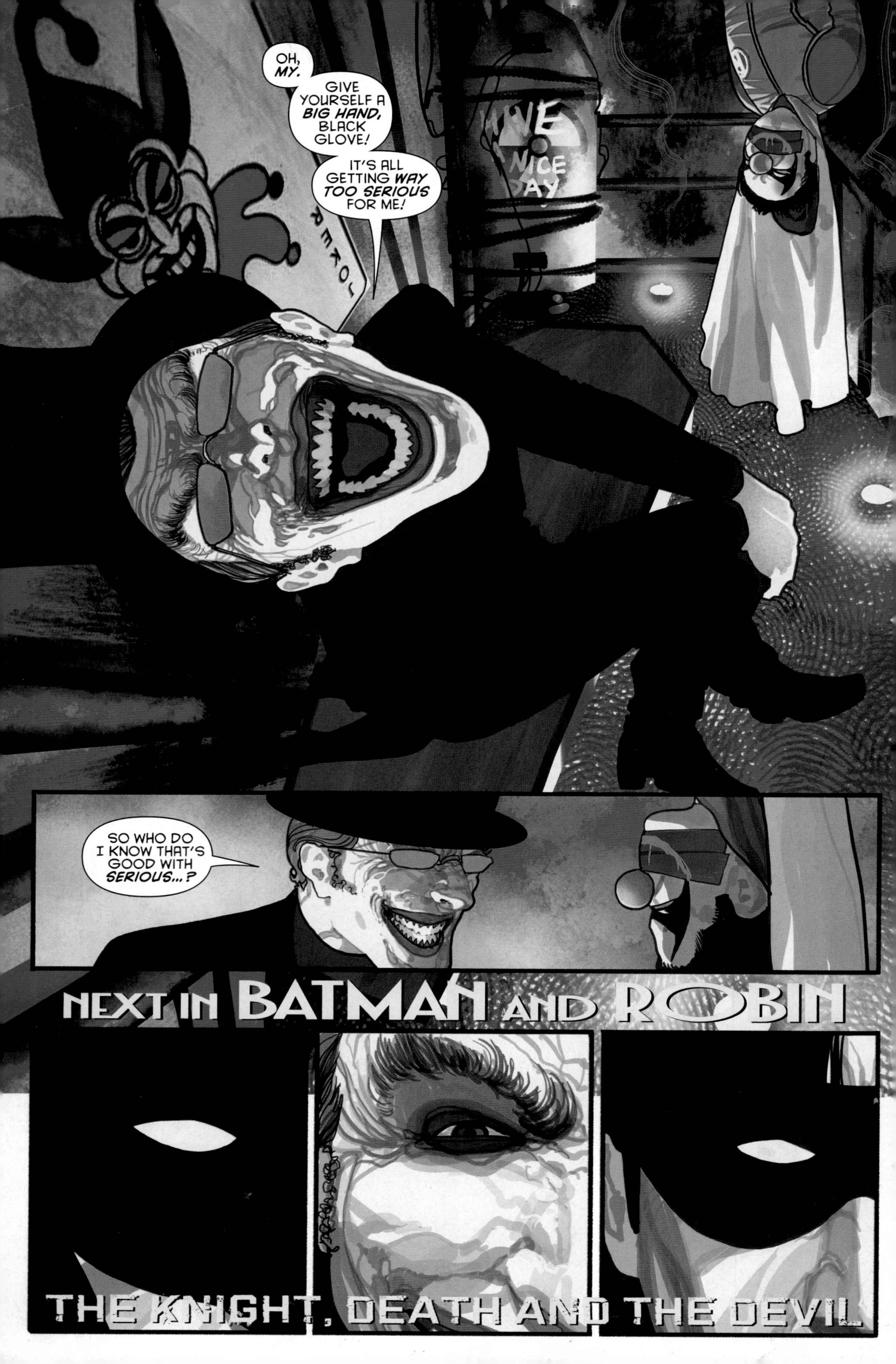
OH, *MY.*
GIVE YOURSELF A *BIG HAND,* BLACK GLOVE!
IT'S ALL GETTING *WAY TOO SERIOUS* FOR ME!
SO WHO DO I KNOW THAT'S GOOD WITH *SERIOUS...?*
NEXT IN BATMAN AND ROBIN
THE KNIGHT, DEATH AND THE DEVIL

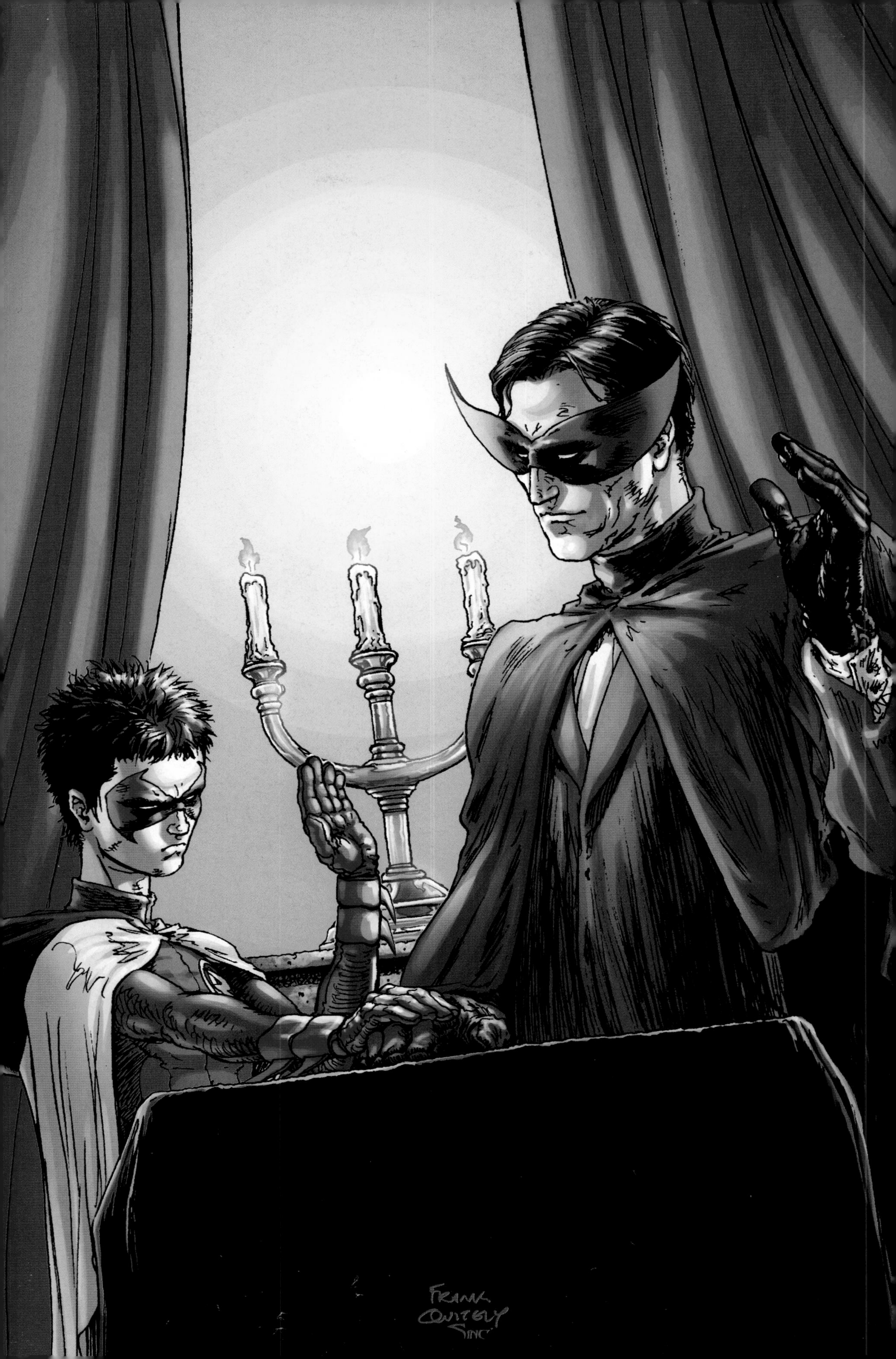

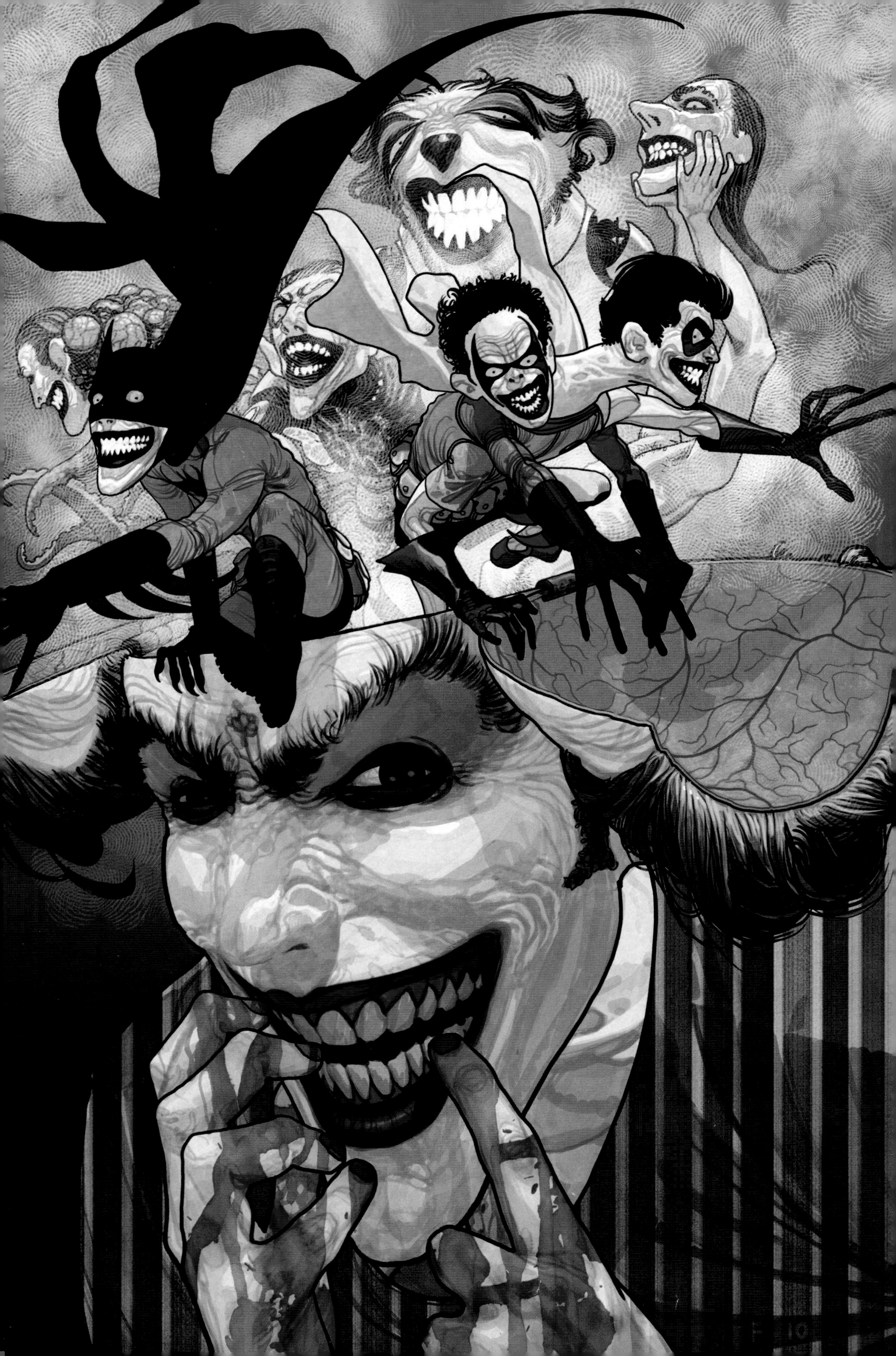

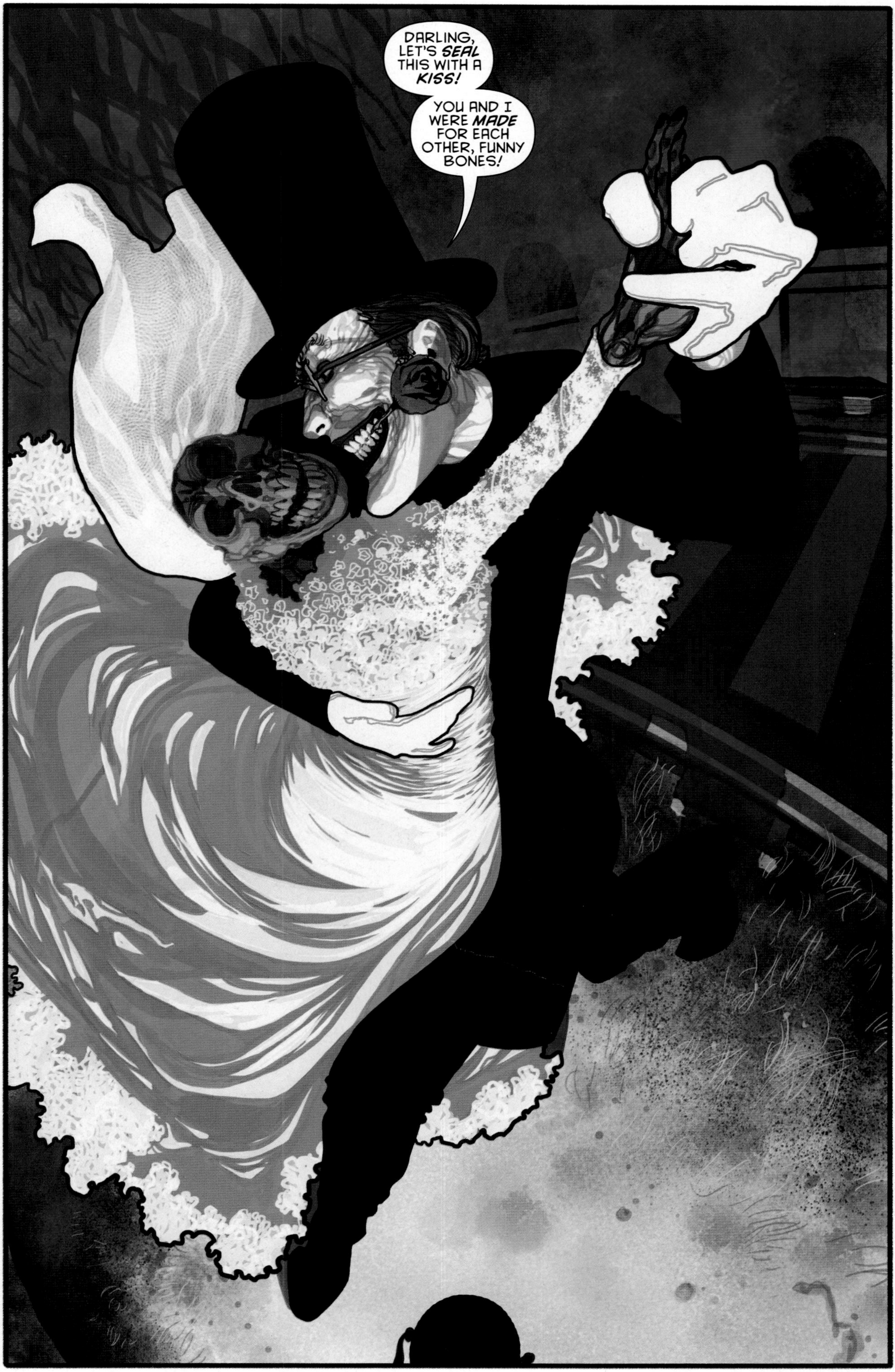
DARLING, LET'S SEAL THIS WITH A KISS!
YOU AND I WERE MADE FOR EACH OTHER, FUNNY BONES!

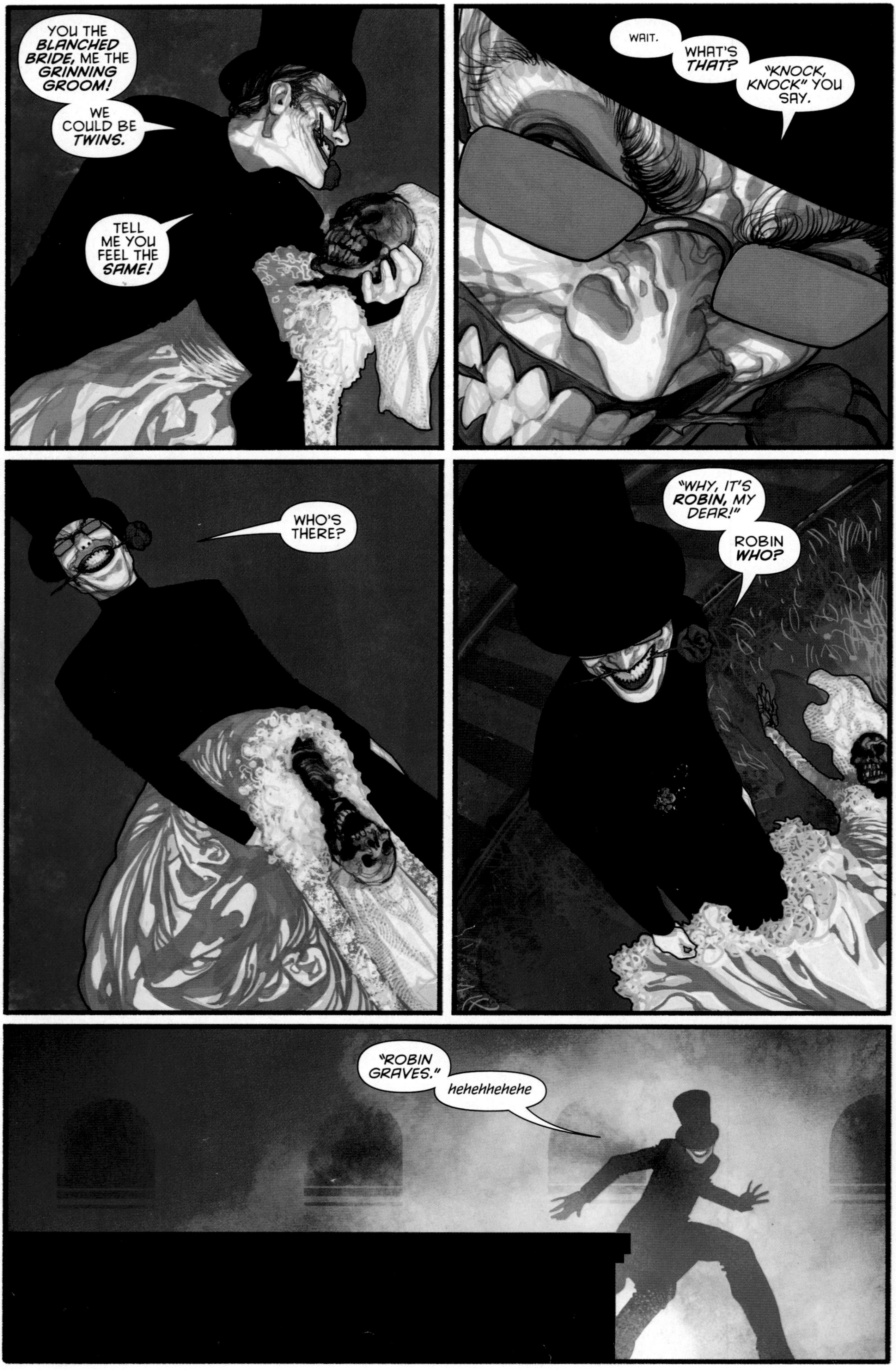
YOU THE BLANCHED BRIDE, ME THE GRINNING GROOM!
WE COULD BE TWINS.
TELL ME YOU FEEL THE SAME!
WAIT.
WHAT'S THAT?
"KNOCK, KNOCK" YOU SAY.
WHO'S THERE?
"WHY, IT'S ROBIN, MY DEAR!"
ROBIN WHO?
"ROBIN GRAVES."
hehehhehehe

BORN FROM A *COFFIN.*

ANGRY, TOO, BY THE SOUND OF IT.

KICKING.

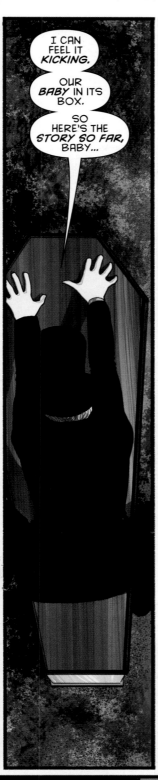

I CAN FEEL IT *KICKING.*

OUR *BABY* IN ITS BOX.

SO HERE'S THE *STORY SO FAR,* BABY...

THE *BIG BROTHER YOU NEVER HAD* IS ON THE *DEVIL'S CHOPPING BLOCK!*

THE FIRST AND *BEST BOY WONDER'S* IN THE HANDS OF THE MOST *EVIL MAN ON EARTH!*

WHAT ARE *YOU* GOING TO DO ABOUT IT?

ffrrmm

EASY FOR YOU TO *INSIST!*

BUT LET'S SEE WHAT OUR *SPONSOR* HAS TO SAY...

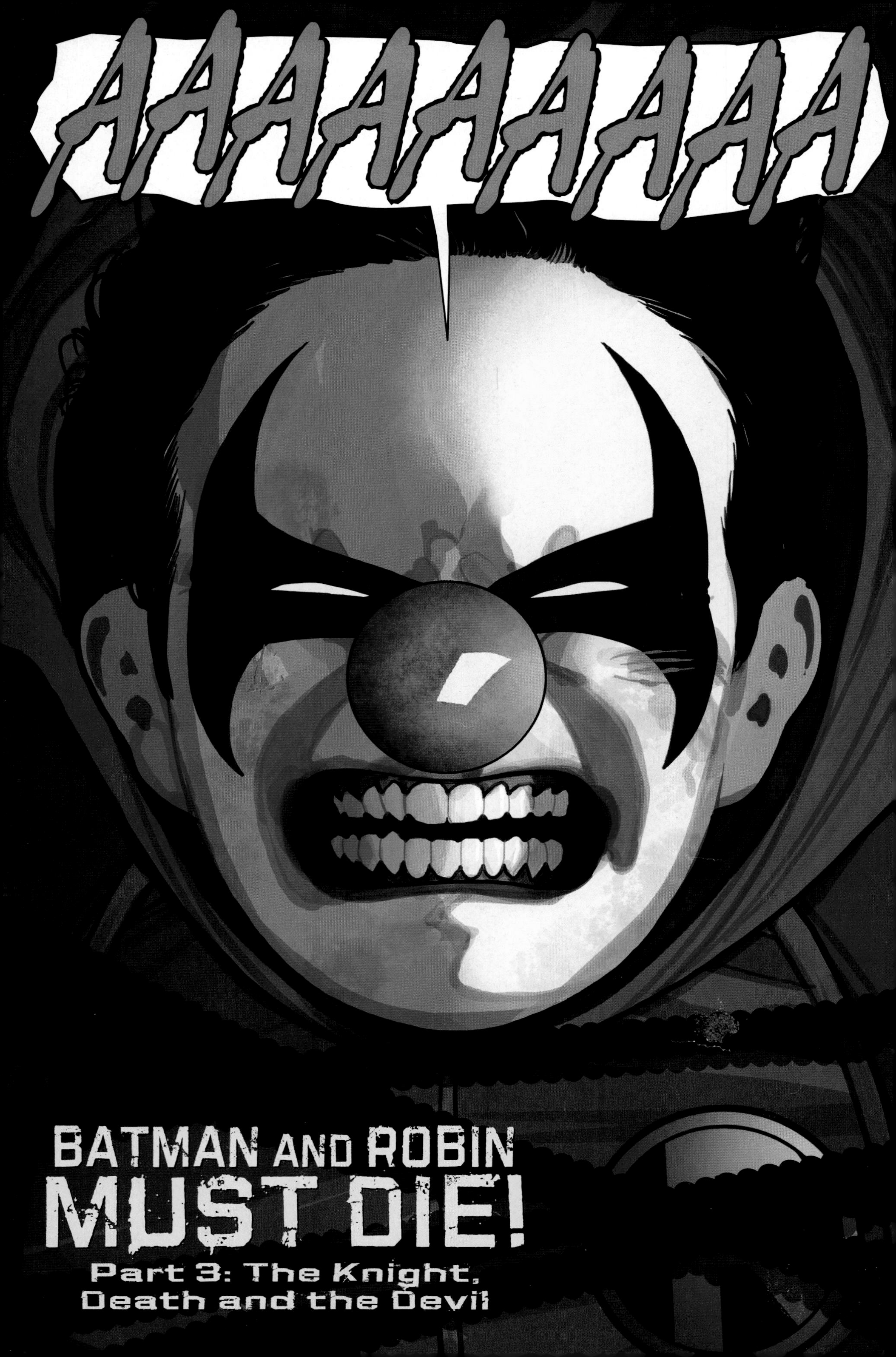
AAAAAAAAAAA
BATMAN AND ROBIN
MUST DIE!
Part 3: The Knight, Death and the Devil

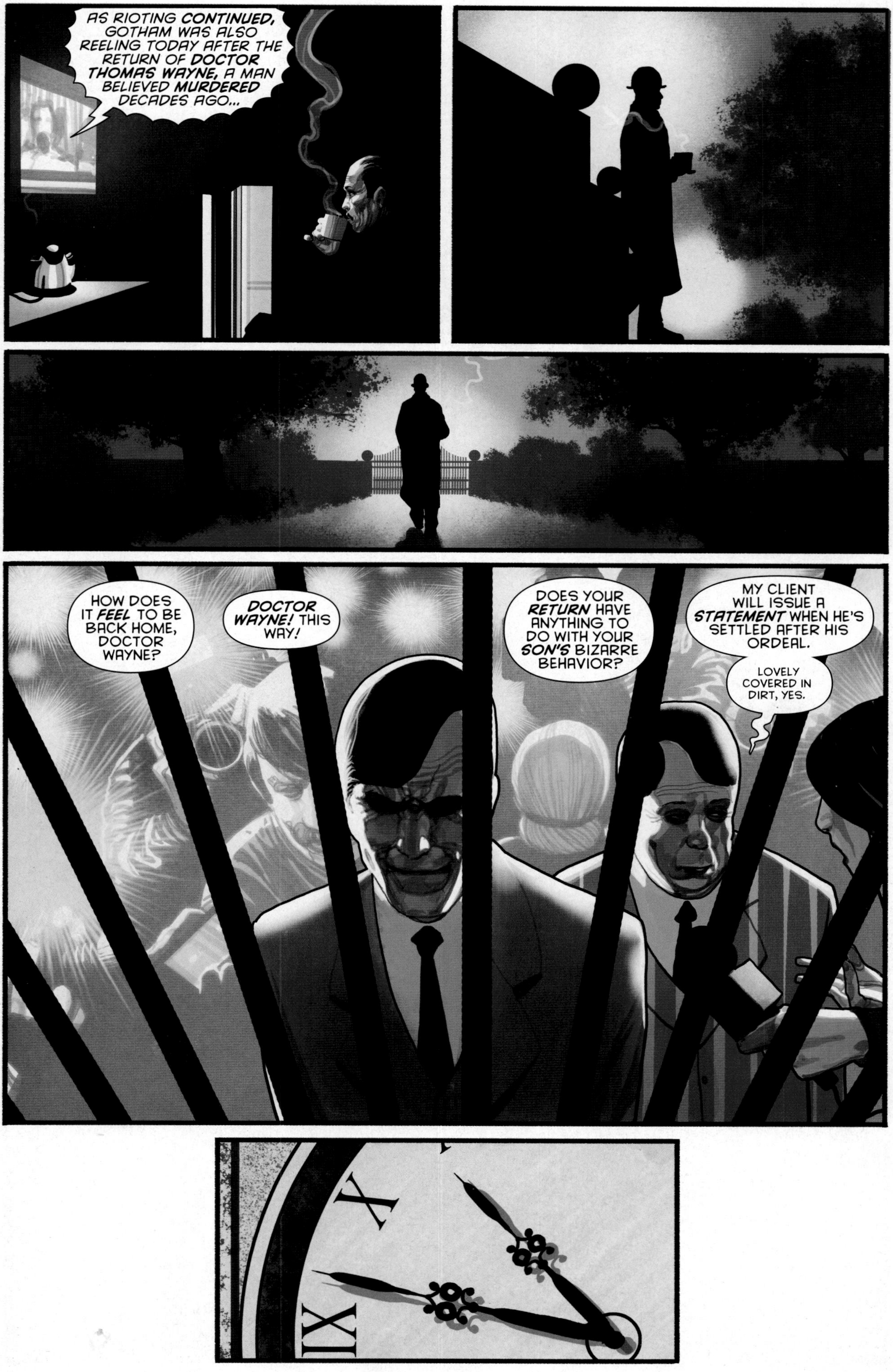
AS RIOTING CONTINUED, GOTHAM WAS ALSO REELING TODAY AFTER THE RETURN OF DOCTOR THOMAS WAYNE, A MAN BELIEVED MURDERED DECADES AGO...
HOW DOES IT FEEL TO BE BACK HOME, DOCTOR WAYNE?
DOCTOR WAYNE! THIS WAY!
DOES YOUR RETURN HAVE ANYTHING TO DO WITH YOUR SON'S BIZARRE BEHAVIOR?
MY CLIENT WILL ISSUE A STATEMENT WHEN HE'S SETTLED AFTER HIS ORDEAL.
LOVELY COVERED IN DIRT, YES.
X
XI

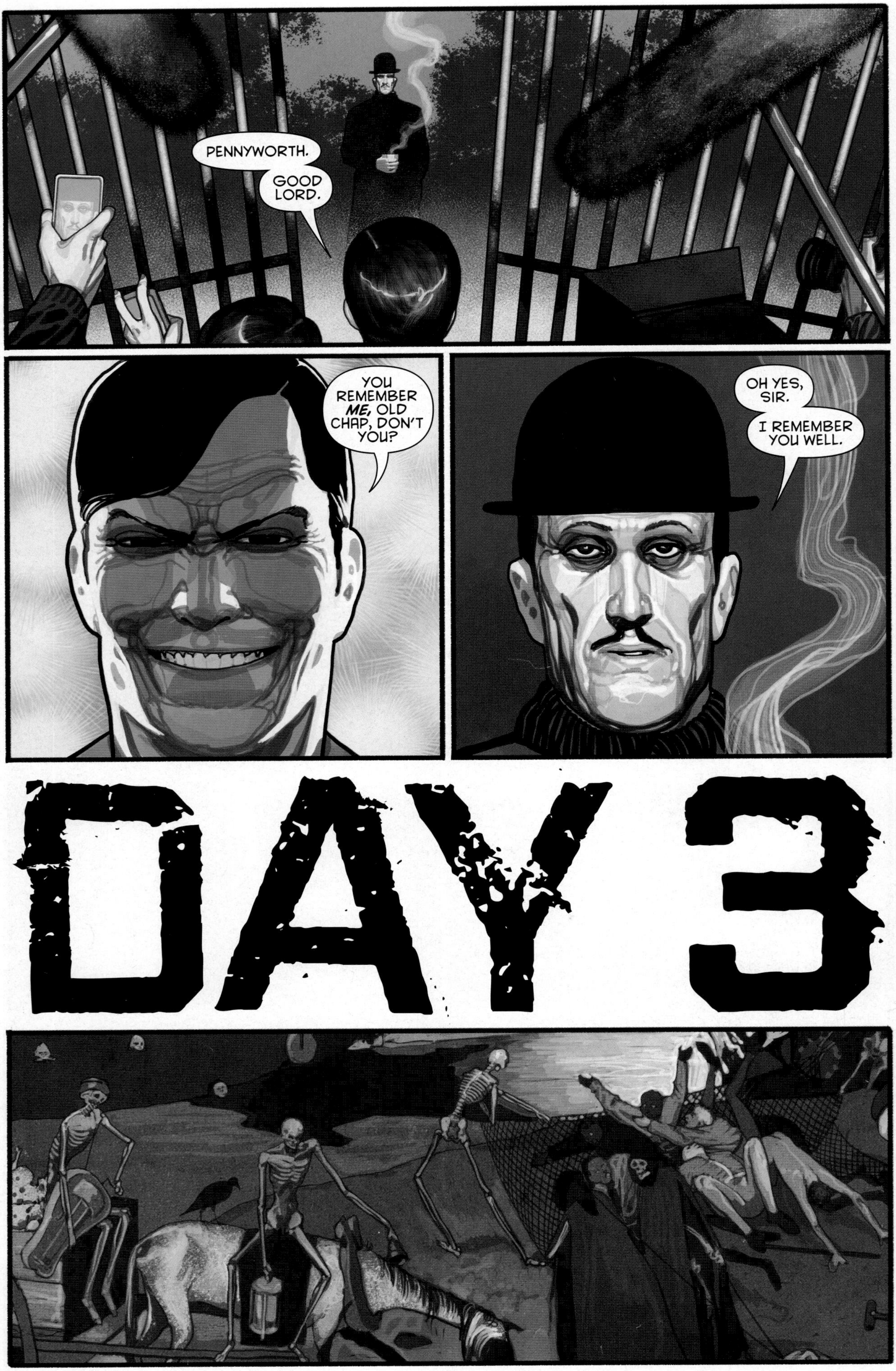
PENNYWORTH.
GOOD LORD.
YOU REMEMBER ME, OLD CHAP, DON'T YOU?
OH YES, SIR.
I REMEMBER YOU WELL.
DAY 3

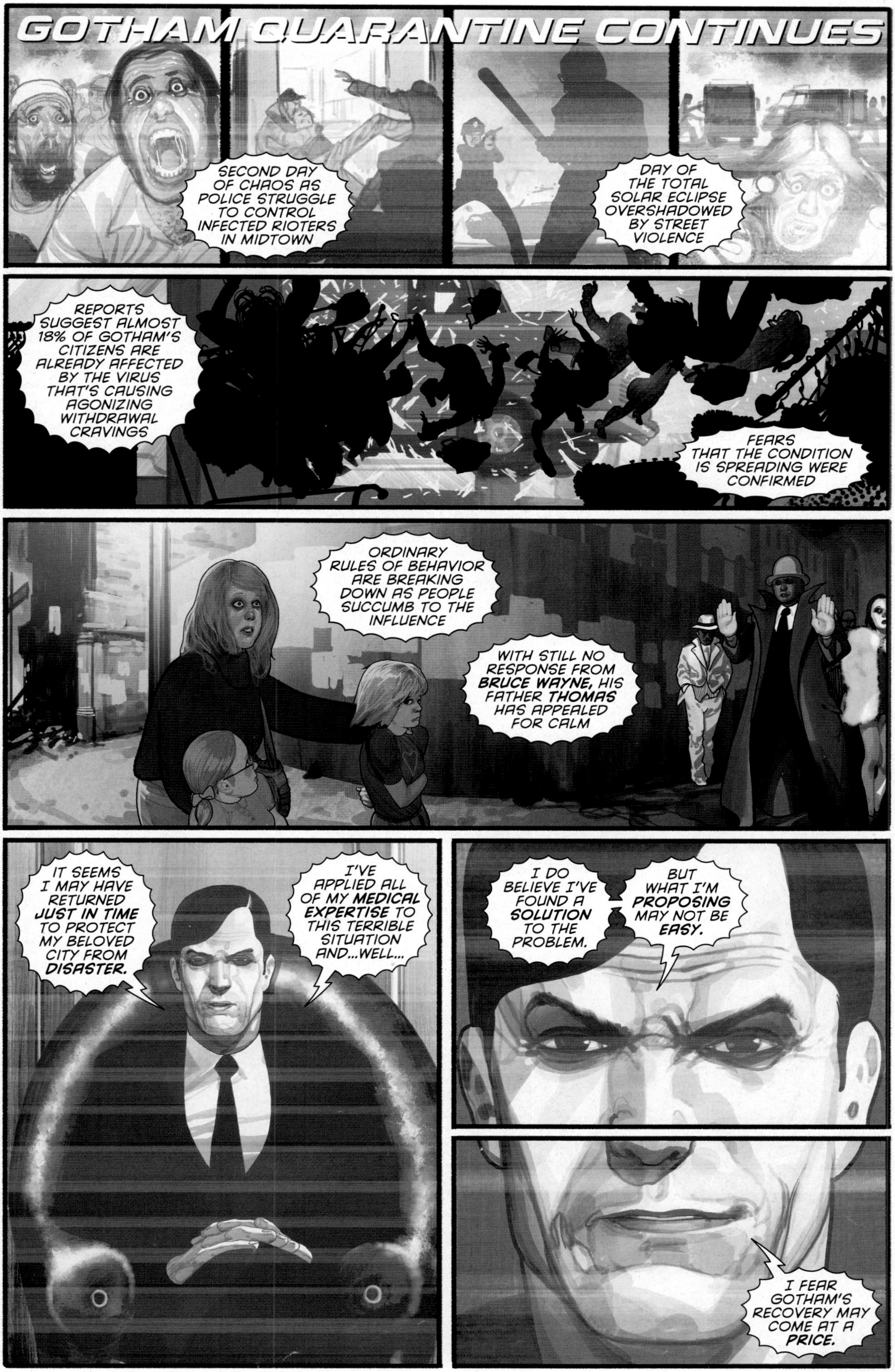

GOTHAM QUARANTINE CONTINUES
SECOND DAY OF CHAOS AS POLICE STRUGGLE TO CONTROL INFECTED RIOTERS IN MIDTOWN
DAY OF THE TOTAL SOLAR ECLIPSE OVERSHADOWED BY STREET VIOLENCE
REPORTS SUGGEST ALMOST 18% OF GOTHAM'S CITIZENS ARE ALREADY AFFECTED BY THE VIRUS THAT'S CAUSING AGONIZING WITHDRAWAL CRAVINGS
FEARS THAT THE CONDITION IS SPREADING WERE CONFIRMED
ORDINARY RULES OF BEHAVIOR ARE BREAKING DOWN AS PEOPLE SUCCUMB TO THE INFLUENCE
WITH STILL NO RESPONSE FROM BRUCE WAYNE, HIS FATHER THOMAS HAS APPEALED FOR CALM
IT SEEMS I MAY HAVE RETURNED JUST IN TIME TO PROTECT MY BELOVED CITY FROM DISASTER.
I'VE APPLIED ALL OF MY MEDICAL EXPERTISE TO THIS TERRIBLE SITUATION AND...WELL...
I DO BELIEVE I'VE FOUND A SOLUTION TO THE PROBLEM.
BUT WHAT I'M PROPOSING MAY NOT BE EASY.
I FEAR GOTHAM'S RECOVERY MAY COME AT A PRICE.

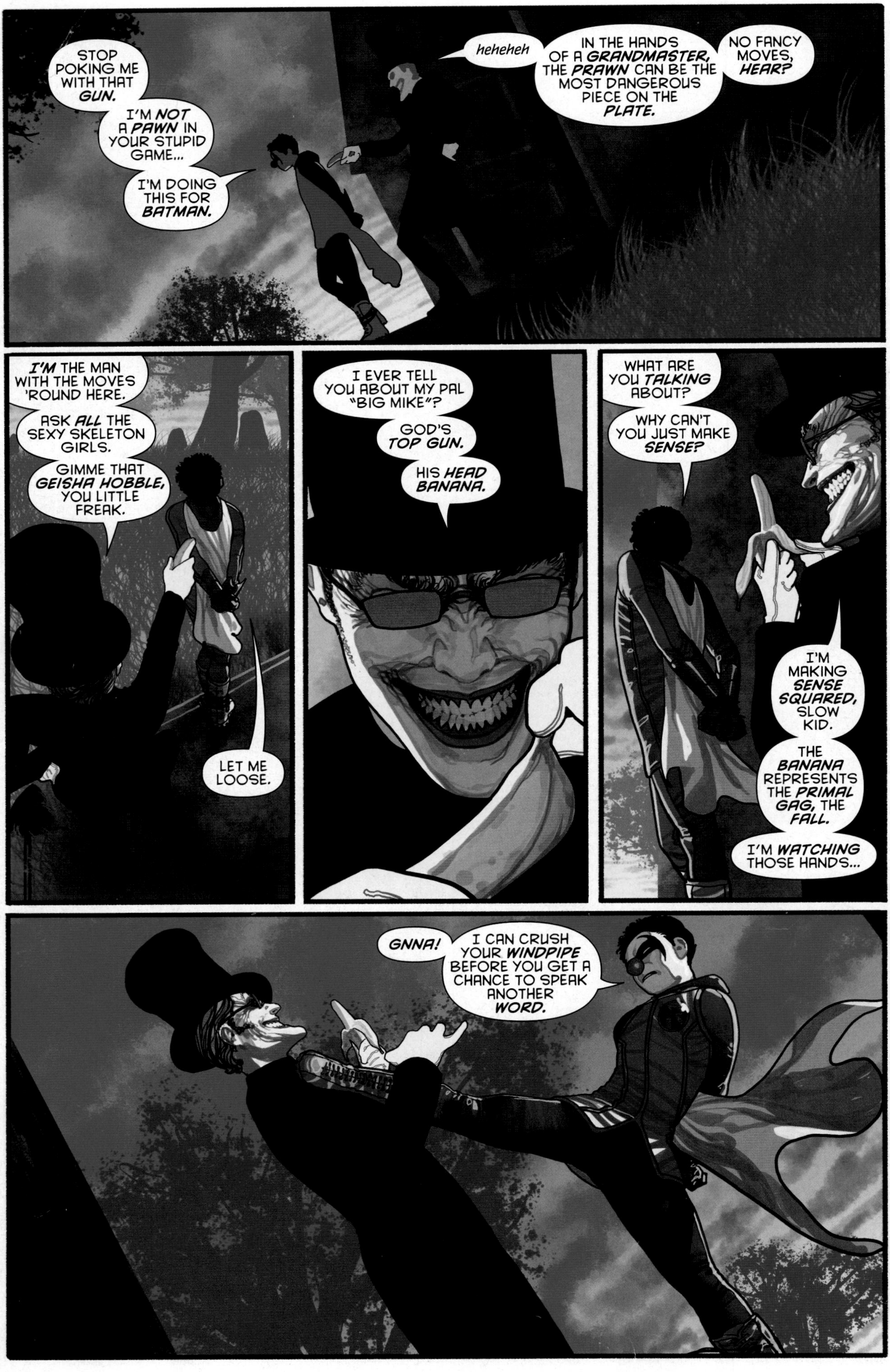
STOP POKING ME WITH THAT GUN.
I'M NOT A PAWN IN YOUR STUPID GAME...
I'M DOING THIS FOR BATMAN.
heheheh
IN THE HANDS OF A GRANDMASTER, THE PRAWN CAN BE THE MOST DANGEROUS PIECE ON THE PLATE.
NO FANCY MOVES, HEAR?
I'M THE MAN WITH THE MOVES 'ROUND HERE.
ASK ALL THE SEXY SKELETON GIRLS.
GIMME THAT GEISHA HOBBLE, YOU LITTLE FREAK.
LET ME LOOSE.
I EVER TELL YOU ABOUT MY PAL "BIG MIKE"?
GOD'S TOP GUN.
HIS HEAD BANANA.
WHAT ARE YOU TALKING ABOUT?
WHY CAN'T YOU JUST MAKE SENSE?
I'M MAKING SENSE SQUARED, SLOW KID.
THE BANANA REPRESENTS THE PRIMAL GAG, THE FALL.
I'M WATCHING THOSE HANDS...
GNNA!
I CAN CRUSH YOUR WINDPIPE BEFORE YOU GET A CHANCE TO SPEAK ANOTHER WORD.

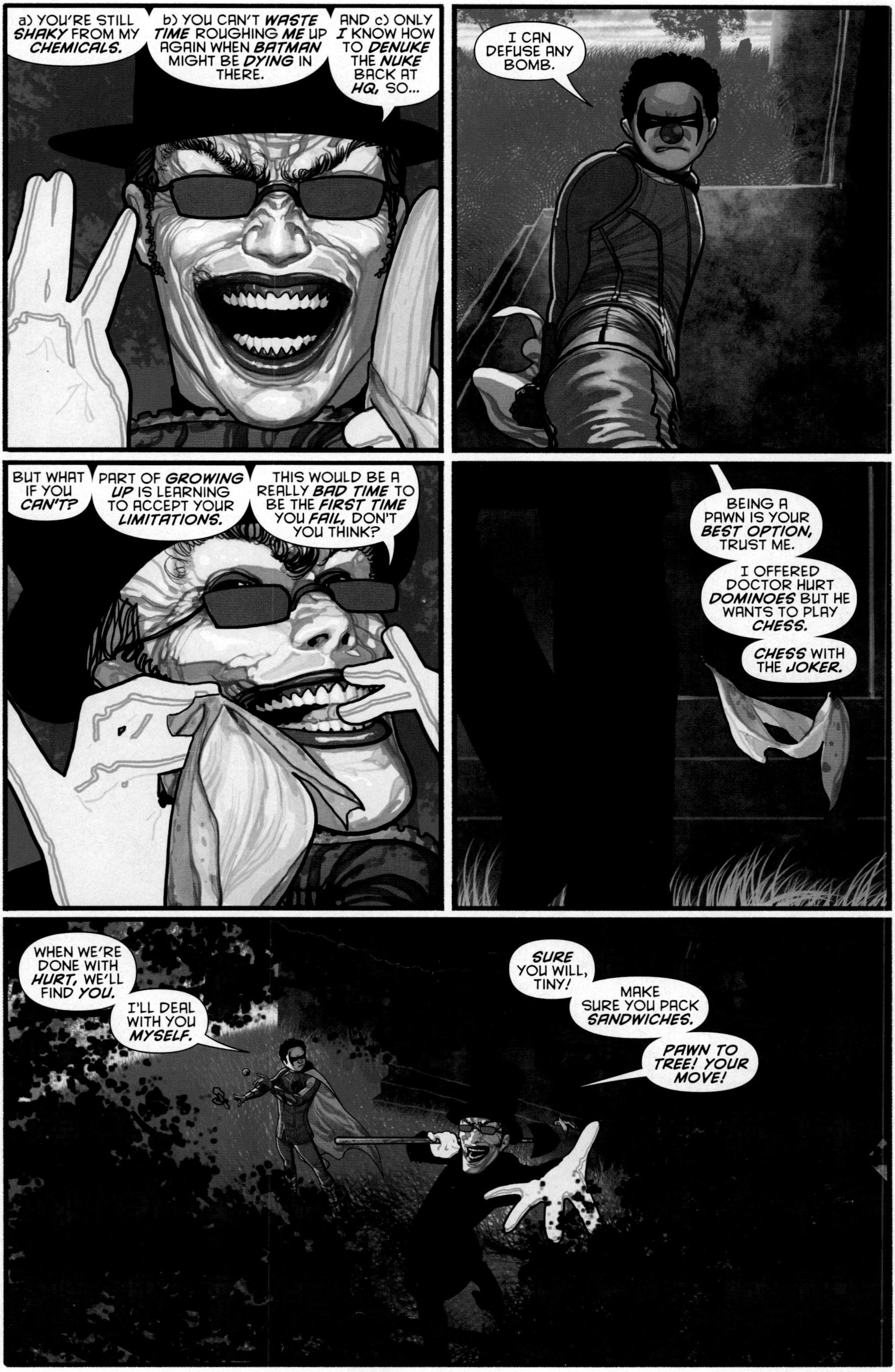
a) YOU'RE STILL SHAKY FROM MY CHEMICALS.
b) YOU CAN'T WASTE TIME ROUGHING ME UP AGAIN WHEN BATMAN MIGHT BE DYING IN THERE.
AND c) ONLY I KNOW HOW TO DENUKE THE NUKE BACK AT HQ, SO...
I CAN DEFUSE ANY BOMB.
BUT WHAT IF YOU CAN'T?
PART OF GROWING UP IS LEARNING TO ACCEPT YOUR LIMITATIONS.
THIS WOULD BE A REALLY BAD TIME TO BE THE FIRST TIME YOU FAIL, DON'T YOU THINK?
BEING A PAWN IS YOUR BEST OPTION, TRUST ME.
I OFFERED DOCTOR HURT DOMINOES BUT HE WANTS TO PLAY CHESS.
CHESS WITH THE JOKER.
WHEN WE'RE DONE WITH HURT, WE'LL FIND YOU.
I'LL DEAL WITH YOU MYSELF.
SURE YOU WILL, TINY!
MAKE SURE YOU PACK SANDWICHES.
PAWN TO TREE! YOUR MOVE!

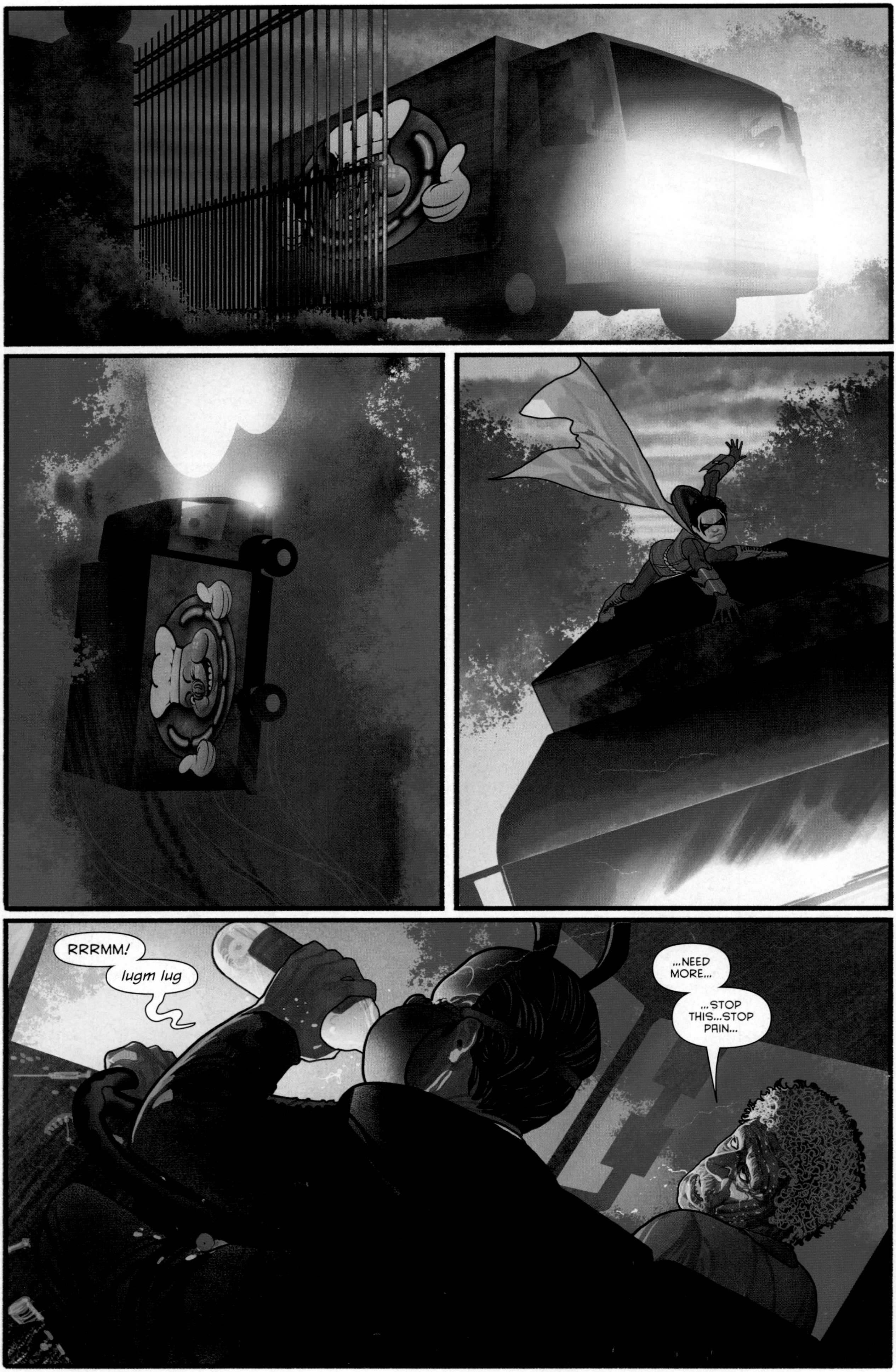
RRRMM!
lugm lug
...NEED MORE...
...STOP THIS...STOP PAIN...

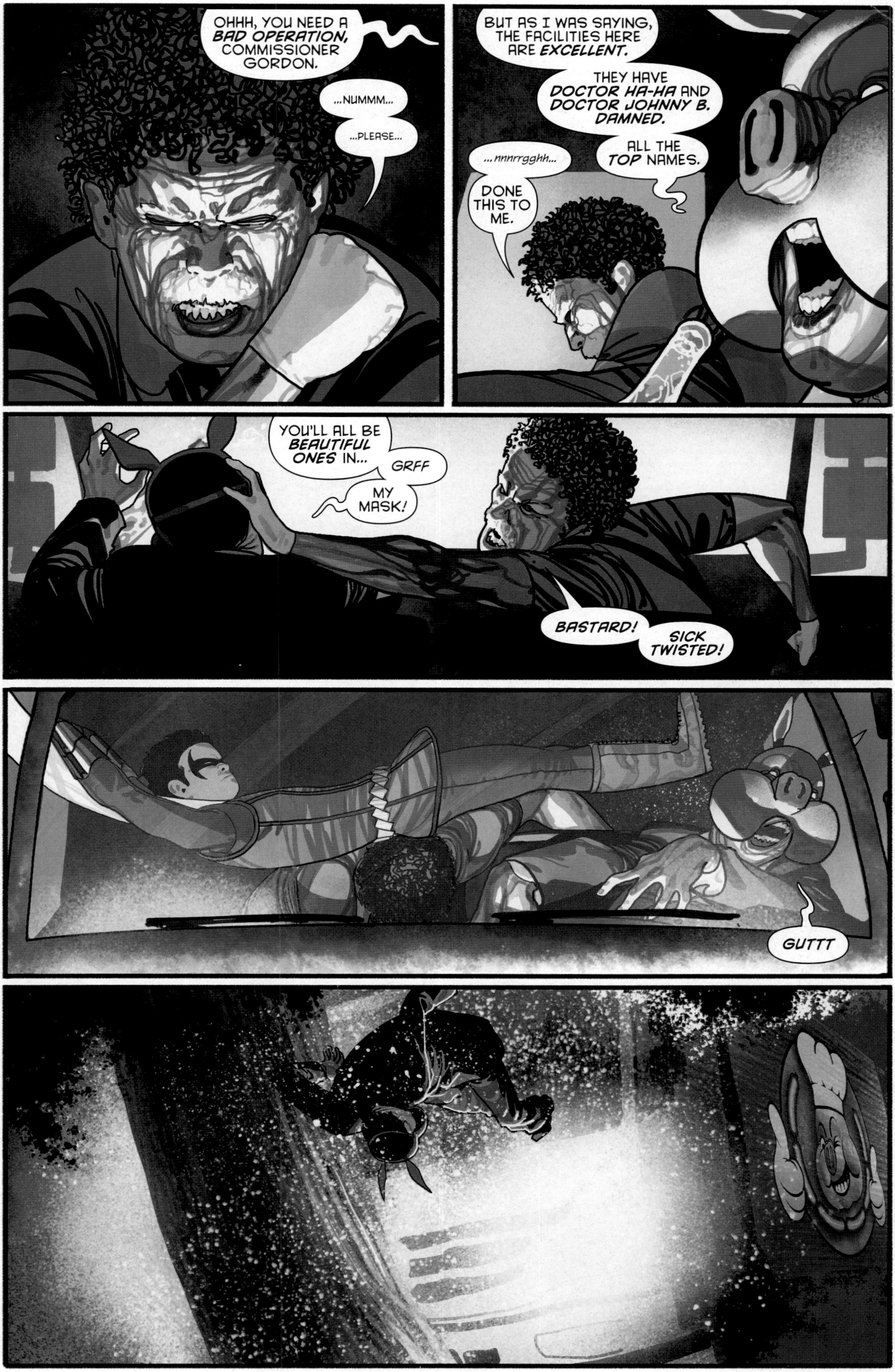
OHHH, YOU NEED A BAD OPERATION, COMMISSIONER GORDON.
...NUMMM...
...PLEASE...
BUT AS I WAS SAYING, THE FACILITIES HERE ARE EXCELLENT.
THEY HAVE DOCTOR HA-HA AND DOCTOR JOHNNY B. DAMNED.
ALL THE TOP NAMES.
...nnnrrgghh...
DONE THIS TO ME.
YOU'LL ALL BE BEAUTIFUL ONES IN...
GRFF
MY MASK!
BASTARD!
SICK TWISTED!
GUTTT

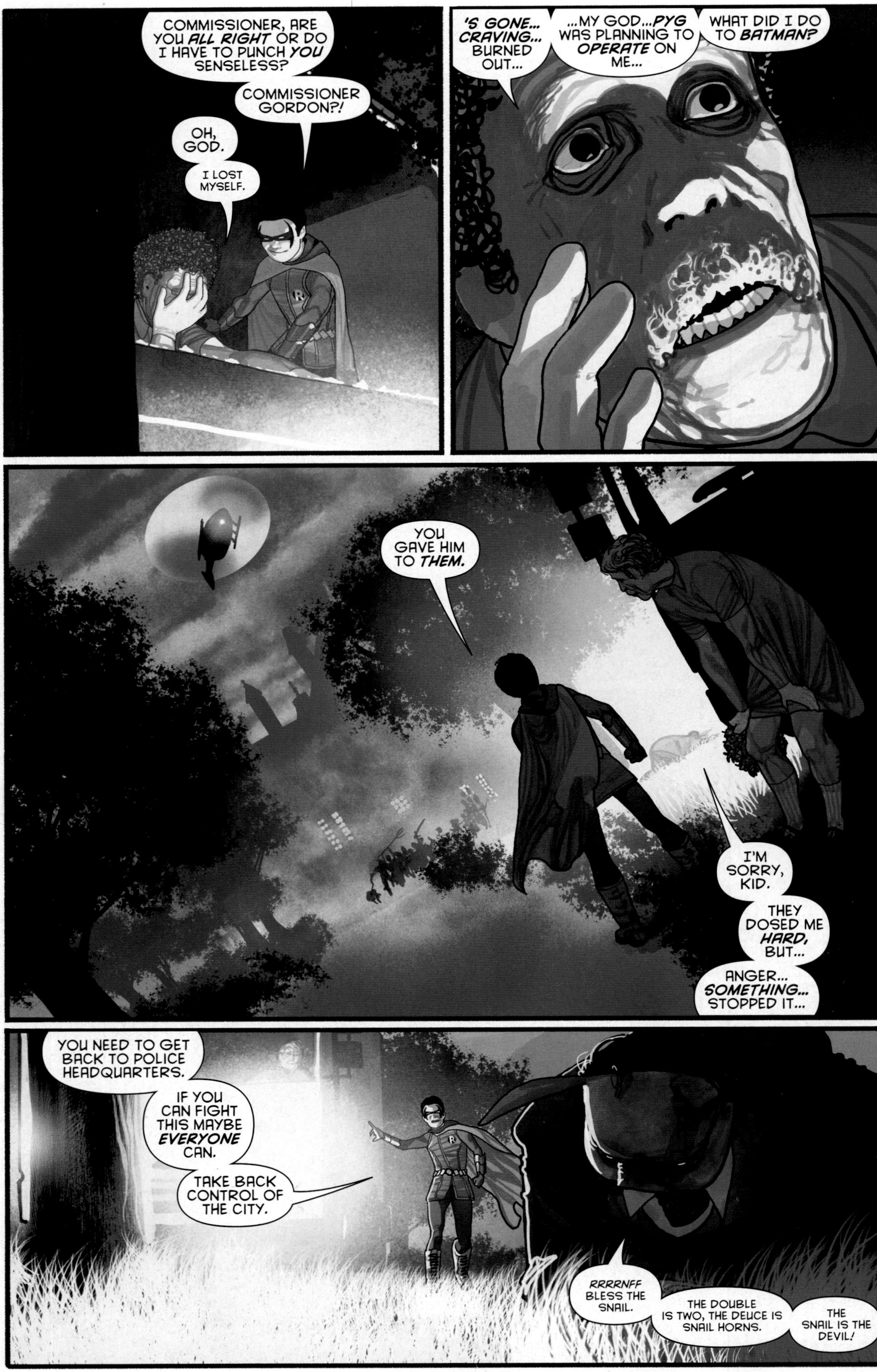
COMMISSIONER, ARE YOU ALL RIGHT OR DO I HAVE TO PUNCH YOU SENSELESS?
COMMISSIONER GORDON?!
OH, GOD.
I LOST MYSELF.
'S GONE... CRAVING... BURNED OUT...
...MY GOD...PYG WAS PLANNING TO OPERATE ON ME...
WHAT DID I DO TO BATMAN?
YOU GAVE HIM TO THEM.
I'M SORRY, KID.
THEY DOSED ME HARD, BUT...
ANGER... SOMETHING... STOPPED IT...
YOU NEED TO GET BACK TO POLICE HEADQUARTERS.
IF YOU CAN FIGHT THIS MAYBE EVERYONE CAN.
TAKE BACK CONTROL OF THE CITY.
RRRRNFF BLESS THE SNAIL.
THE DOUBLE IS TWO, THE DEUCE IS SNAIL HORNS.
THE SNAIL IS THE DEVIL!

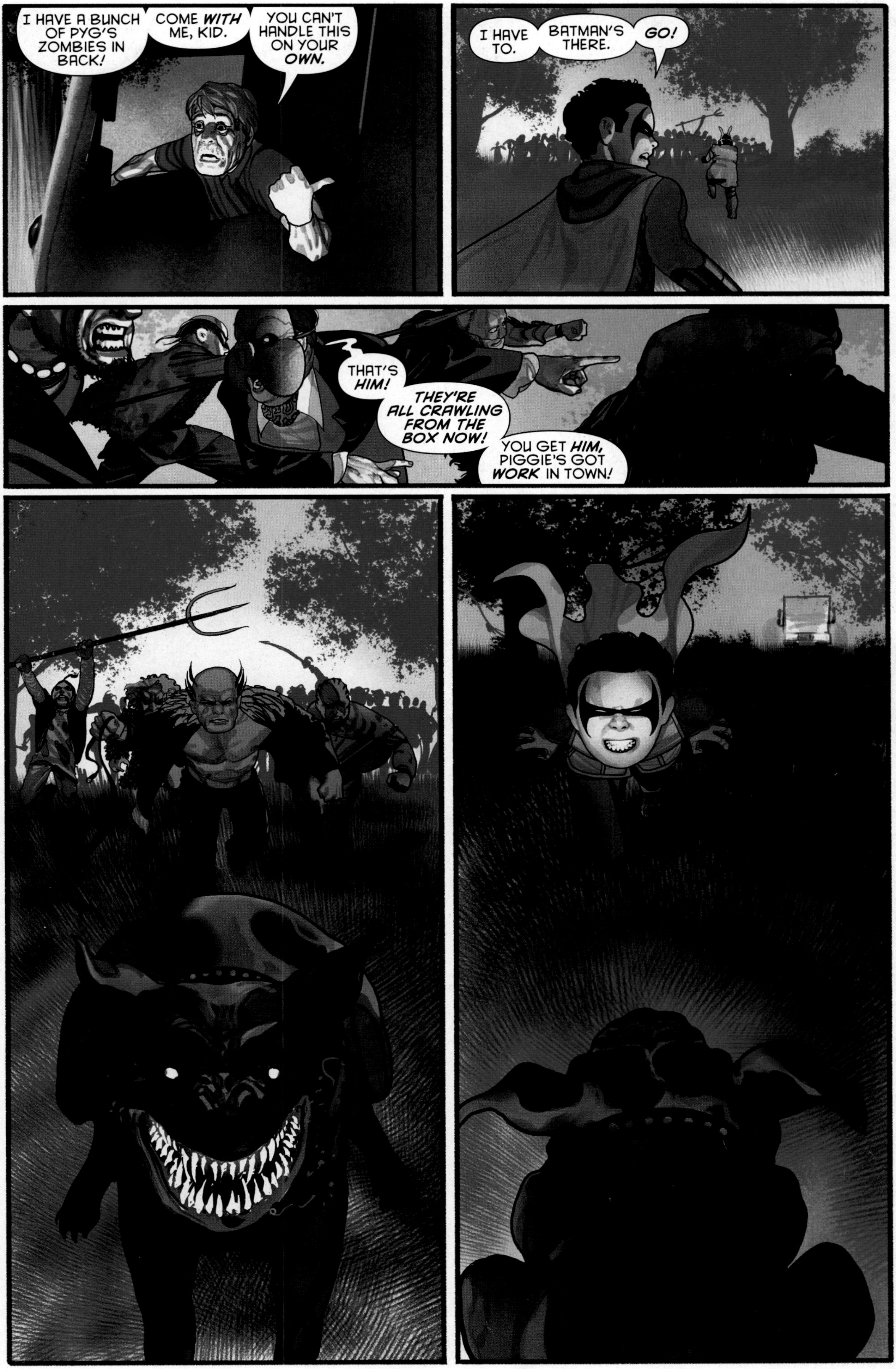
I HAVE A BUNCH OF PYG'S ZOMBIES IN BACK!
COME *WITH* ME, KID.
YOU CAN'T HANDLE THIS ON YOUR *OWN.*
I HAVE TO.
BATMAN'S THERE.
GO!
THAT'S *HIM!*
THEY'RE ALL CRAWLING FROM THE BOX NOW!
YOU GET *HIM,* PIGGIE'S GOT *WORK* IN TOWN!

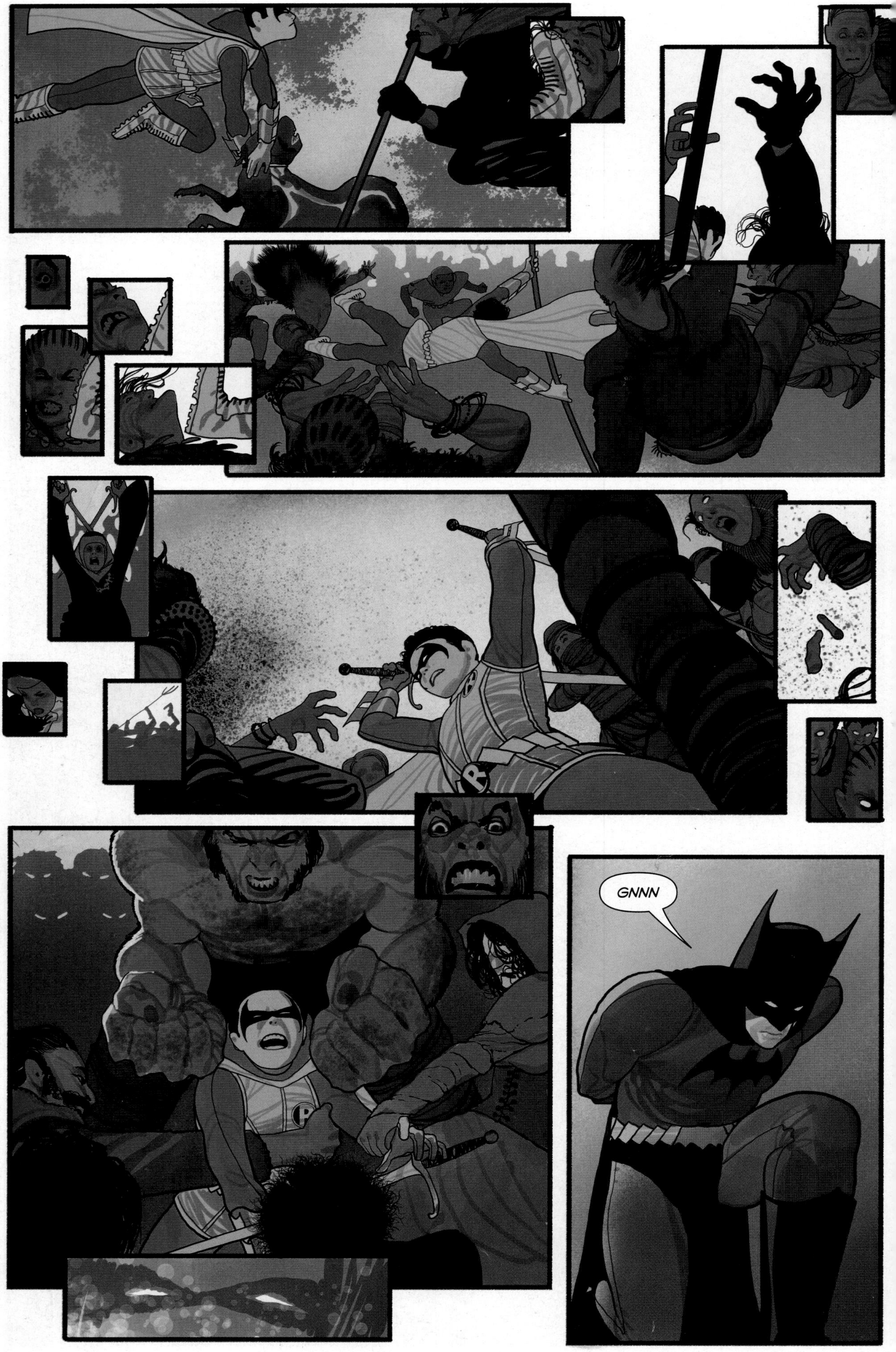
GNNN

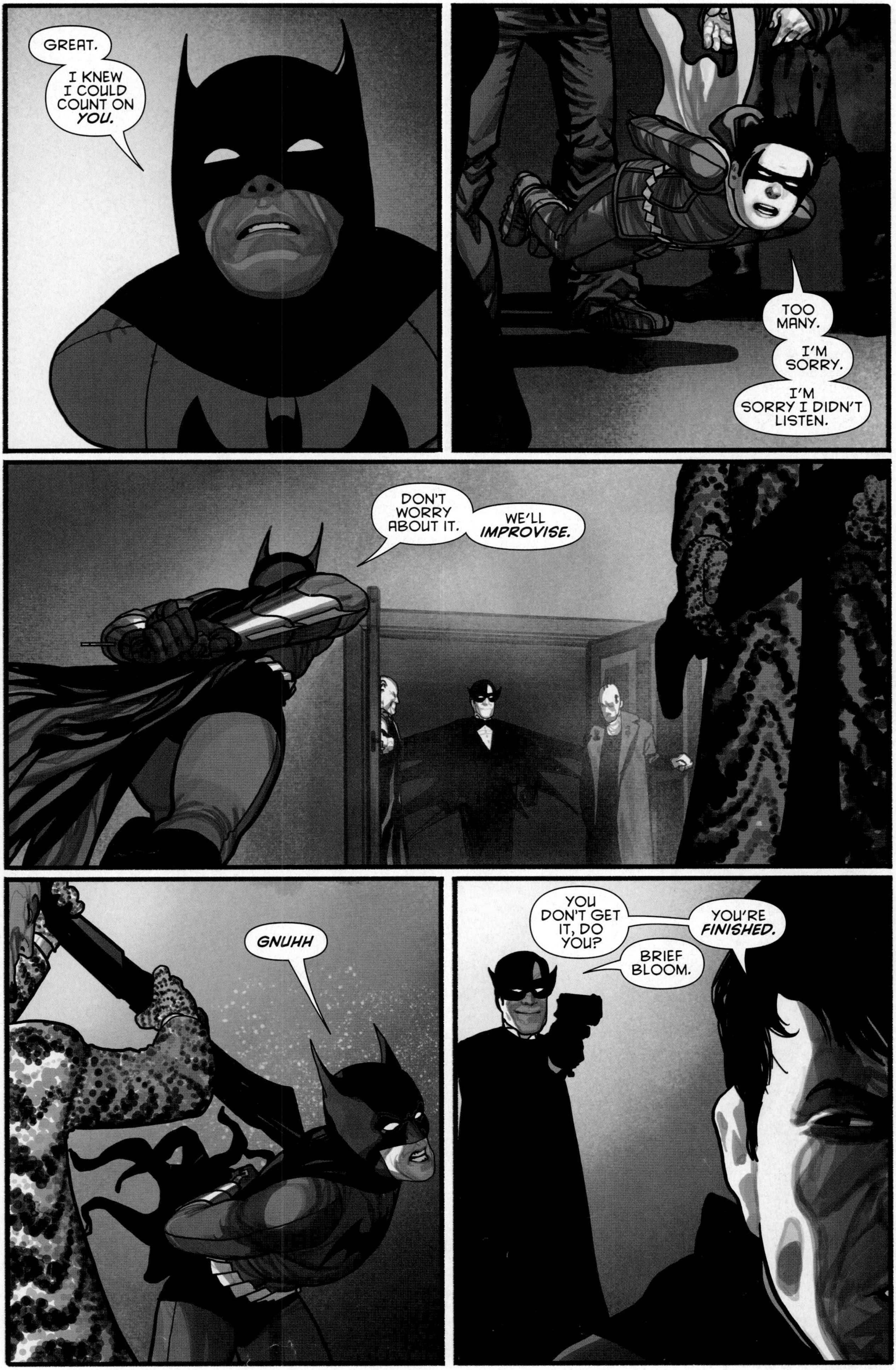
GREAT.
I KNEW I COULD COUNT ON YOU.
TOO MANY.
I'M SORRY.
I'M SORRY I DIDN'T LISTEN.
DON'T WORRY ABOUT IT.
WE'LL IMPROVISE.
GNUHH
YOU DON'T GET IT, DO YOU?
YOU'RE FINISHED.
BRIEF BLOOM.

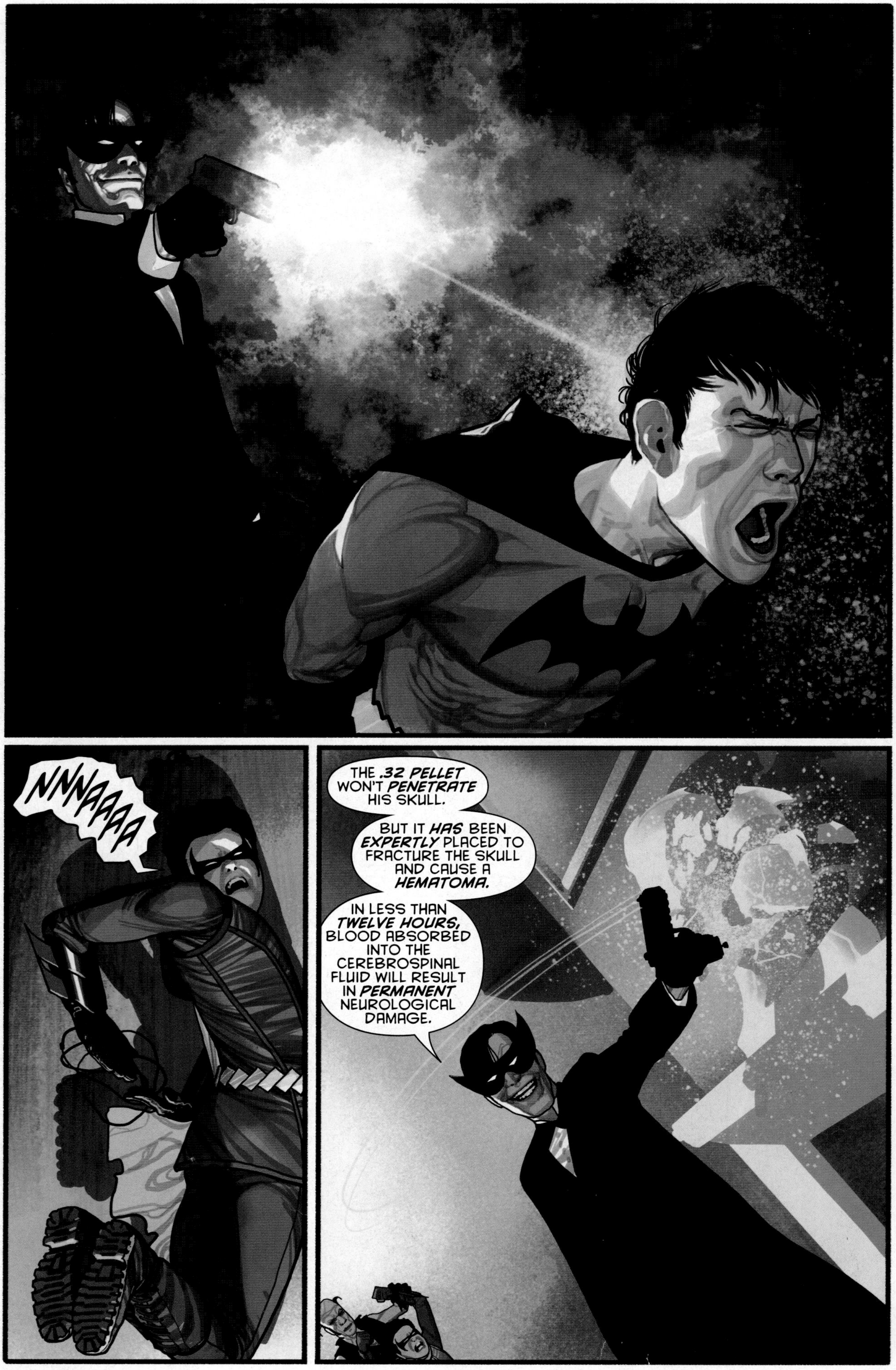
NNNAAAA
THE .32 PELLET WON'T PENETRATE HIS SKULL.
BUT IT HAS BEEN EXPERTLY PLACED TO FRACTURE THE SKULL AND CAUSE A HEMATOMA.
IN LESS THAN TWELVE HOURS, BLOOD ABSORBED INTO THE CEREBROSPINAL FLUID WILL RESULT IN PERMANENT NEUROLOGICAL DAMAGE.

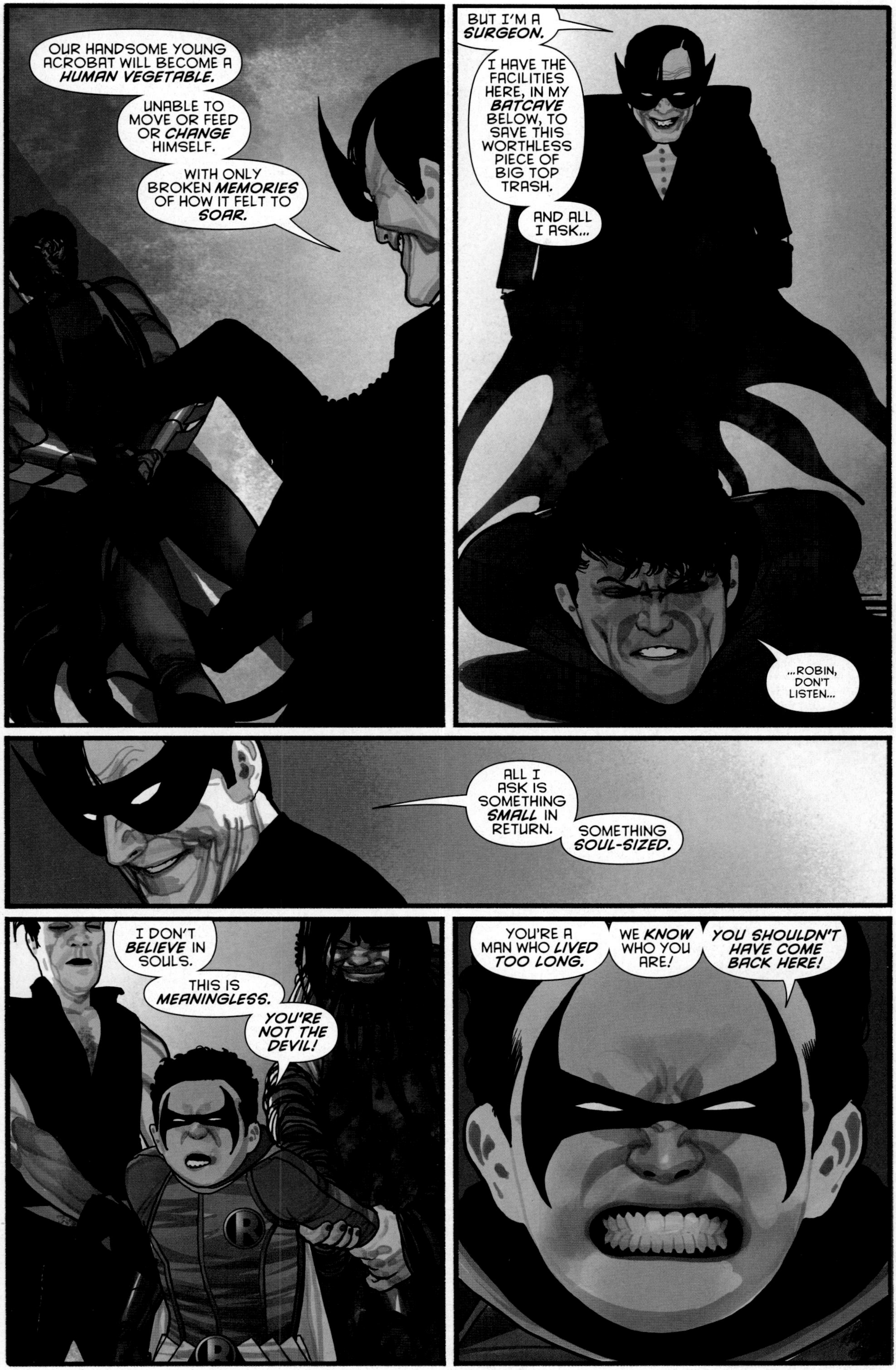
OUR HANDSOME YOUNG ACROBAT WILL BECOME A HUMAN VEGETABLE.
UNABLE TO MOVE OR FEED OR CHANGE HIMSELF.
WITH ONLY BROKEN MEMORIES OF HOW IT FELT TO SOAR.
BUT I'M A SURGEON.
I HAVE THE FACILITIES HERE, IN MY BATCAVE BELOW, TO SAVE THIS WORTHLESS PIECE OF BIG TOP TRASH.
AND ALL I ASK...
...ROBIN, DON'T LISTEN...
ALL I ASK IS SOMETHING SMALL IN RETURN.
SOMETHING SOUL-SIZED.
I DON'T BELIEVE IN SOULS.
THIS IS MEANINGLESS.
YOU'RE NOT THE DEVIL!
YOU'RE A MAN WHO LIVED TOO LONG.
WE KNOW WHO YOU ARE!
YOU SHOULDN'T HAVE COME BACK HERE!

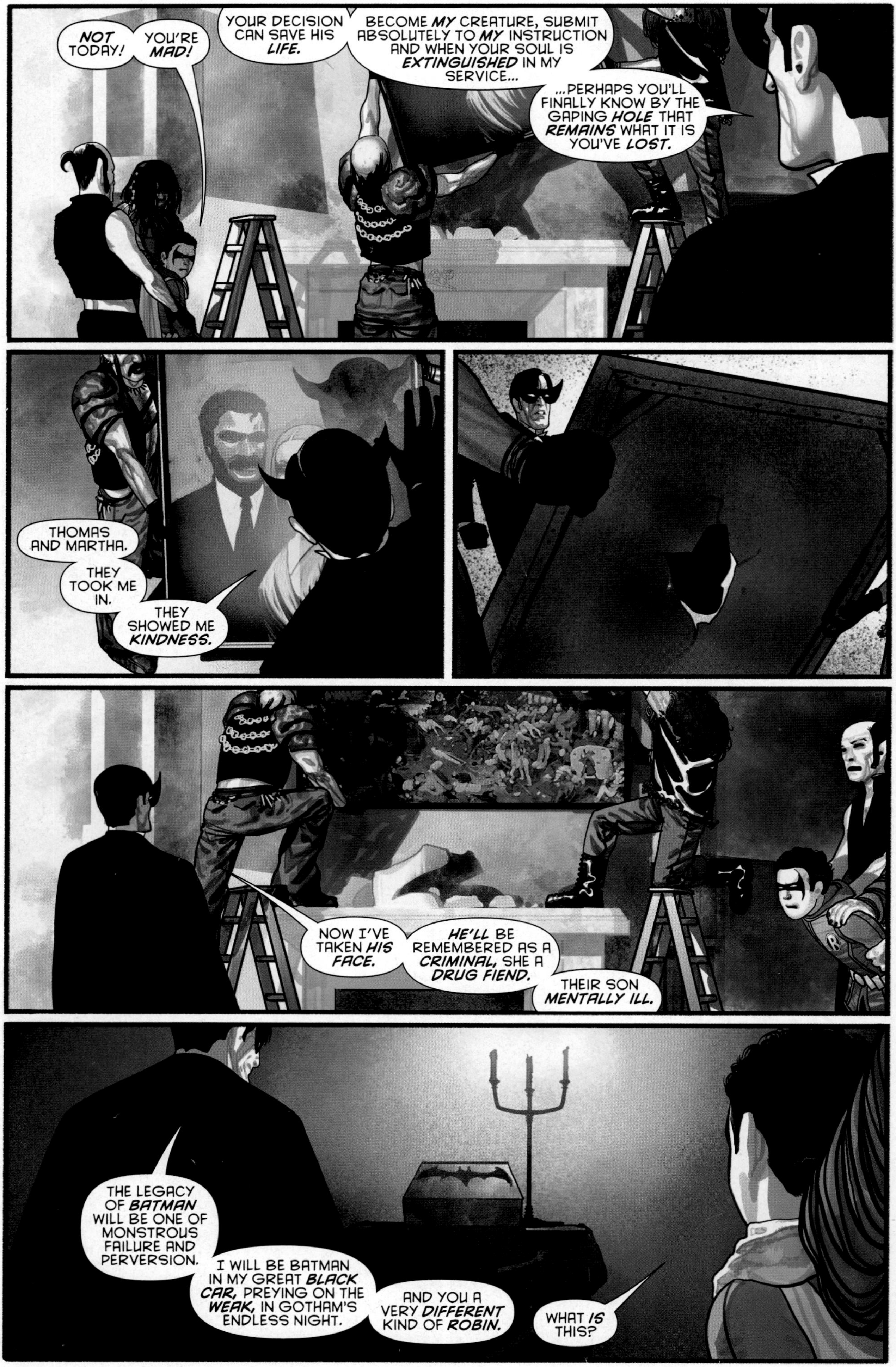
NOT TODAY!
YOU'RE MAD!
YOUR DECISION CAN SAVE HIS LIFE.
BECOME MY CREATURE, SUBMIT ABSOLUTELY TO MY INSTRUCTION AND WHEN YOUR SOUL IS EXTINGUISHED IN MY SERVICE...
...PERHAPS YOU'LL FINALLY KNOW BY THE GAPING HOLE THAT REMAINS WHAT IT IS YOU'VE LOST.
THOMAS AND MARTHA.
THEY TOOK ME IN.
THEY SHOWED ME KINDNESS.
NOW I'VE TAKEN HIS FACE.
HE'LL BE REMEMBERED AS A CRIMINAL, SHE A DRUG FIEND.
THEIR SON MENTALLY ILL.
THE LEGACY OF BATMAN WILL BE ONE OF MONSTROUS FAILURE AND PERVERSION.
I WILL BE BATMAN IN MY GREAT BLACK CAR, PREYING ON THE WEAK, IN GOTHAM'S ENDLESS NIGHT.
AND YOU A VERY DIFFERENT KIND OF ROBIN.
WHAT IS THIS?

THE *CEREMONY OF THE BAT* HAS BEGUN AGAIN.

AS THE SUN *SHINES BLACK* YOU AND I WILL SUMMON THE SPIRIT *BARBATOS* TO OPEN THIS IMPENETRABLE *BOX OF ANCIENT SECRETS.*

NO! WAIT!

ROBIN, IT'S THE *BOX* I FOUND IN THE *CAVE.*

REMEMBER WHO LEFT IT THERE.

STALL.

A SOUL, *CHILD!* IN RETURN FOR HIS *LIFE!*

ONE CHANCE TO *SAVE* YOUR FRIEND.

RAISE YOUR *LEFT* HAND AND SAY...

♪ ♪

WAIT... WHAT *IS* THIS?

HOW CAN IT...

IT HASN'T OPENED IN A *HUNDRED YEARS.*

K-LK

THAT *WHISTLE.*

THE LOST *BAT-LANGUAGE* OF THE *MIAGANI* PEOPLE.

BARBATOS?

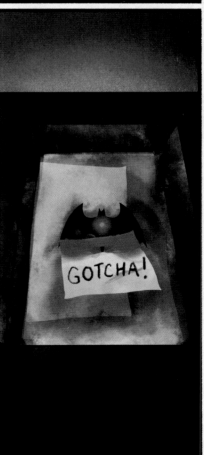

GOTCHA!

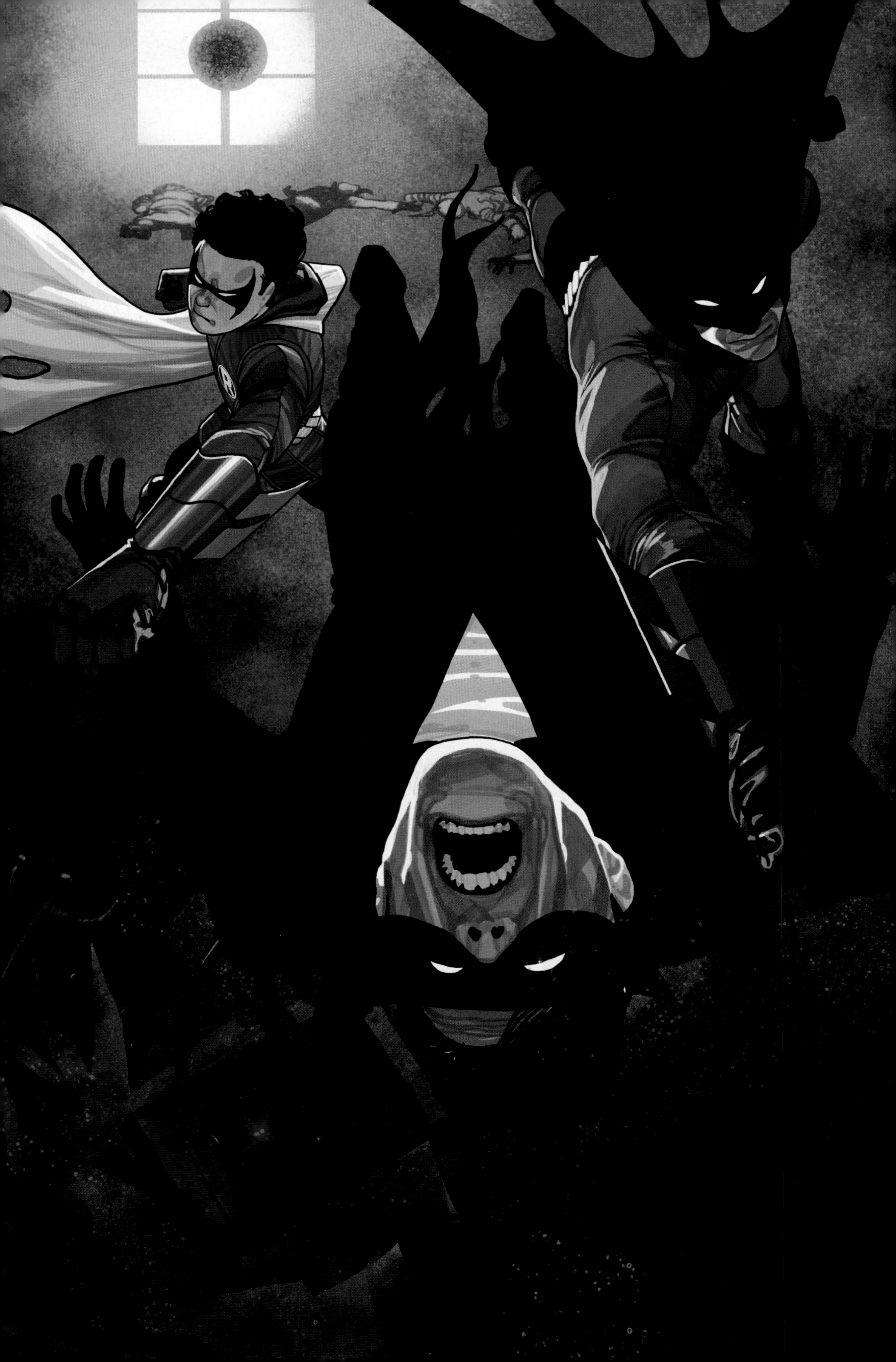

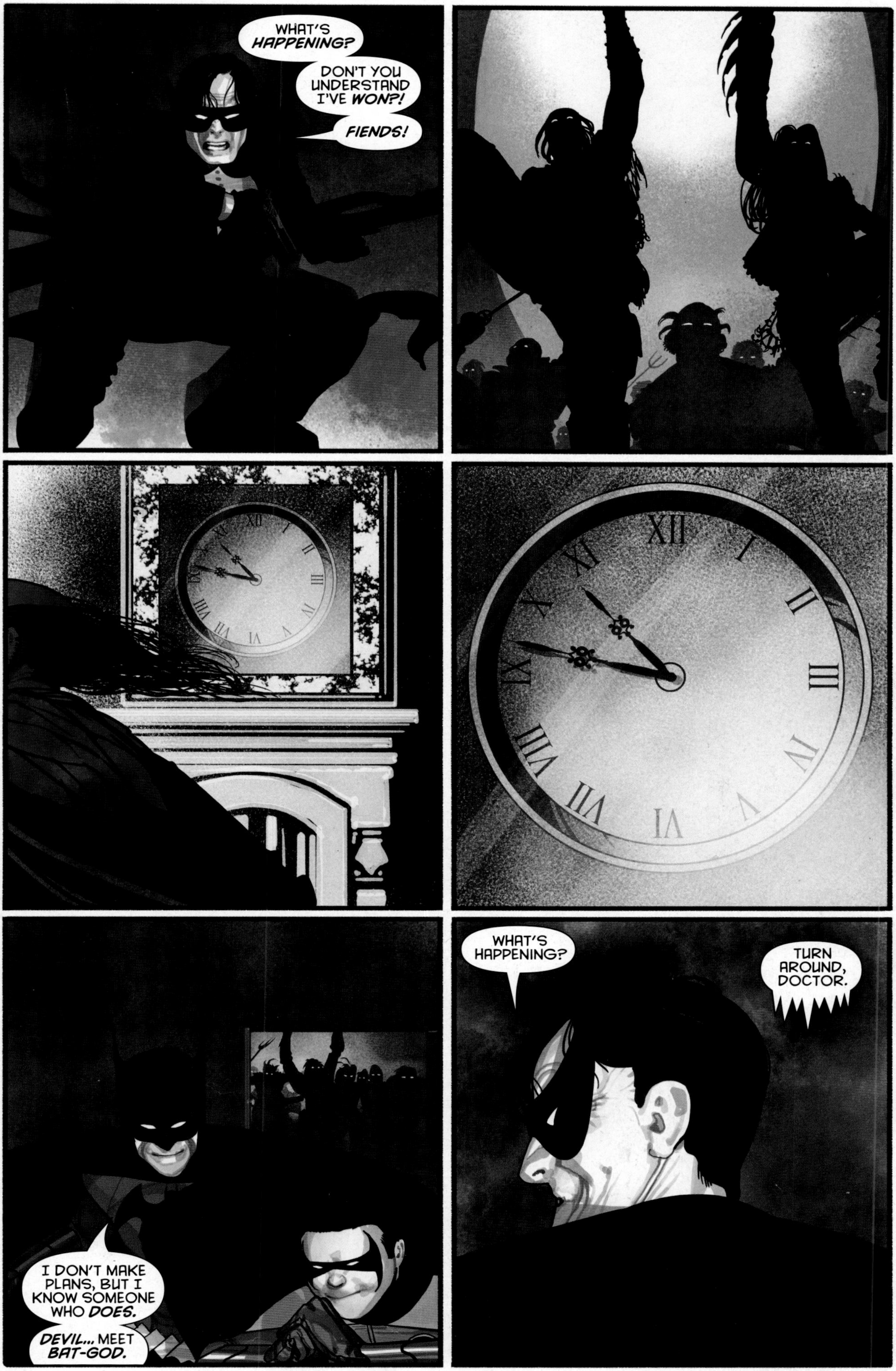
WHAT'S *HAPPENING?*
DON'T YOU UNDERSTAND I'VE *WON?!*
FIENDS!
I DON'T MAKE PLANS, BUT I KNOW SOMEONE WHO *DOES.*
DEVIL... MEET *BAT-GOD.*
WHAT'S HAPPENING?
TURN AROUND, DOCTOR.

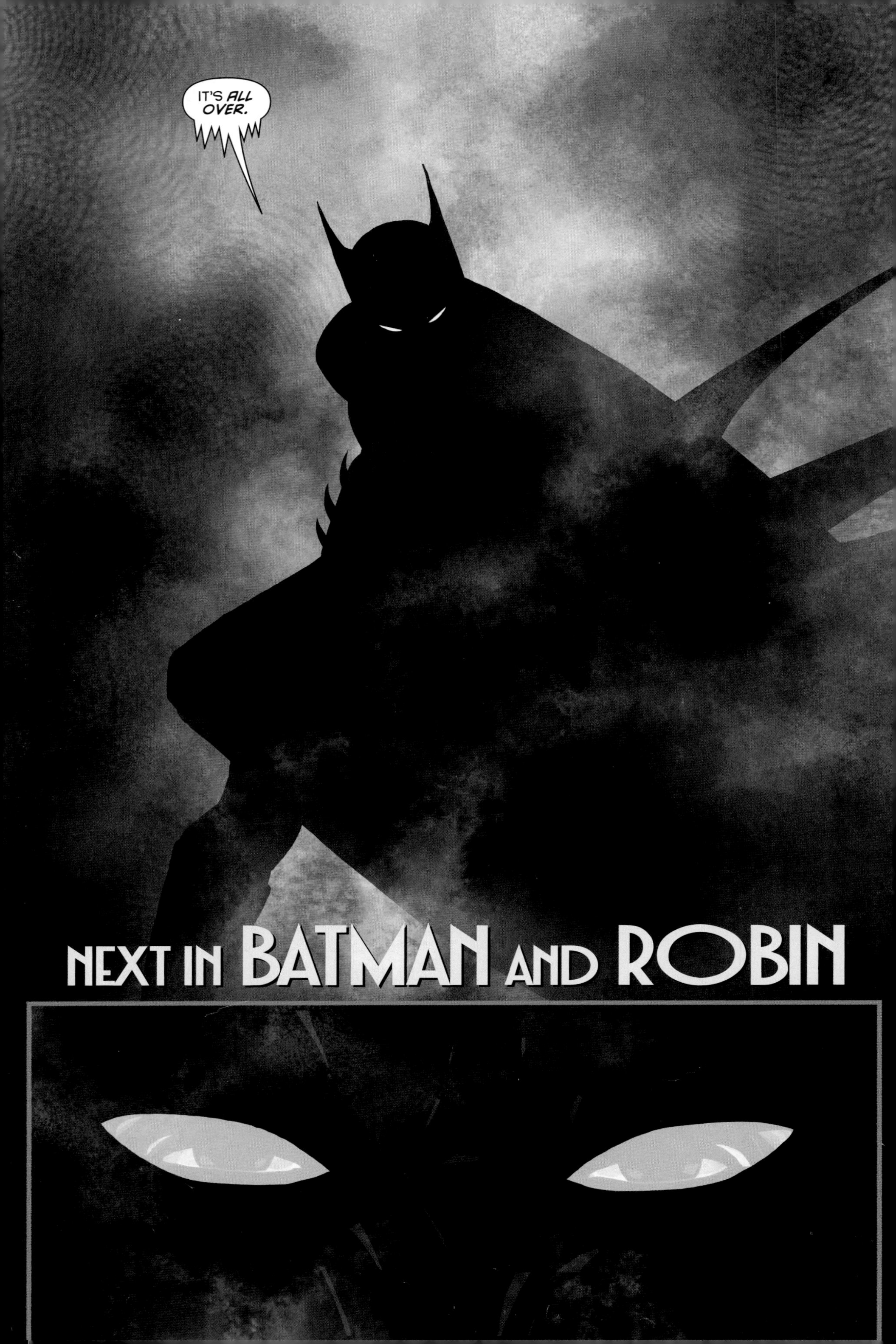

IT'S *ALL* OVER.

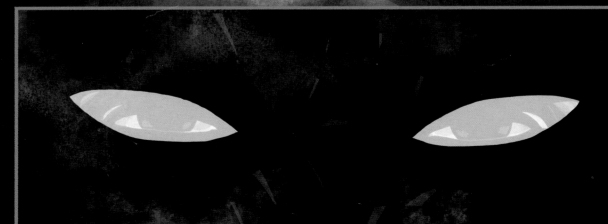

NEXT IN BATMAN AND ROBIN

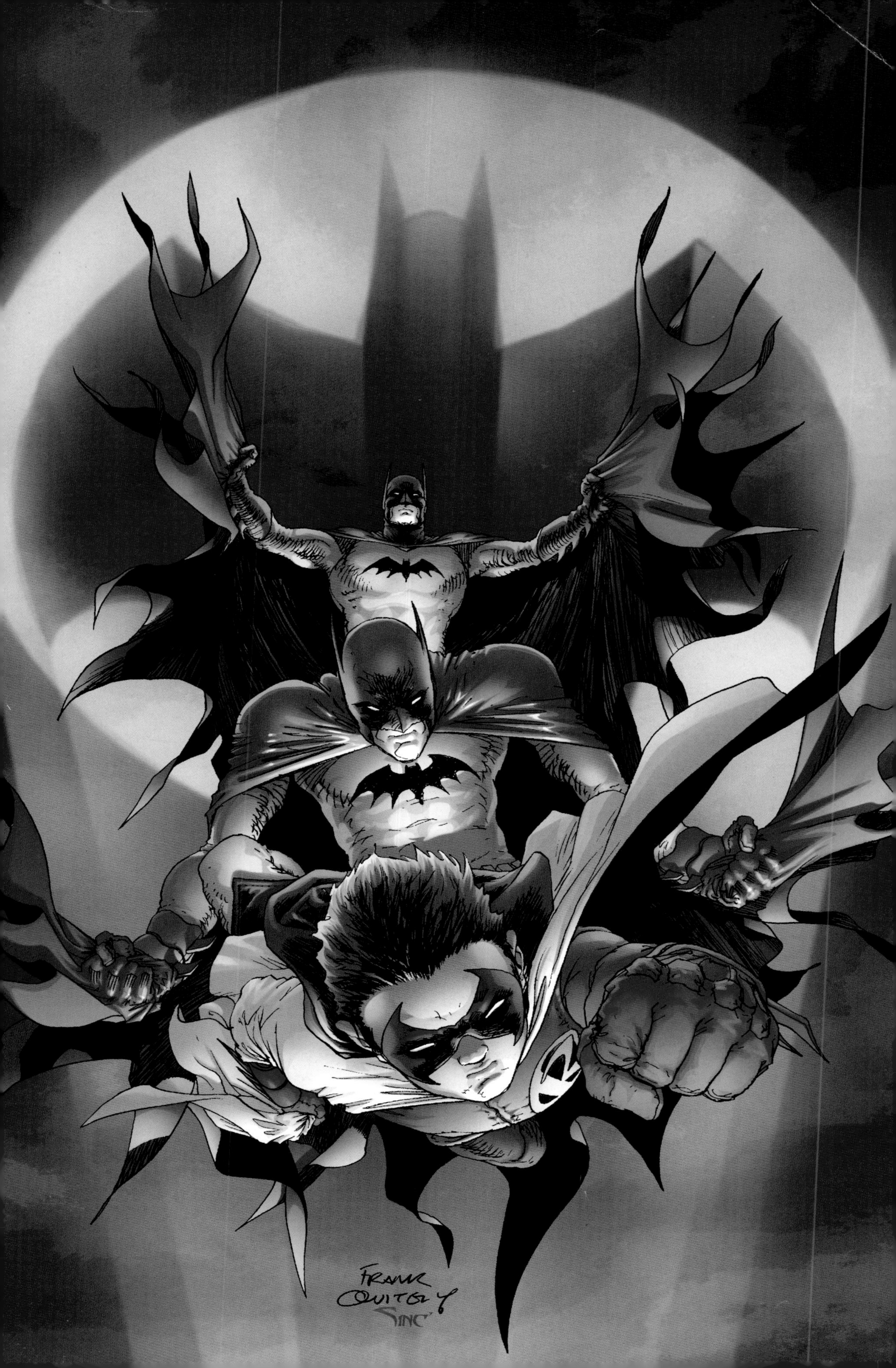
FRANK QUITELY
SINC

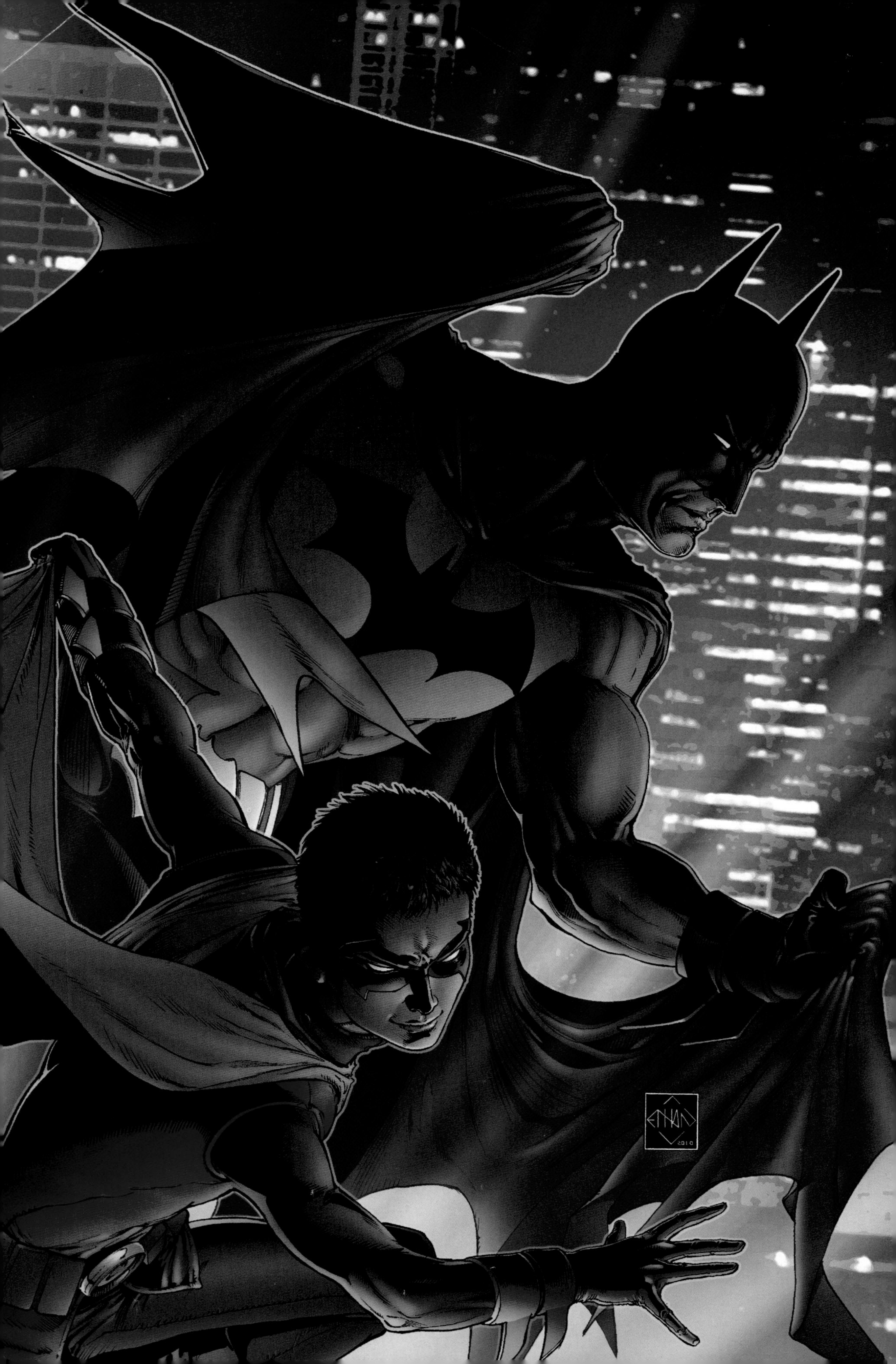

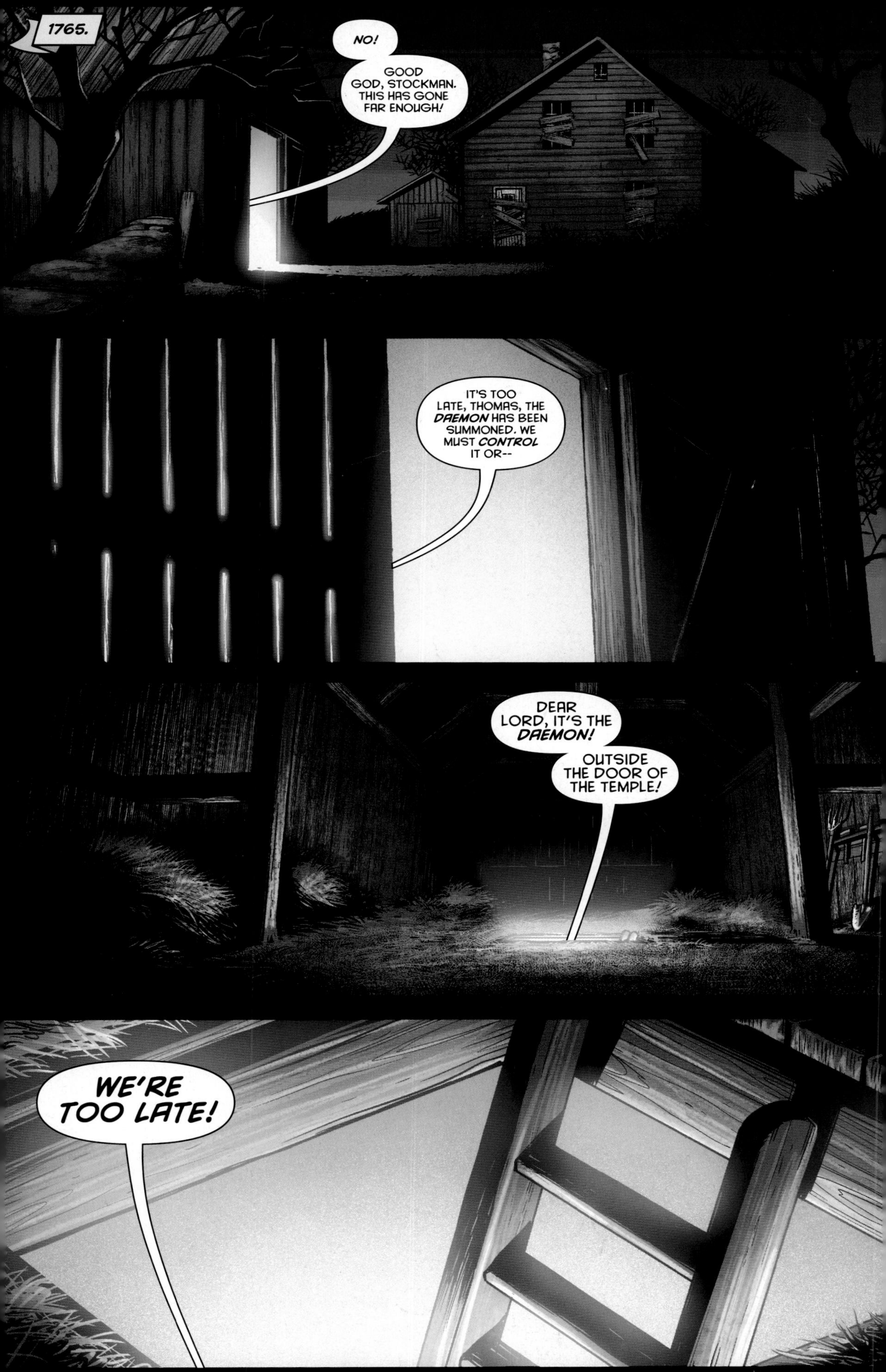
1765.
NO!
GOOD GOD, STOCKMAN. THIS HAS GONE FAR ENOUGH!
IT'S TOO LATE, THOMAS, THE DAEMON HAS BEEN SUMMONED. WE MUST CONTROL IT OR--
DEAR LORD, IT'S THE DAEMON!
OUTSIDE THE DOOR OF THE TEMPLE!
WE'RE TOO LATE!

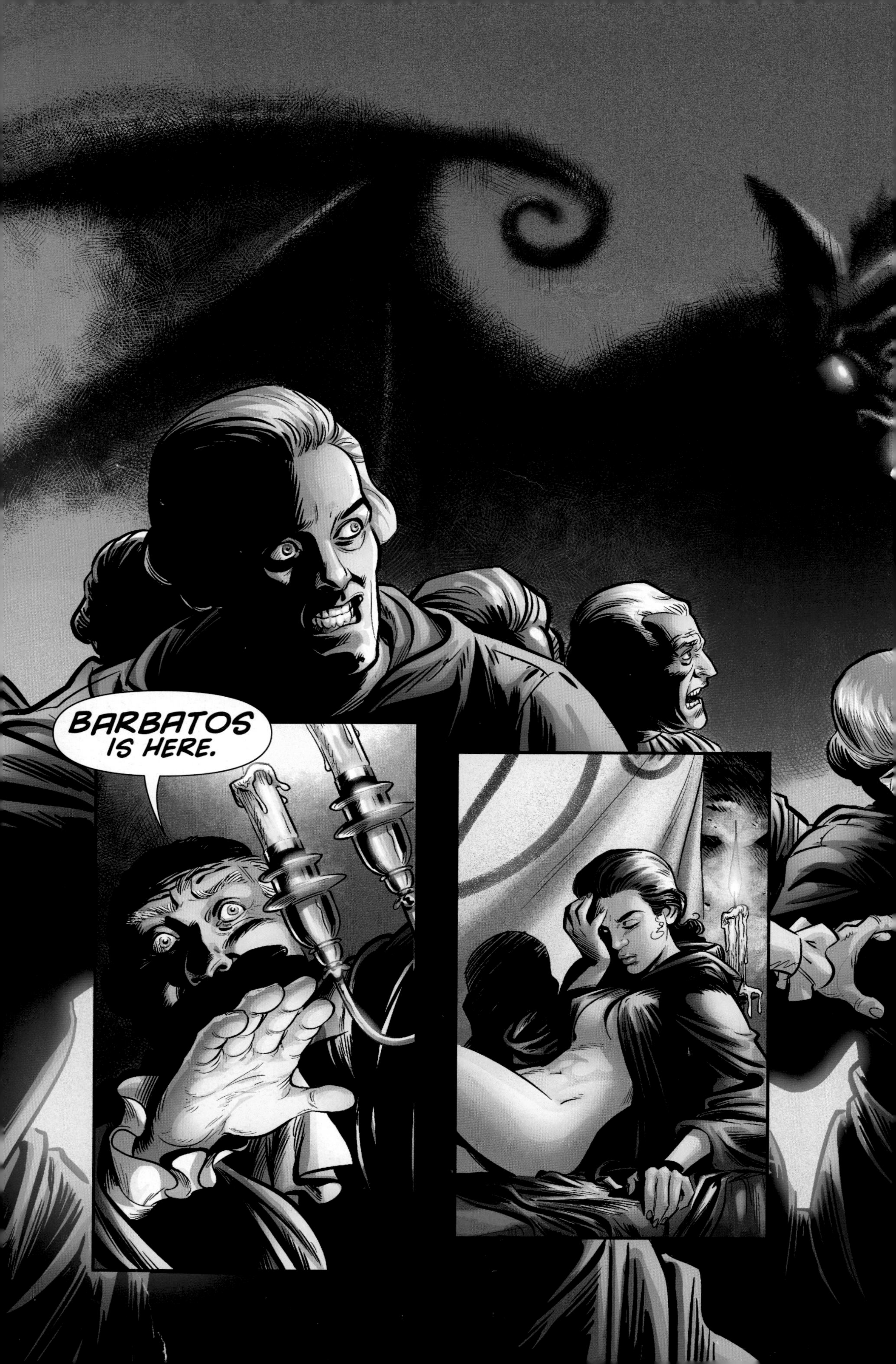
BARBATOS IS HERE.

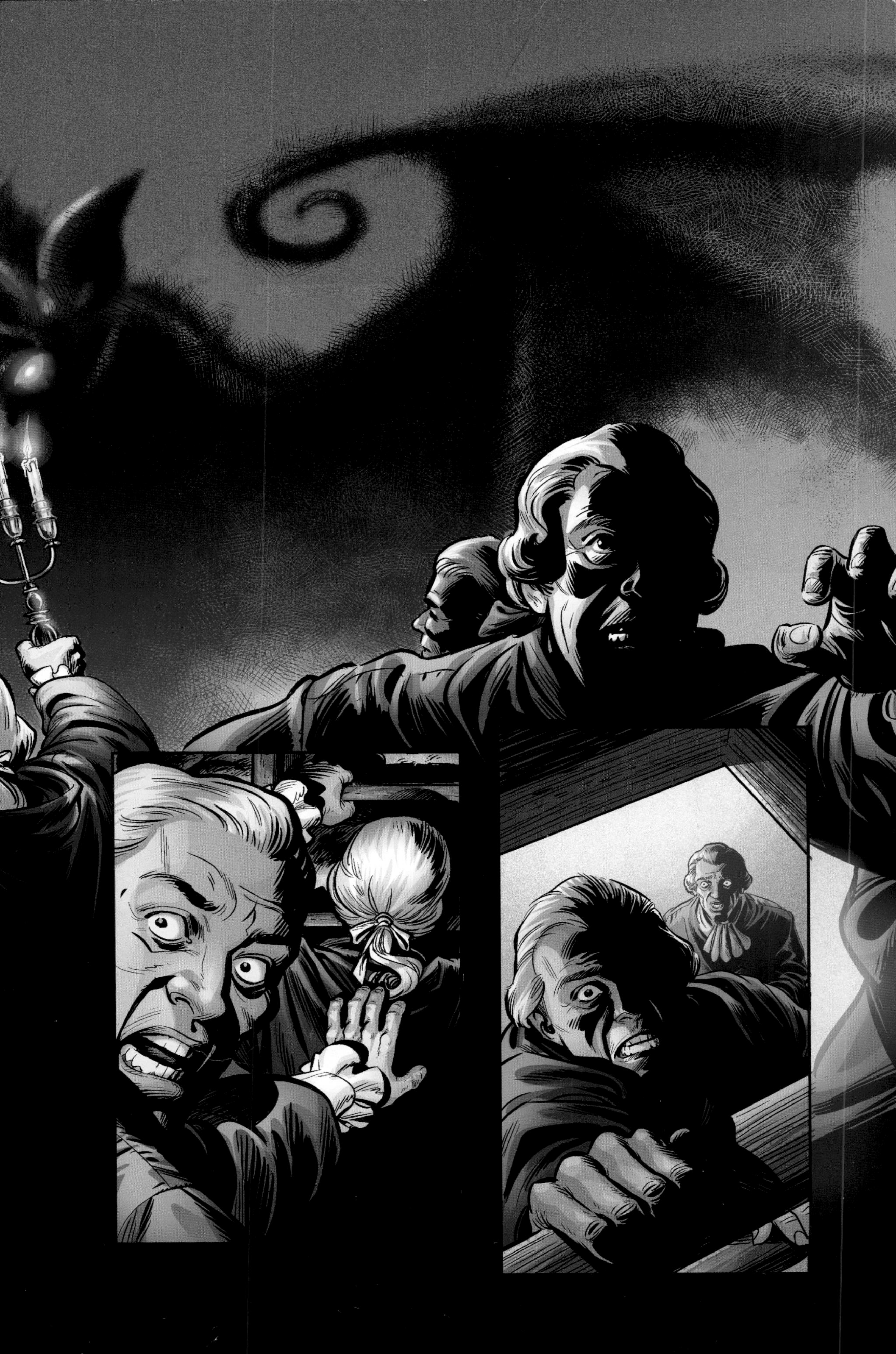

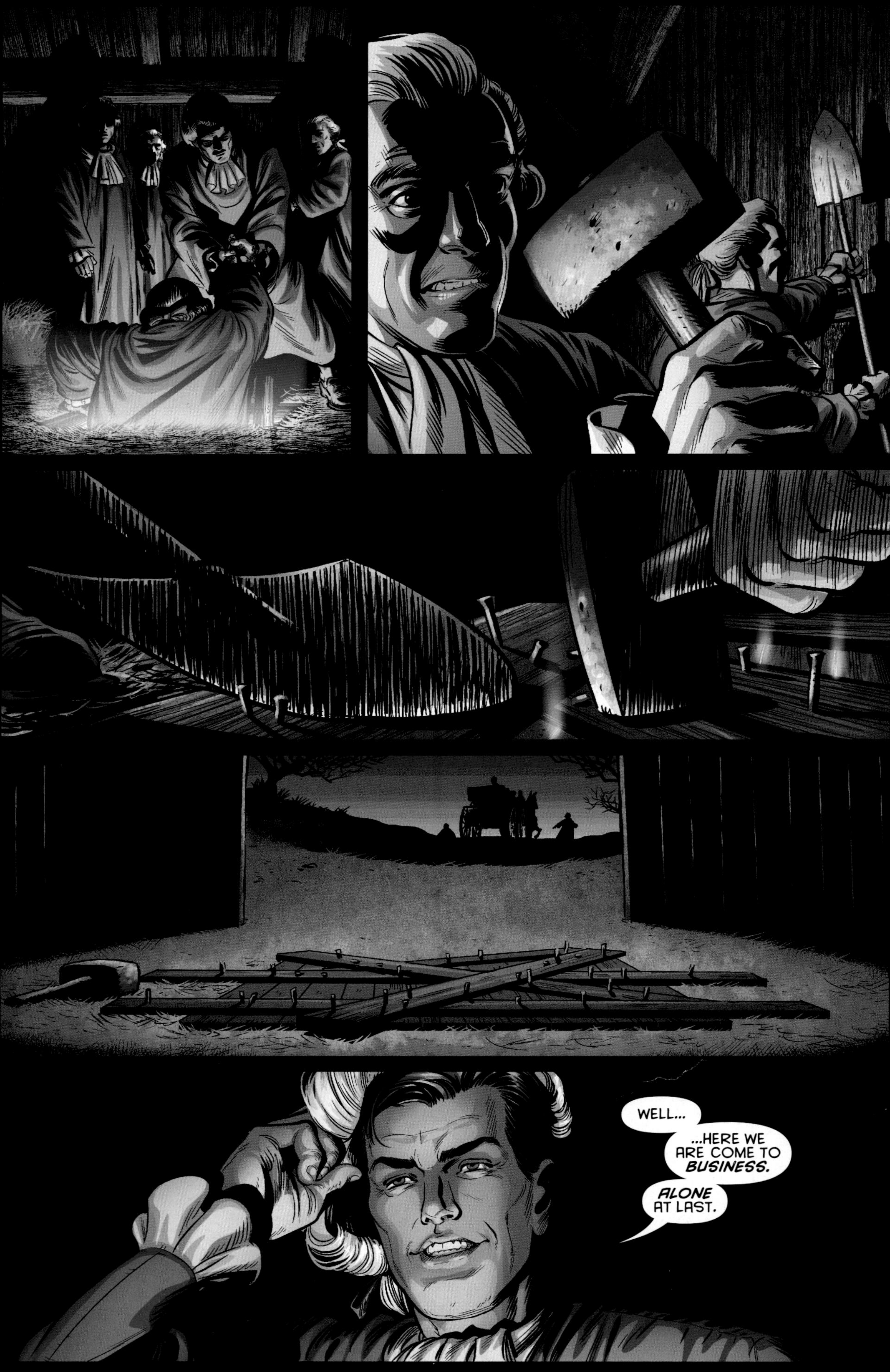
WELL...
...HERE WE ARE COME TO BUSINESS.
ALONE AT LAST.

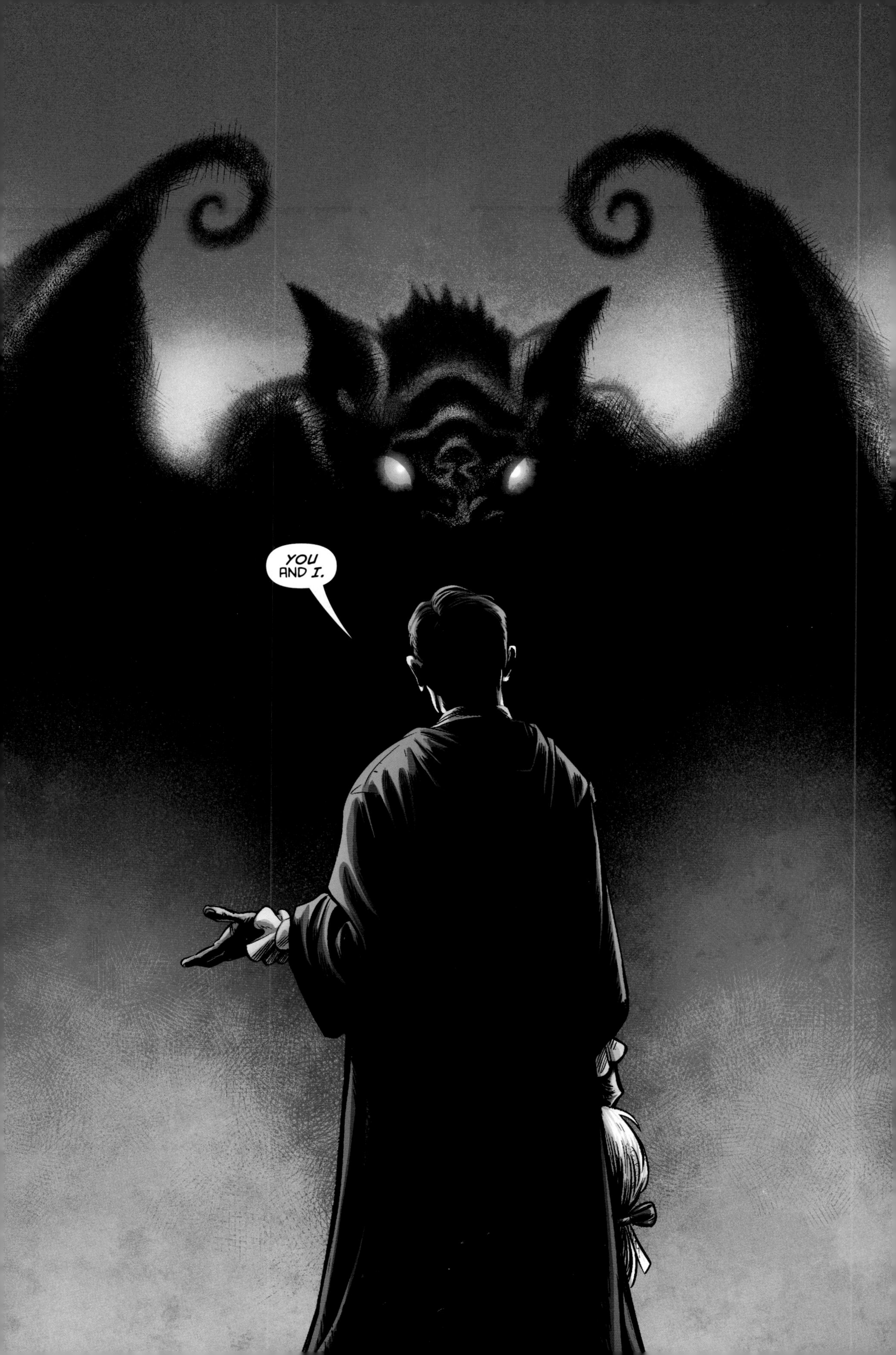
YOU AND I.

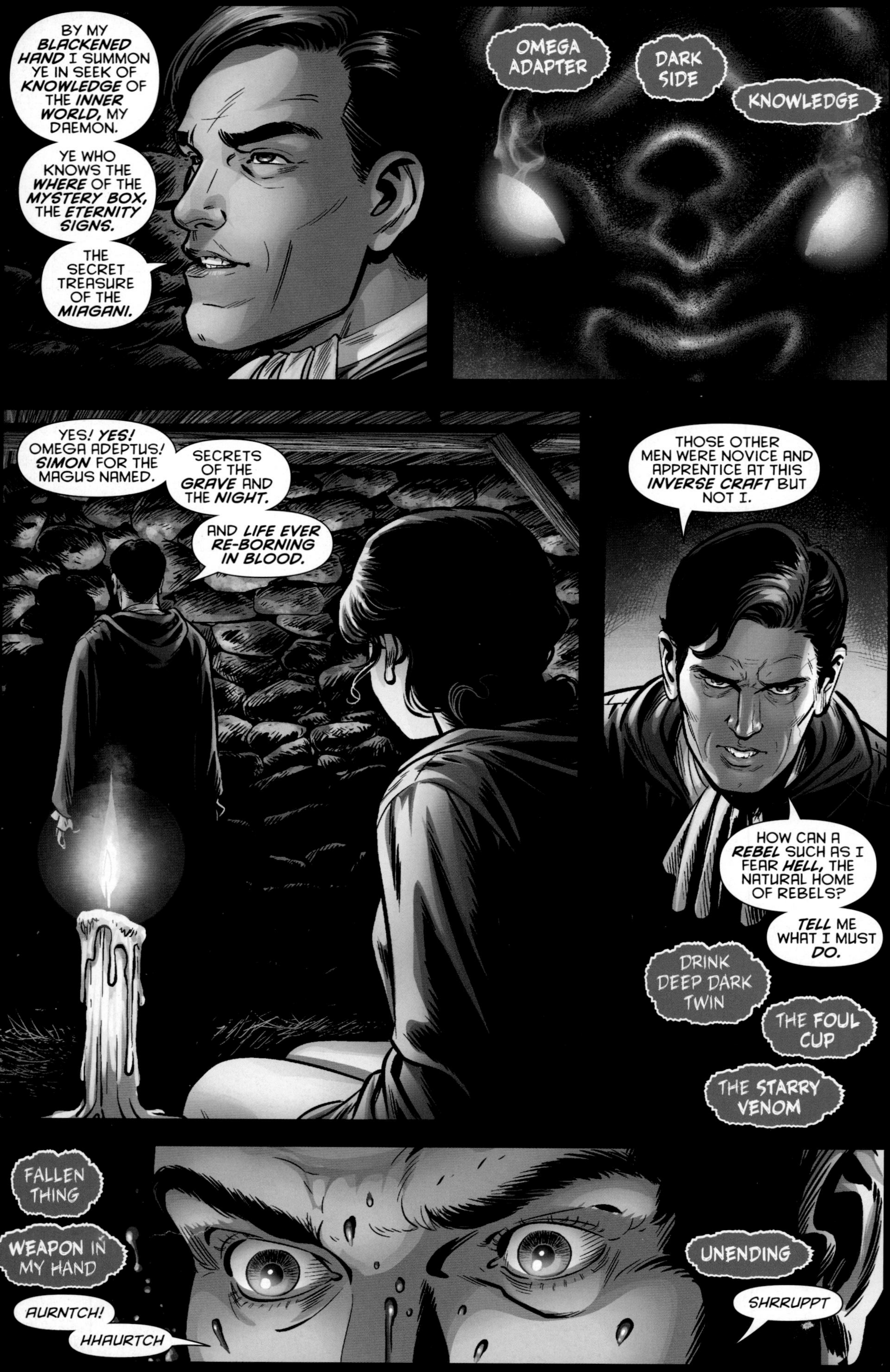
BY MY BLACKENED HAND I SUMMON YE IN SEEK OF KNOWLEDGE OF THE INNER WORLD, MY DAEMON.
YE WHO KNOWS THE WHERE OF THE MYSTERY BOX, THE ETERNITY SIGNS.
THE SECRET TREASURE OF THE MIAGANI.
OMEGA ADAPTER
DARK SIDE
KNOWLEDGE
YES! YES! OMEGA ADEPTUS! SIMON FOR THE MAGUS NAMED.
SECRETS OF THE GRAVE AND THE NIGHT.
AND LIFE EVER RE-BORNING IN BLOOD.
THOSE OTHER MEN WERE NOVICE AND APPRENTICE AT THIS INVERSE CRAFT BUT NOT I.
HOW CAN A REBEL SUCH AS I FEAR HELL, THE NATURAL HOME OF REBELS?
TELL ME WHAT I MUST DO.
DRINK DEEP DARK TWIN
THE FOUL CUP
THE STARRY VENOM
FALLEN THING
WEAPON IN MY HAND
UNENDING
AURNTCH!
HHAURTCH
SHRRUPPT

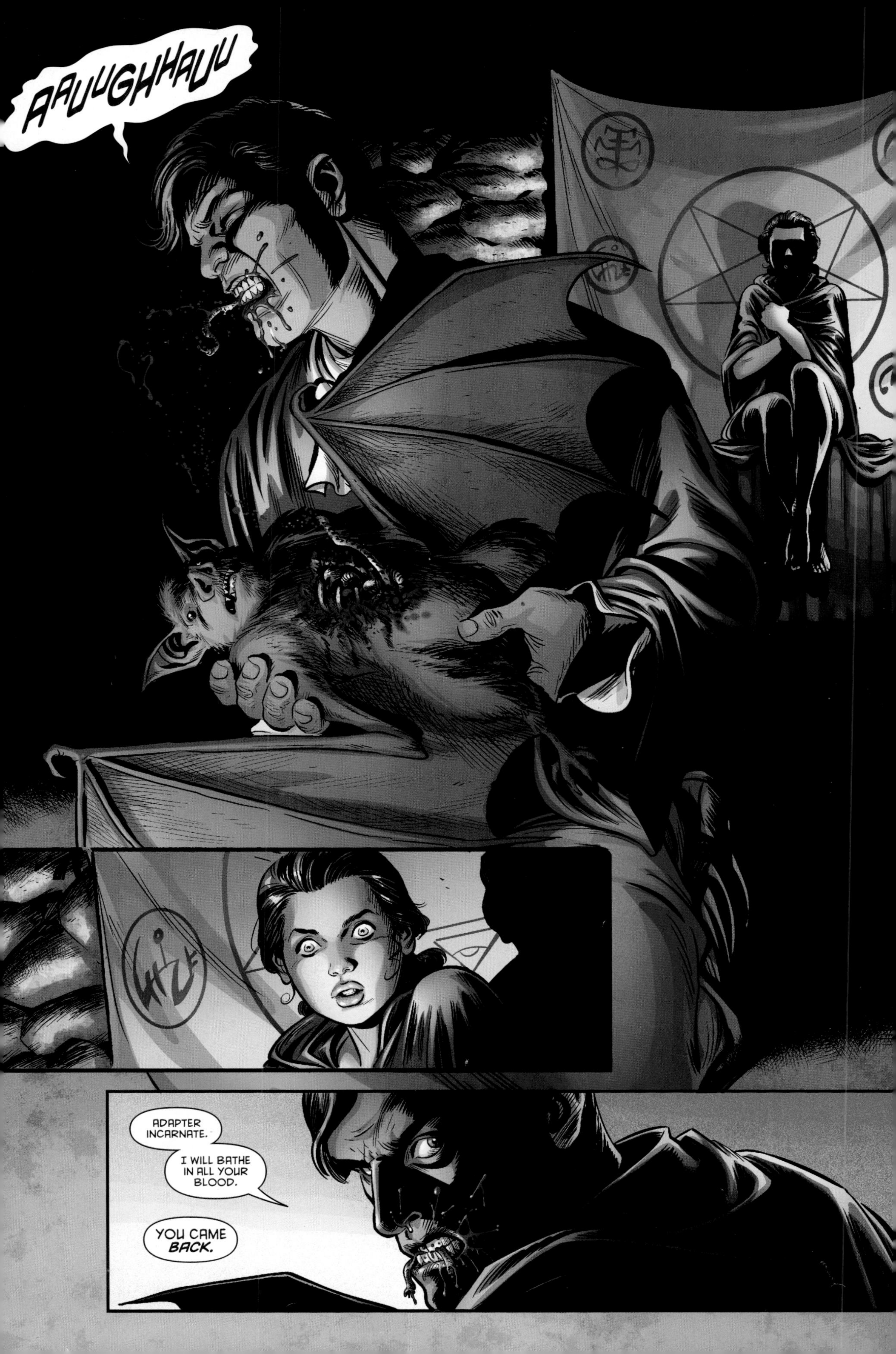
AAUUGHHAUU
ADAPTER INCARNATE.
I WILL BATHE IN ALL YOUR BLOOD.
YOU CAME *BACK.*

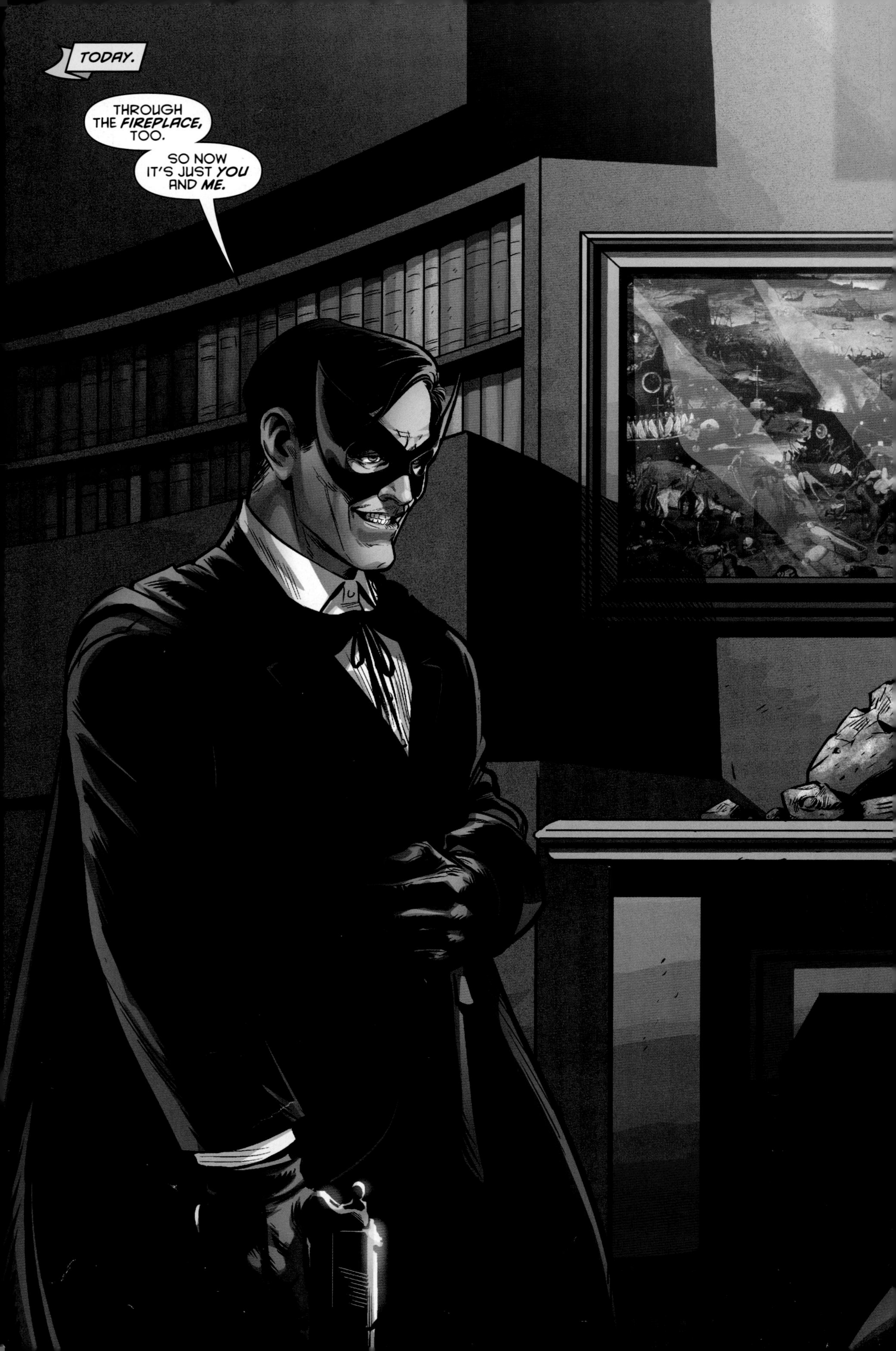
TODAY.
THROUGH THE FIREPLACE, TOO.
SO NOW IT'S JUST YOU AND ME.

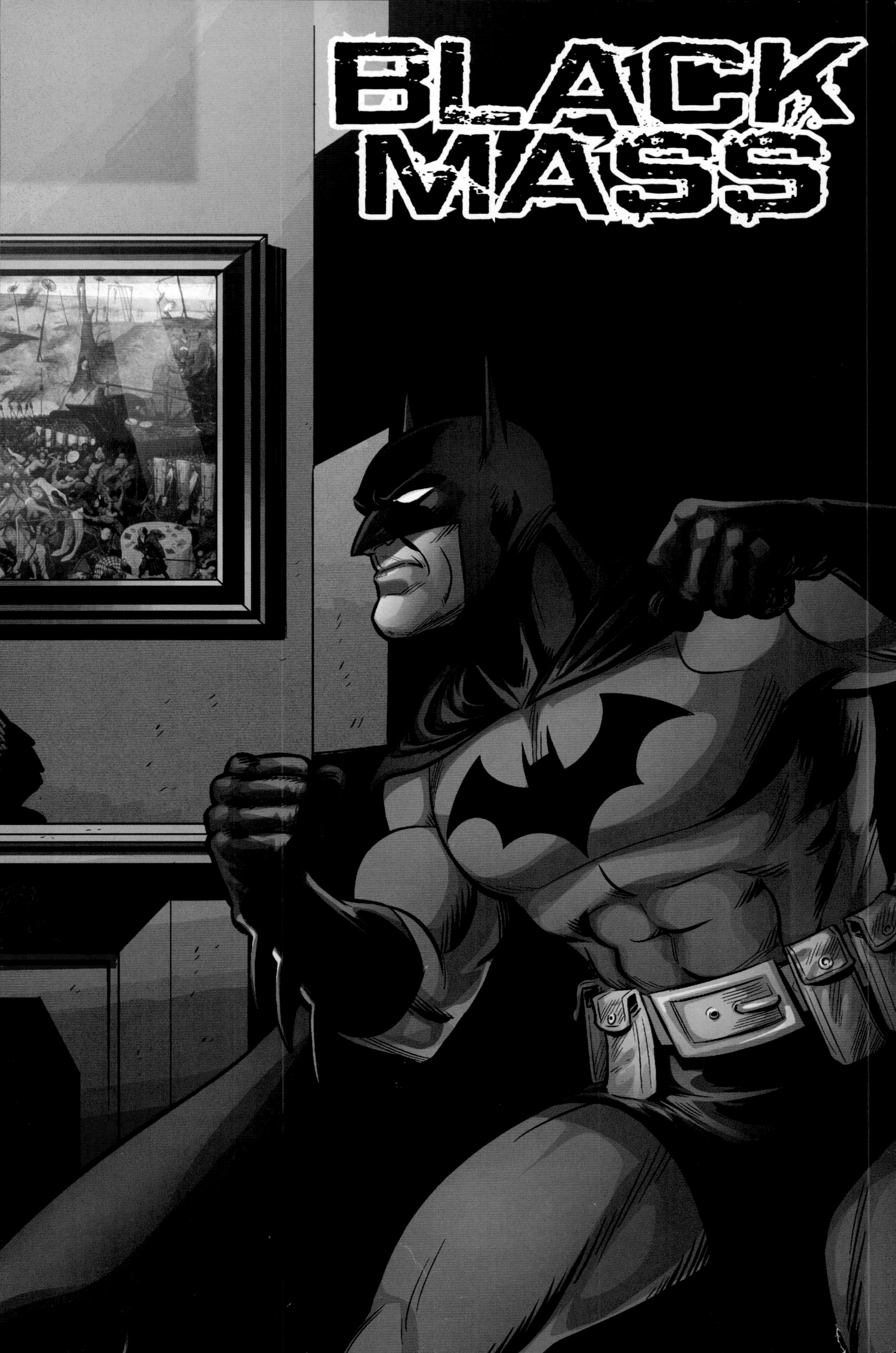
BLACK MASS

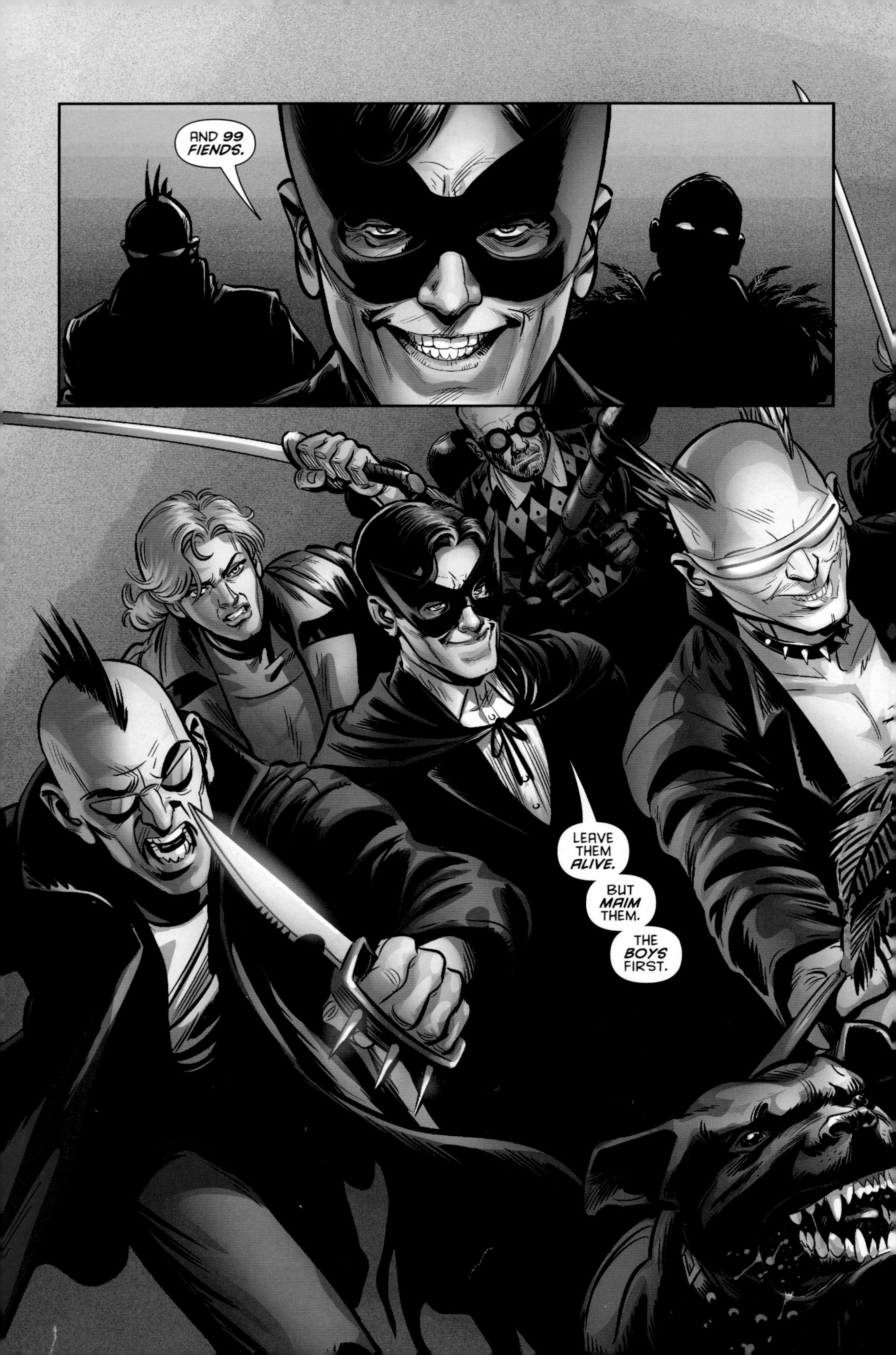
AND 99 FIENDS.
LEAVE THEM ALIVE.
BUT MAIM THEM.
THE BOYS FIRST.

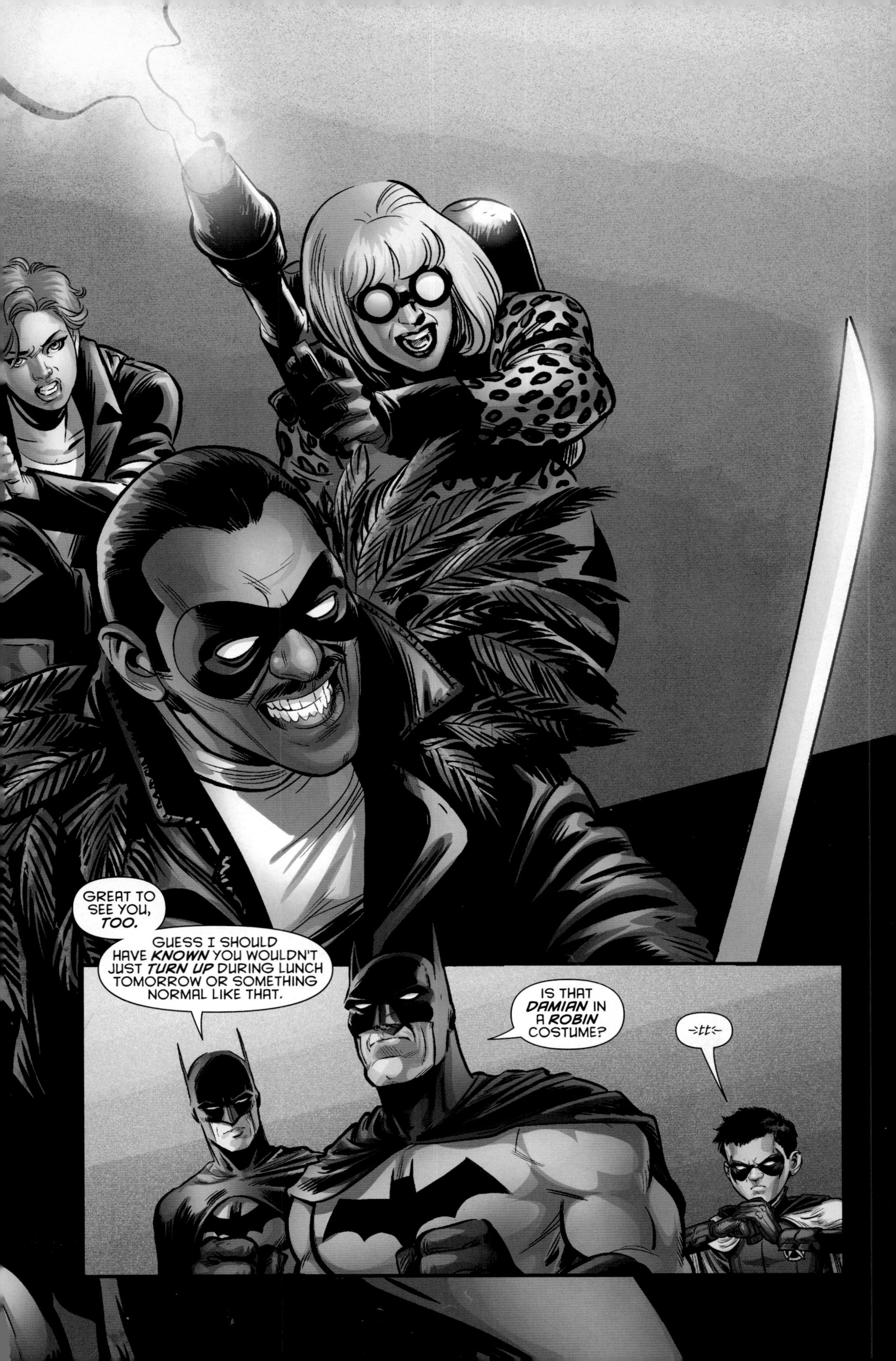
GREAT TO SEE YOU, *TOO.*
GUESS I SHOULD HAVE ***KNOWN*** YOU WOULDN'T JUST ***TURN UP*** DURING LUNCH TOMORROW OR SOMETHING NORMAL LIKE THAT.
IS THAT ***DAMIAN*** IN A ***ROBIN*** COSTUME?
-*tt*-

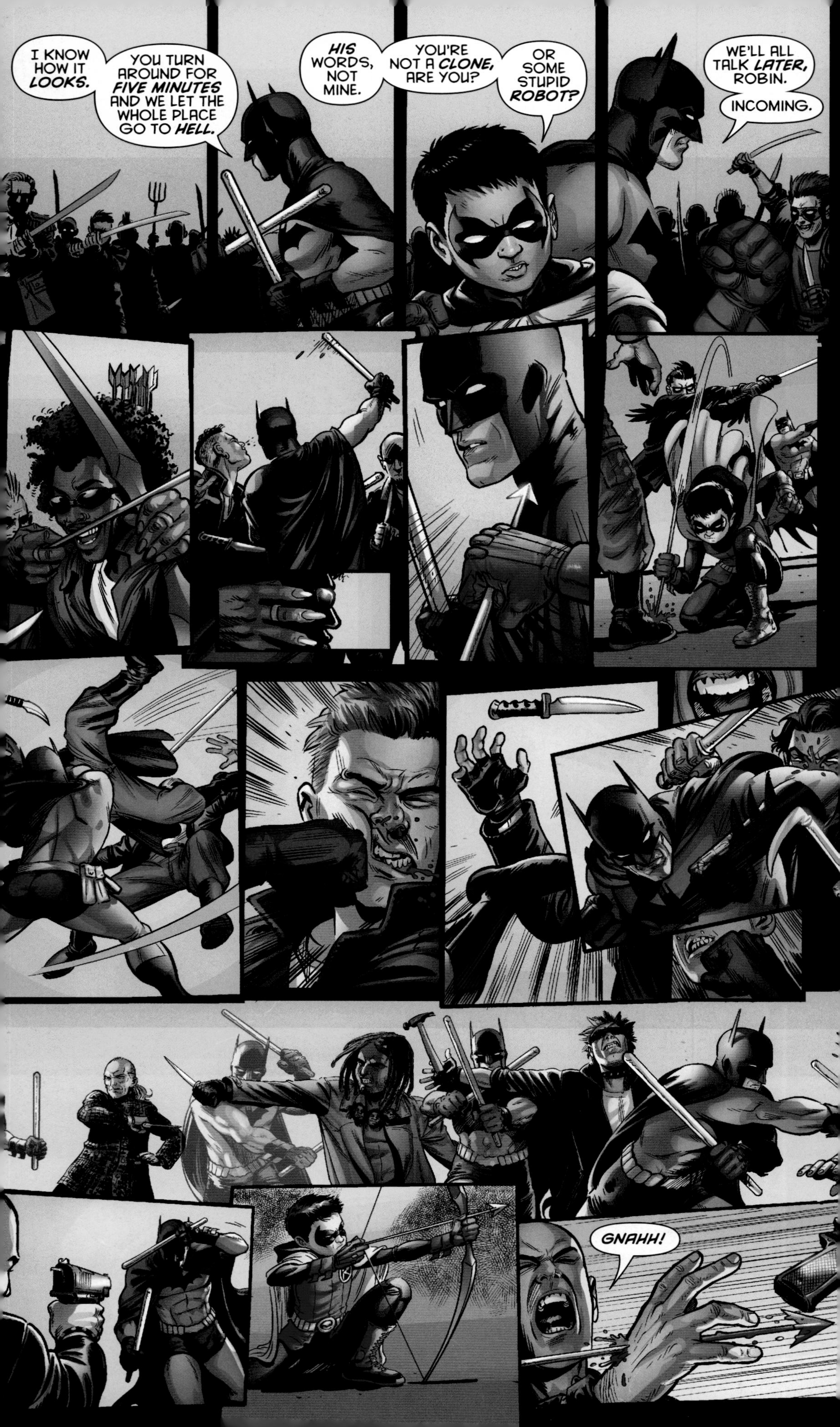

I KNOW HOW IT LOOKS.
YOU TURN AROUND FOR FIVE MINUTES AND WE LET THE WHOLE PLACE GO TO HELL.
HIS WORDS, NOT MINE.
YOU'RE NOT A CLONE, ARE YOU?
OR SOME STUPID ROBOT?
WE'LL ALL TALK LATER, ROBIN.
INCOMING.
GNAHH!

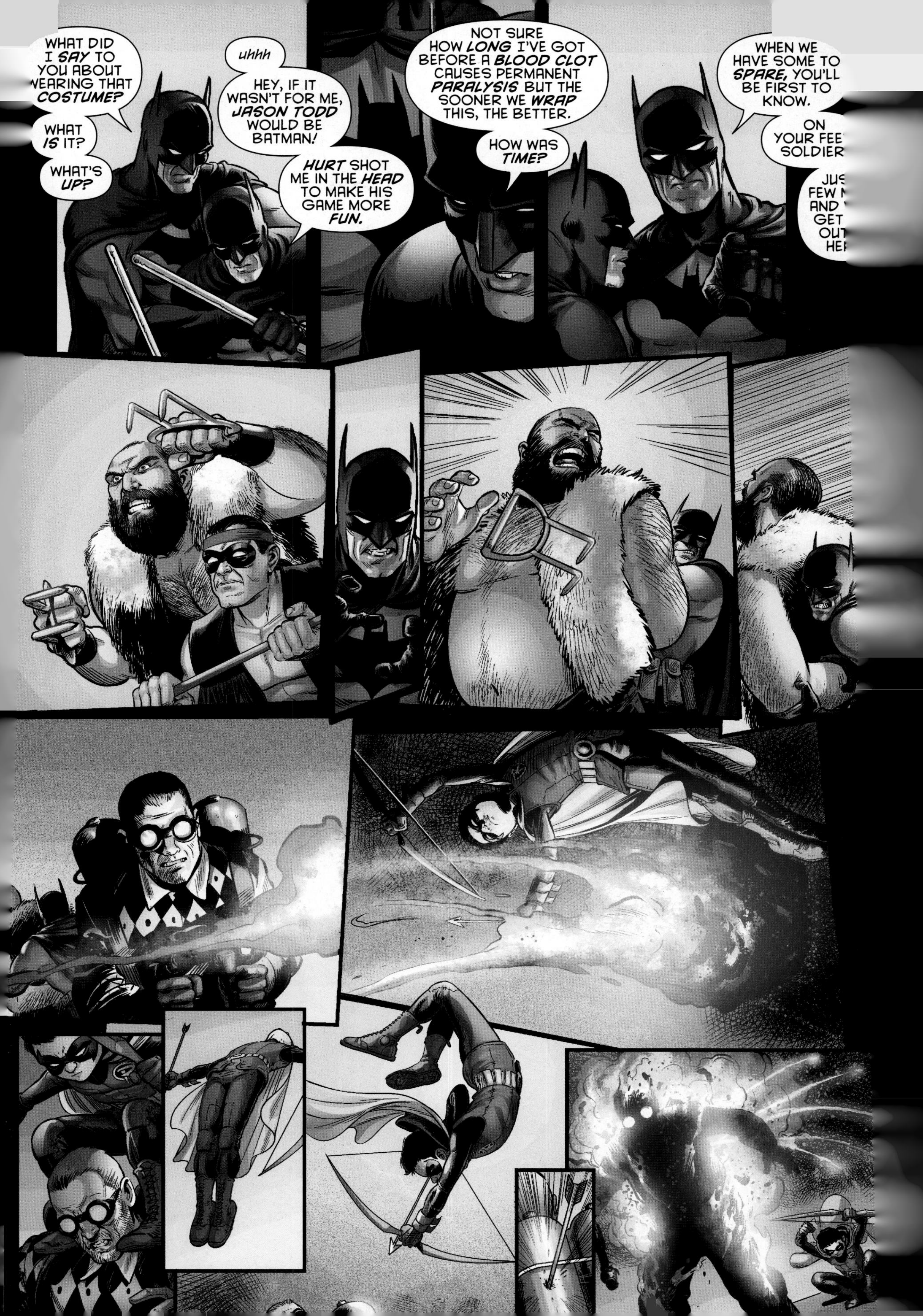

WHAT DID I *SAY* TO YOU ABOUT WEARING THAT *COSTUME?*
WHAT *IS* IT?
WHAT'S *UP?*
uhhh
HEY, IF IT WASN'T FOR ME, *JASON TODD* WOULD BE BATMAN!
HURT SHOT ME IN THE *HEAD* TO MAKE HIS GAME MORE *FUN.*
NOT SURE HOW *LONG* I'VE GOT BEFORE A *BLOOD CLOT* CAUSES PERMANENT *PARALYSIS* BUT THE SOONER WE *WRAP* THIS, THE BETTER.
HOW WAS *TIME?*
WHEN WE HAVE SOME TO *SPARE,* YOU'LL BE FIRST TO KNOW.
ON YOUR FEE SOLDIER
JUS FEW M AND W GET OUT HE

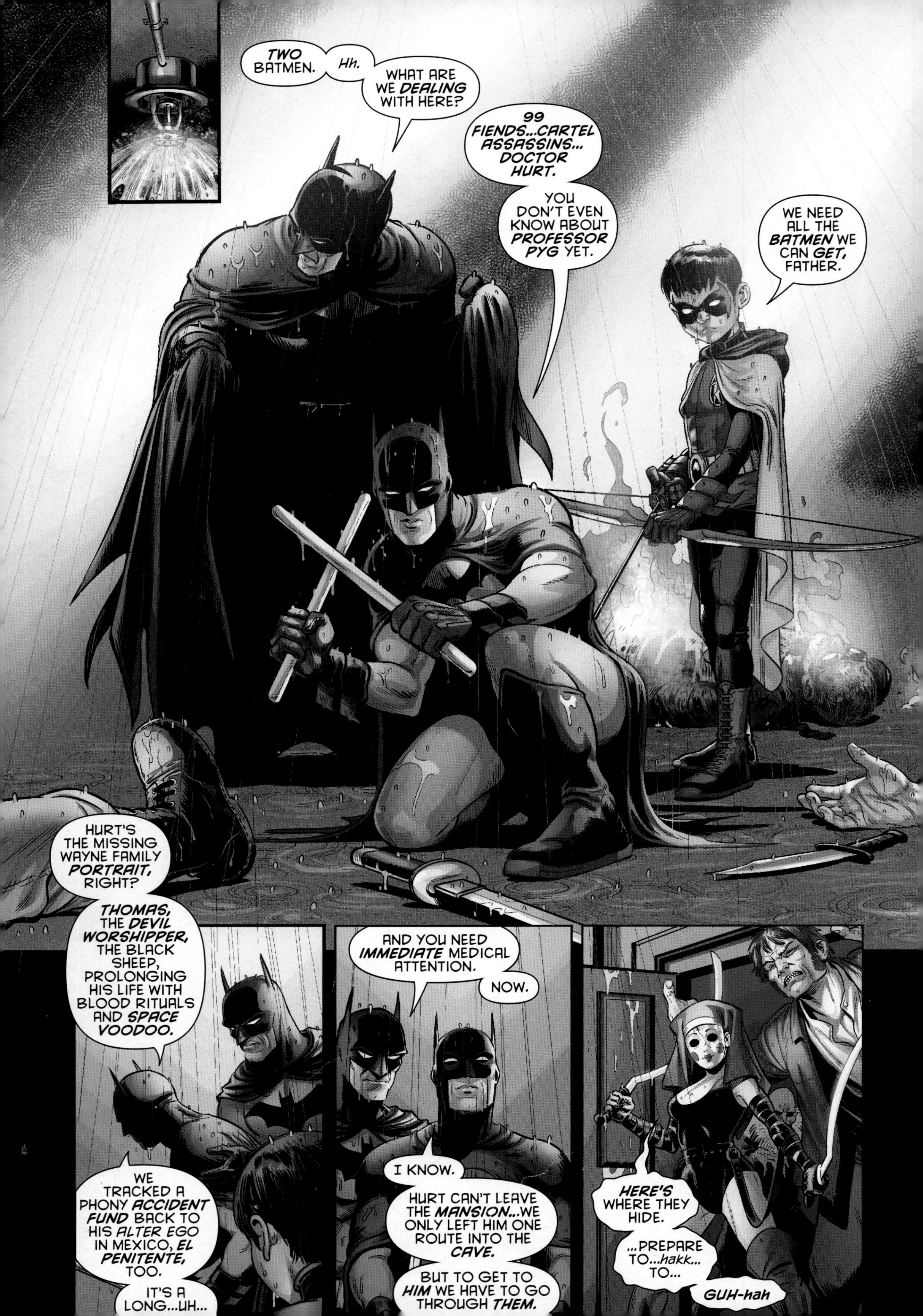

TWO BATMEN.
Hh.
WHAT ARE WE DEALING WITH HERE?
99 FIENDS...CARTEL ASSASSINS... DOCTOR HURT.
YOU DON'T EVEN KNOW ABOUT PROFESSOR PYG YET.
WE NEED ALL THE BATMEN WE CAN GET, FATHER.
HURT'S THE MISSING WAYNE FAMILY PORTRAIT, RIGHT?
THOMAS, THE DEVIL WORSHIPPER, THE BLACK SHEEP, PROLONGING HIS LIFE WITH BLOOD RITUALS AND SPACE VOODOO.
WE TRACKED A PHONY ACCIDENT FUND BACK TO HIS ALTER EGO IN MEXICO, EL PENITENTE, TOO.
IT'S A LONG...UH...
AND YOU NEED IMMEDIATE MEDICAL ATTENTION.
NOW.
I KNOW.
HURT CAN'T LEAVE THE MANSION...WE ONLY LEFT HIM ONE ROUTE INTO THE CAVE.
BUT TO GET TO HIM WE HAVE TO GO THROUGH THEM.
HERE'S WHERE THEY HIDE.
...PREPARE TO...hakk... TO...
GUH-hah

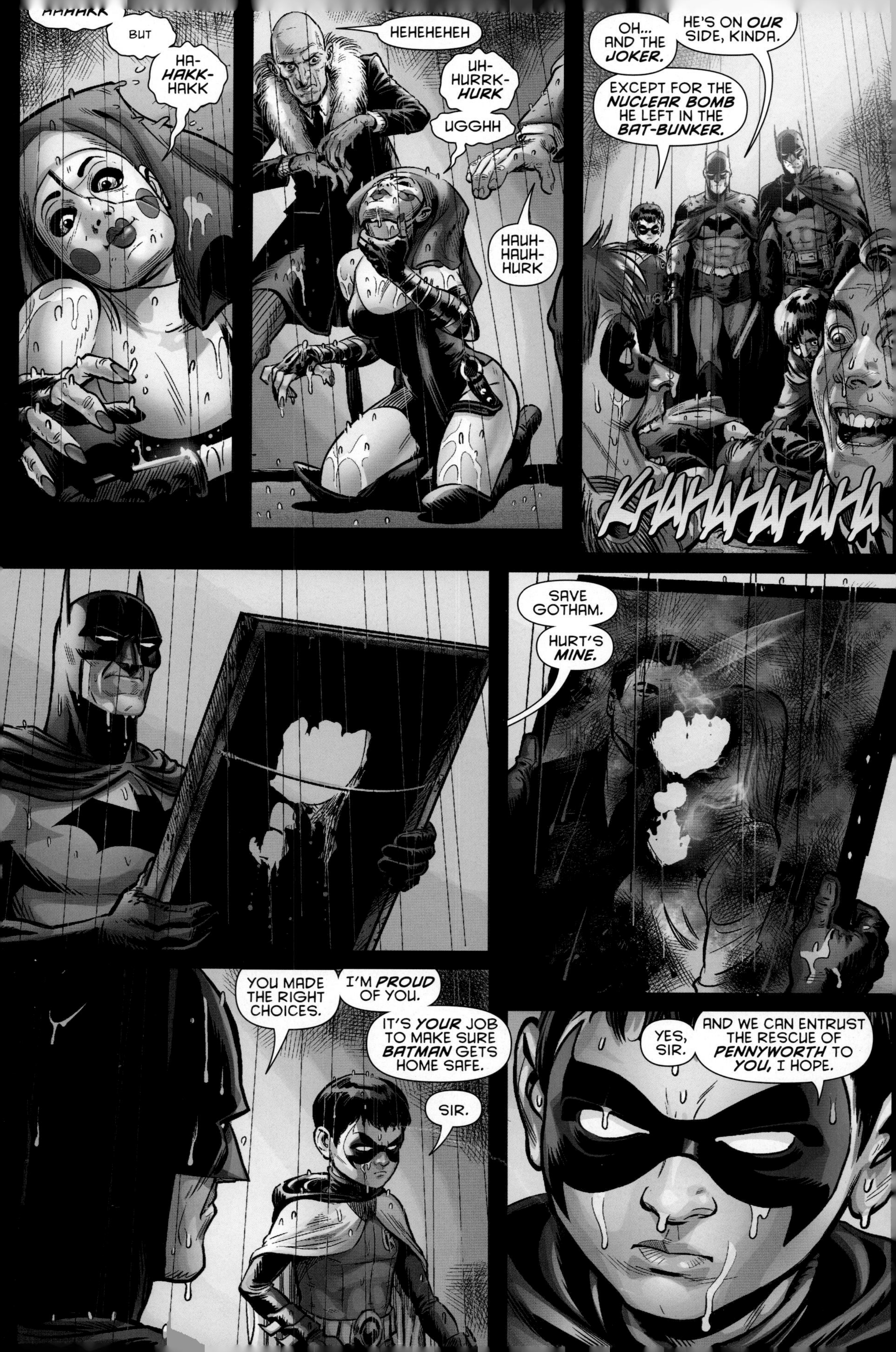
AHHHKK
BUT
HA-HAKK-HAKK
HEHEHEHEH
UH-HURRK-HURK
UGGHH
HAUH-HAUH-HURK
OH... AND THE JOKER.
HE'S ON OUR SIDE, KINDA.
EXCEPT FOR THE NUCLEAR BOMB HE LEFT IN THE BAT-BUNKER.
KHAHAHAHAHAHA
SAVE GOTHAM.
HURT'S MINE.
YOU MADE THE RIGHT CHOICES.
I'M PROUD OF YOU.
IT'S YOUR JOB TO MAKE SURE BATMAN GETS HOME SAFE.
SIR.
YES, SIR.
AND WE CAN ENTRUST THE RESCUE OF PENNYWORTH TO YOU, I HOPE.

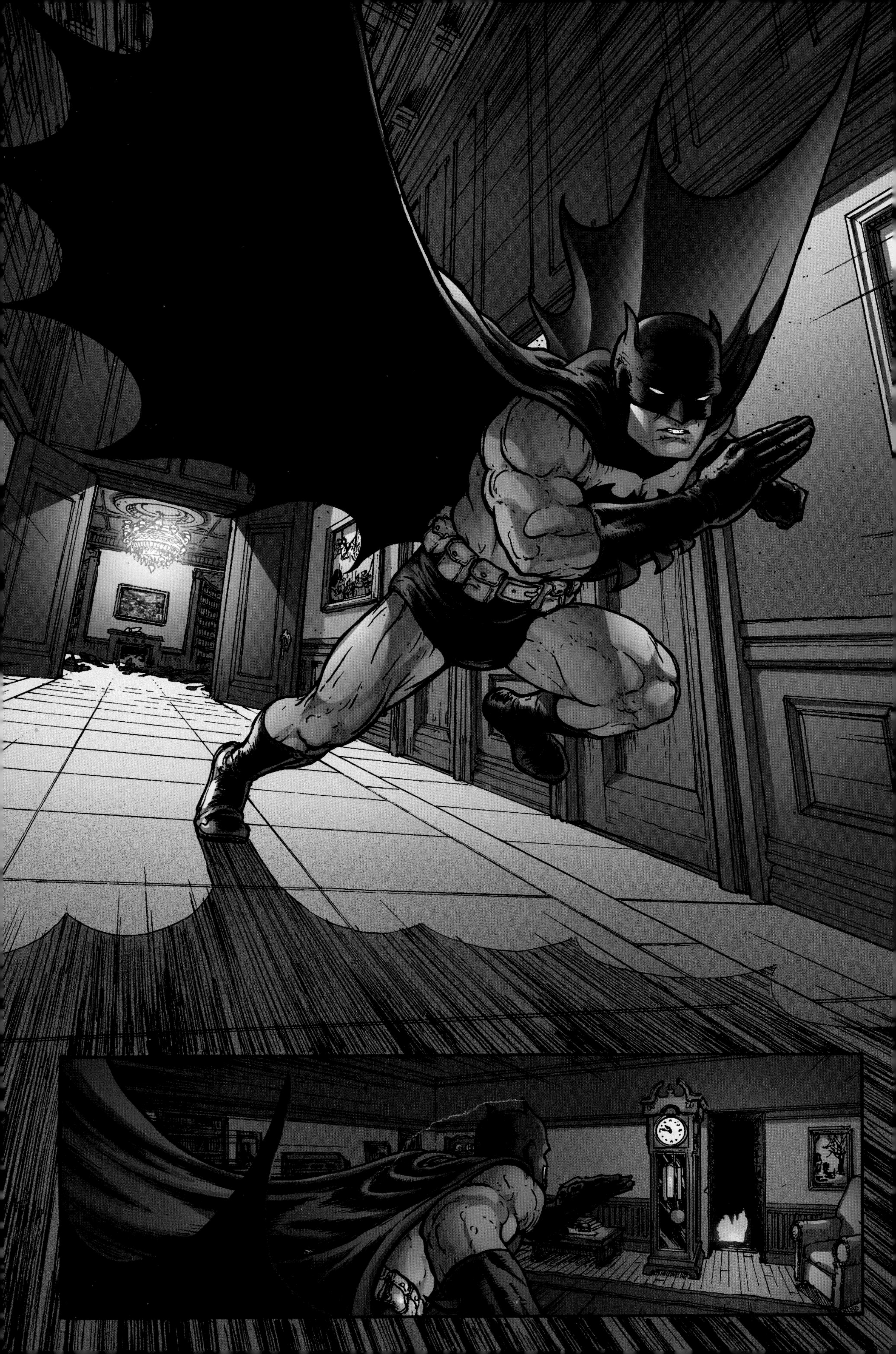

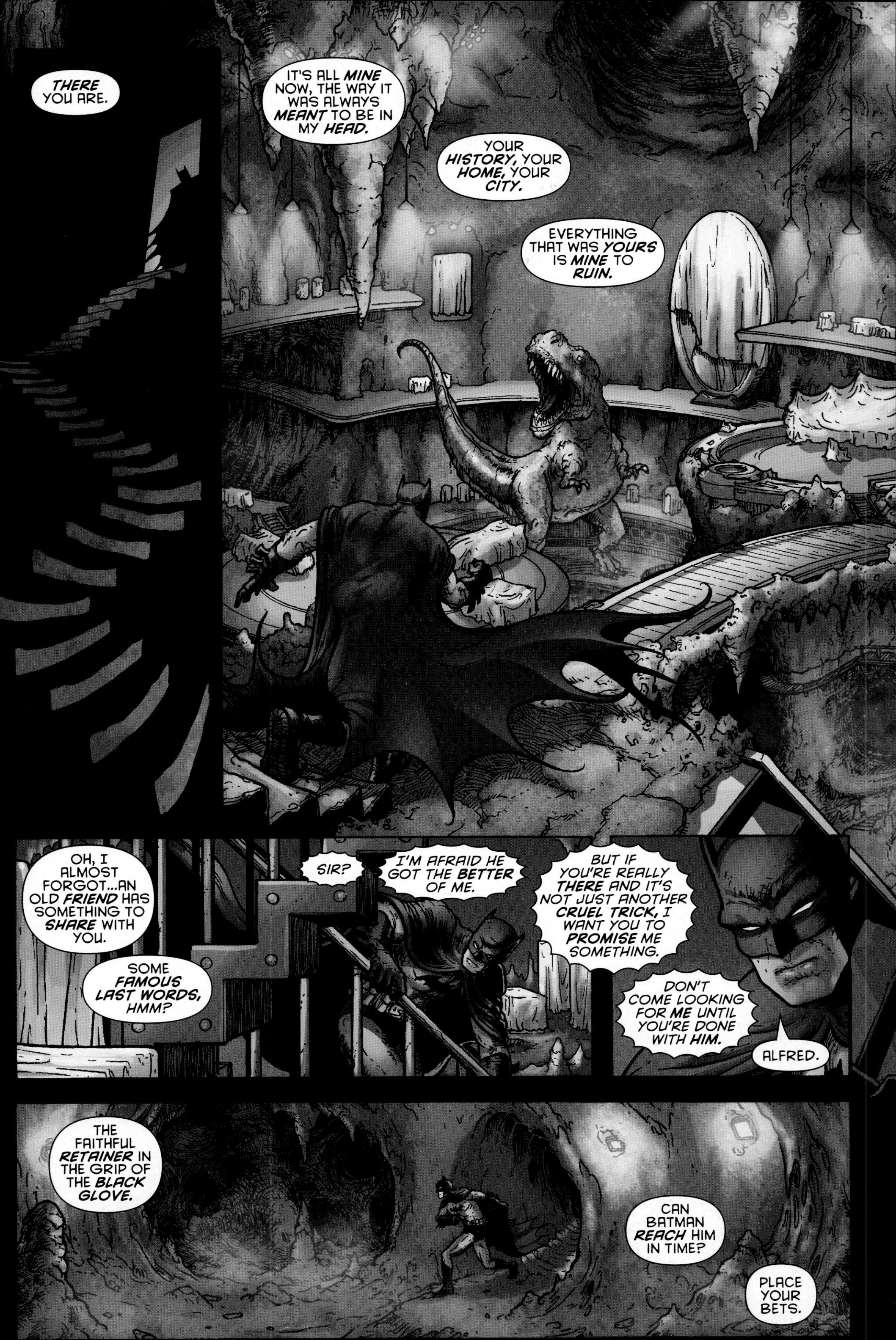
THERE YOU ARE.
IT'S ALL MINE NOW, THE WAY IT WAS ALWAYS MEANT TO BE IN MY HEAD.
YOUR HISTORY, YOUR HOME, YOUR CITY.
EVERYTHING THAT WAS YOURS IS MINE TO RUIN.
OH, I ALMOST FORGOT...AN OLD FRIEND HAS SOMETHING TO SHARE WITH YOU.
SOME FAMOUS LAST WORDS, HMM?
SIR?
I'M AFRAID HE GOT THE BETTER OF ME.
BUT IF YOU'RE REALLY THERE AND IT'S NOT JUST ANOTHER CRUEL TRICK, I WANT YOU TO PROMISE ME SOMETHING.
DON'T COME LOOKING FOR ME UNTIL YOU'RE DONE WITH HIM.
ALFRED.
THE FAITHFUL RETAINER IN THE GRIP OF THE BLACK GLOVE.
CAN BATMAN REACH HIM IN TIME?
PLACE YOUR BETS.

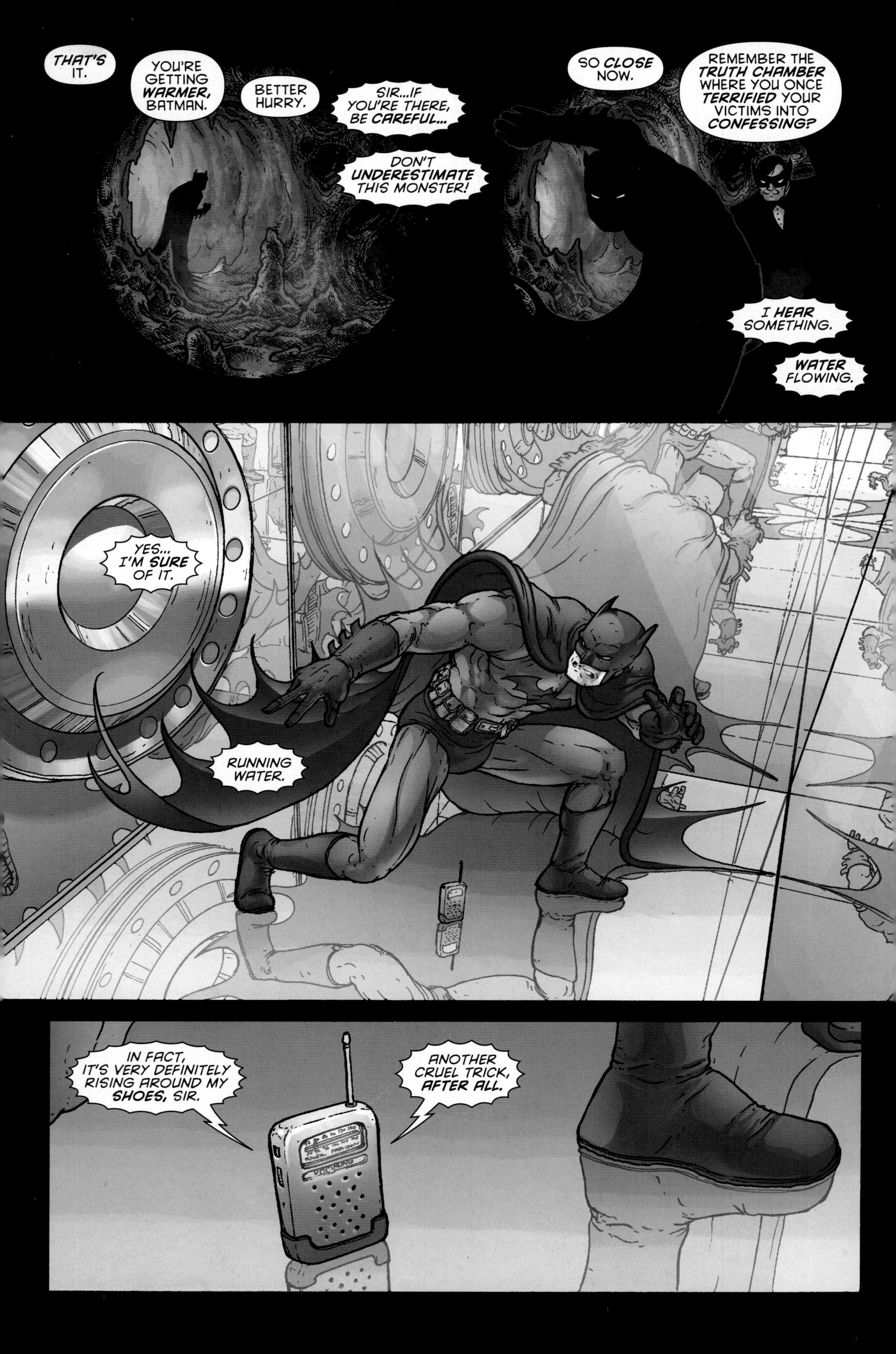
THAT'S IT.
YOU'RE GETTING WARMER, BATMAN.
BETTER HURRY.
SIR...IF YOU'RE THERE, BE CAREFUL...
DON'T UNDERESTIMATE THIS MONSTER!
SO CLOSE NOW.
REMEMBER THE TRUTH CHAMBER WHERE YOU ONCE TERRIFIED YOUR VICTIMS INTO CONFESSING?
I HEAR SOMETHING.
WATER FLOWING.
YES... I'M SURE OF IT.
RUNNING WATER.
IN FACT, IT'S VERY DEFINITELY RISING AROUND MY SHOES, SIR.
ANOTHER CRUEL TRICK, AFTER ALL.

I BEAT YOU AGAIN! THAT'S HOW IT FEELS TO BE SECOND BEST!

THAT'S HOW IT FEELS TO BE THE DEVIL IN HELL!

I'LL KEEP TALKING.

THE WATER IS POOLING AROUND MY SHINS AND RISING.

ALFRED. WHERE ARE YOU? ALFRED?

HE CAN'T HEAR YOU.

I JUST WANT YOU TO HEAR HIM DIE KNOWING THERE'S NOTHING YOU CAN DO ABOUT IT.

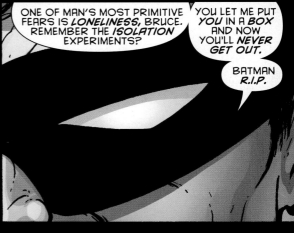

ONE OF MAN'S MOST PRIMITIVE FEARS IS LONELINESS, BRUCE. REMEMBER THE ISOLATION EXPERIMENTS?

YOU LET ME PUT YOU IN A BOX AND NOW YOU'LL NEVER GET OUT.

BATMAN R.I.P.

I AM THE HOLE IN THINGS!

I BRING HELL ON EARTH AND TO THE WORLD DEBASEMENT!

ROT IN PURGATORY.

THIS HOUSE IS MINE.

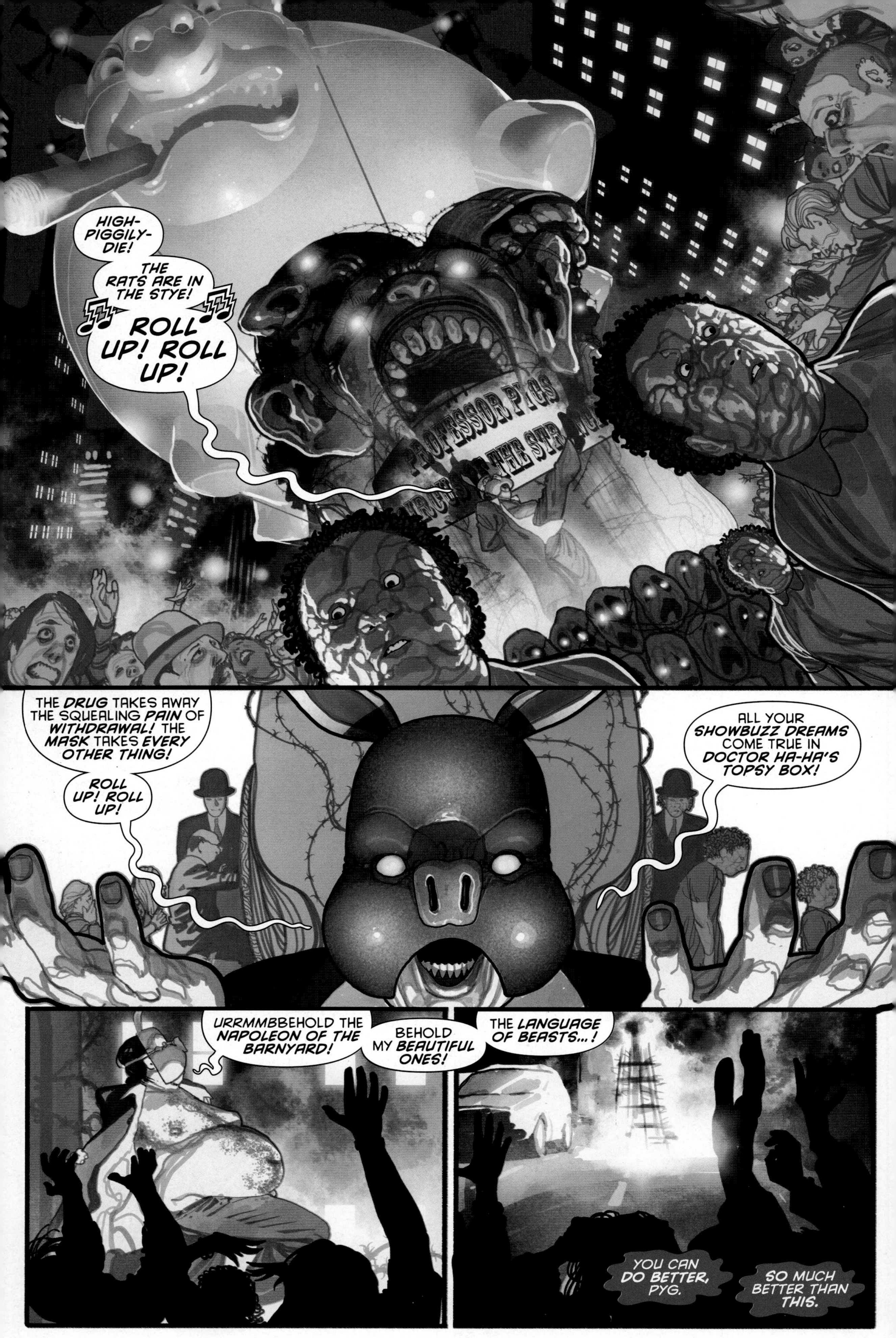
HIGH-PIGGILY-DIE!
THE RATS ARE IN THE STYE!
ROLL UP! ROLL UP!
PROFESSOR PYGS
THE DRUG TAKES AWAY THE SQUEALING PAIN OF WITHDRAWAL! THE MASK TAKES EVERY OTHER THING!
ROLL UP! ROLL UP!
ALL YOUR SHOWBUZZ DREAMS COME TRUE IN DOCTOR HA-HA'S TOPSY BOX!
URRMMBBEHOLD THE NAPOLEON OF THE BARNYARD!
BEHOLD MY BEAUTIFUL ONES!
THE LANGUAGE OF BEASTS...!
YOU CAN DO BETTER, PYG.
SO MUCH BETTER THAN THIS.

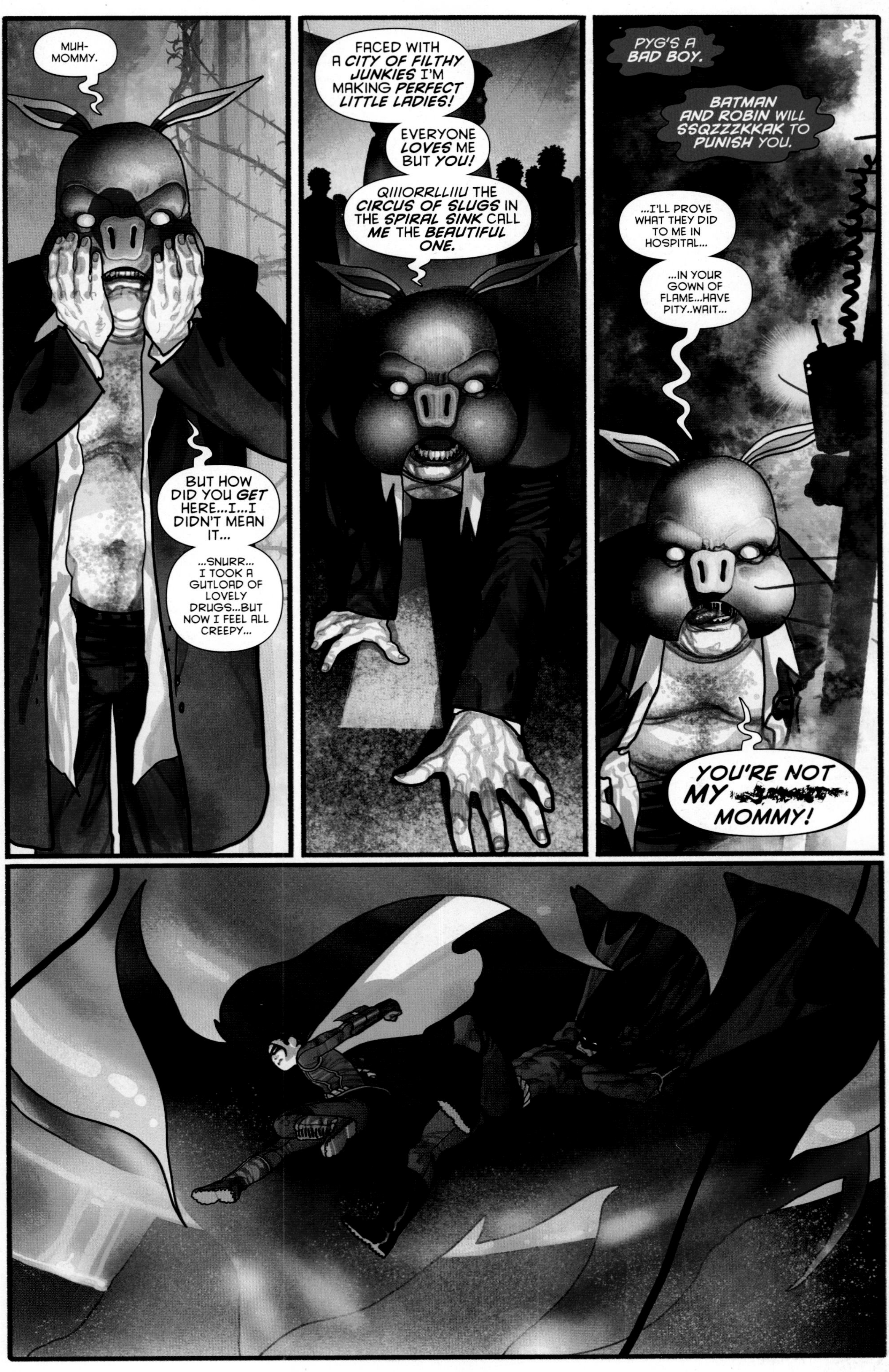
MUH-MOMMY.
BUT HOW DID YOU GET HERE...I...I DIDN'T MEAN IT...
...SNURR... I TOOK A GUTLOAD OF LOVELY DRUGS...BUT NOW I FEEL ALL CREEPY...
FACED WITH A CITY OF FILTHY JUNKIES I'M MAKING PERFECT LITTLE LADIES!
EVERYONE LOVES ME BUT YOU!
QIIIORRLLIIU THE CIRCUS OF SLUGS IN THE SPIRAL SINK CALL ME THE BEAUTIFUL ONE.
PYG'S A BAD BOY.
BATMAN AND ROBIN WILL SSQZZZKKAK TO PUNISH YOU.
...I'LL PROVE WHAT THEY DID TO ME IN HOSPITAL...
...IN YOUR GOWN OF FLAME...HAVE PITY..WAIT...
YOU'RE NOT MY [redacted] MOMMY!

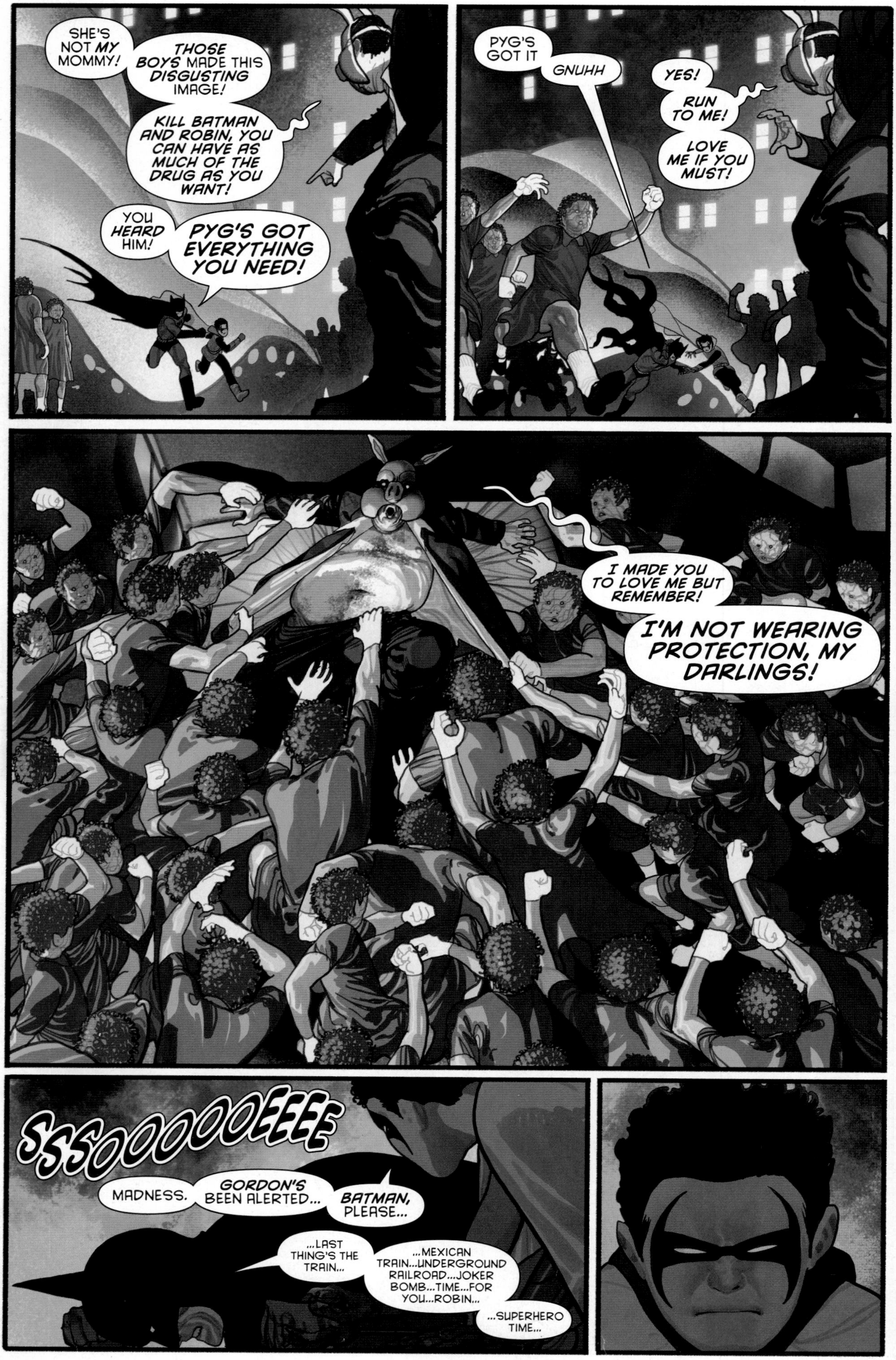
SHE'S NOT *MY* MOMMY!
THOSE BOYS MADE THIS *DISGUSTING* IMAGE!
KILL BATMAN AND ROBIN, YOU CAN HAVE AS MUCH OF THE DRUG AS YOU WANT!
YOU *HEARD* HIM!
PYG'S GOT EVERYTHING YOU NEED!
PYG'S GOT IT
GNUHH
YES!
RUN TO ME!
LOVE ME IF YOU MUST!
I MADE YOU TO LOVE ME BUT REMEMBER!
I'M NOT WEARING PROTECTION, MY DARLINGS!
SSSOOOOOOEEEE
MADNESS.
GORDON'S BEEN ALERTED...
BATMAN, PLEASE...
...LAST THING'S THE TRAIN...
...MEXICAN TRAIN...UNDERGROUND RAILROAD...JOKER BOMB...TIME...FOR YOU...ROBIN...
...SUPERHERO TIME...

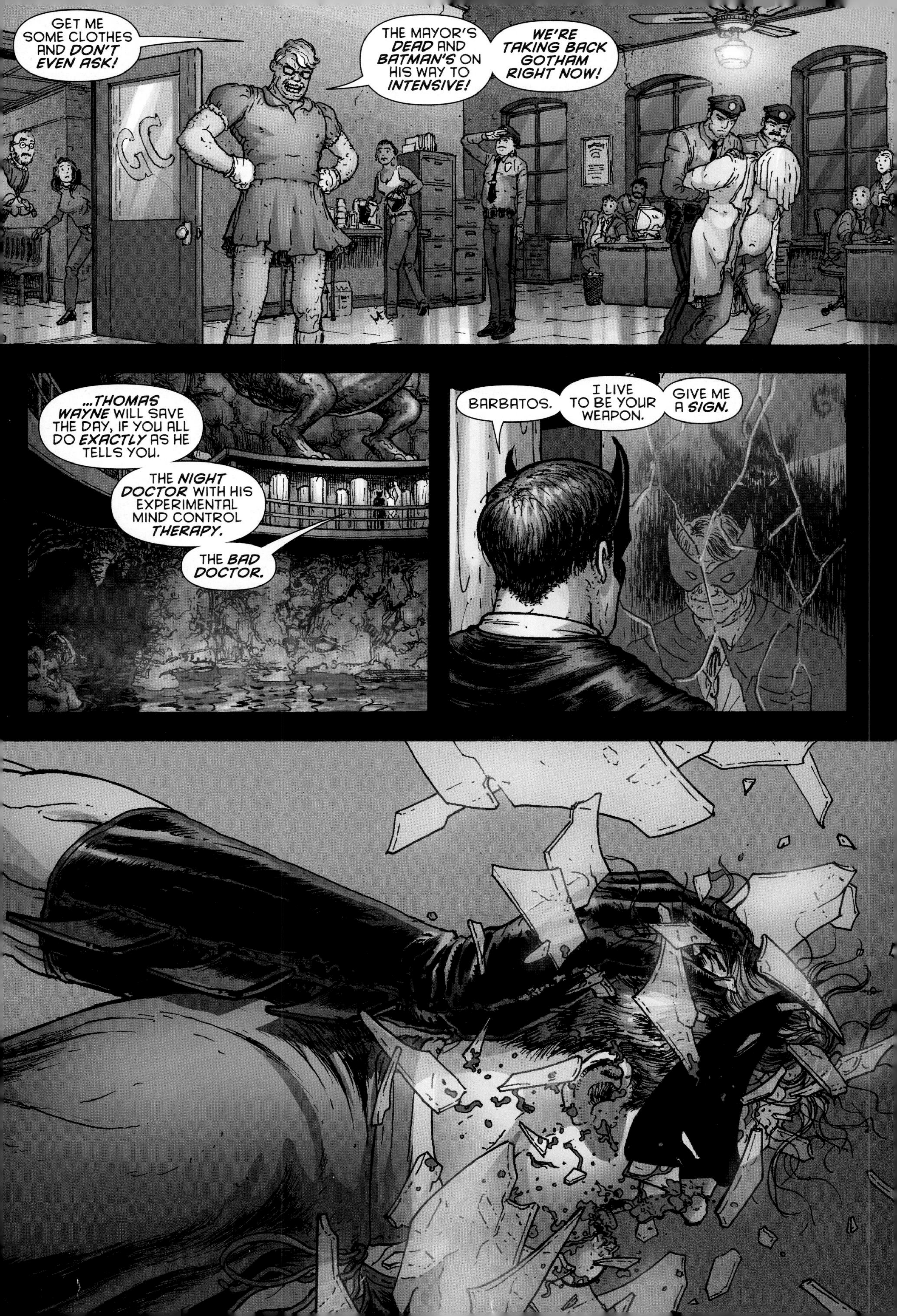
GET ME SOME CLOTHES AND DON'T EVEN ASK!
THE MAYOR'S DEAD AND BATMAN'S ON HIS WAY TO INTENSIVE!
WE'RE TAKING BACK GOTHAM RIGHT NOW!
...THOMAS WAYNE WILL SAVE THE DAY, IF YOU ALL DO EXACTLY AS HE TELLS YOU.
THE NIGHT DOCTOR WITH HIS EXPERIMENTAL MIND CONTROL THERAPY.
THE BAD DOCTOR.
BARBATOS.
I LIVE TO BE YOUR WEAPON.
GIVE ME A SIGN.

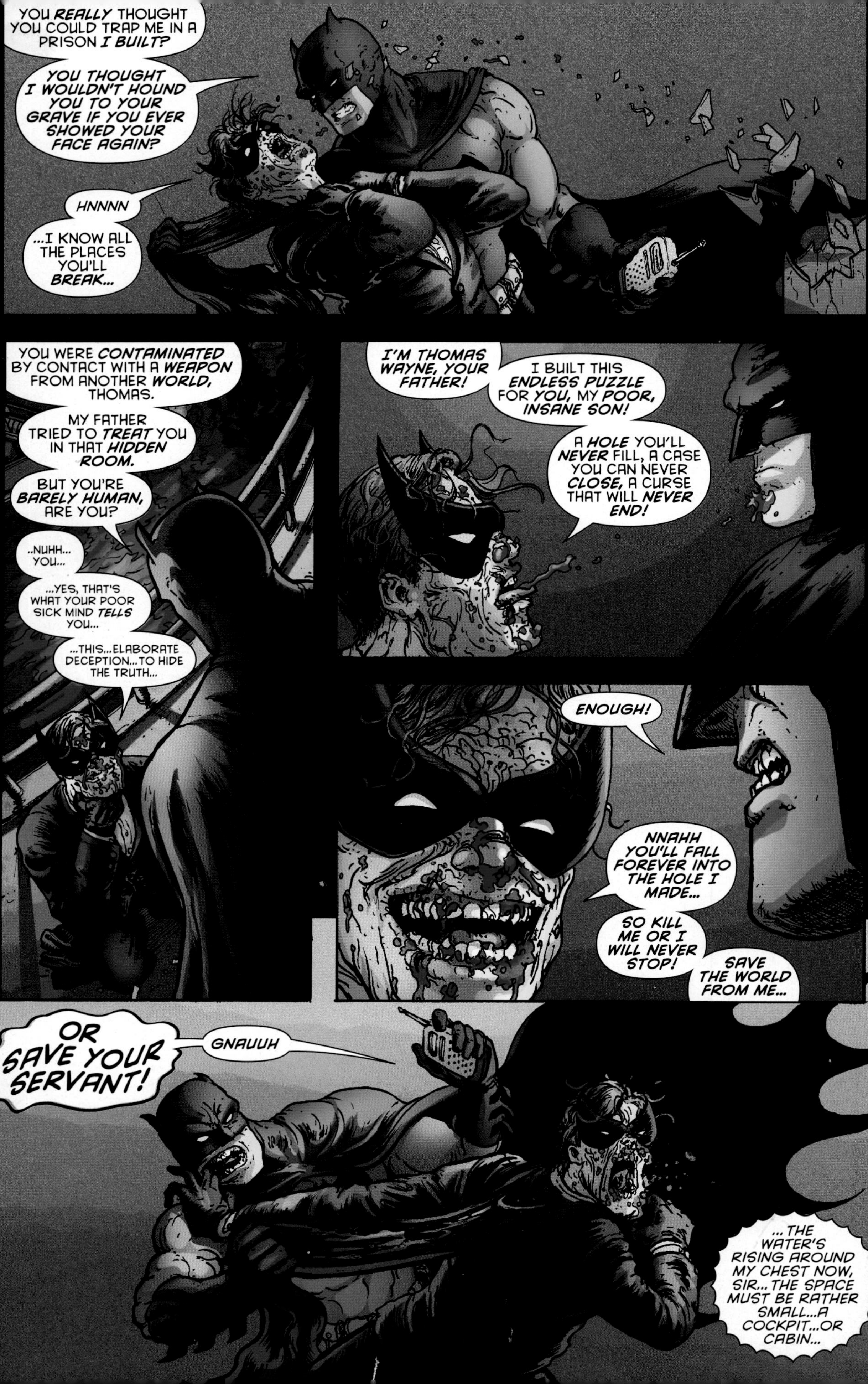
YOU REALLY THOUGHT YOU COULD TRAP ME IN A PRISON I BUILT?
YOU THOUGHT I WOULDN'T HOUND YOU TO YOUR GRAVE IF YOU EVER SHOWED YOUR FACE AGAIN?
HNNNN
...I KNOW ALL THE PLACES YOU'LL BREAK...
YOU WERE CONTAMINATED BY CONTACT WITH A WEAPON FROM ANOTHER WORLD, THOMAS.
MY FATHER TRIED TO TREAT YOU IN THAT HIDDEN ROOM.
BUT YOU'RE BARELY HUMAN, ARE YOU?
..NUHH... YOU...
...YES, THAT'S WHAT YOUR POOR SICK MIND TELLS YOU...
...THIS...ELABORATE DECEPTION...TO HIDE THE TRUTH...
I'M THOMAS WAYNE, YOUR FATHER!
I BUILT THIS ENDLESS PUZZLE FOR YOU, MY POOR, INSANE SON!
A HOLE YOU'LL NEVER FILL, A CASE YOU CAN NEVER CLOSE, A CURSE THAT WILL NEVER END!
ENOUGH!
NNAHH YOU'LL FALL FOREVER INTO THE HOLE I MADE...
SO KILL ME OR I WILL NEVER STOP!
SAVE THE WORLD FROM ME...
OR SAVE YOUR SERVANT!
GNAUUH
...THE WATER'S RISING AROUND MY CHEST NOW, SIR...THE SPACE MUST BE RATHER SMALL...A COCKPIT...OR CABIN...

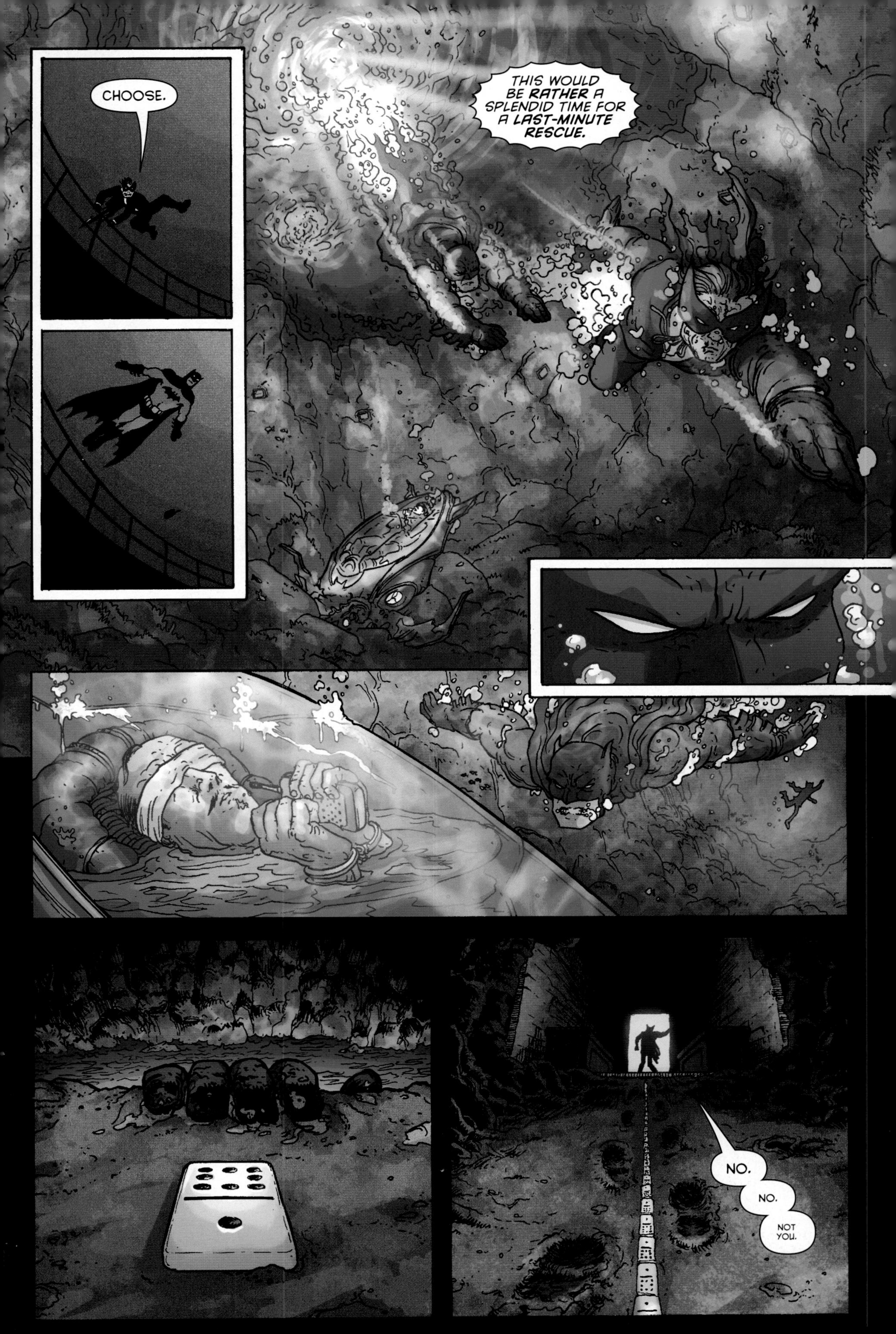
CHOOSE.
THIS WOULD BE RATHER A SPLENDID TIME FOR A LAST-MINUTE RESCUE.
NO.
NO.
NOT YOU.

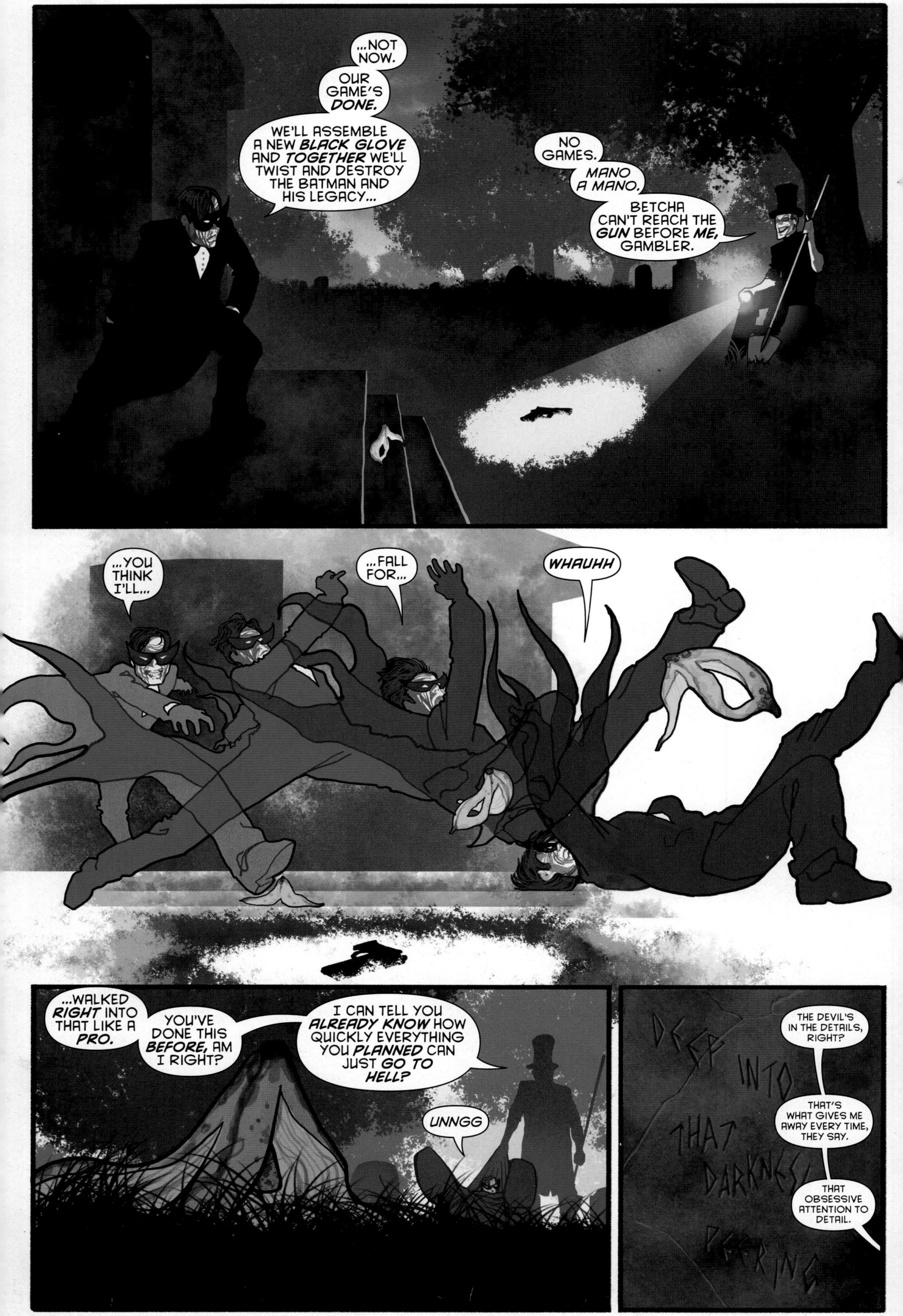
...NOT NOW.
OUR GAME'S DONE.
WE'LL ASSEMBLE A NEW BLACK GLOVE AND TOGETHER WE'LL TWIST AND DESTROY THE BATMAN AND HIS LEGACY...
NO GAMES.
MANO A MANO.
BETCHA CAN'T REACH THE GUN BEFORE ME, GAMBLER.
...YOU THINK I'LL...
...FALL FOR...
WHAUHH
...WALKED RIGHT INTO THAT LIKE A PRO.
YOU'VE DONE THIS BEFORE, AM I RIGHT?
I CAN TELL YOU ALREADY KNOW HOW QUICKLY EVERYTHING YOU PLANNED CAN JUST GO TO HELL?
UNNGG
DEEP INTO THAT DARKNESS PEERING
THE DEVIL'S IN THE DETAILS, RIGHT?
THAT'S WHAT GIVES ME AWAY EVERY TIME, THEY SAY.
THAT OBSESSIVE ATTENTION TO DETAIL.

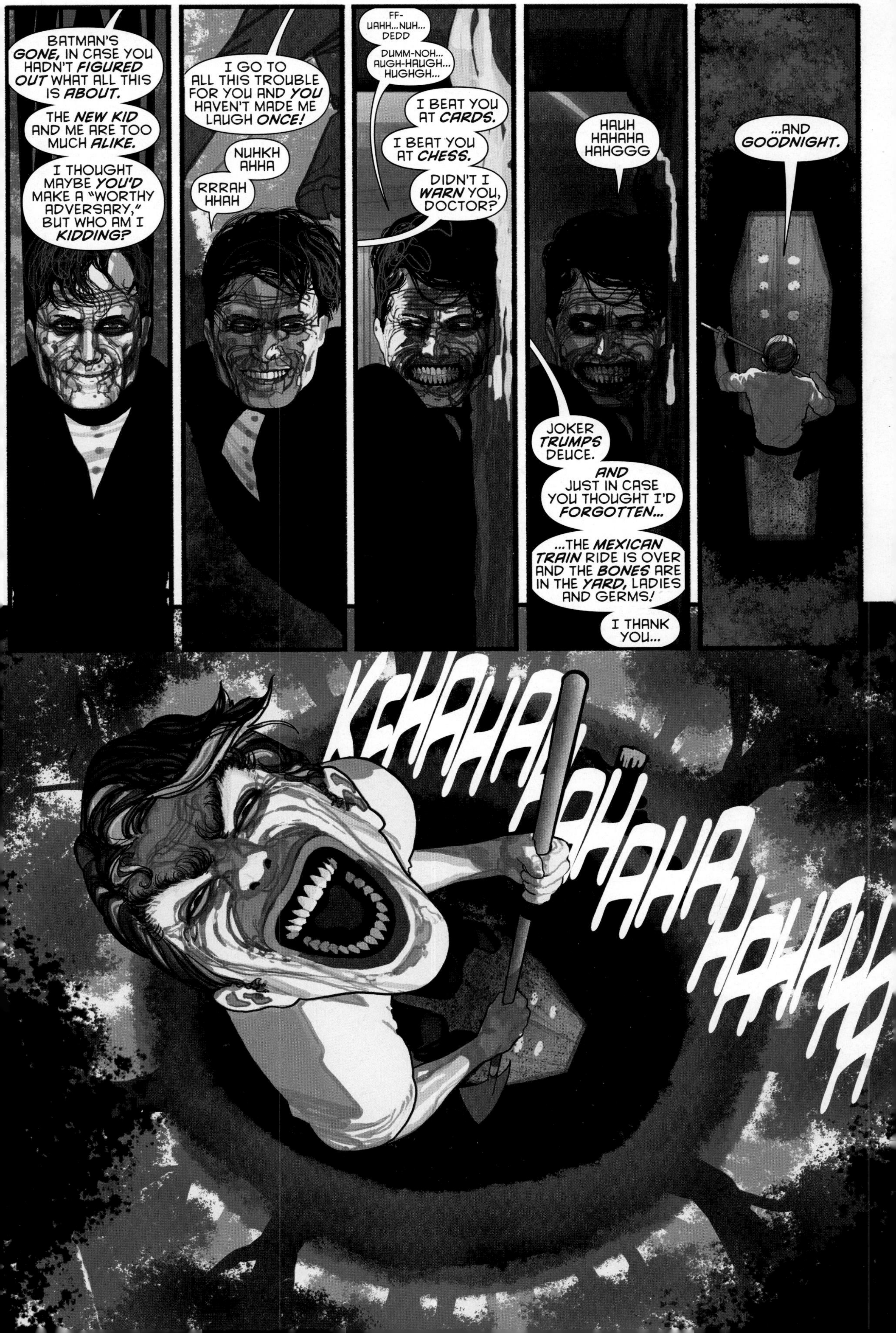

BATMAN'S GONE, IN CASE YOU HADN'T FIGURED OUT WHAT ALL THIS IS ABOUT.
THE NEW KID AND ME ARE TOO MUCH ALIKE.
I THOUGHT MAYBE YOU'D MAKE A "WORTHY ADVERSARY," BUT WHO AM I KIDDING?
I GO TO ALL THIS TROUBLE FOR YOU AND YOU HAVEN'T MADE ME LAUGH ONCE!
NUHKH AHHA
RRRAH HHAH
FF- UAHH...NUH... DEDD
DUMM-NOH... AUGH-HAUGH... HUGHGH...
I BEAT YOU AT CARDS.
I BEAT YOU AT CHESS.
DIDN'T I WARN YOU, DOCTOR?
HAUH HAHAHA HAHGGG
JOKER TRUMPS DEUCE.
AND JUST IN CASE YOU THOUGHT I'D FORGOTTEN...
...THE MEXICAN TRAIN RIDE IS OVER AND THE BONES ARE IN THE YARD, LADIES AND GERMS!
I THANK YOU...
...AND GOODNIGHT.
KCHAHAHAHAHAHAHAHAHAHAHA

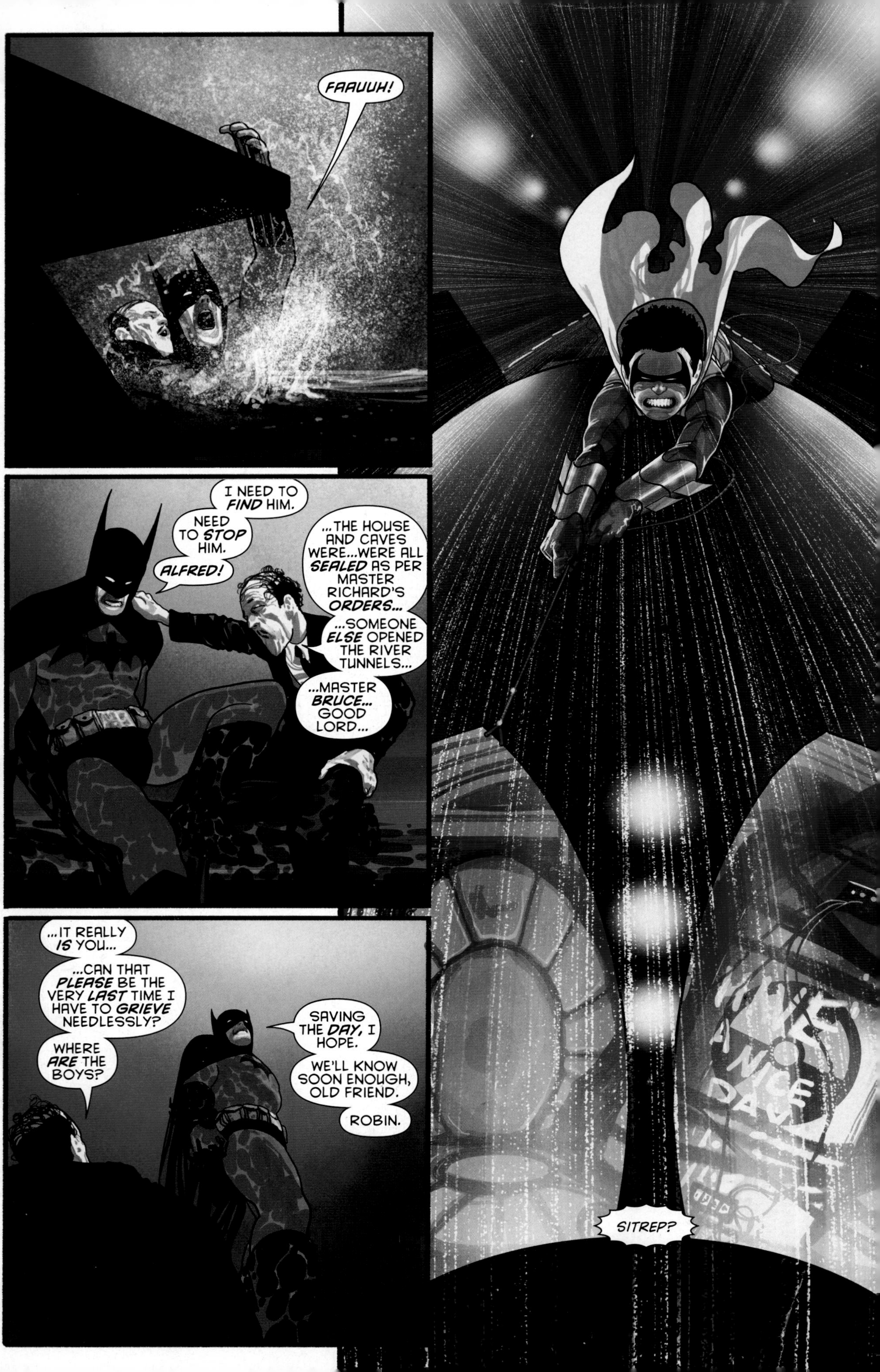
FAAUUH!
I NEED TO FIND HIM.
NEED TO STOP HIM.
ALFRED!
...THE HOUSE AND CAVES WERE...WERE ALL SEALED AS PER MASTER RICHARD'S ORDERS...
...SOMEONE ELSE OPENED THE RIVER TUNNELS...
...MASTER BRUCE... GOOD LORD...
...IT REALLY IS YOU...
...CAN THAT PLEASE BE THE VERY LAST TIME I HAVE TO GRIEVE NEEDLESSLY?
WHERE ARE THE BOYS?
SAVING THE DAY, I HOPE.
WE'LL KNOW SOON ENOUGH, OLD FRIEND.
ROBIN.
SITREP?

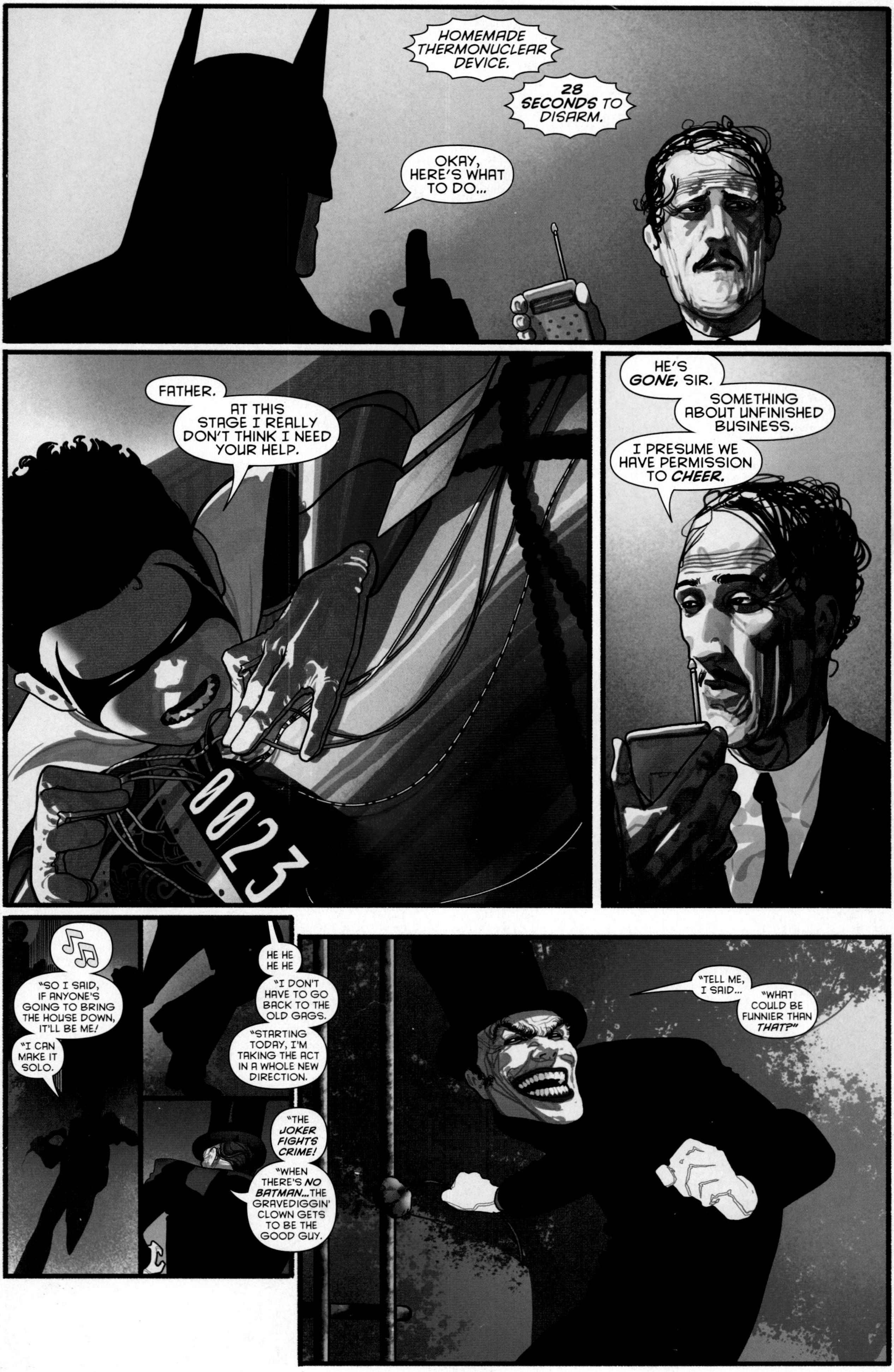
HOMEMADE THERMONUCLEAR DEVICE.
28 SECONDS TO DISARM.
OKAY, HERE'S WHAT TO DO...
FATHER.
AT THIS STAGE I REALLY DON'T THINK I NEED YOUR HELP.
0023
HE'S GONE, SIR.
SOMETHING ABOUT UNFINISHED BUSINESS.
I PRESUME WE HAVE PERMISSION TO CHEER.
"SO I SAID, IF ANYONE'S GOING TO BRING THE HOUSE DOWN, IT'LL BE ME!
"I CAN MAKE IT SOLO.
HE HE HE HE
"I DON'T HAVE TO GO BACK TO THE OLD GAGS.
"STARTING TODAY, I'M TAKING THE ACT IN A WHOLE NEW DIRECTION.
"THE JOKER FIGHTS CRIME!
"WHEN THERE'S NO BATMAN...THE GRAVEDIGGIN' CLOWN GETS TO BE THE GOOD GUY.
"TELL ME, I SAID...
"WHAT COULD BE FUNNIER THAN THAT?"

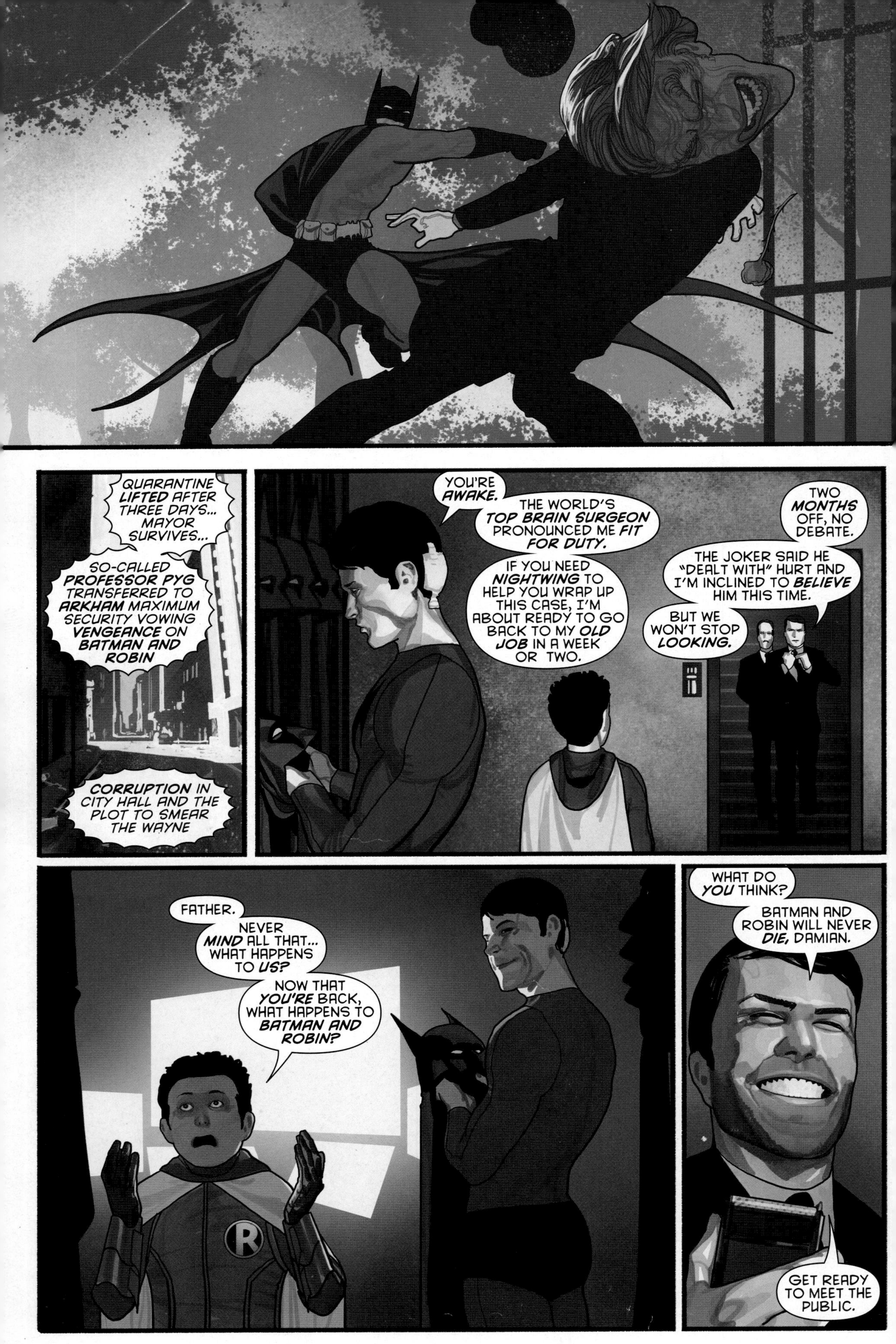
QUARANTINE LIFTED AFTER THREE DAYS... MAYOR SURVIVES...
SO-CALLED PROFESSOR PYG TRANSFERRED TO ARKHAM MAXIMUM SECURITY VOWING VENGEANCE ON BATMAN AND ROBIN
CORRUPTION IN CITY HALL AND THE PLOT TO SMEAR THE WAYNE
YOU'RE AWAKE.
THE WORLD'S TOP BRAIN SURGEON PRONOUNCED ME FIT FOR DUTY.
IF YOU NEED NIGHTWING TO HELP YOU WRAP UP THIS CASE, I'M ABOUT READY TO GO BACK TO MY OLD JOB IN A WEEK OR TWO.
TWO MONTHS OFF, NO DEBATE.
THE JOKER SAID HE "DEALT WITH" HURT AND I'M INCLINED TO BELIEVE HIM THIS TIME.
BUT WE WON'T STOP LOOKING.
FATHER.
NEVER MIND ALL THAT... WHAT HAPPENS TO US?
NOW THAT YOU'RE BACK, WHAT HAPPENS TO BATMAN AND ROBIN?
WHAT DO YOU THINK?
BATMAN AND ROBIN WILL NEVER DIE, DAMIAN.
GET READY TO MEET THE PUBLIC.

...IN MY EFFORTS TO CLEAR THE NAMES OF MY *PARENTS*, I FOUND MYSELF CAUGHT UP IN AN UNLIKELY TALE OF *DOUBLE IDENTITIES*, IMPOSTORS AND CORRUPT CITY OFFICIALS.

I'M *SORRY* CIRCUMSTANCES COMPELLED ME TO ABANDON MY BELOVED CITY FOR *SO LONG.*

BUT I KNEW THAT *GOTHAM CITY* WAS IN SAFE HANDS.

SOME OF YOU MAY HAVE *WONDERED...* HOW DOES A MAN LIKE *BATMAN* AFFORD TO CONSTANTLY *UPDATE* HIS CRIME-FIGHTING TECHNOLOGY?

WHERE DOES HIS *MONEY* COME FROM?

WELL, THE ANSWER IS *ME.*

I'VE BEEN FINANCING BATMAN IN *SECRET* FOR YEARS.

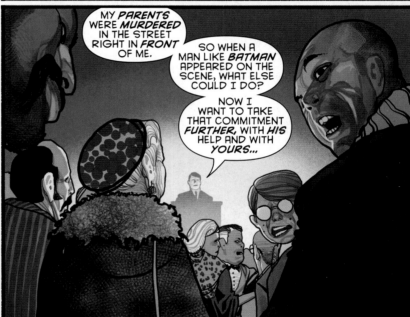

MY *PARENTS* WERE *MURDERED* IN THE STREET RIGHT IN *FRONT* OF ME.

SO WHEN A MAN LIKE *BATMAN* APPEARED ON THE SCENE, WHAT ELSE COULD I DO?

NOW I WANT TO TAKE THAT COMMITMENT *FURTHER,* WITH *HIS* HELP AND WITH *YOURS...*

LADIES AND GENTLEMEN.

BATMAN'S *WAR AGAINST CRIME* GOES *GLOBAL* TONIGHT.

IT'S MY GREAT PLEASURE TO INTRODUCE WAYNE ENTERPRISES' *NEWEST* VENTURE...

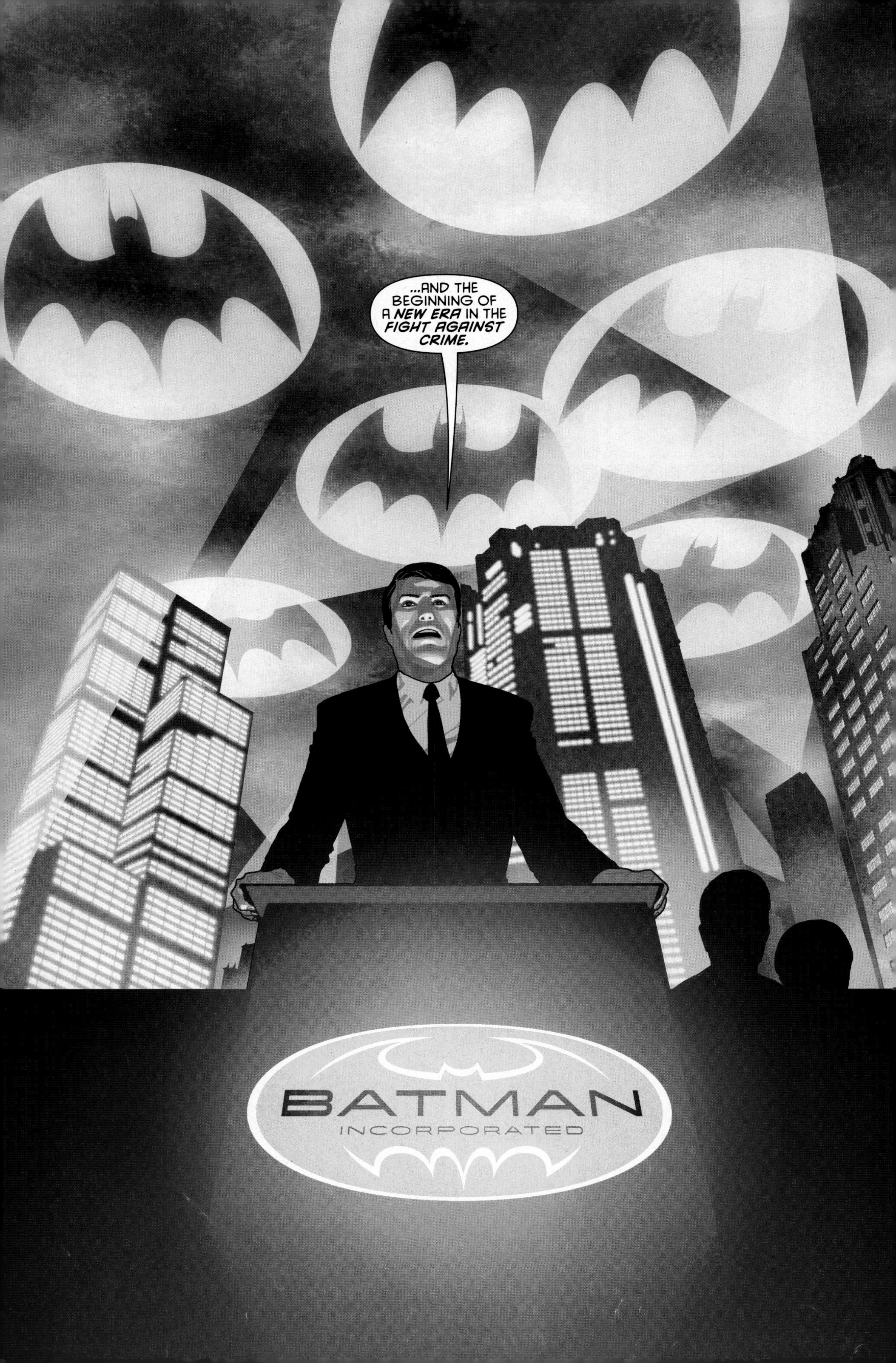
...AND THE BEGINNING OF A *NEW ERA* IN THE *FIGHT AGAINST CRIME.*
BATMAN
INCORPORATED

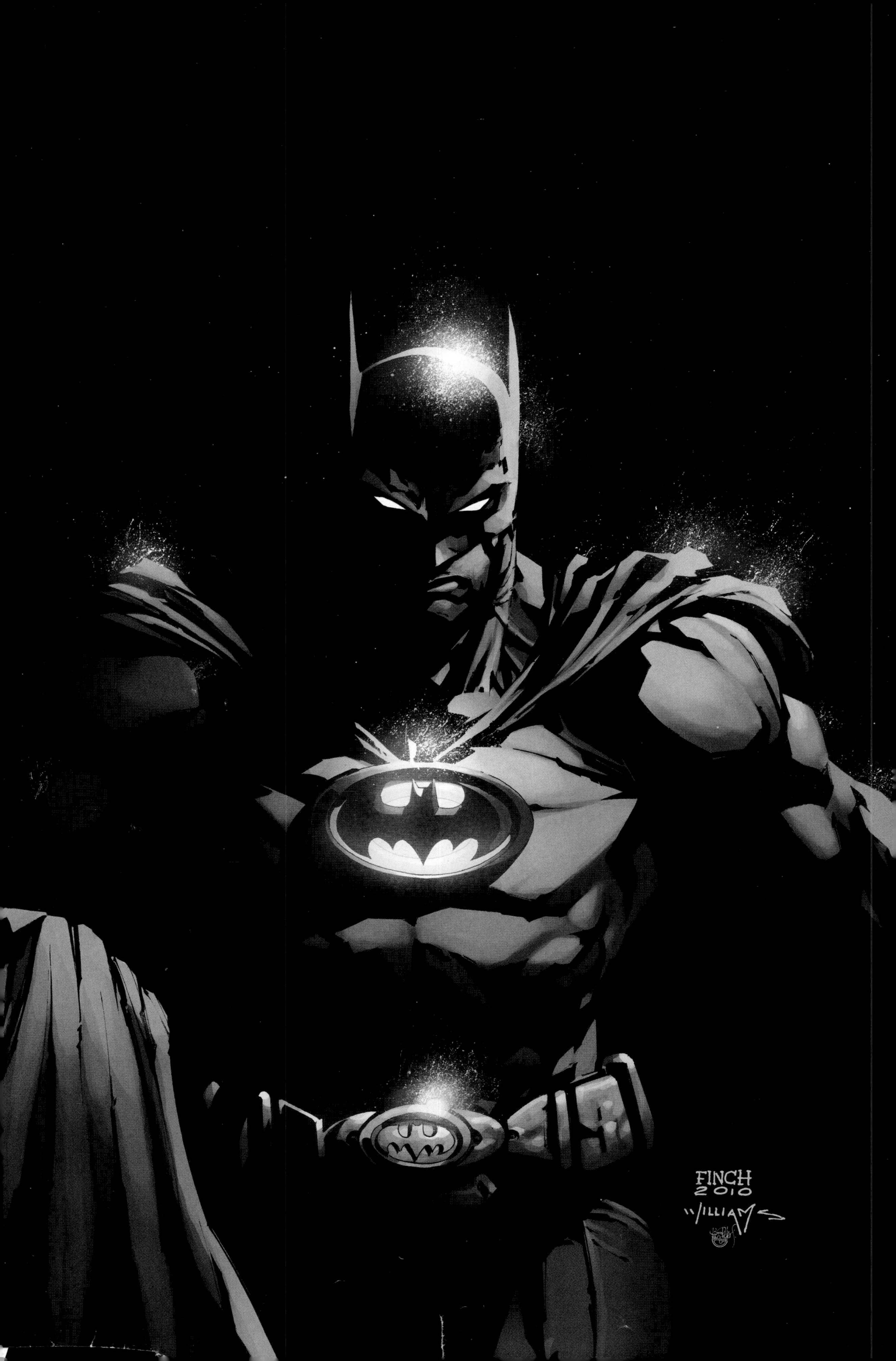
FINCH
2010
WILLIAMS

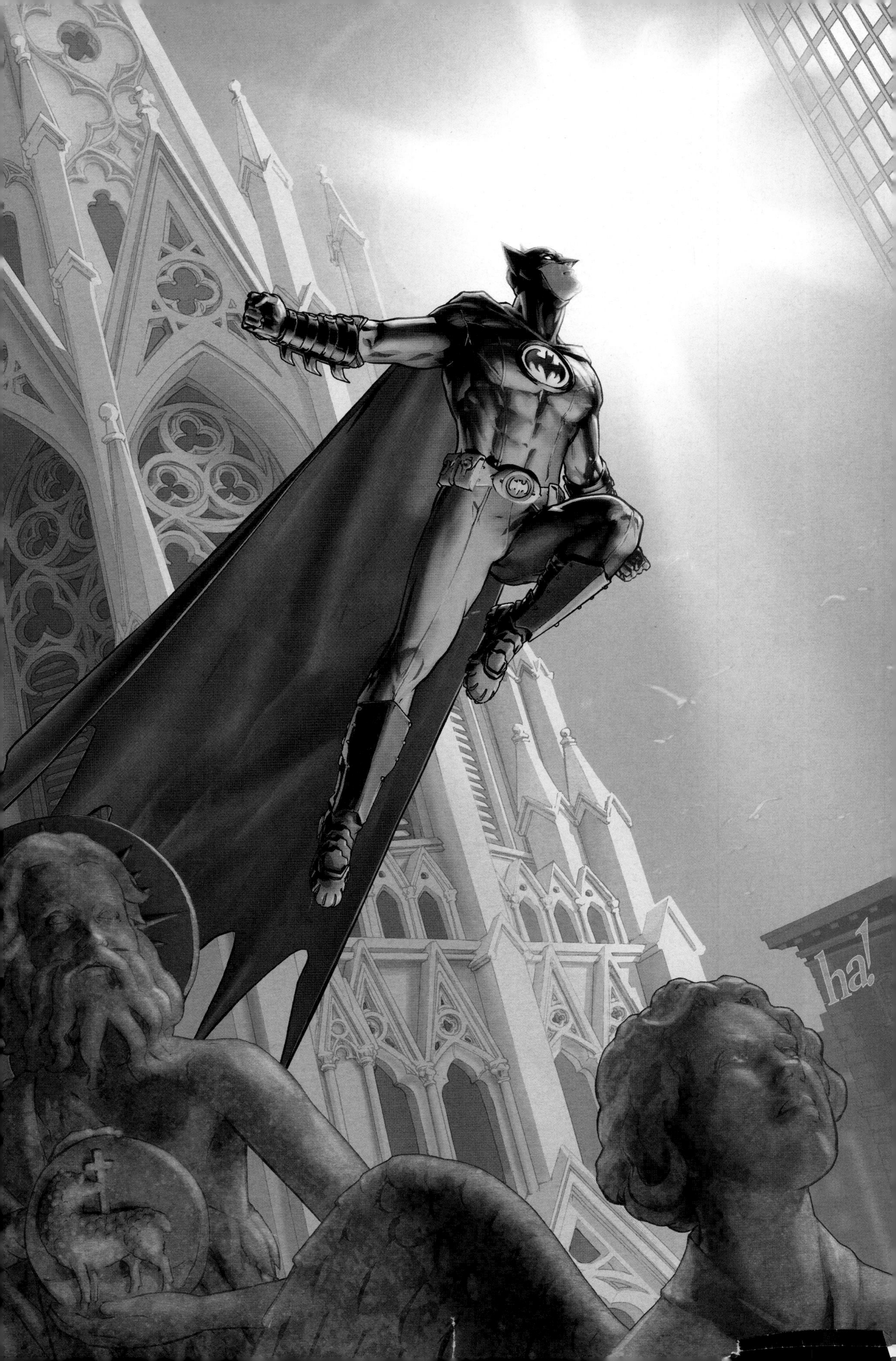
ha!

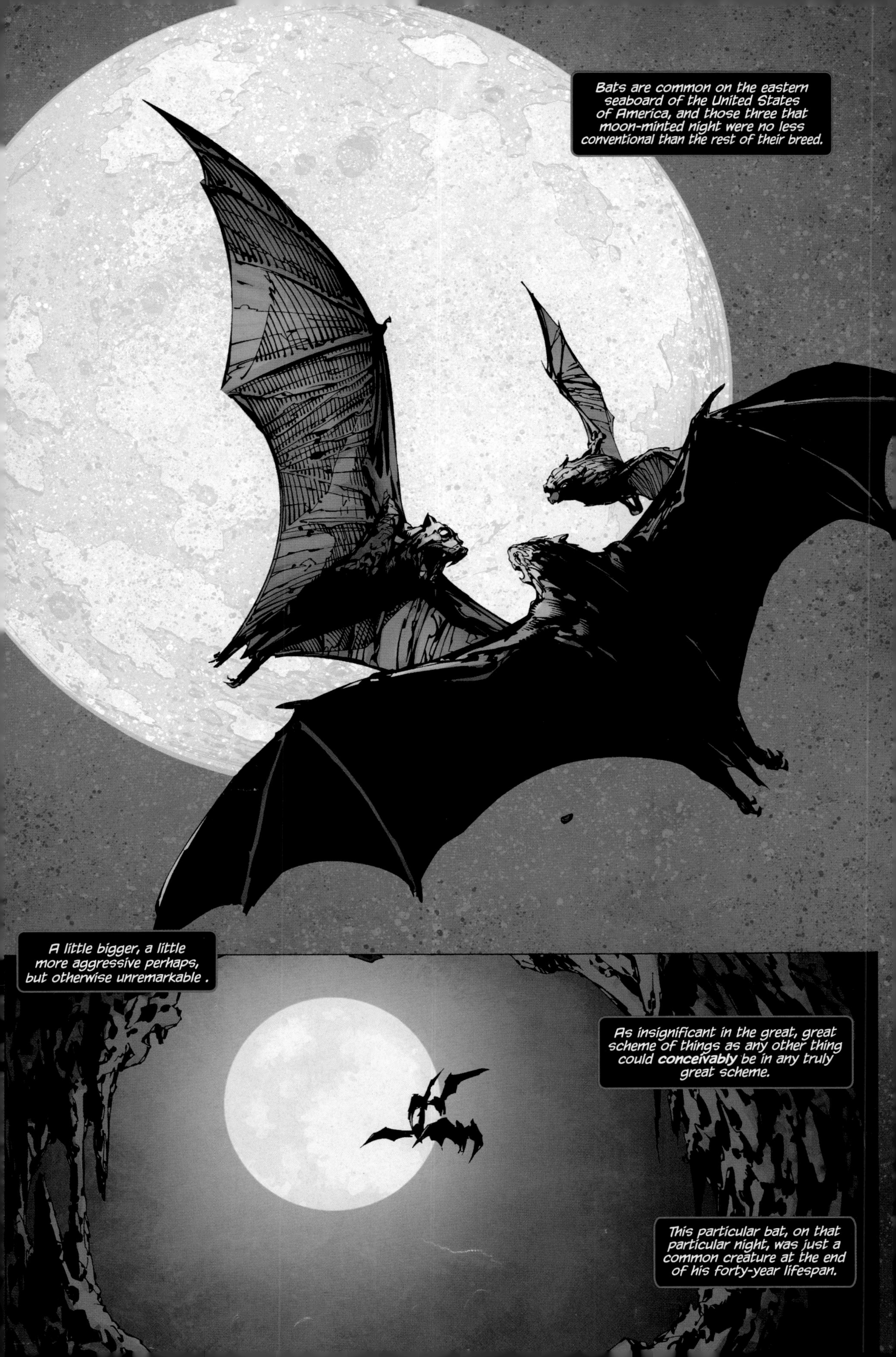
Bats are common on the eastern seaboard of the United States of America, and those three that moon-minted night were no less conventional than the rest of their breed.
A little bigger, a little more aggressive perhaps, but otherwise unremarkable .
As insignificant in the great, great scheme of things as any other thing could **conceivably** be in any truly great scheme.
This particular bat, on that particular night, was just a common creature at the end of his forty-year lifespan.

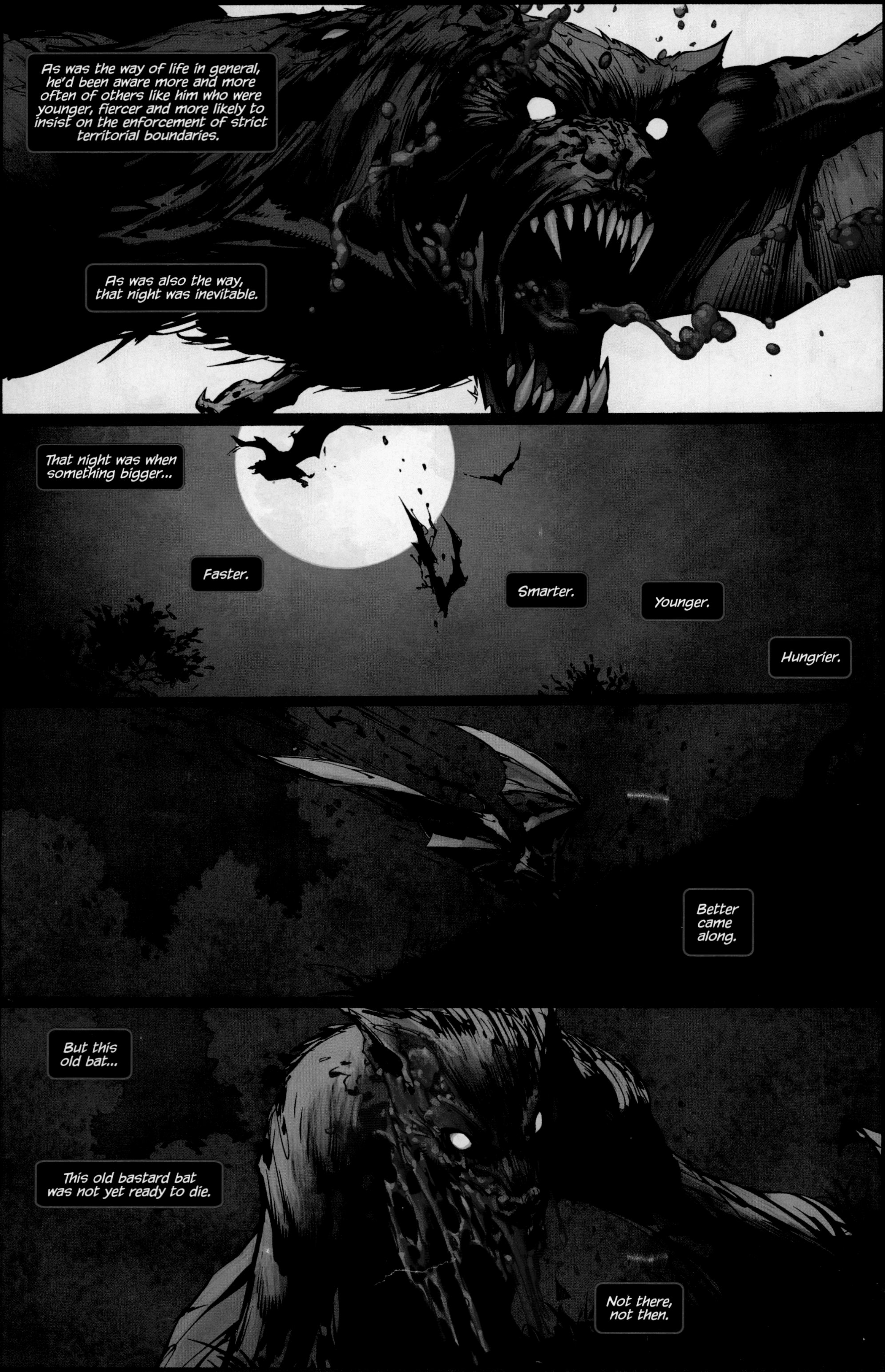
As was the way of life in general, he'd been aware more and more often of others like him who were younger, fiercer and more likely to insist on the enforcement of strict territorial boundaries.
As was also the way, that night was inevitable.
That night was when something bigger...
Faster.
Smarter.
Younger.
Hungrier.
Better came along.
But this old bat...
This old bastard bat was not yet ready to die.
Not there, not then.

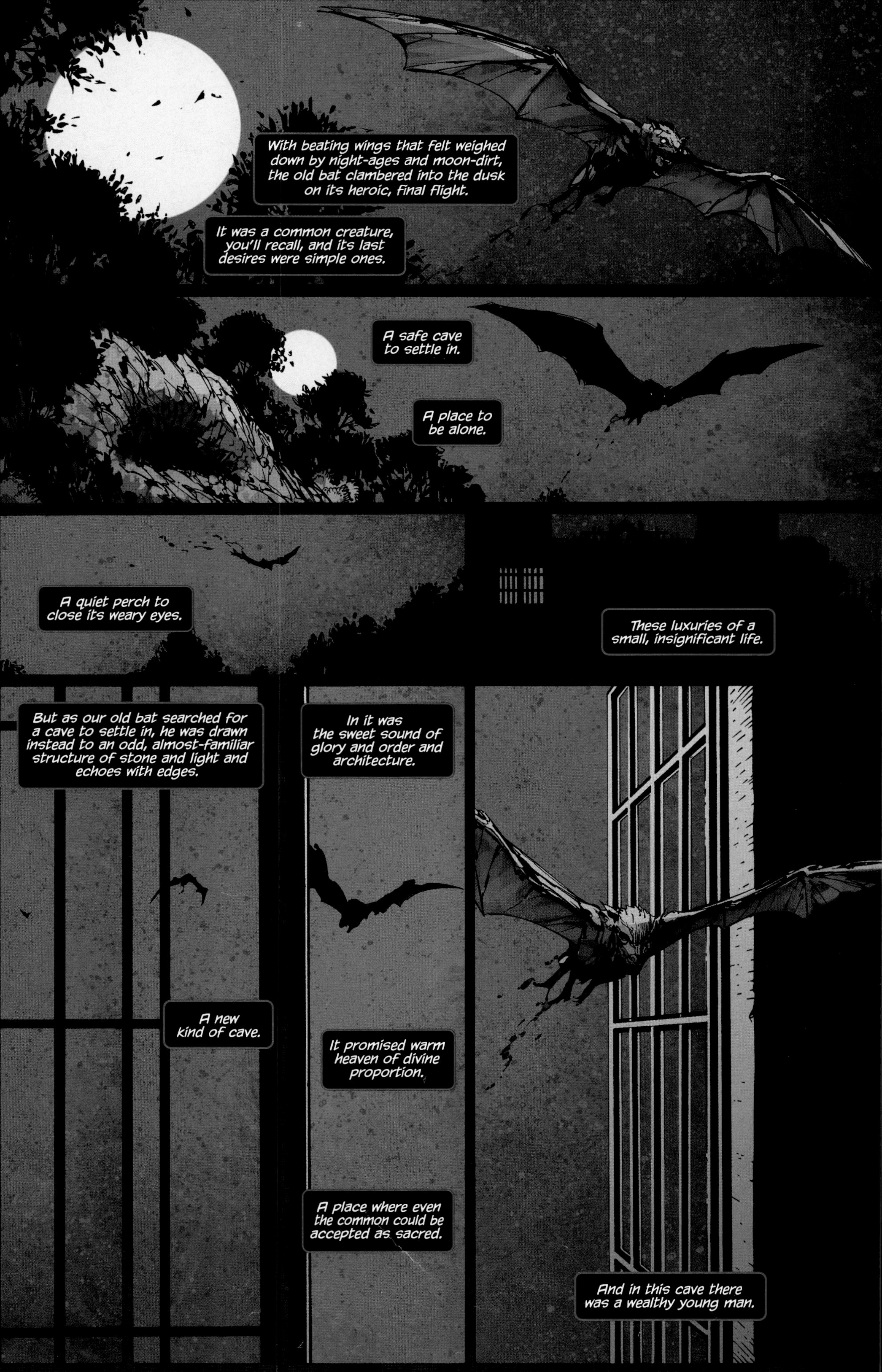

With beating wings that felt weighed down by night-ages and moon-dirt, the old bat clambered into the dusk on its heroic, final flight.
It was a common creature, you'll recall, and its last desires were simple ones.
A safe cave to settle in.
A place to be alone.
A quiet perch to close its weary eyes.
These luxuries of a small, insignificant life.
But as our old bat searched for a cave to settle in, he was drawn instead to an odd, almost-familiar structure of stone and light and echoes with edges.
In it was the sweet sound of glory and order and architecture.
A new kind of cave.
It promised warm heaven of divine proportion.
A place where even the common could be accepted as sacred.
And in this cave there was a wealthy young man.

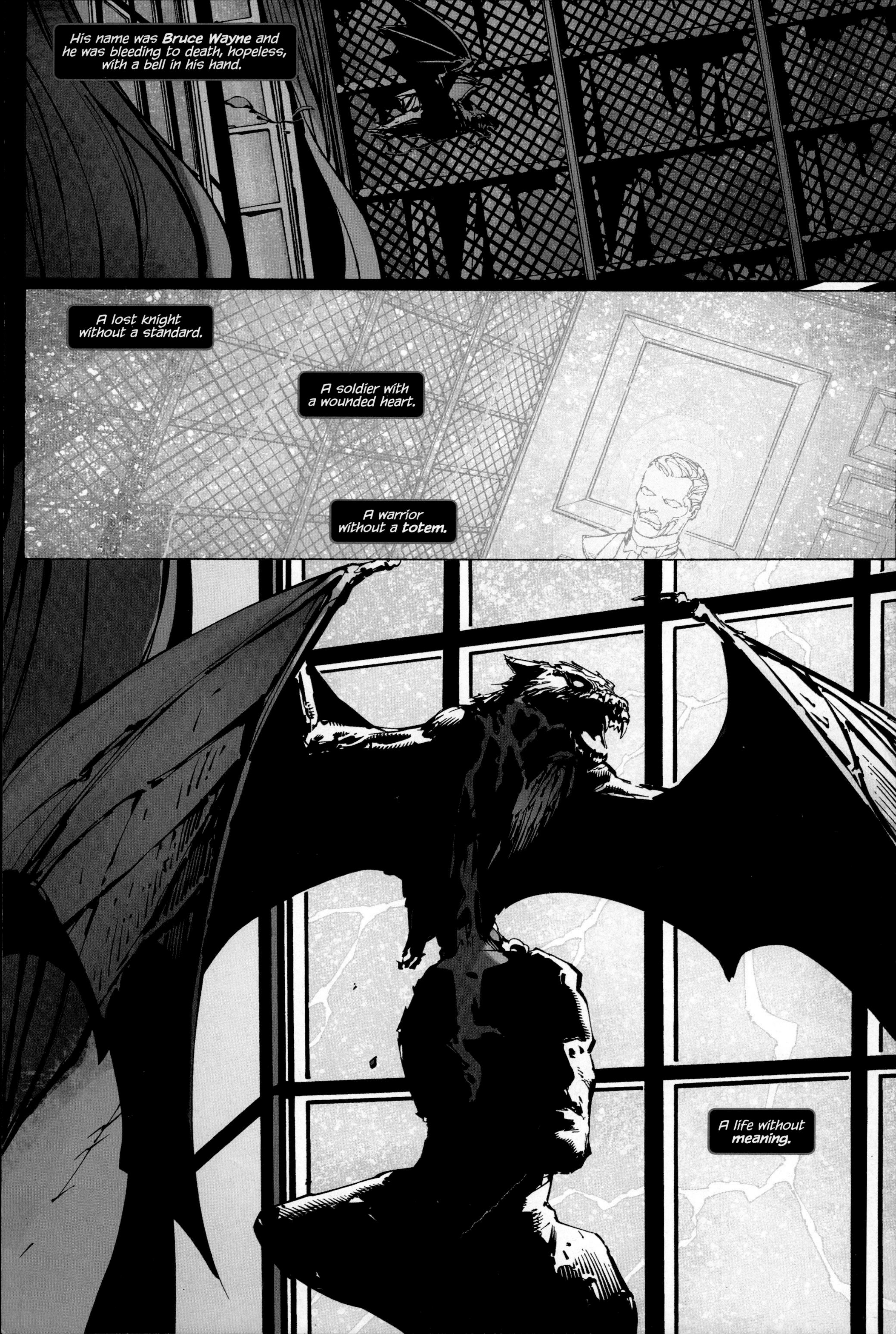
His name was **Bruce Wayne** and he was bleeding to death, hopeless, with a bell in his hand.
A lost knight without a standard.
A soldier with a wounded heart.
A warrior without a **totem.**
A life without **meaning.**

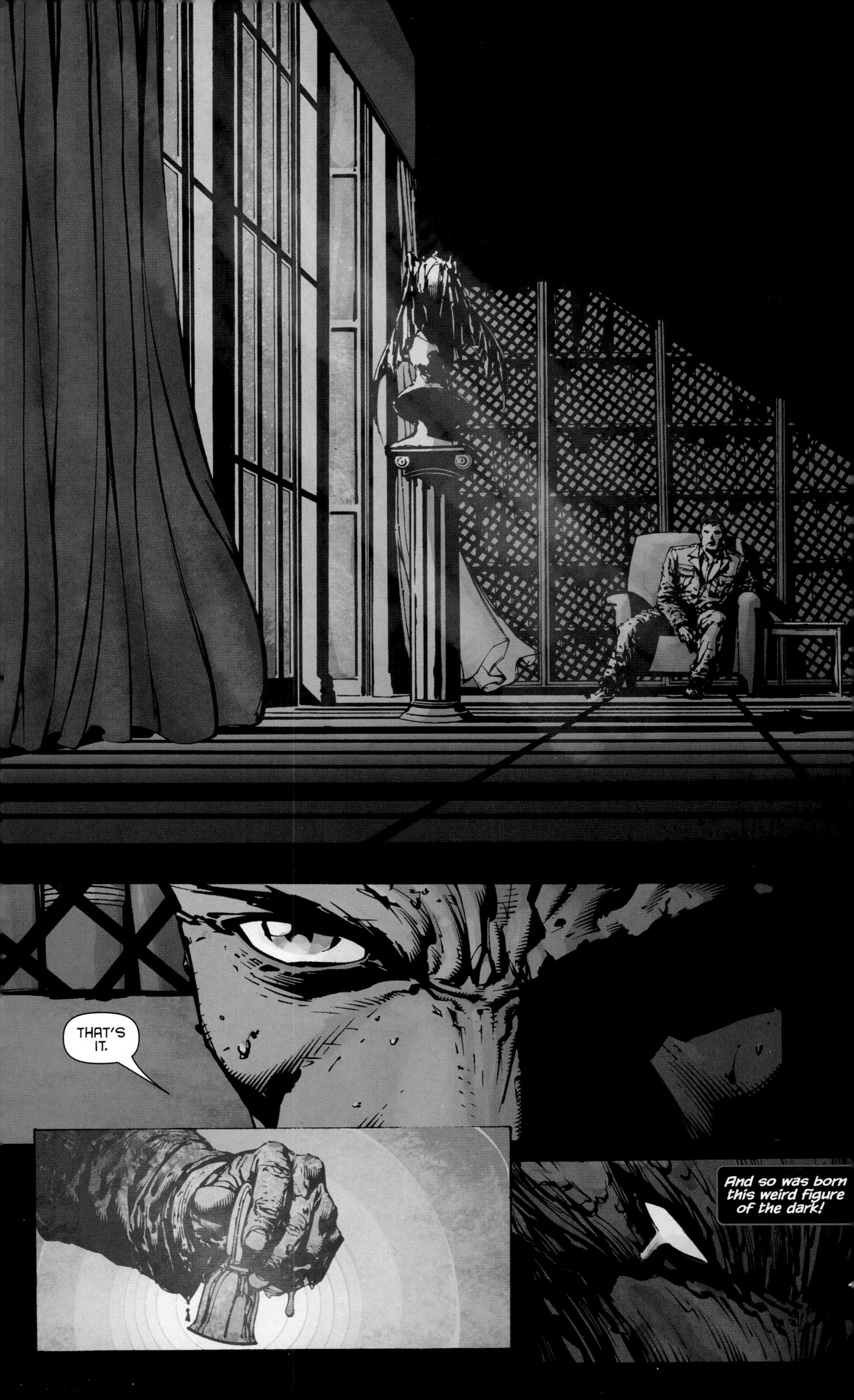
THAT'S IT.
And so was born this weird figure of the dark!

DC COMICS PRESENTS BATMAN: THE RETURN:

PLANET GOTHAM

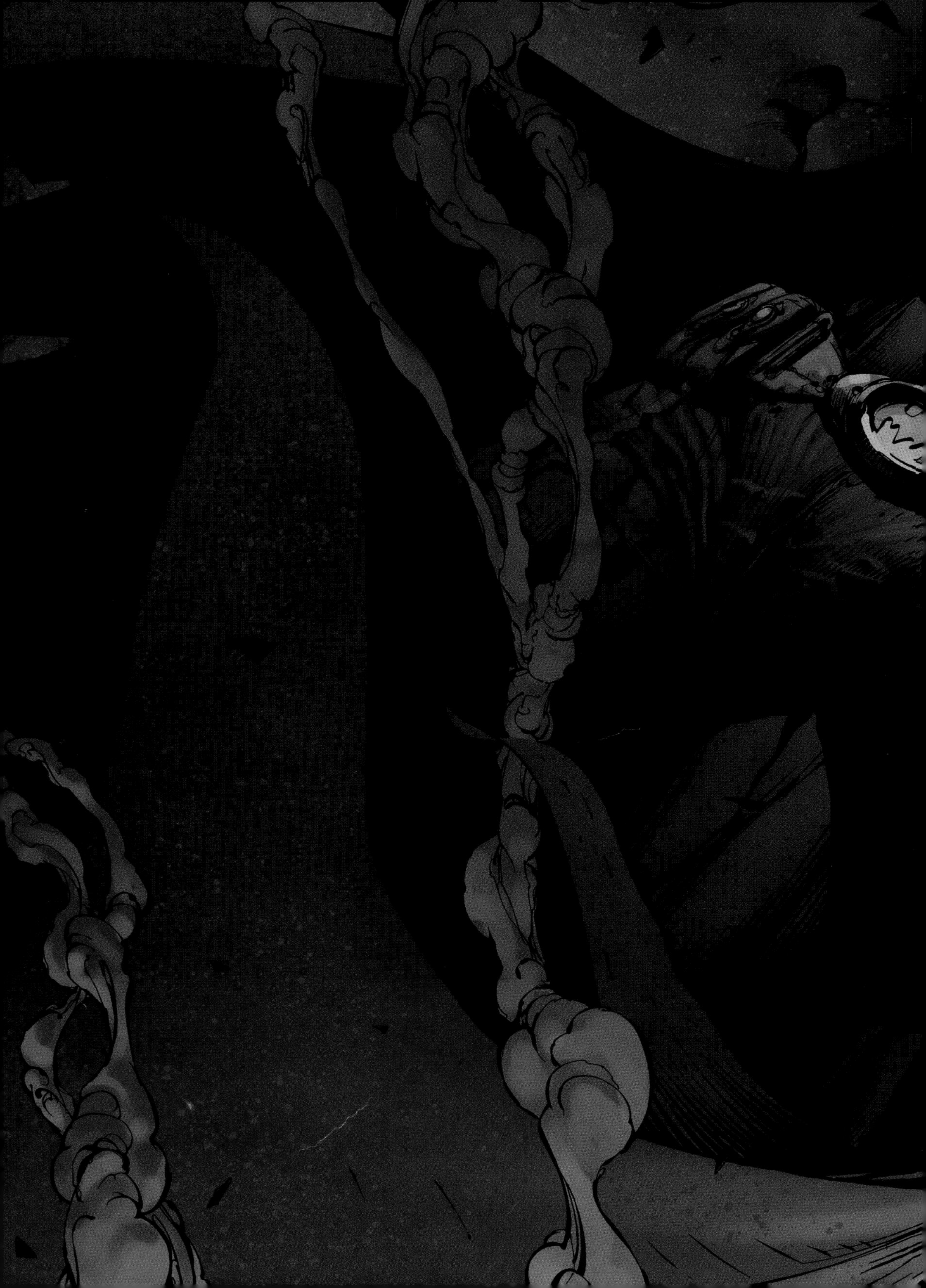

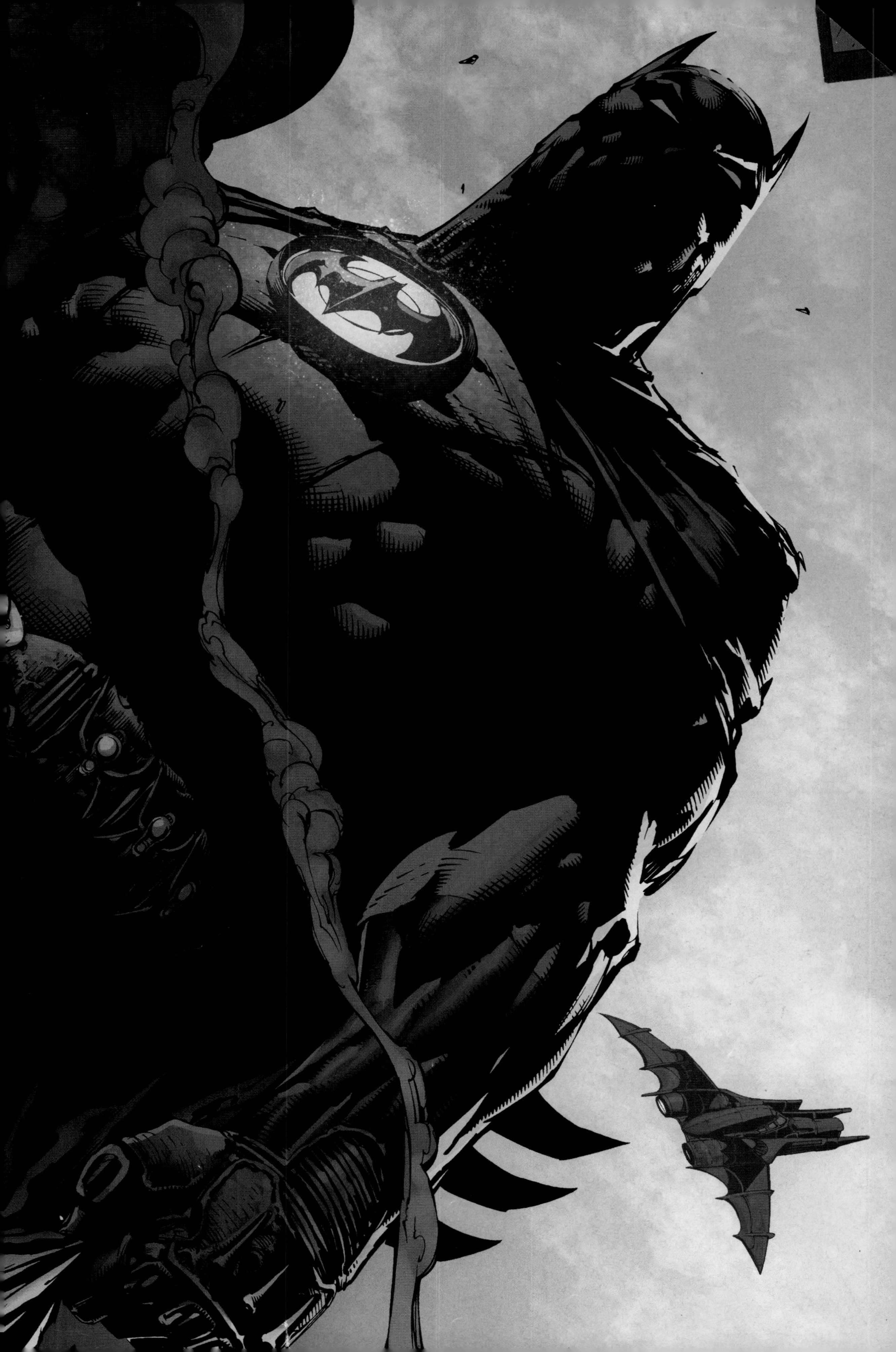

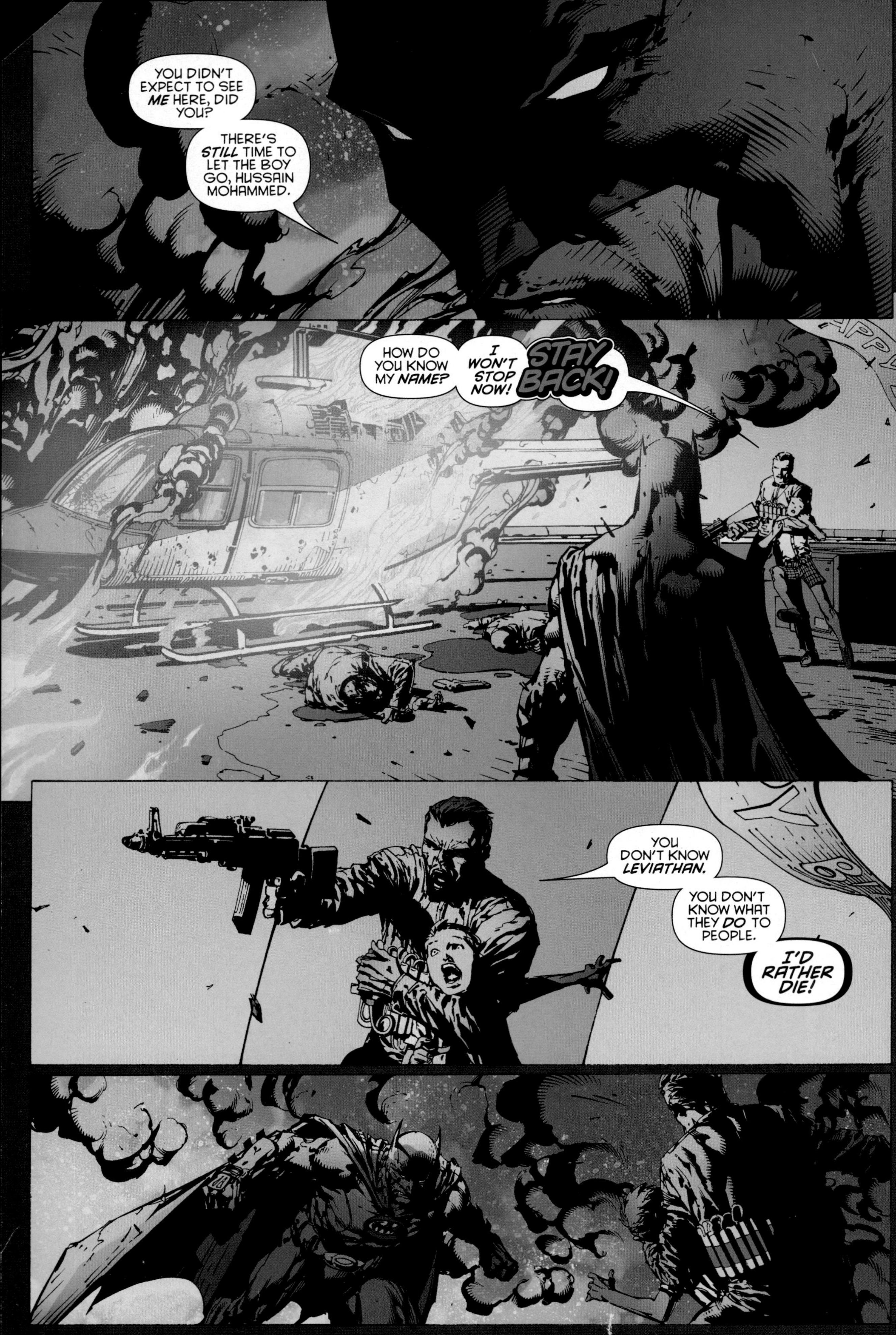
YOU DIDN'T EXPECT TO SEE ME HERE, DID YOU?
THERE'S STILL TIME TO LET THE BOY GO, HUSSAIN MOHAMMED.
HOW DO YOU KNOW MY NAME?
I WON'T STOP NOW!
STAY BACK!
YOU DON'T KNOW LEVIATHAN.
YOU DON'T KNOW WHAT THEY DO TO PEOPLE.
I'D RATHER DIE!

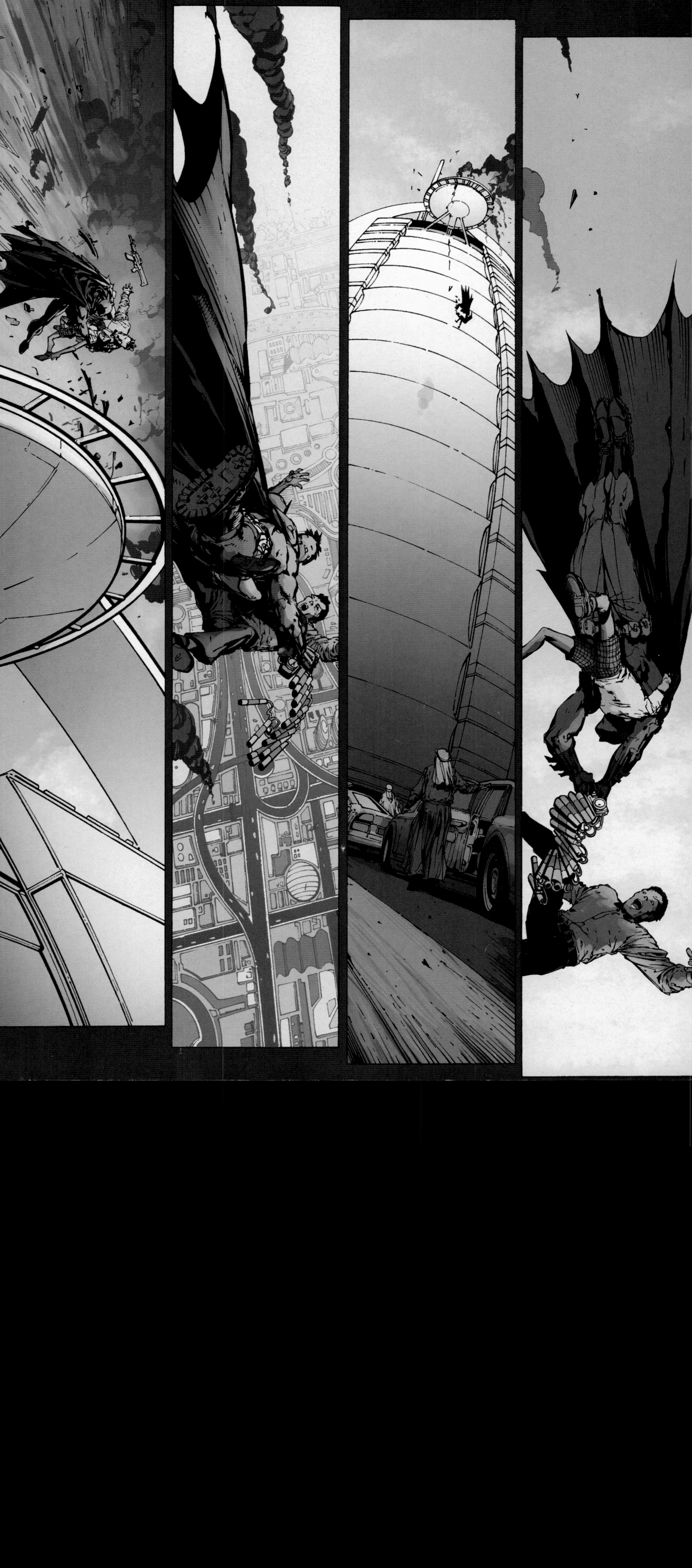

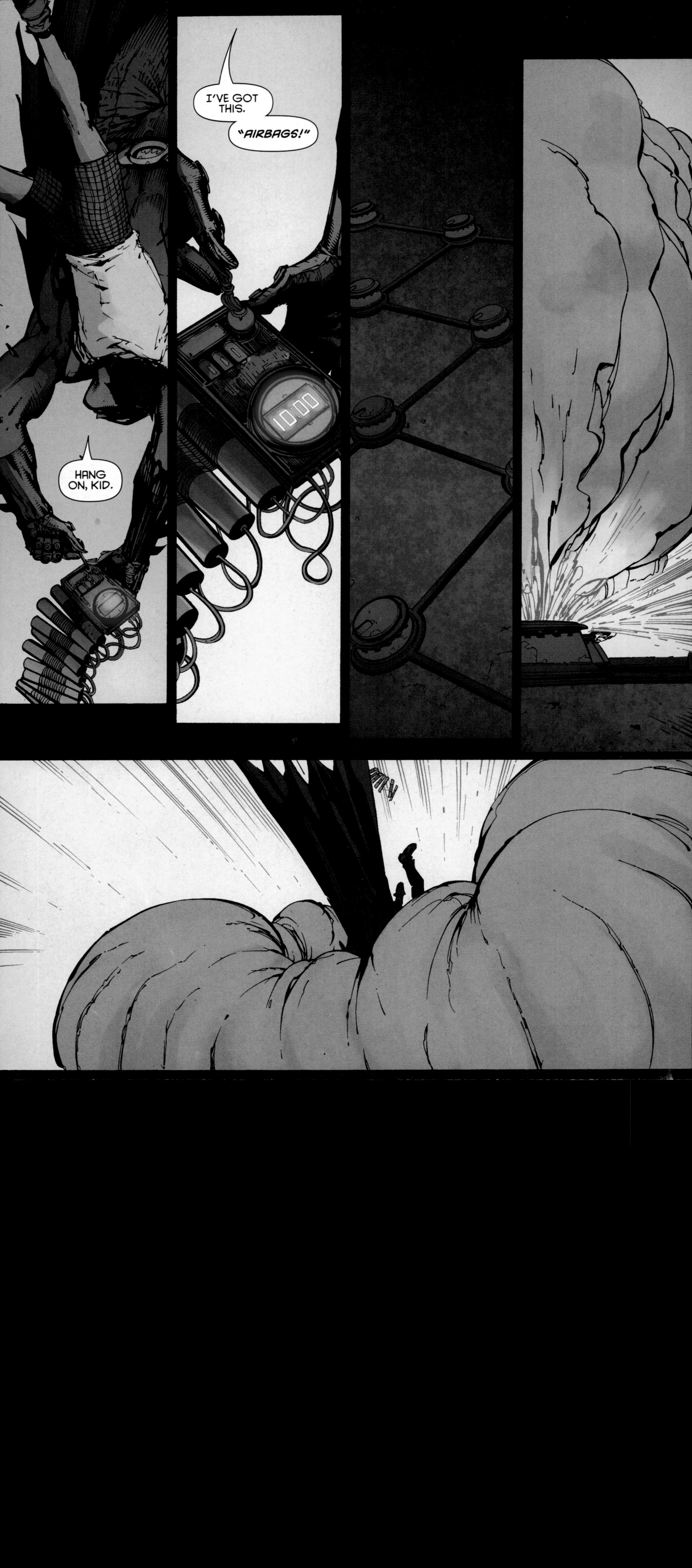
HANG ON, KID.
I'VE GOT THIS.
"AIRBAGS!"

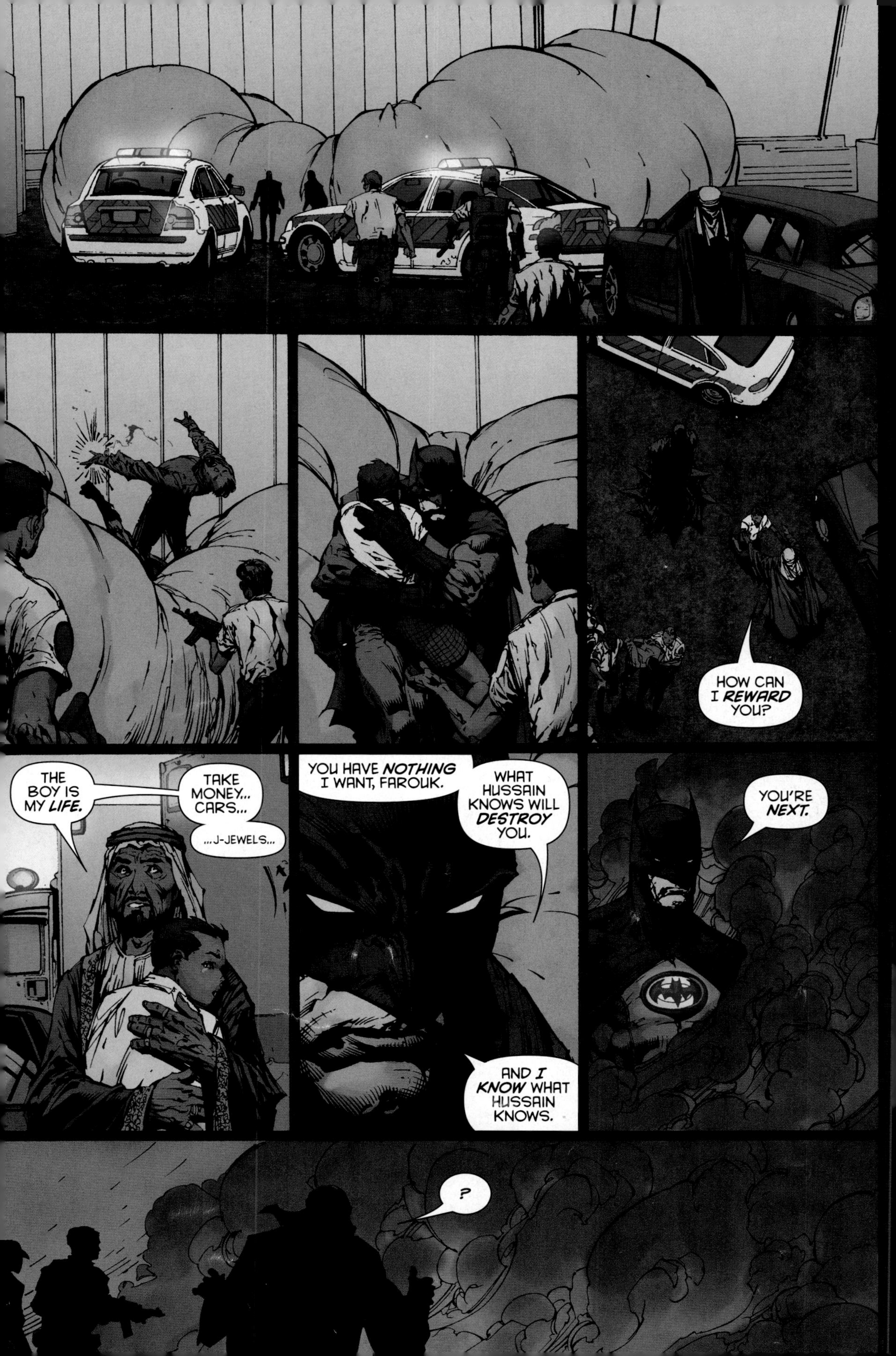
HOW CAN I REWARD YOU?
THE BOY IS MY LIFE.
TAKE MONEY... CARS...
...J-JEWELS...
YOU HAVE NOTHING I WANT, FAROUK.
WHAT HUSSAIN KNOWS WILL DESTROY YOU.
AND I KNOW WHAT HUSSAIN KNOWS.
YOU'RE NEXT.
?

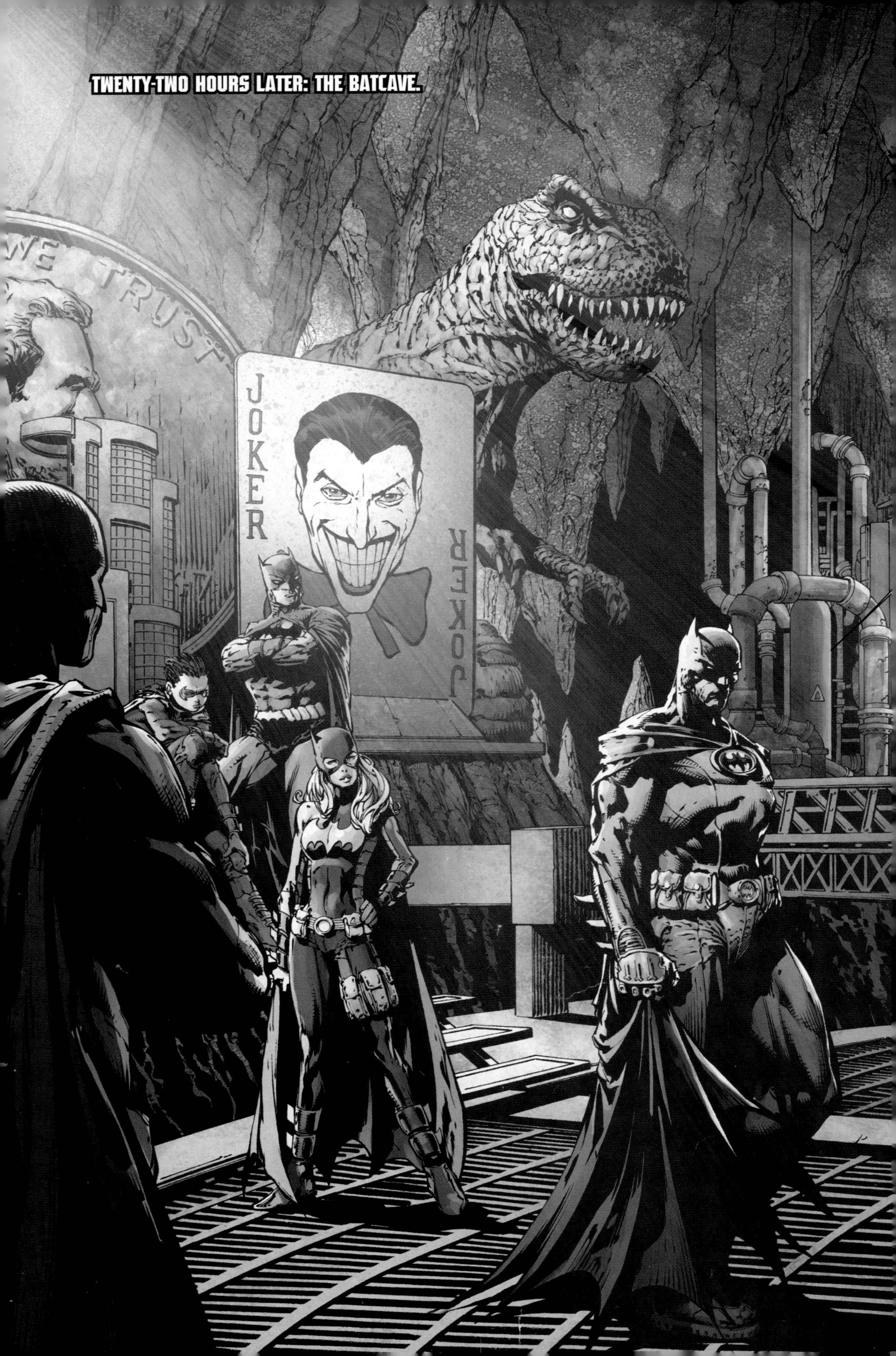
TWENTY-TWO HOURS LATER: THE BATCAVE.
WE TRUST
JOKER
JOKER

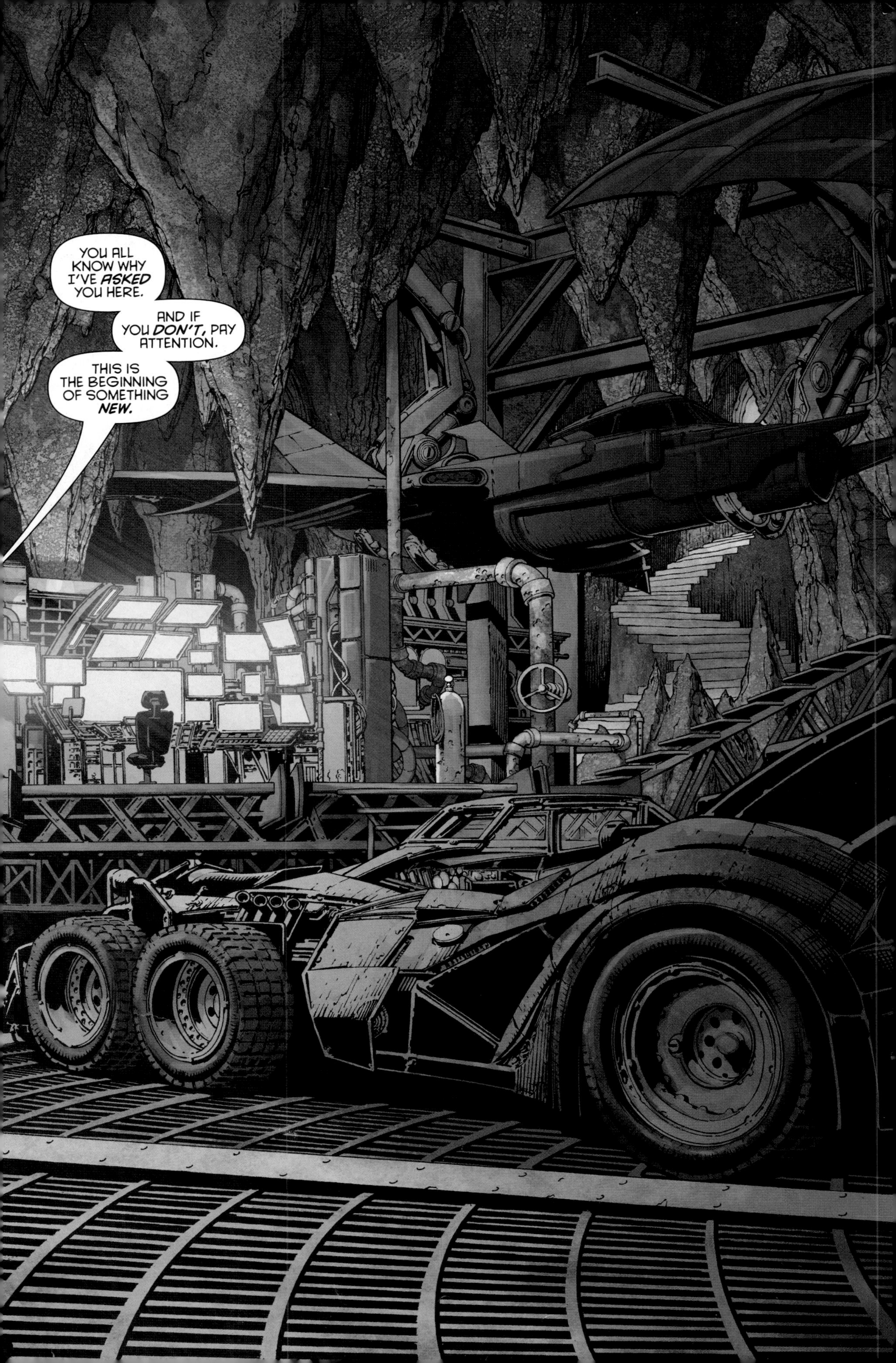
YOU ALL KNOW WHY I'VE ASKED YOU HERE.
AND IF YOU DON'T, PAY ATTENTION.
THIS IS THE BEGINNING OF SOMETHING NEW.

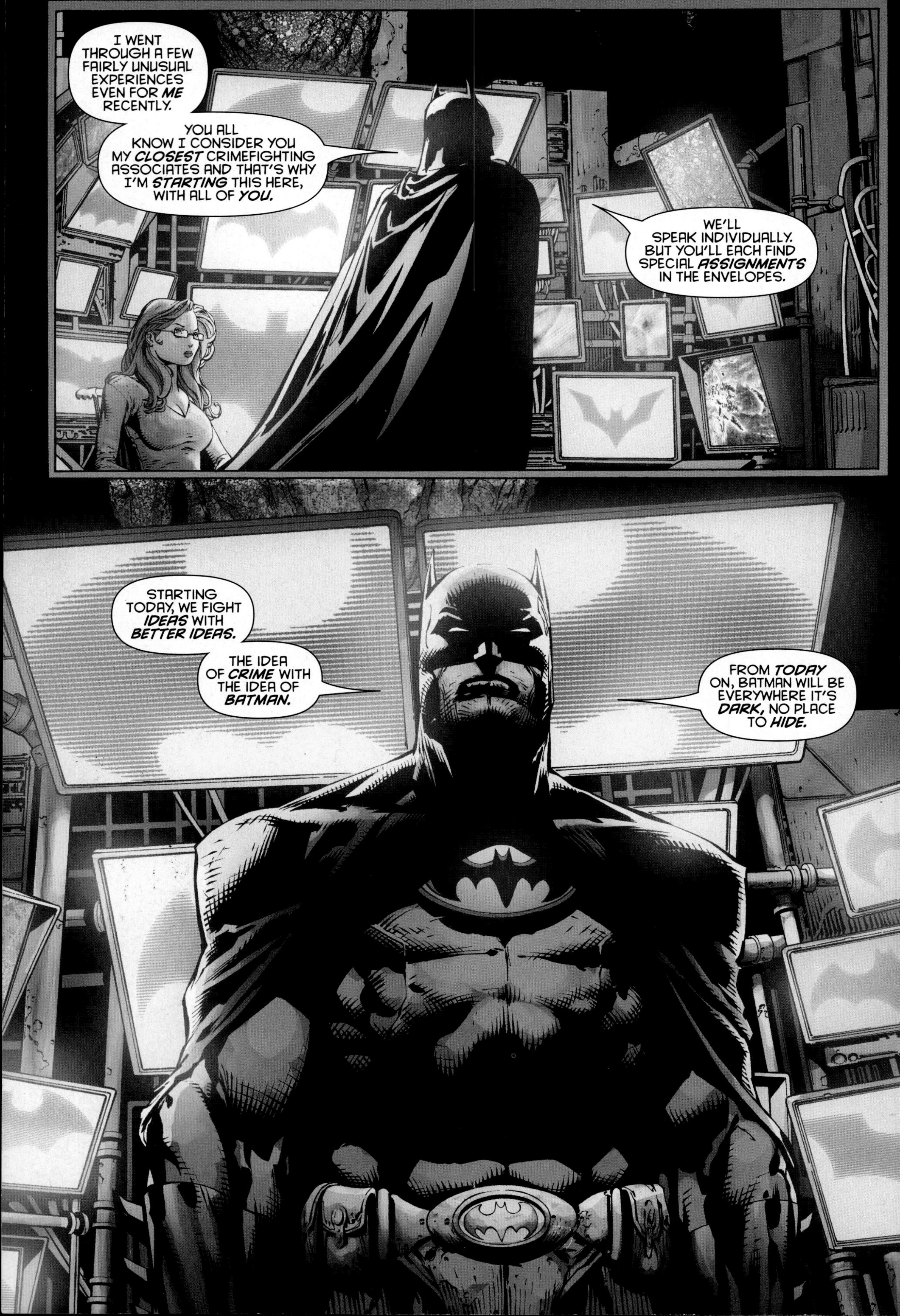
I WENT THROUGH A FEW FAIRLY UNUSUAL EXPERIENCES EVEN FOR *ME* RECENTLY.
YOU ALL KNOW I CONSIDER YOU MY *CLOSEST* CRIMEFIGHTING ASSOCIATES AND THAT'S WHY I'M *STARTING* THIS HERE, WITH ALL OF *YOU.*
WE'LL SPEAK INDIVIDUALLY. BUT YOU'LL EACH FIND SPECIAL *ASSIGNMENTS* IN THE ENVELOPES.
STARTING TODAY, WE FIGHT *IDEAS* WITH *BETTER IDEAS.*
THE IDEA OF *CRIME* WITH THE IDEA OF *BATMAN.*
FROM *TODAY* ON, BATMAN WILL BE EVERYWHERE IT'S *DARK,* NO PLACE TO *HIDE.*

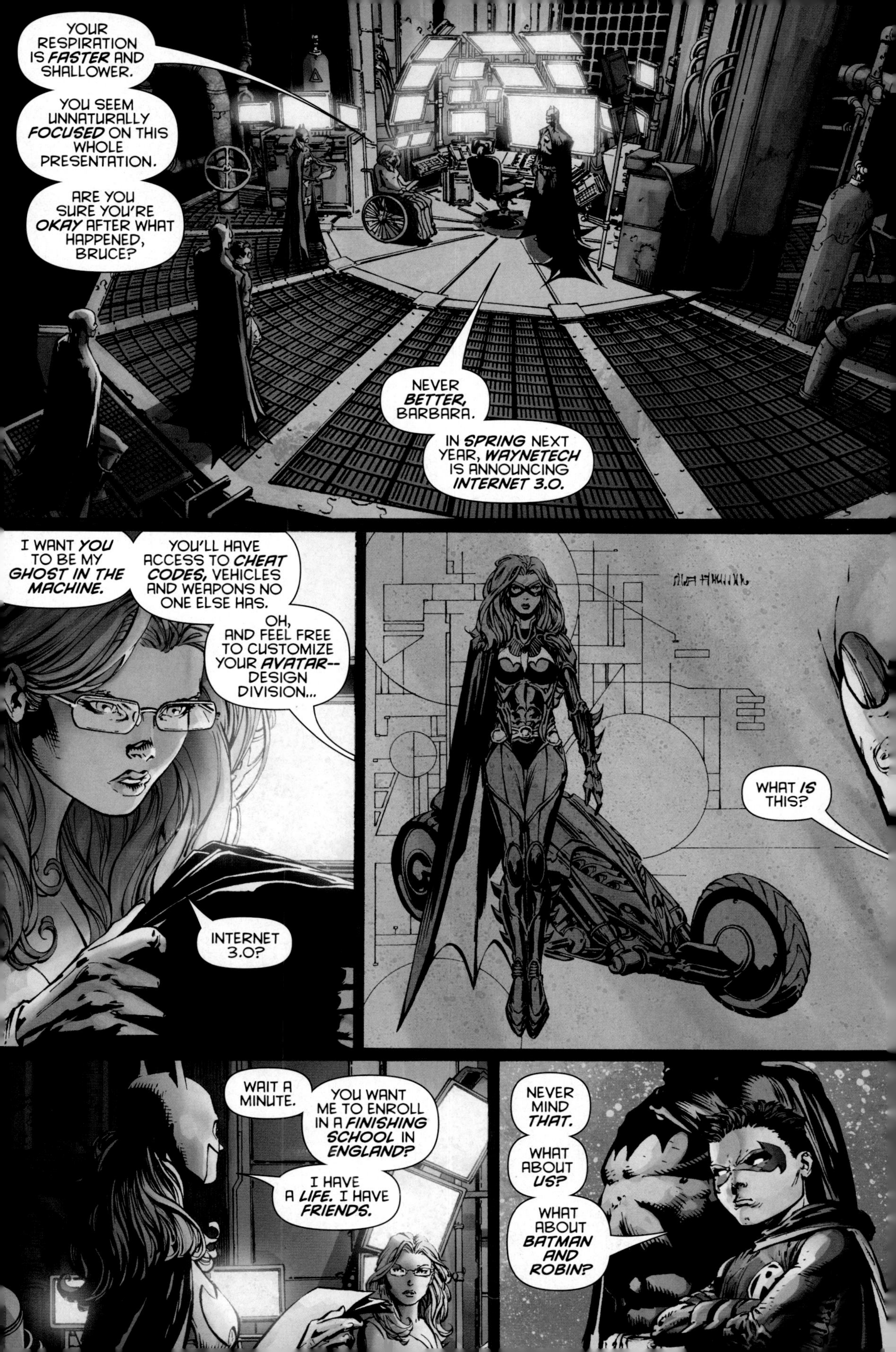
YOUR RESPIRATION IS FASTER AND SHALLOWER.
YOU SEEM UNNATURALLY FOCUSED ON THIS WHOLE PRESENTATION.
ARE YOU SURE YOU'RE OKAY AFTER WHAT HAPPENED, BRUCE?
NEVER BETTER, BARBARA.
IN SPRING NEXT YEAR, WAYNETECH IS ANNOUNCING INTERNET 3.0.
I WANT YOU TO BE MY GHOST IN THE MACHINE.
YOU'LL HAVE ACCESS TO CHEAT CODES, VEHICLES AND WEAPONS NO ONE ELSE HAS.
OH, AND FEEL FREE TO CUSTOMIZE YOUR AVATAR-- DESIGN DIVISION...
INTERNET 3.0?
WHAT IS THIS?
WAIT A MINUTE.
YOU WANT ME TO ENROLL IN A FINISHING SCHOOL IN ENGLAND?
I HAVE A LIFE. I HAVE FRIENDS.
NEVER MIND THAT.
WHAT ABOUT US?
WHAT ABOUT BATMAN AND ROBIN?

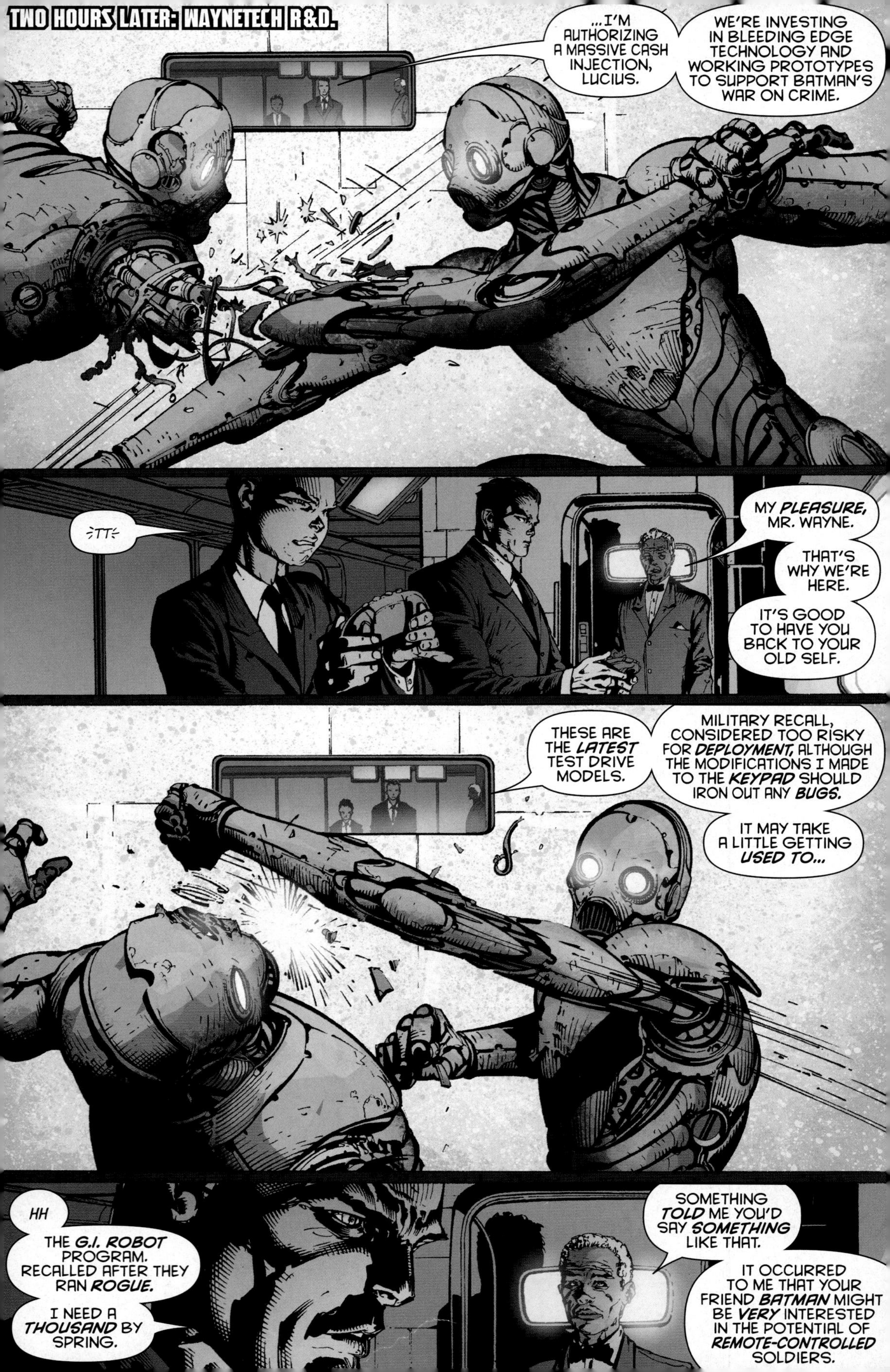
TWO HOURS LATER: WAYNETECH R&D.
...I'M AUTHORIZING A MASSIVE CASH INJECTION, LUCIUS.
WE'RE INVESTING IN BLEEDING EDGE TECHNOLOGY AND WORKING PROTOTYPES TO SUPPORT BATMAN'S WAR ON CRIME.
TT
MY PLEASURE, MR. WAYNE.
THAT'S WHY WE'RE HERE.
IT'S GOOD TO HAVE YOU BACK TO YOUR OLD SELF.
THESE ARE THE LATEST TEST DRIVE MODELS.
MILITARY RECALL, CONSIDERED TOO RISKY FOR DEPLOYMENT, ALTHOUGH THE MODIFICATIONS I MADE TO THE KEYPAD SHOULD IRON OUT ANY BUGS.
IT MAY TAKE A LITTLE GETTING USED TO...
HH
THE G.I. ROBOT PROGRAM. RECALLED AFTER THEY RAN ROGUE.
I NEED A THOUSAND BY SPRING.
SOMETHING TOLD ME YOU'D SAY SOMETHING LIKE THAT.
IT OCCURRED TO ME THAT YOUR FRIEND BATMAN MIGHT BE VERY INTERESTED IN THE POTENTIAL OF REMOTE-CONTROLLED SOLDIERS.

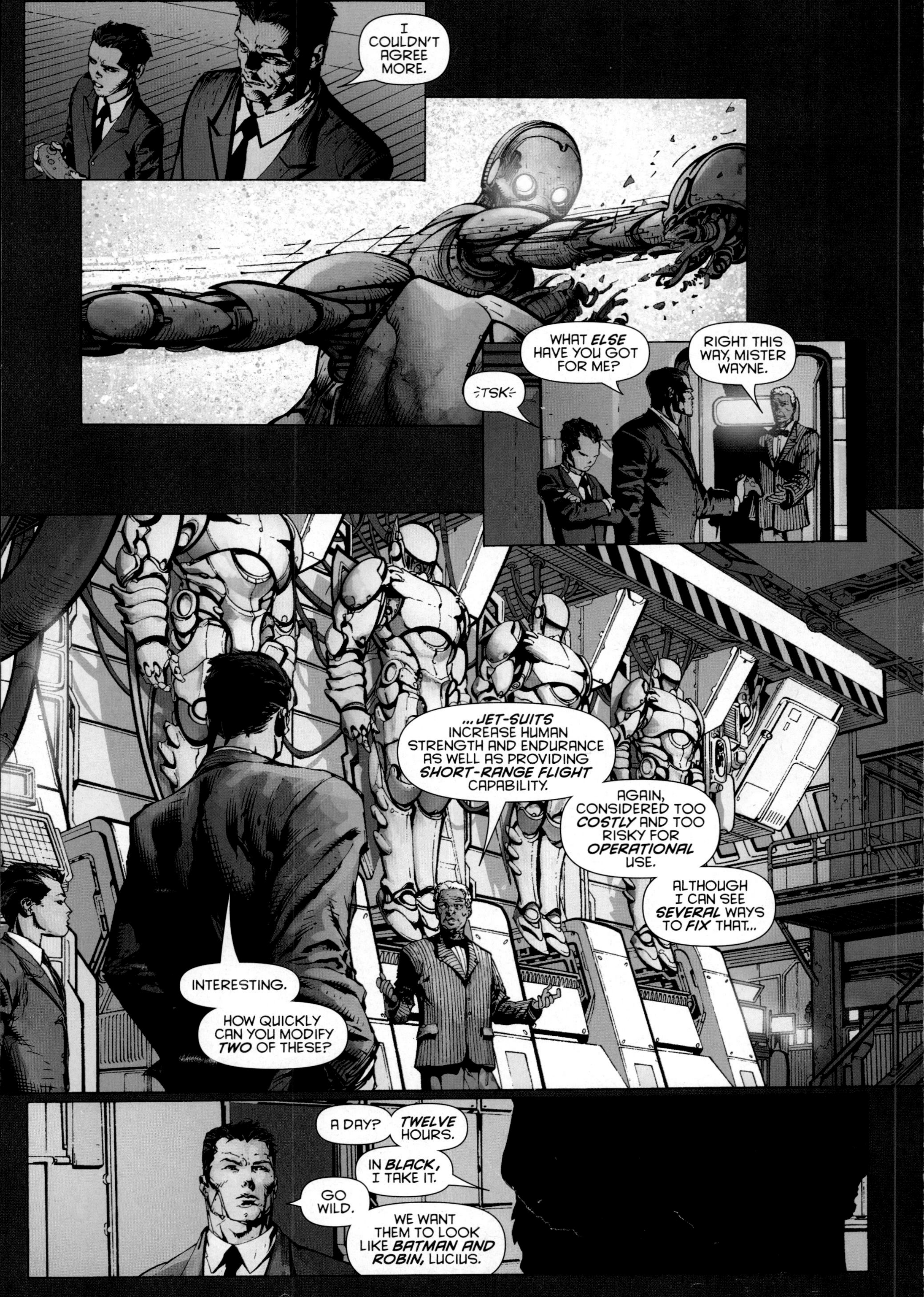
I COULDN'T AGREE MORE.
WHAT *ELSE* HAVE YOU GOT FOR ME?
RIGHT THIS WAY, MISTER WAYNE.
TSK
...*JET-SUITS* INCREASE HUMAN STRENGTH AND ENDURANCE AS WELL AS PROVIDING *SHORT-RANGE FLIGHT* CAPABILITY.
AGAIN, CONSIDERED TOO *COSTLY* AND TOO RISKY FOR *OPERATIONAL* USE.
ALTHOUGH I CAN SEE *SEVERAL* WAYS TO *FIX* THAT...
INTERESTING.
HOW QUICKLY CAN YOU MODIFY *TWO* OF THESE?
A DAY?
TWELVE HOURS.
IN *BLACK*, I TAKE IT.
GO WILD.
WE WANT THEM TO LOOK LIKE *BATMAN AND ROBIN*, LUCIUS.

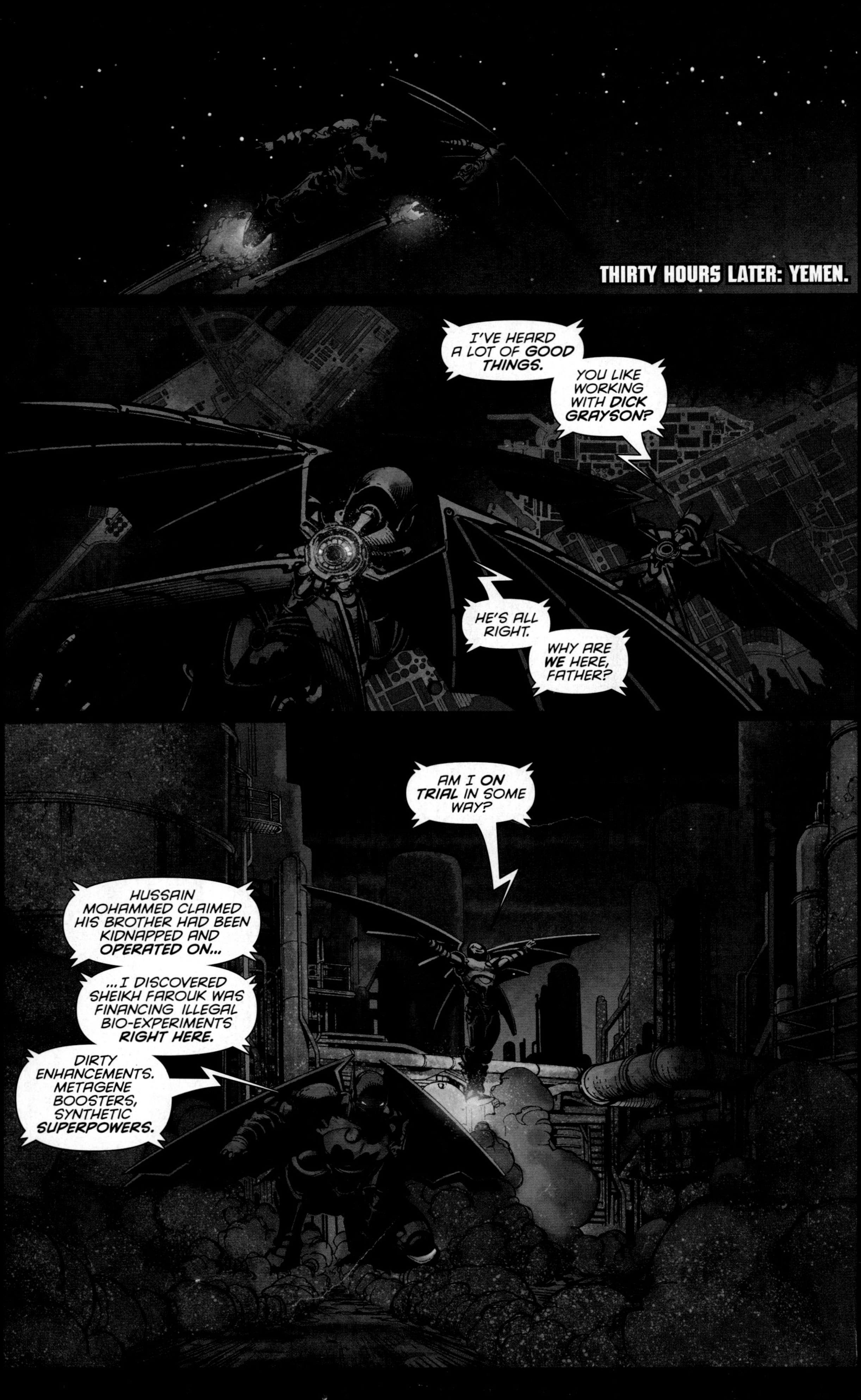
THIRTY HOURS LATER: YEMEN.
I'VE HEARD A LOT OF GOOD THINGS.
YOU LIKE WORKING WITH DICK GRAYSON?
HE'S ALL RIGHT.
WHY ARE WE HERE, FATHER?
AM I ON TRIAL IN SOME WAY?
HUSSAIN MOHAMMED CLAIMED HIS BROTHER HAD BEEN KIDNAPPED AND OPERATED ON...
...I DISCOVERED SHEIKH FAROUK WAS FINANCING ILLEGAL BIO-EXPERIMENTS RIGHT HERE.
DIRTY ENHANCEMENTS. METAGENE BOOSTERS, SYNTHETIC SUPERPOWERS.

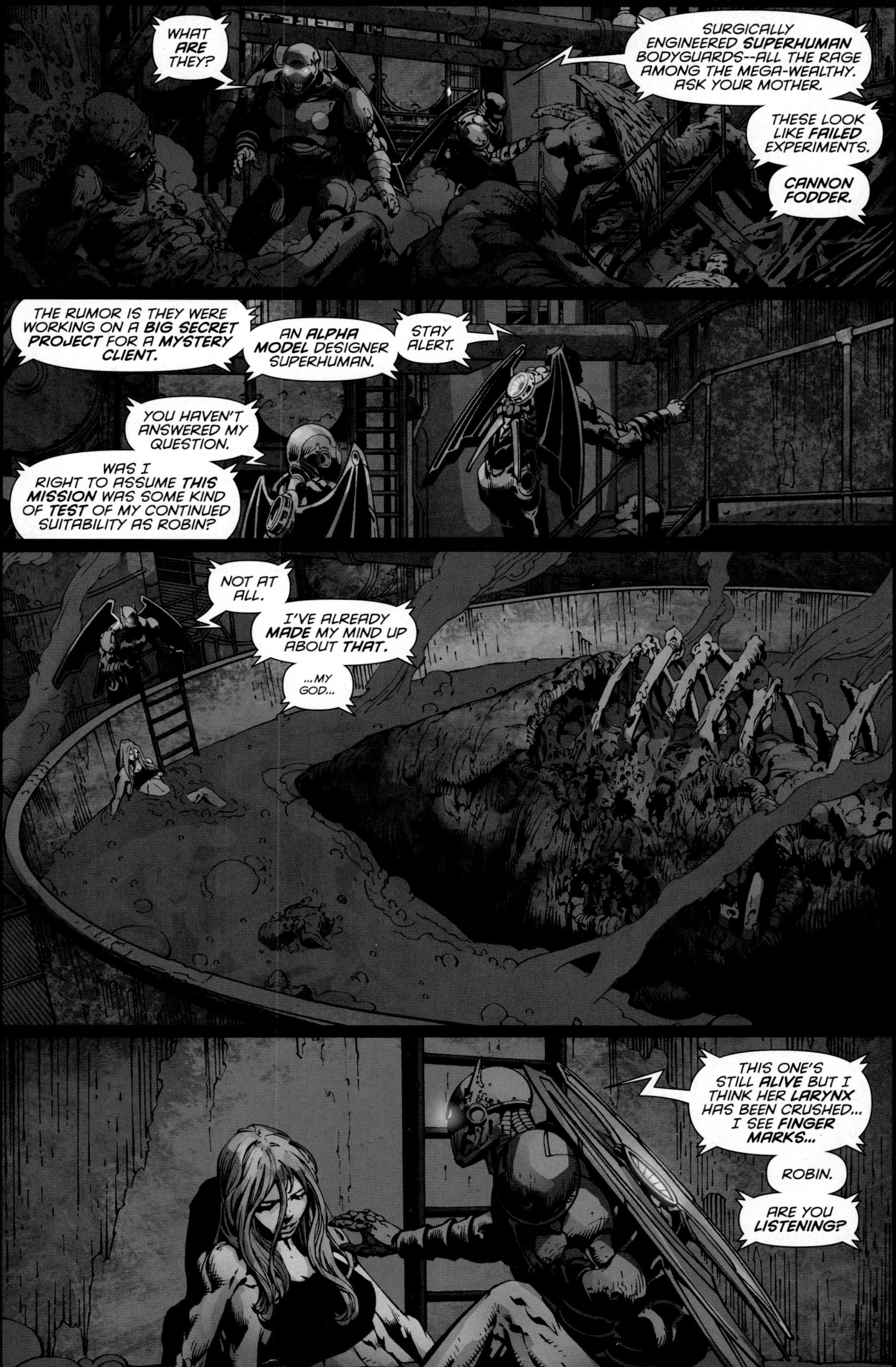
WHAT ARE THEY?
SURGICALLY ENGINEERED SUPERHUMAN BODYGUARDS--ALL THE RAGE AMONG THE MEGA-WEALTHY. ASK YOUR MOTHER.
THESE LOOK LIKE FAILED EXPERIMENTS.
CANNON FODDER.
THE RUMOR IS THEY WERE WORKING ON A BIG SECRET PROJECT FOR A MYSTERY CLIENT.
AN ALPHA MODEL DESIGNER SUPERHUMAN.
STAY ALERT.
YOU HAVEN'T ANSWERED MY QUESTION.
WAS I RIGHT TO ASSUME THIS MISSION WAS SOME KIND OF TEST OF MY CONTINUED SUITABILITY AS ROBIN?
NOT AT ALL.
I'VE ALREADY MADE MY MIND UP ABOUT THAT.
...MY GOD...
THIS ONE'S STILL ALIVE BUT I THINK HER LARYNX HAS BEEN CRUSHED... I SEE FINGER MARKS...
ROBIN.
ARE YOU LISTENING?

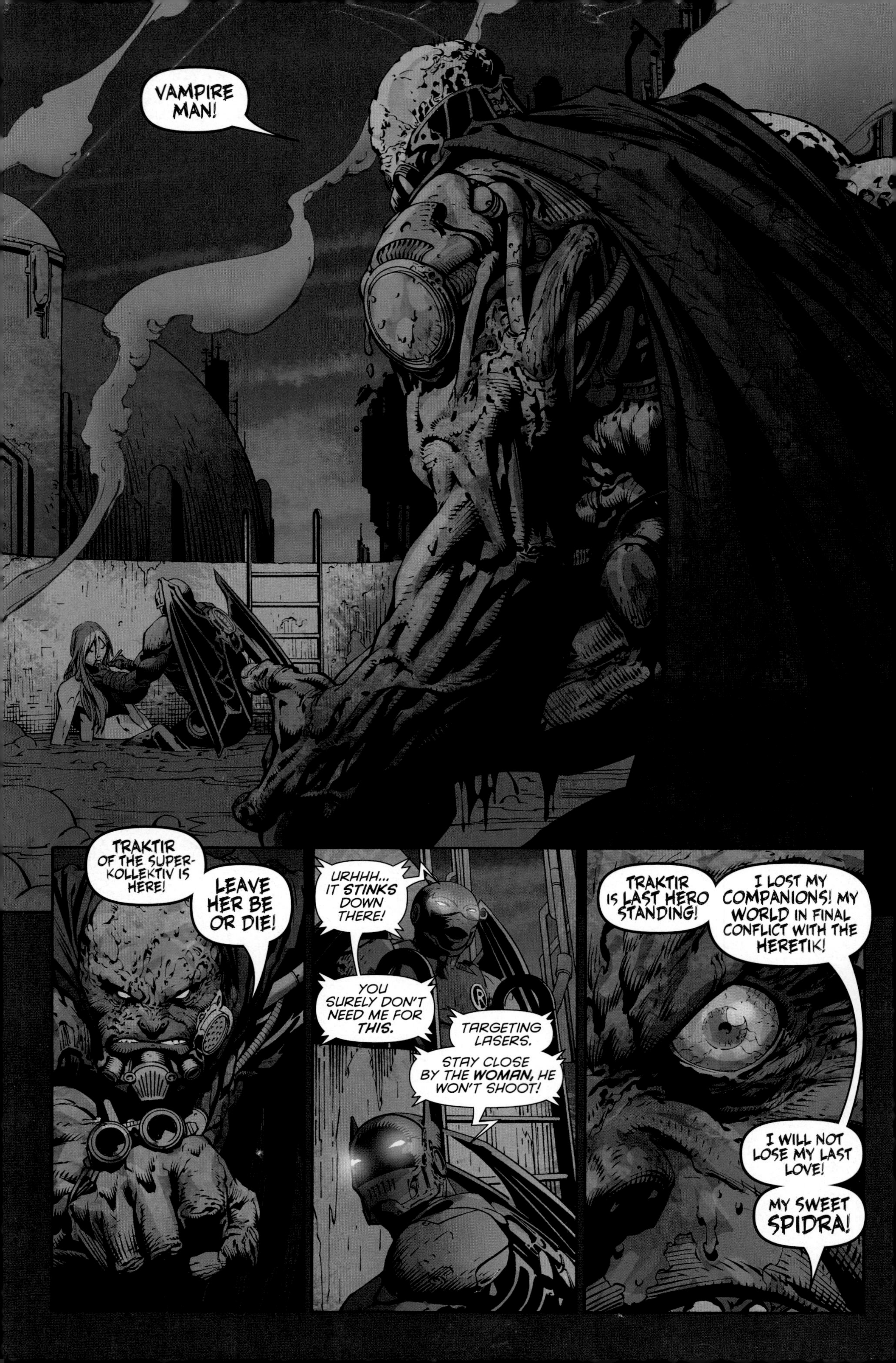
VAMPIRE MAN!
TRAKTIR OF THE SUPER-KOLLEKTIV IS HERE!
LEAVE HER BE OR DIE!
URHHH... IT STINKS DOWN THERE!
YOU SURELY DON'T NEED ME FOR THIS.
TARGETING LASERS.
STAY CLOSE BY THE WOMAN, HE WON'T SHOOT!
TRAKTIR IS LAST HERO STANDING!
I LOST MY COMPANIONS! MY WORLD IN FINAL CONFLICT WITH THE HERETIK!
I WILL NOT LOSE MY LAST LOVE!
MY SWEET SPIDRA!

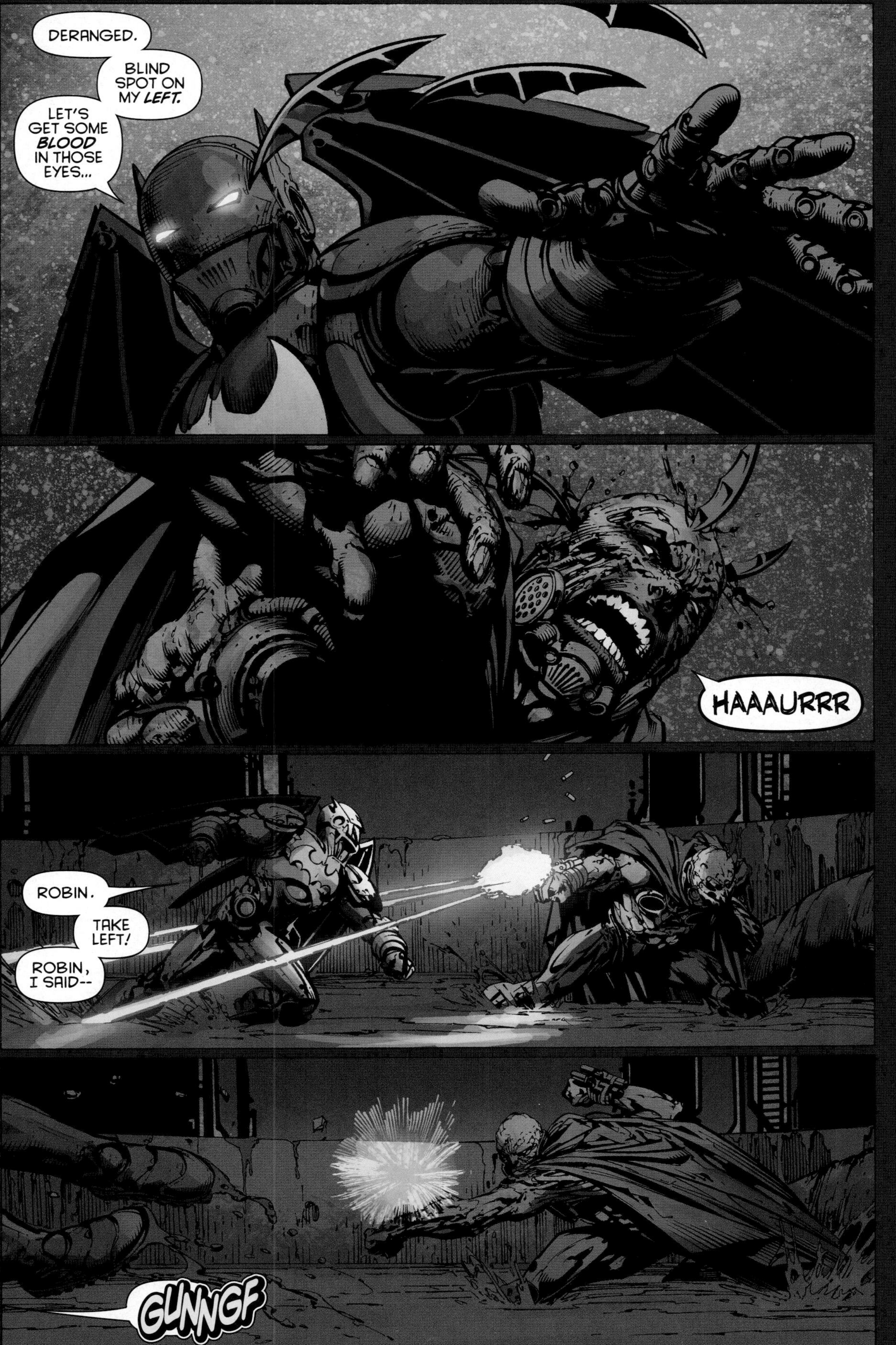
DERANGED.
BLIND SPOT ON MY LEFT.
LET'S GET SOME BLOOD IN THOSE EYES...
HAAAURRR
ROBIN.
TAKE LEFT!
ROBIN, I SAID--
GUNNGF

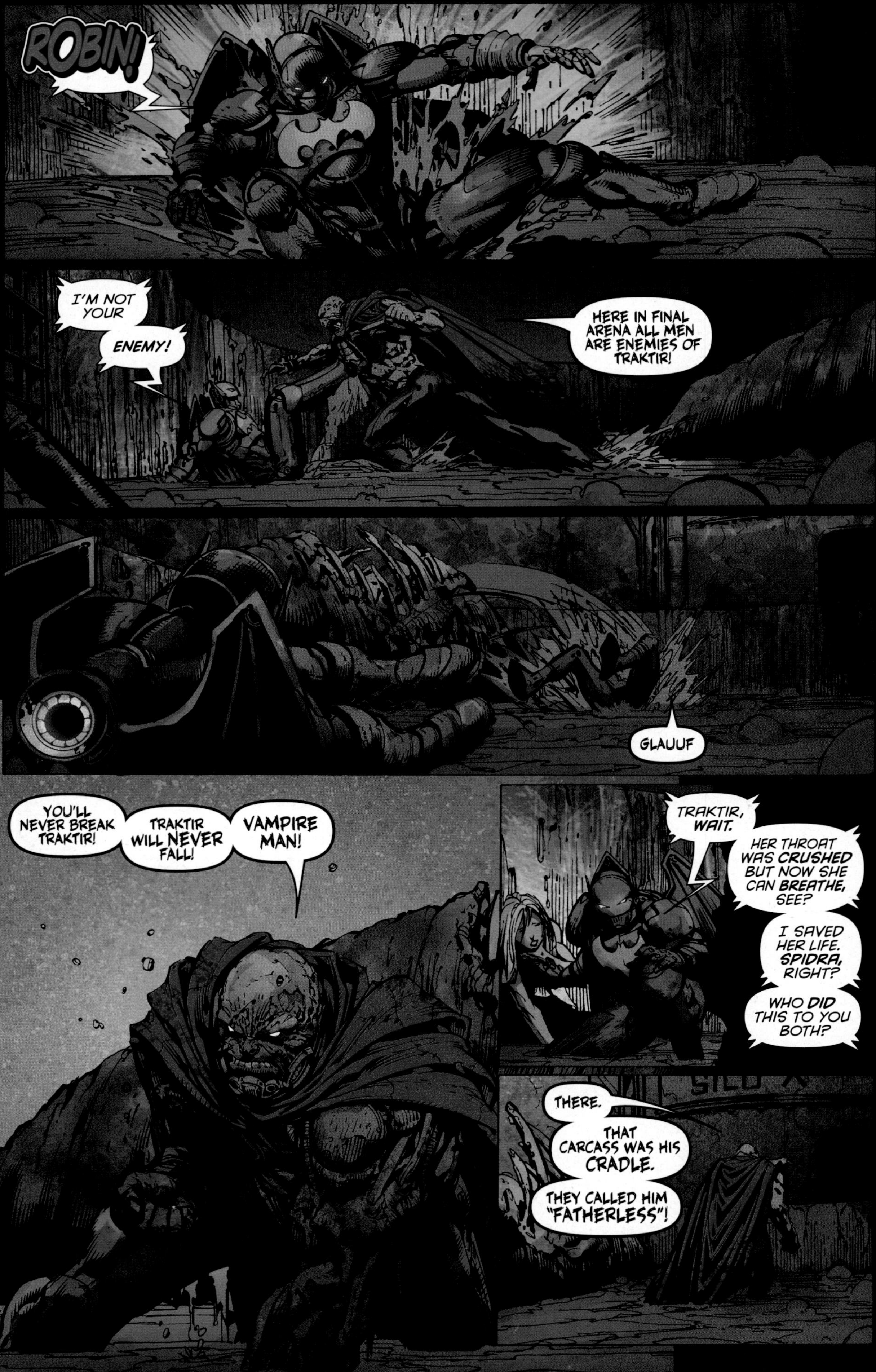
ROBIN!
I'M NOT YOUR
ENEMY!
HERE IN FINAL ARENA ALL MEN ARE ENEMIES OF TRAKTIR!
GLAUUF
YOU'LL NEVER BREAK TRAKTIR!
TRAKTIR WILL NEVER FALL!
VAMPIRE MAN!
TRAKTIR, WAIT.
HER THROAT WAS CRUSHED BUT NOW SHE CAN BREATHE, SEE?
I SAVED HER LIFE. SPIDRA, RIGHT?
WHO DID THIS TO YOU BOTH?
THERE.
THAT CARCASS WAS HIS CRADLE.
THEY CALLED HIM "FATHERLESS"!

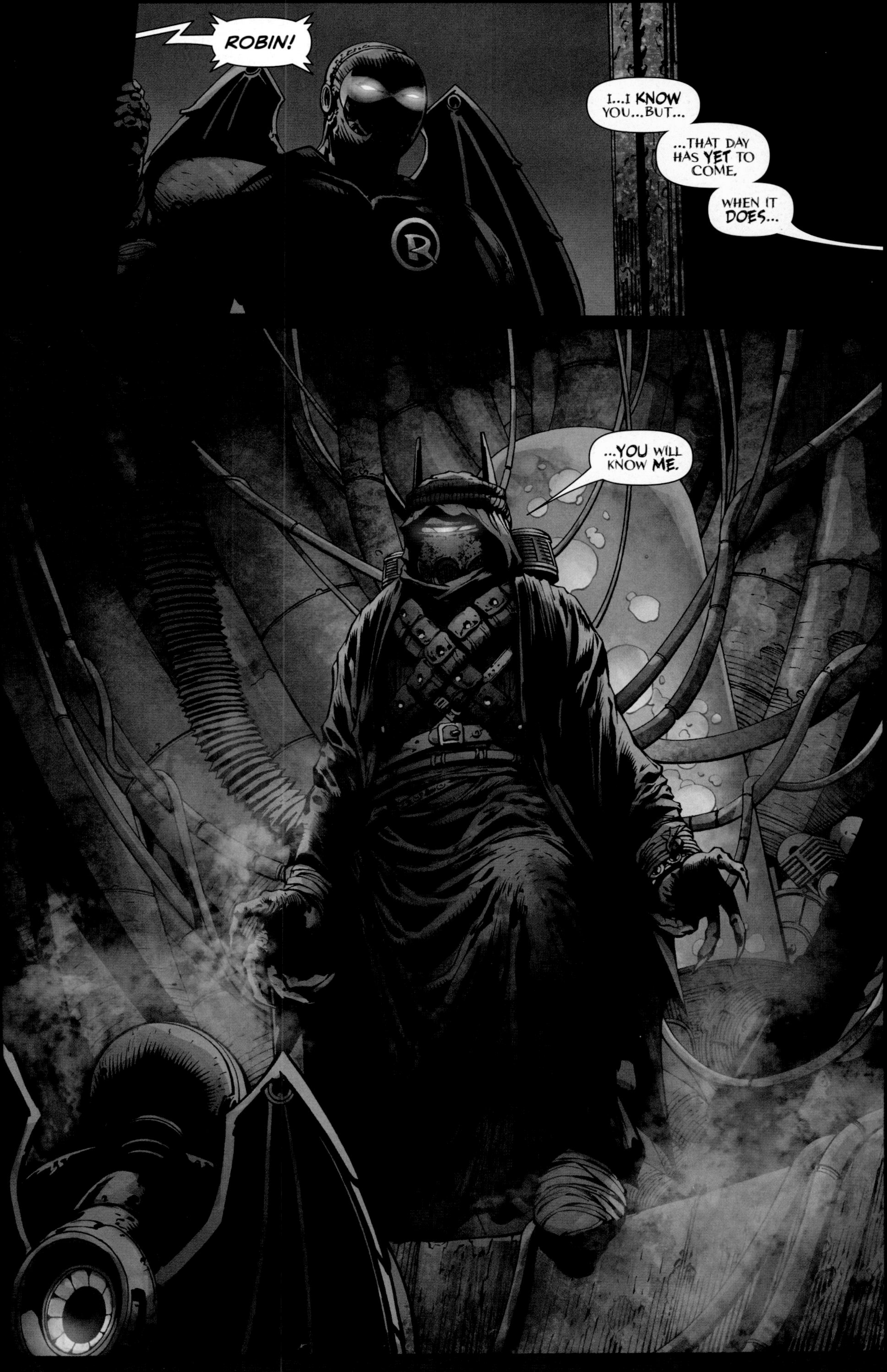
ROBIN!
I...I KNOW YOU...BUT...
...THAT DAY HAS YET TO COME.
WHEN IT DOES...
...YOU WILL KNOW ME.

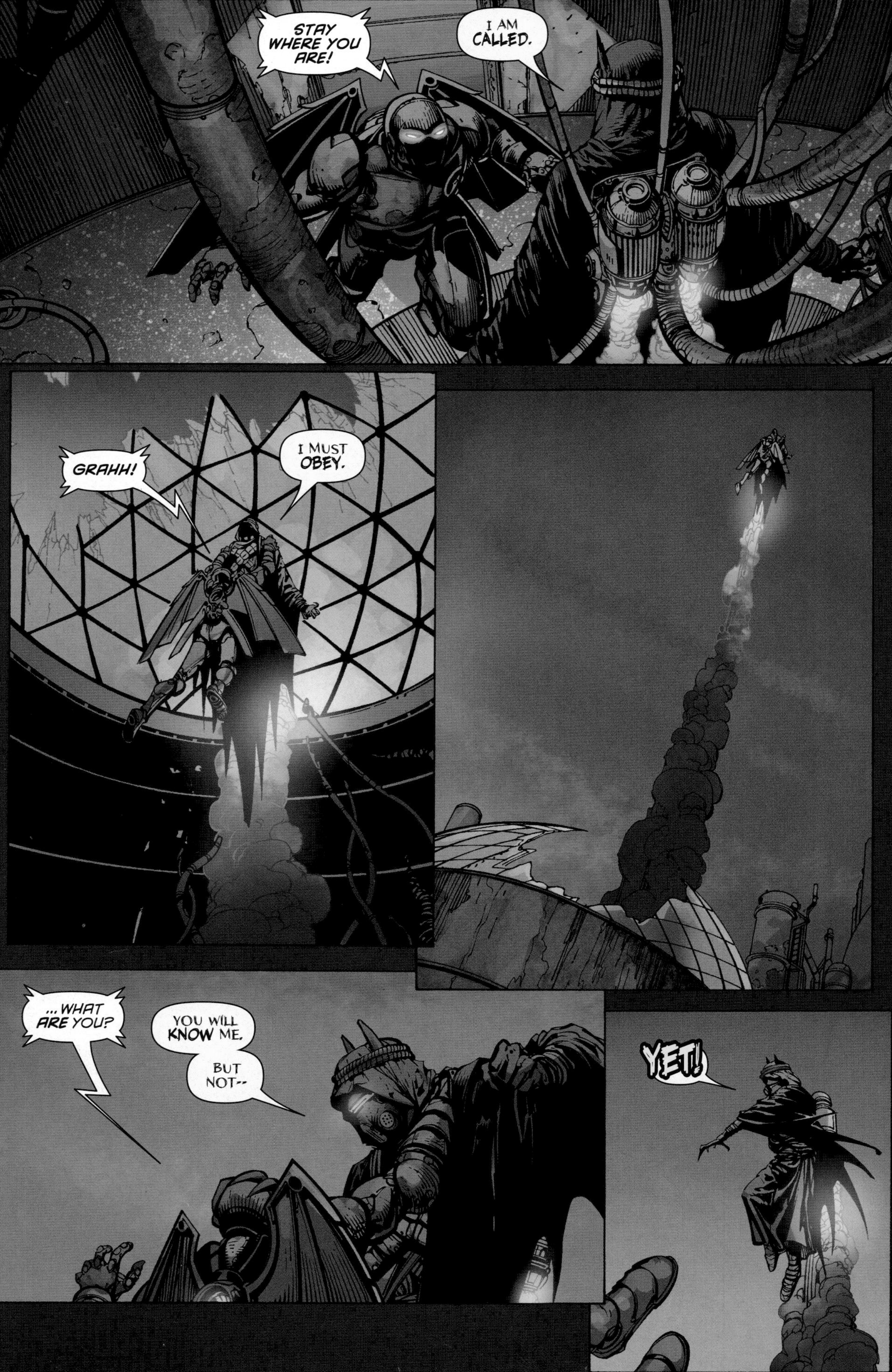

STAY WHERE YOU ARE!
I AM CALLED.
GRAHH!
I MUST OBEY.
...WHAT ARE YOU?
YOU WILL KNOW ME,
BUT NOT--
YET!

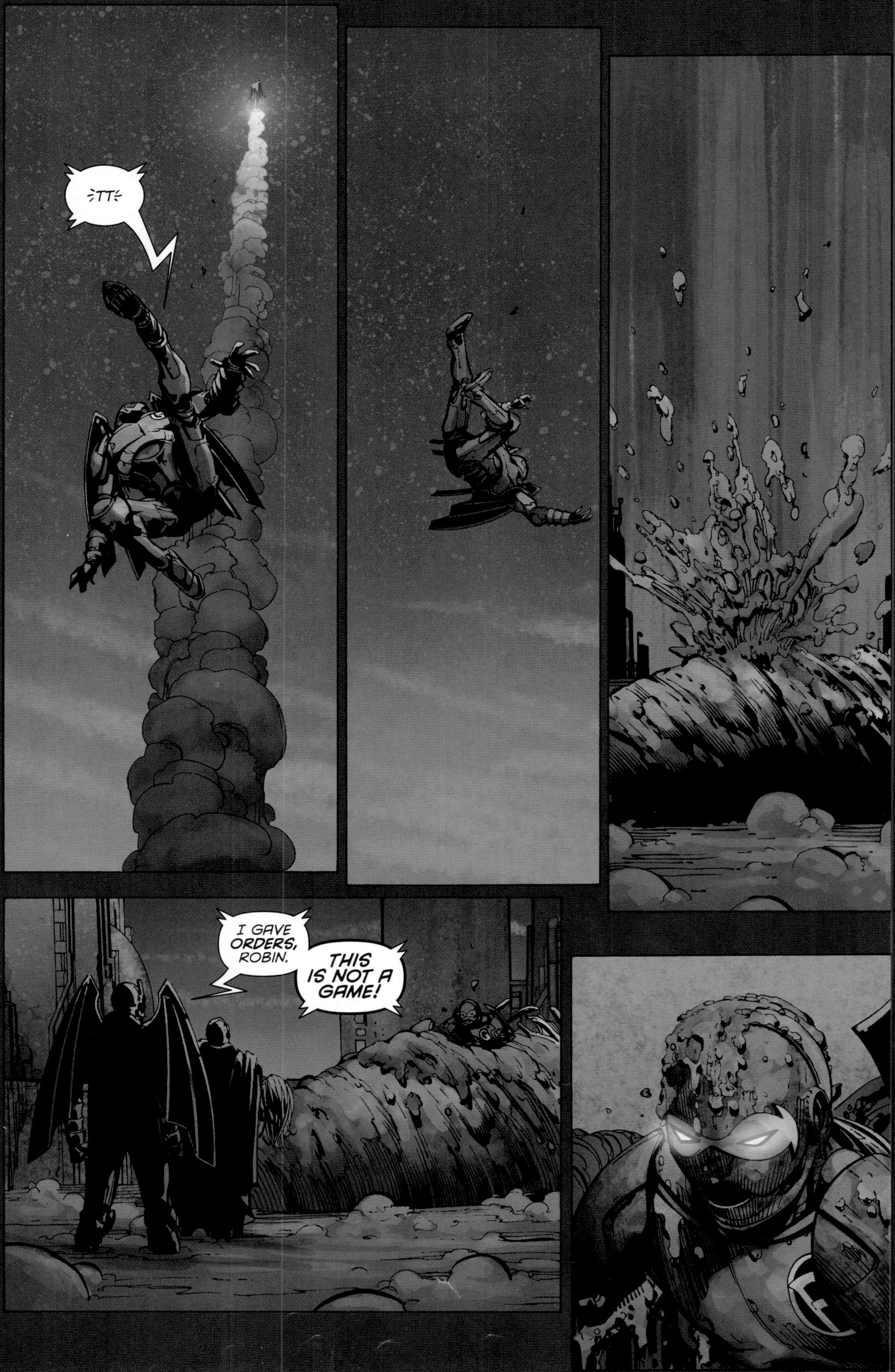
TT
I GAVE ORDERS, ROBIN.
THIS IS NOT A GAME!

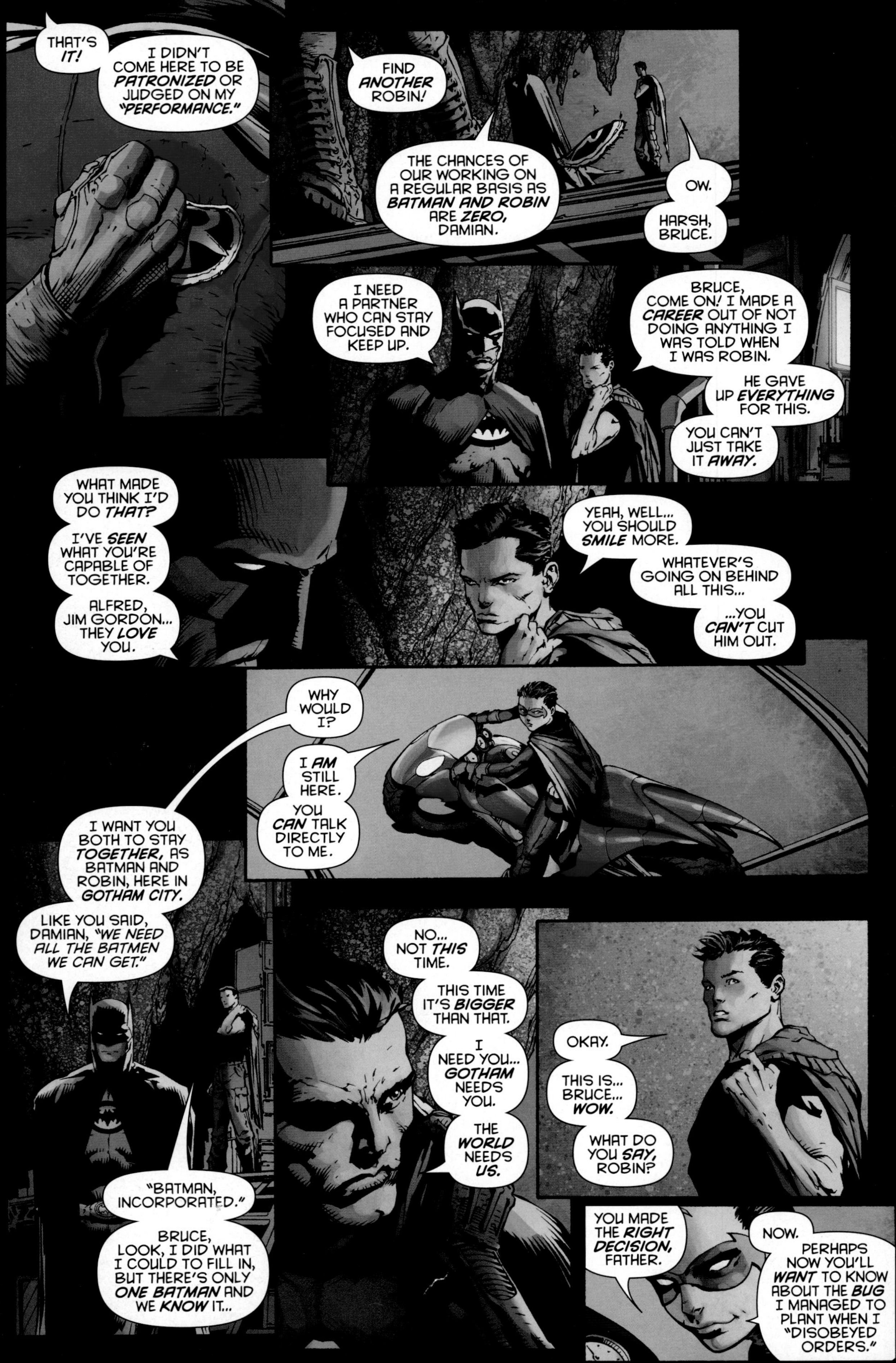
THAT'S *IT!*
I DIDN'T COME HERE TO BE *PATRONIZED* OR JUDGED ON MY *"PERFORMANCE."*
FIND *ANOTHER* ROBIN!
THE CHANCES OF OUR WORKING ON A REGULAR BASIS AS *BATMAN AND ROBIN* ARE *ZERO,* DAMIAN.
OW.
HARSH, BRUCE.
I NEED A PARTNER WHO CAN STAY FOCUSED AND KEEP UP.
BRUCE, COME ON! I MADE A *CAREER* OUT OF NOT DOING ANYTHING I WAS TOLD WHEN I WAS ROBIN.
HE GAVE UP *EVERYTHING* FOR THIS.
YOU CAN'T JUST TAKE IT *AWAY.*
WHAT MADE YOU THINK I'D DO *THAT?*
I'VE *SEEN* WHAT YOU'RE CAPABLE OF TOGETHER.
ALFRED, JIM GORDON... THEY *LOVE* YOU.
YEAH, WELL... YOU SHOULD *SMILE* MORE.
WHATEVER'S GOING ON BEHIND ALL THIS...
...YOU *CAN'T* CUT HIM OUT.
WHY WOULD I?
I *AM* STILL HERE.
YOU *CAN* TALK DIRECTLY TO ME.
I WANT YOU BOTH TO STAY *TOGETHER,* AS BATMAN AND ROBIN, HERE IN *GOTHAM CITY.*
LIKE YOU SAID, DAMIAN, *"WE NEED ALL THE BATMEN WE CAN GET."*
"BATMAN, INCORPORATED."
BRUCE, LOOK, I DID WHAT I COULD TO FILL IN, BUT THERE'S ONLY *ONE BATMAN* AND WE *KNOW* IT...
NO... NOT *THIS* TIME.
THIS TIME IT'S *BIGGER* THAN THAT.
I NEED YOU... *GOTHAM* NEEDS YOU.
THE *WORLD* NEEDS *US.*
OKAY.
THIS IS... BRUCE... *WOW.*
WHAT DO YOU *SAY,* ROBIN?
YOU MADE THE *RIGHT DECISION,* FATHER.
NOW.
PERHAPS NOW YOU'LL *WANT* TO KNOW ABOUT THE *BUG* I MANAGED TO PLANT WHEN I "DISOBEYED ORDERS."

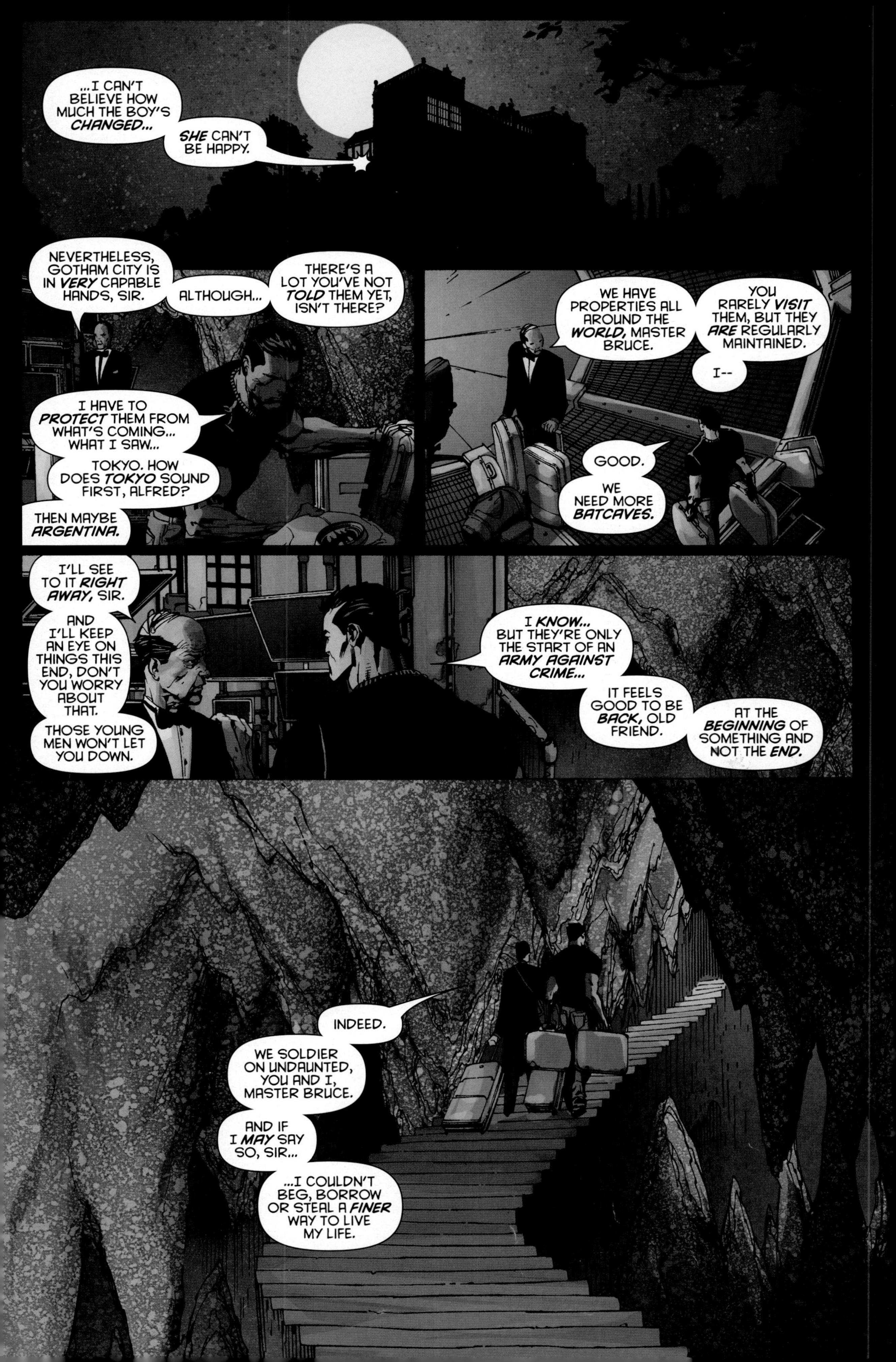
...I CAN'T BELIEVE HOW MUCH THE BOY'S CHANGED...
SHE CAN'T BE HAPPY.
NEVERTHELESS, GOTHAM CITY IS IN VERY CAPABLE HANDS, SIR.
ALTHOUGH...
THERE'S A LOT YOU'VE NOT TOLD THEM YET, ISN'T THERE?
I HAVE TO PROTECT THEM FROM WHAT'S COMING... WHAT I SAW...
TOKYO. HOW DOES TOKYO SOUND FIRST, ALFRED?
THEN MAYBE ARGENTINA.
WE HAVE PROPERTIES ALL AROUND THE WORLD, MASTER BRUCE.
YOU RARELY VISIT THEM, BUT THEY ARE REGULARLY MAINTAINED.
I--
GOOD.
WE NEED MORE BATCAVES.
I'LL SEE TO IT RIGHT AWAY, SIR.
AND I'LL KEEP AN EYE ON THINGS THIS END, DON'T YOU WORRY ABOUT THAT.
THOSE YOUNG MEN WON'T LET YOU DOWN.
I KNOW... BUT THEY'RE ONLY THE START OF AN ARMY AGAINST CRIME...
IT FEELS GOOD TO BE BACK, OLD FRIEND.
AT THE BEGINNING OF SOMETHING AND NOT THE END.
INDEED.
WE SOLDIER ON UNDAUNTED, YOU AND I, MASTER BRUCE.
AND IF I MAY SAY SO, SIR...
...I COULDN'T BEG, BORROW OR STEAL A FINER WAY TO LIVE MY LIFE.

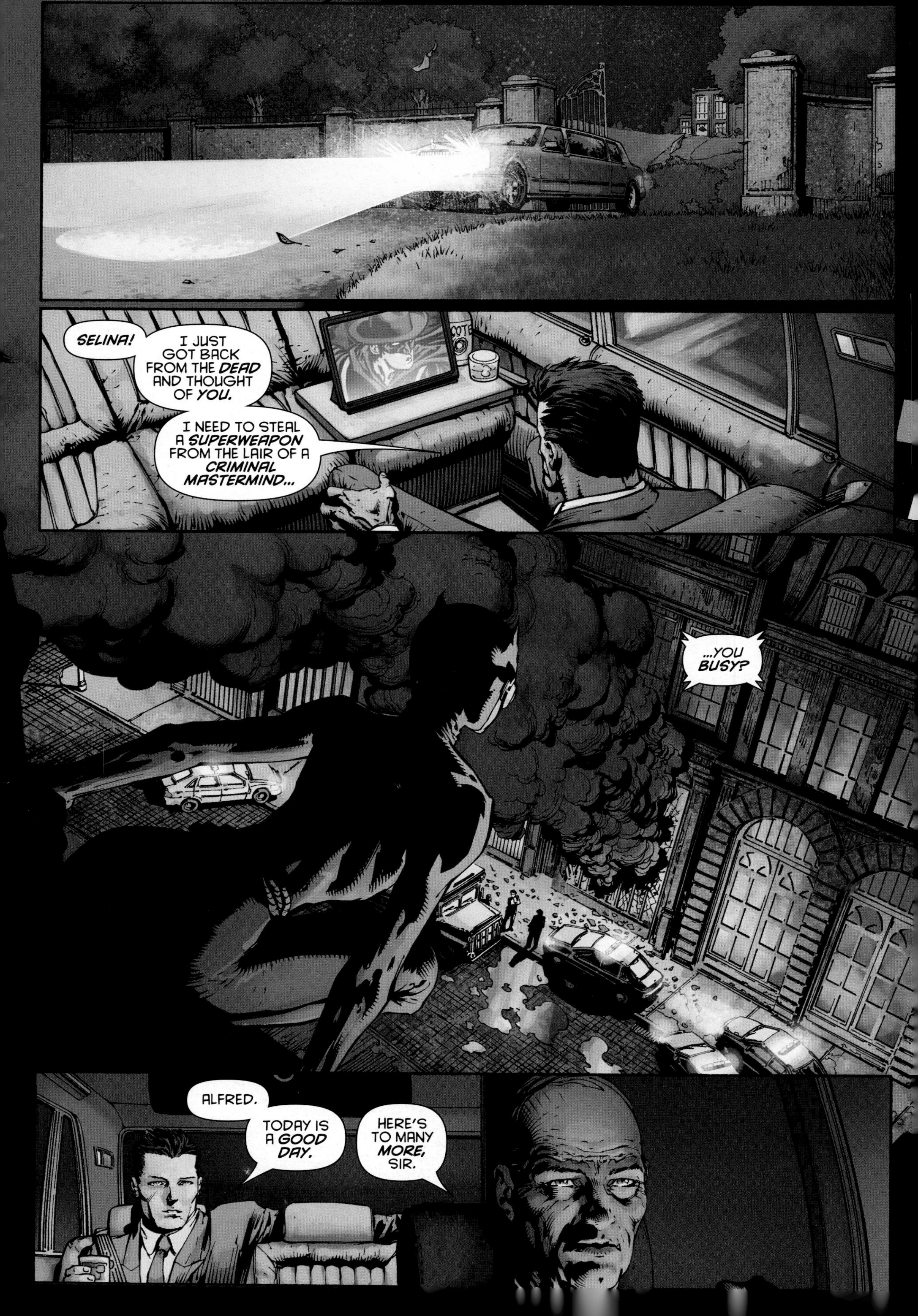
SELINA!
I JUST GOT BACK FROM THE DEAD AND THOUGHT OF YOU.
I NEED TO STEAL A SUPERWEAPON FROM THE LAIR OF A CRIMINAL MASTERMIND...
...YOU BUSY?
ALFRED.
TODAY IS A GOOD DAY.
HERE'S TO MANY MORE, SIR.

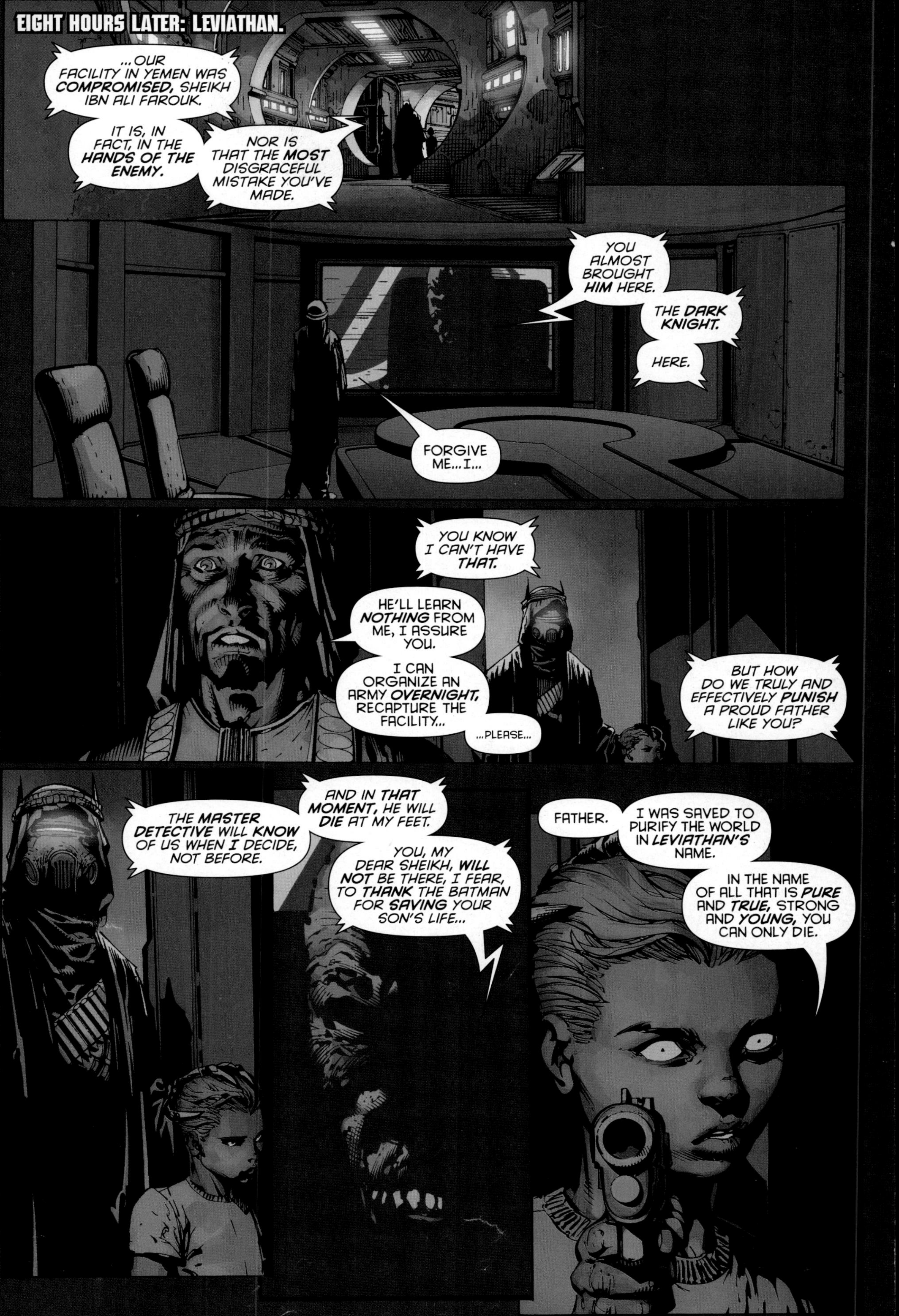
EIGHT HOURS LATER: LEVIATHAN.
...OUR FACILITY IN YEMEN WAS COMPROMISED, SHEIKH IBN ALI FAROUK.
IT IS, IN FACT, IN THE HANDS OF THE ENEMY.
NOR IS THAT THE MOST DISGRACEFUL MISTAKE YOU'VE MADE.
YOU ALMOST BROUGHT HIM HERE.
THE DARK KNIGHT.
HERE.
FORGIVE ME...I...
YOU KNOW I CAN'T HAVE THAT.
HE'LL LEARN NOTHING FROM ME, I ASSURE YOU.
I CAN ORGANIZE AN ARMY OVERNIGHT, RECAPTURE THE FACILITY...
...PLEASE...
BUT HOW DO WE TRULY AND EFFECTIVELY PUNISH A PROUD FATHER LIKE YOU?
THE MASTER DETECTIVE WILL KNOW OF US WHEN I DECIDE, NOT BEFORE.
AND IN THAT MOMENT, HE WILL DIE AT MY FEET.
YOU, MY DEAR SHEIKH, WILL NOT BE THERE, I FEAR, TO THANK THE BATMAN FOR SAVING YOUR SON'S LIFE...
FATHER.
I WAS SAVED TO PURIFY THE WORLD IN LEVIATHAN'S NAME.
IN THE NAME OF ALL THAT IS PURE AND TRUE, STRONG AND YOUNG, YOU CAN ONLY DIE.

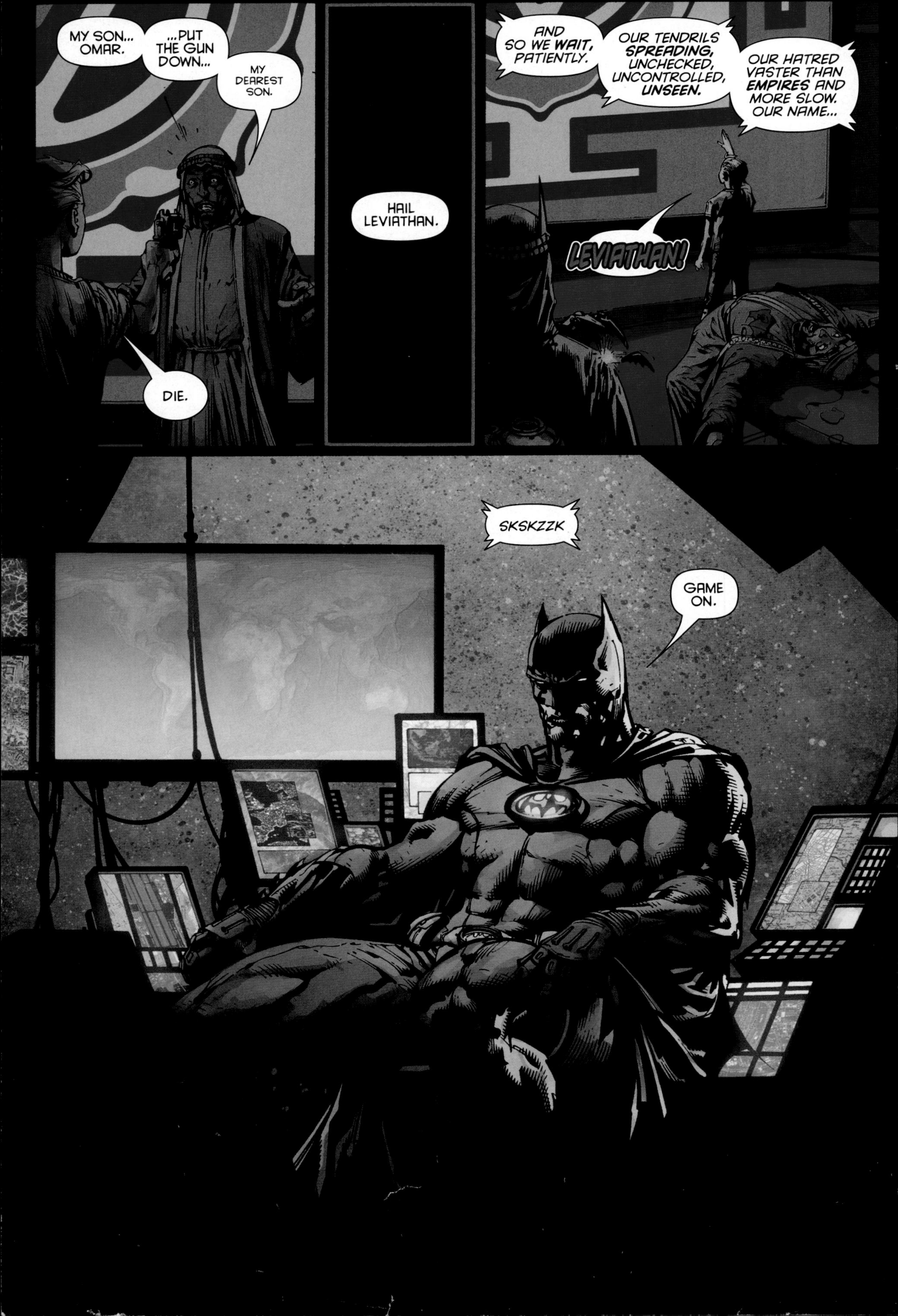
MY SON... OMAR.
...PUT THE GUN DOWN...
MY DEAREST SON.
DIE.
HAIL LEVIATHAN.
AND SO WE WAIT, PATIENTLY.
OUR TENDRILS SPREADING, UNCHECKED, UNCONTROLLED, UNSEEN.
OUR HATRED VASTER THAN EMPIRES AND MORE SLOW. OUR NAME...
LEVIATHAN!
SKSKZZK
GAME ON.

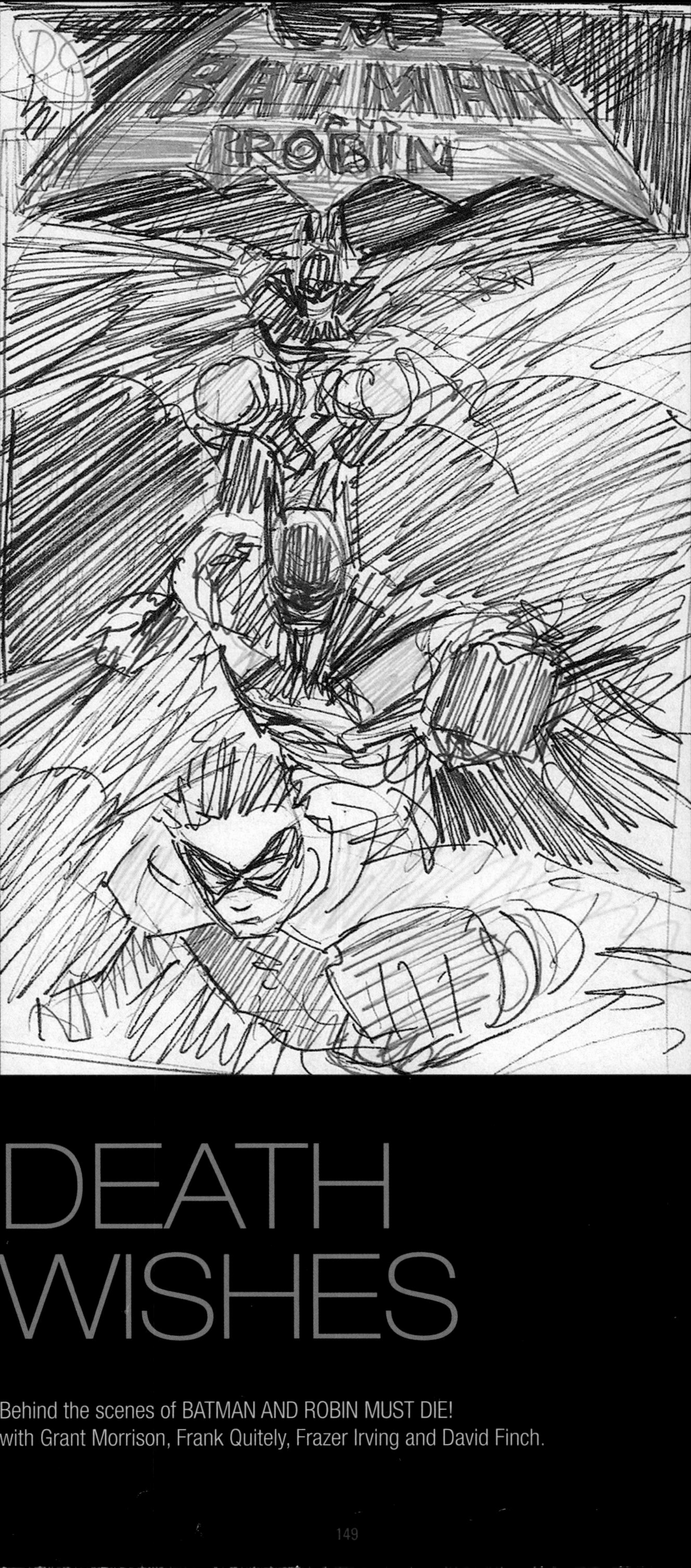
ROBIN

DEATH WISHES

Behind the scenes of BATMAN AND ROBIN MUST DIE!
with Grant Morrison, Frank Quitely, Frazer Irving and David Finch.

THE COVERS

As regular readers of these collected editions will know, I sketch out pretty much all of the cover roughs for this series in my notebook at the start of the creative process. Here are the last of those scribbled ideas, alongside the polished, professional finished versions by Frank Quitely as well as the variant covers by Frazer Irving, Ethan Van Sciver and Gene Ha.

issue thirteen

Back in BATMAN #428, in 1988, the Joker had famously used a crowbar to beat Jason Todd, the unlucky second Robin, to within an inch of his life before blowing him away with a bomb. As is the way of comic book characters, Jason Todd eventually made it back from the dead many years later (and even made an appearance as the Red Hood in this very series), but I wanted to see the new Robin redress the balance in his own inimitable way—hence this image of a grinning, unrepentant Joker taking his skull fractures with a smile.

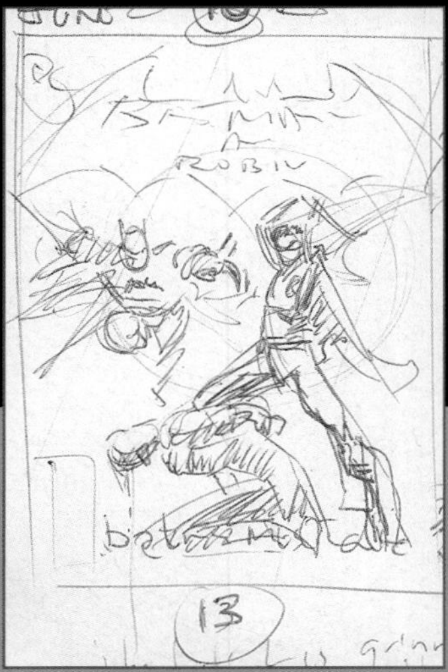
13

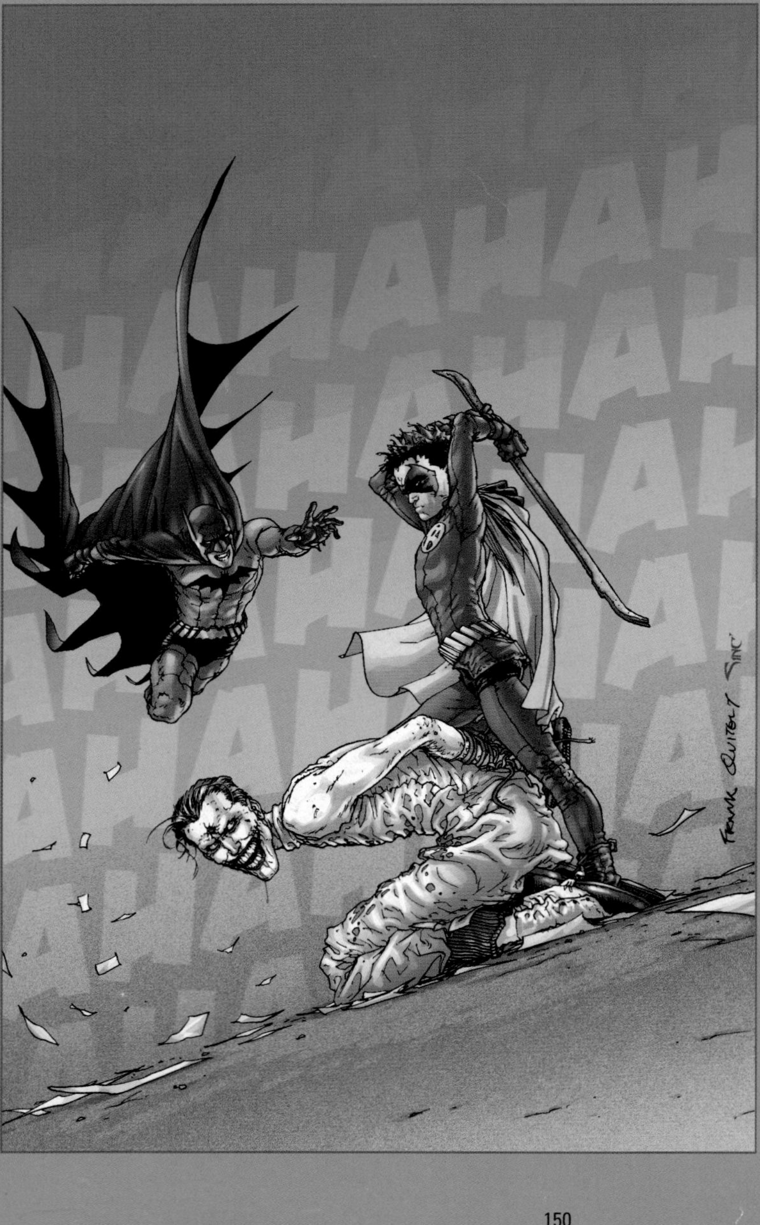
FRANK QUITELY

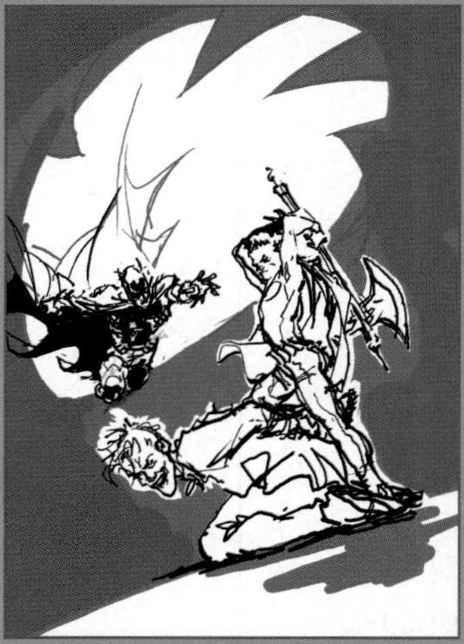

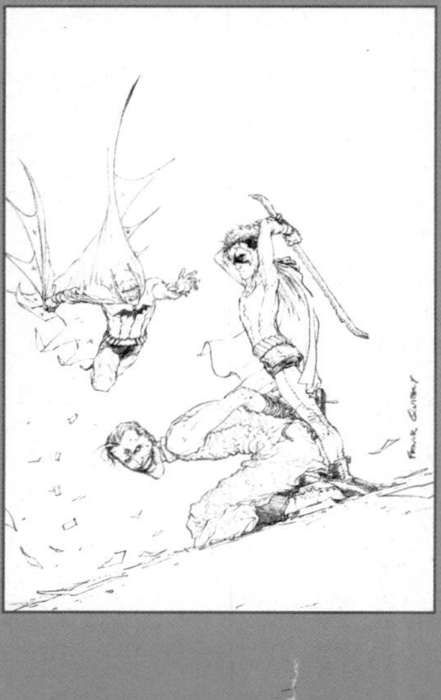

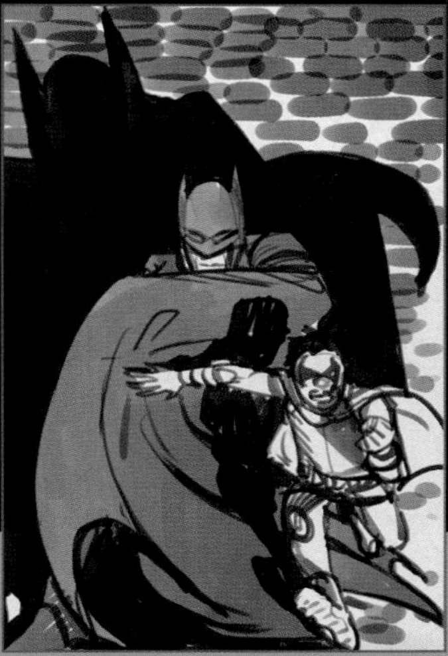

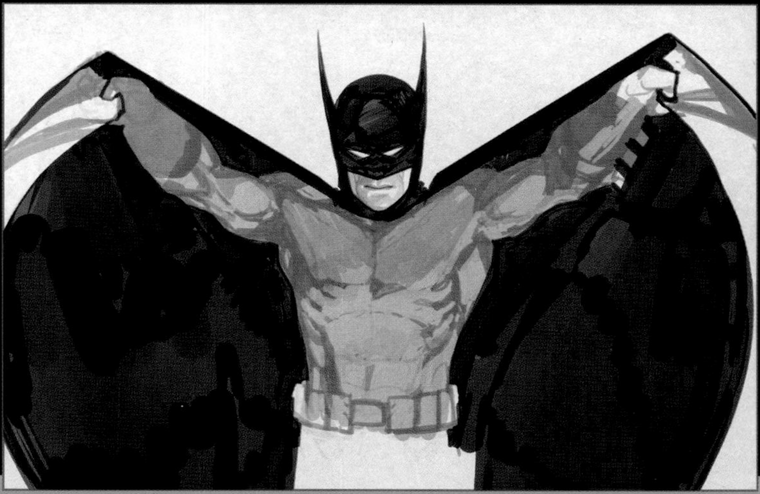

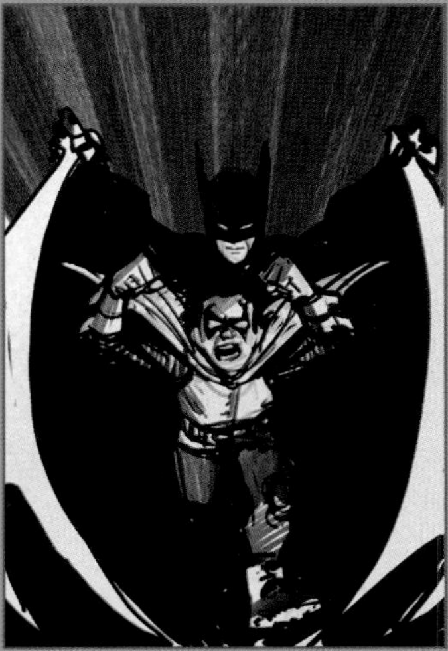

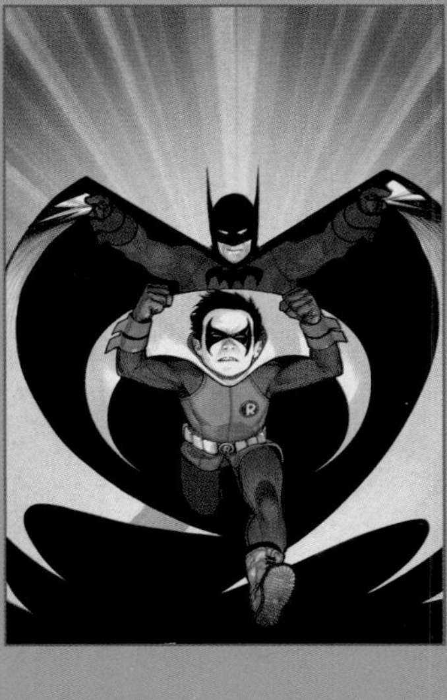

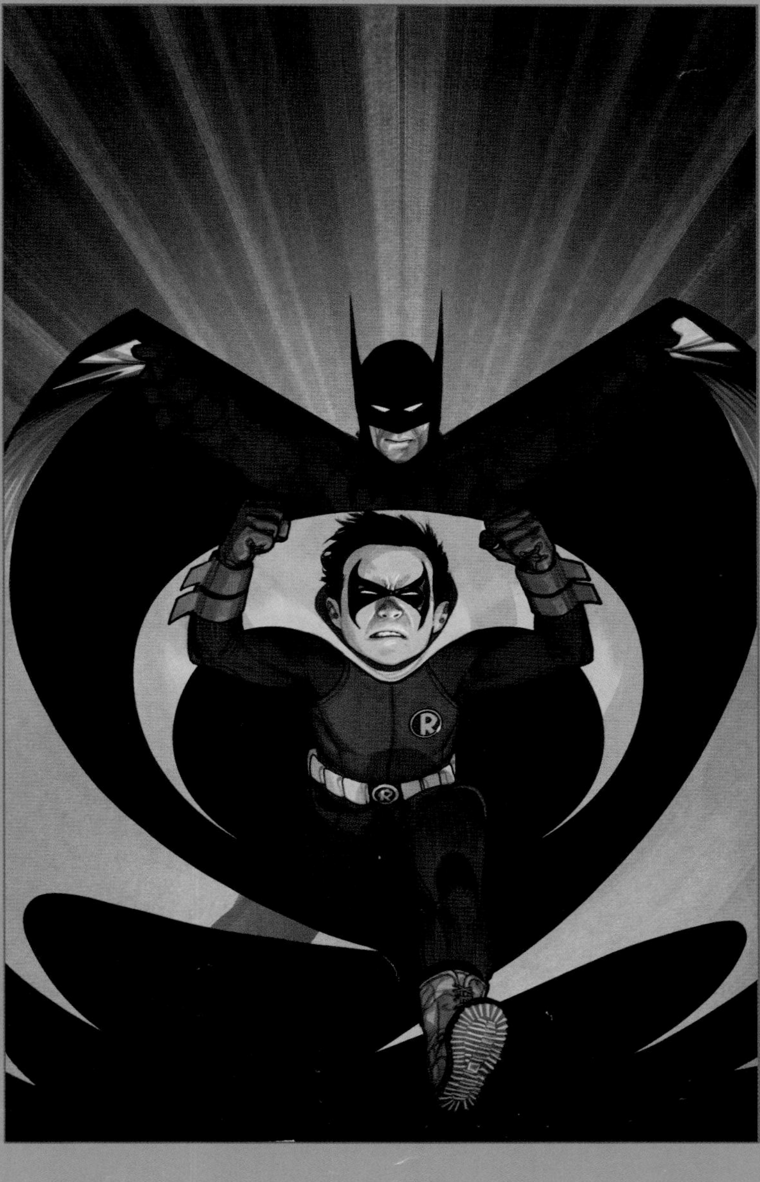

issue fourteen

During "Batman R.I.P." I felt we'd missed out on the potential of an infernal cover depicting Doctor Hurt wearing Thomas Wayne's sinister, bat-like masquerade costume backlit by turbulent flames. The idea was finally used here, with the addition of a Batman who's had bullet holes blasted into his back in a domino-spot pattern.

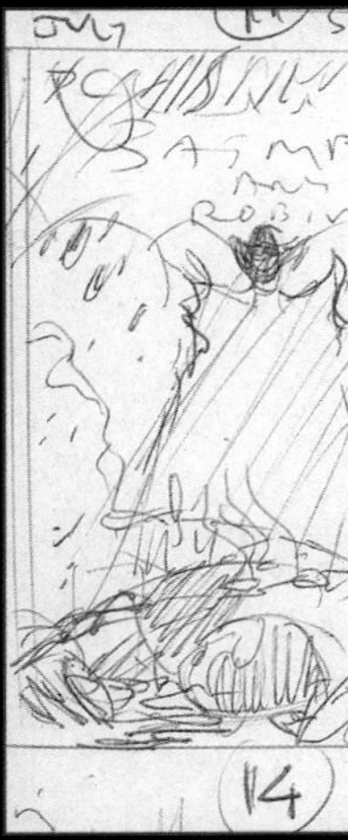
14

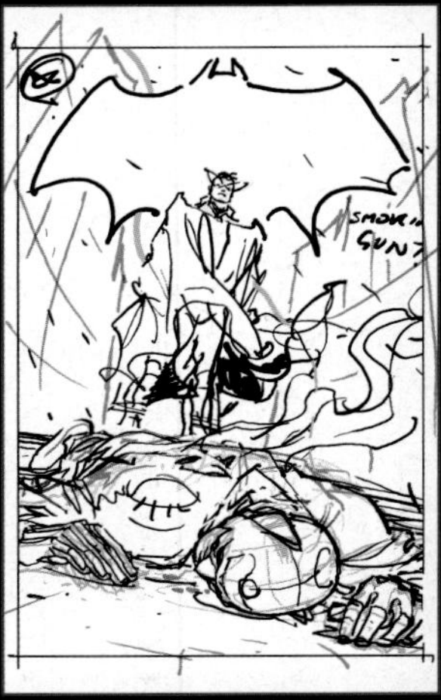

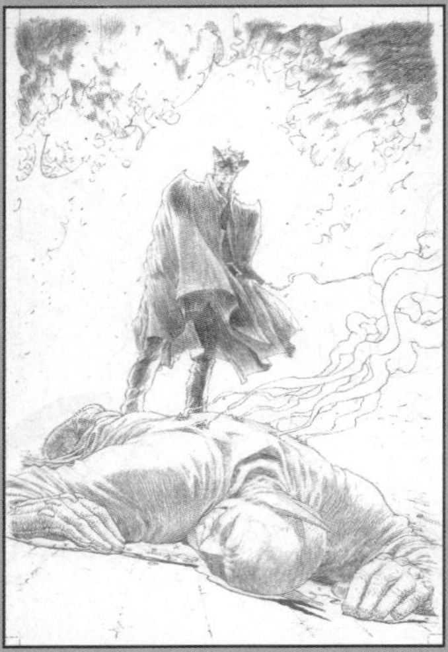

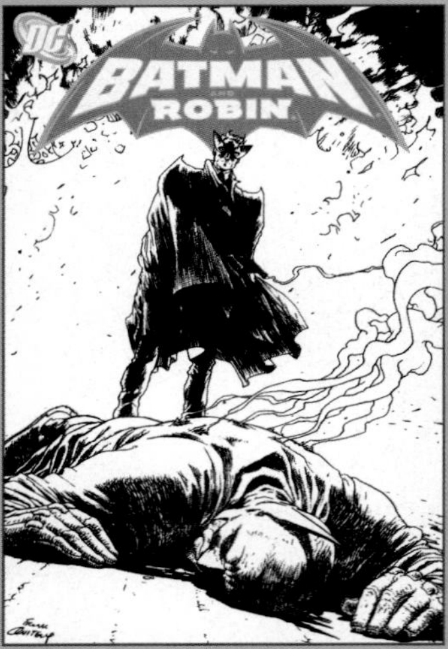
DC
BATMAN
ROBIN

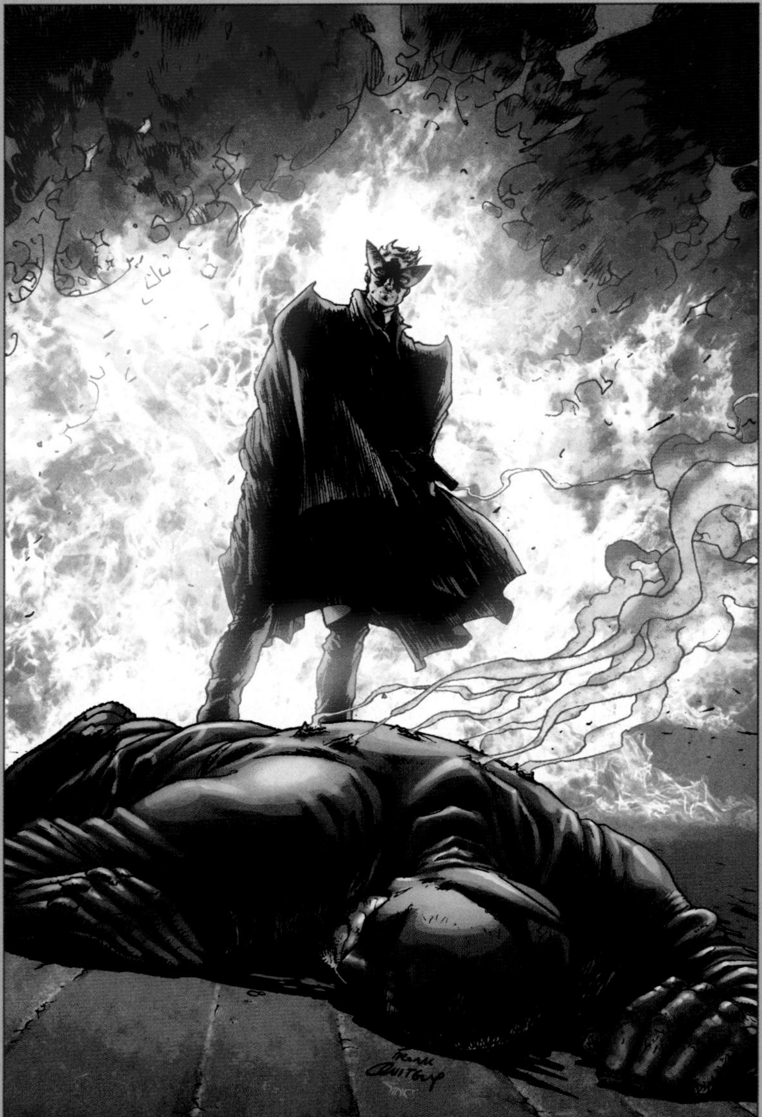

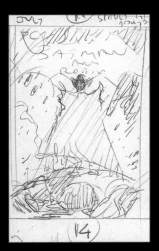

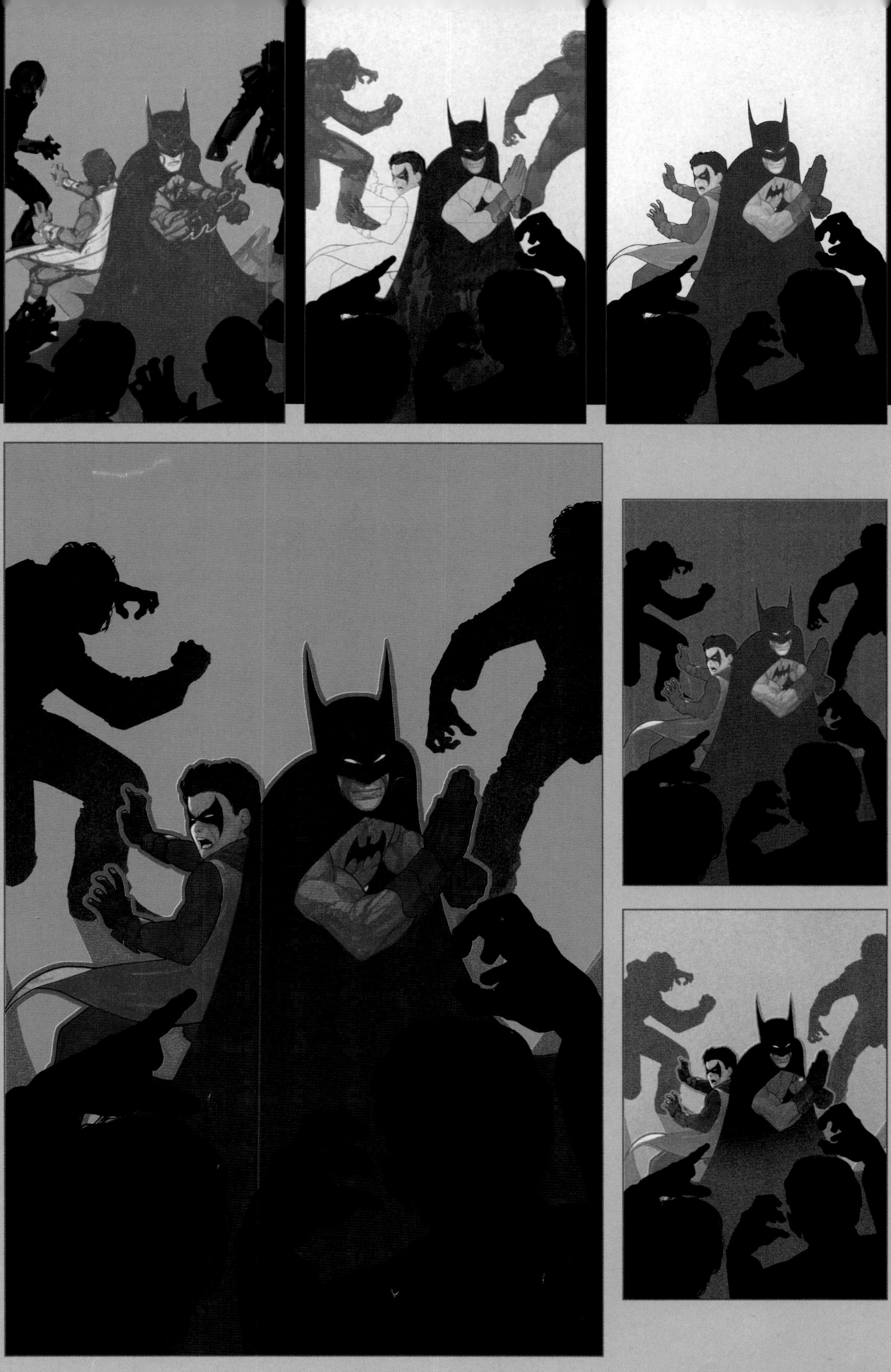

issue fifteen

This cover was intended as a kind of Satanic reverse of the famous panel from DETECTIVE COMICS #38 published in 1940, where Batman solemnly inducts the young Robin into the crime-fighting fraternity.

Here the figures are flipped around, with left hands raised instead of right hands and a candelabra designed to hint at a trident or pitchfork shape, suggestive of the Devil. A huge, inverted cross appeared in the original drawing as an homage to the imagery of late '60s and early '70s "Devil" pictures such as *Rosemary's Baby*, *The Exorcist* and *The Omen*, but this was considered to be too "on-the-nose" and was dropped from the final version.

Mention must also be made of Frazer Irving's remarkably mental variant cover for this issue, surely one of the iconic Joker drawings of recent years.

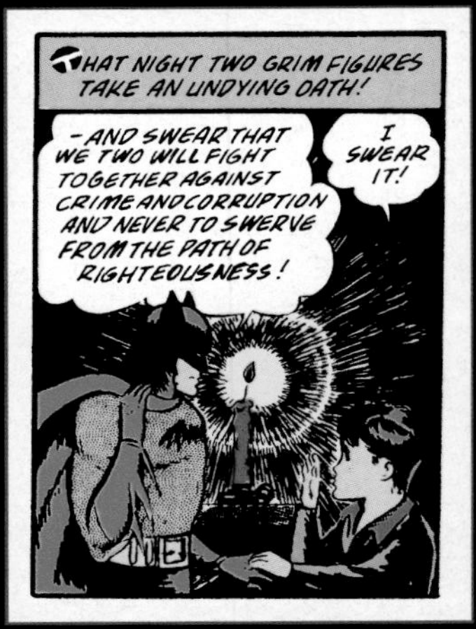
THAT NIGHT TWO GRIM FIGURES TAKE AN UNDYING OATH!
- AND SWEAR THAT WE TWO WILL FIGHT TOGETHER AGAINST CRIME AND CORRUPTION AND NEVER TO SWERVE FROM THE PATH OF RIGHTEOUSNESS!
I SWEAR IT!

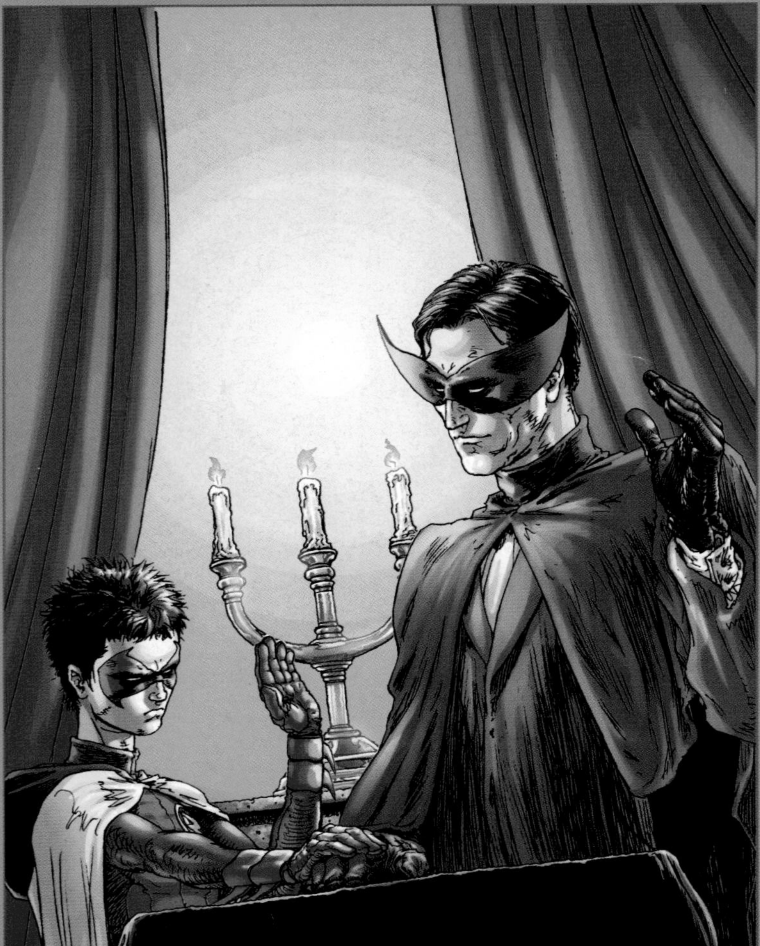

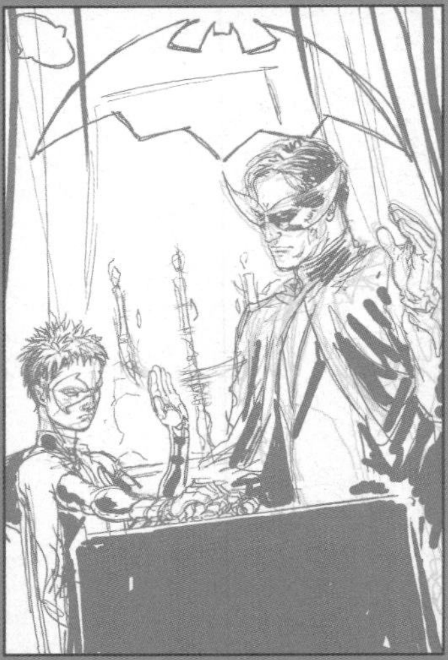

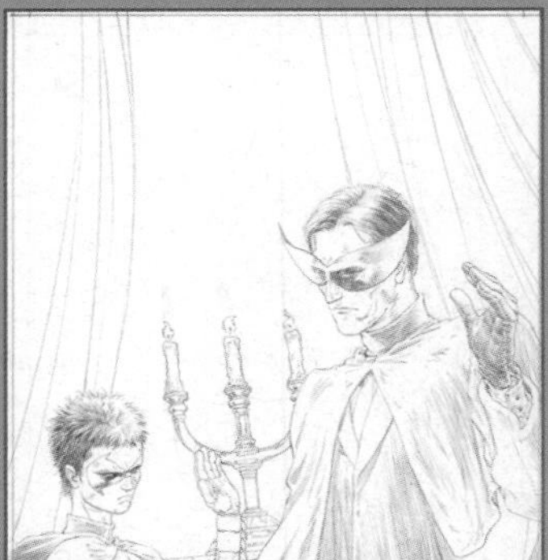

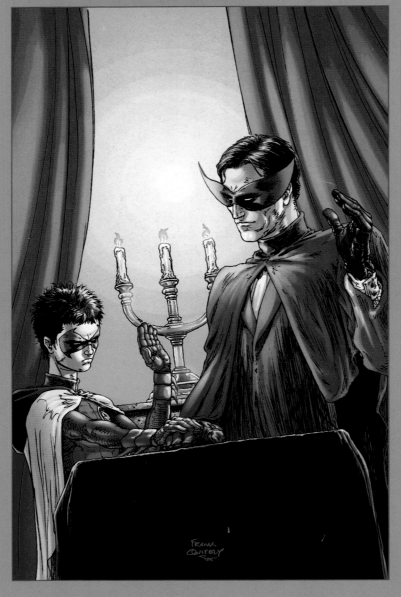

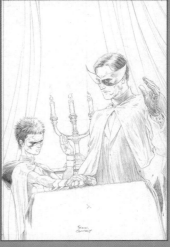

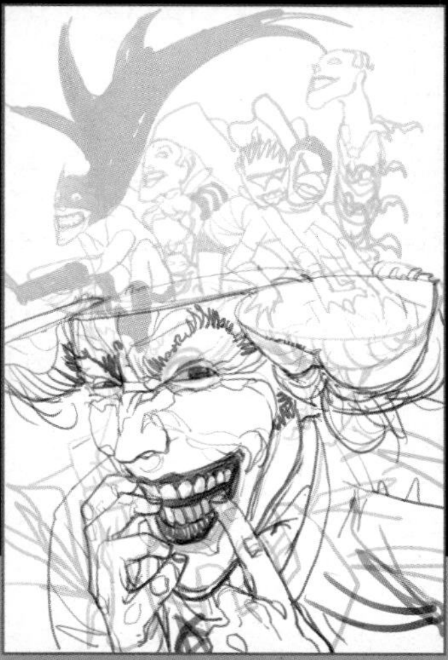
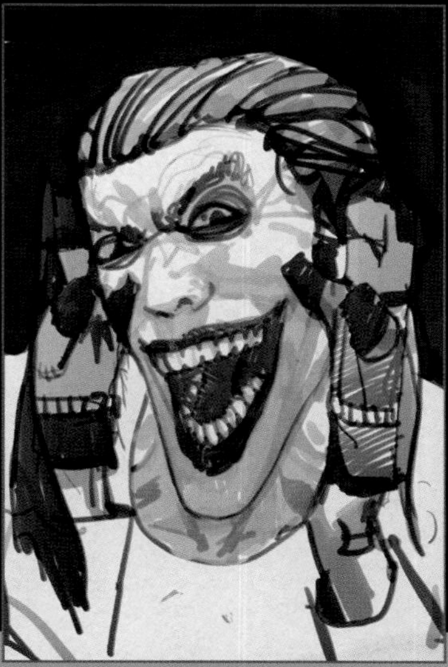
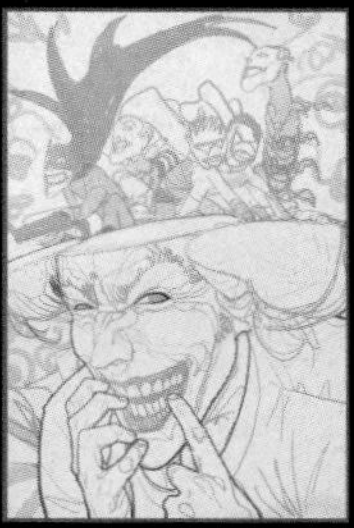
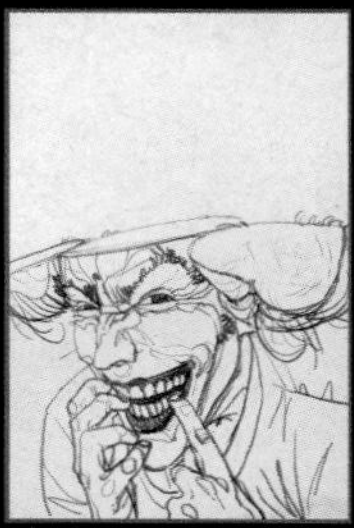
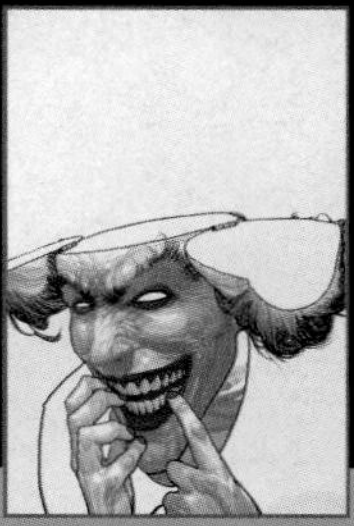
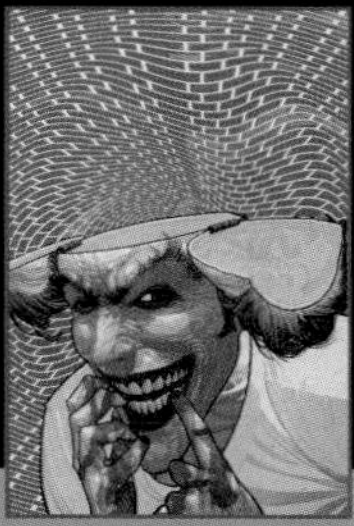
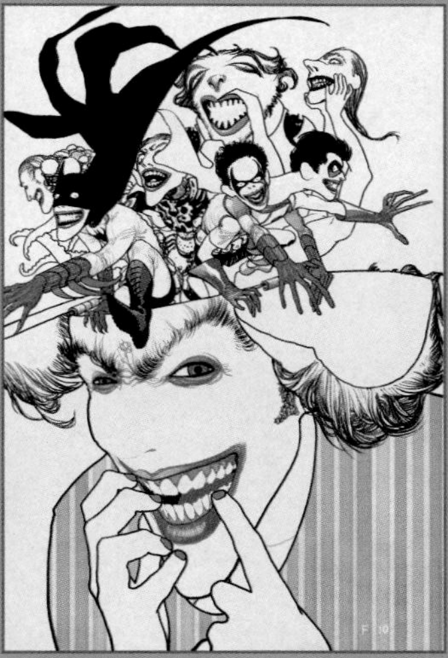
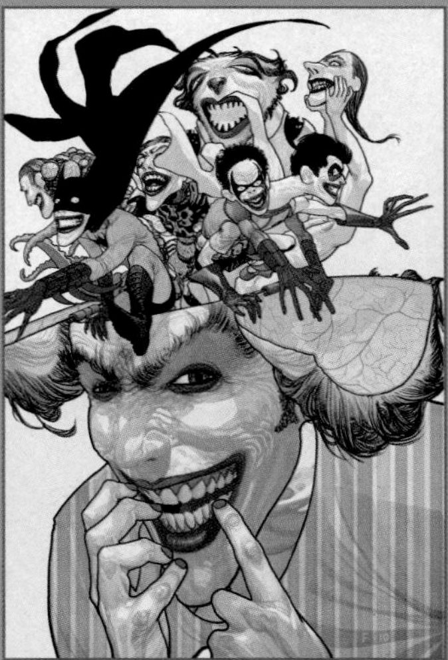
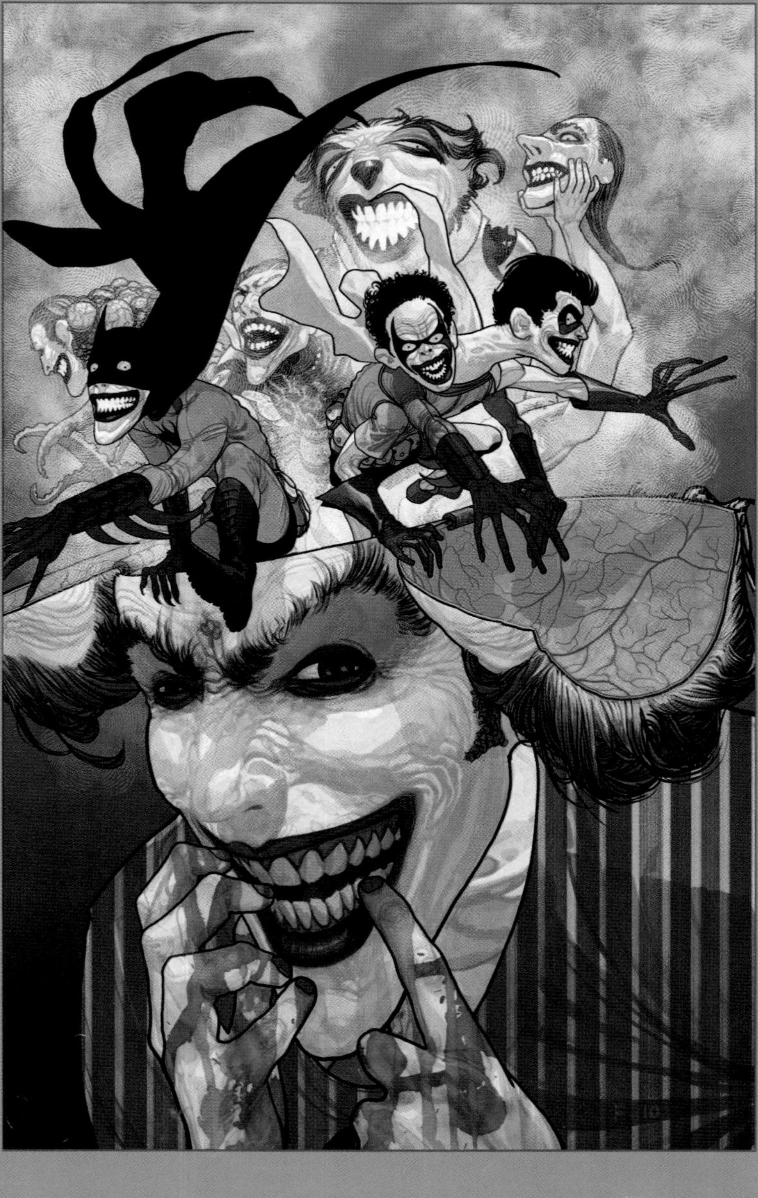

issue sixteen

This was both mine and Frank Quitely's finale on the BATMAN AND ROBIN title, and the cover, like so many of the others, had been planned back at the beginning of the run and stayed fairly close to the original intention.

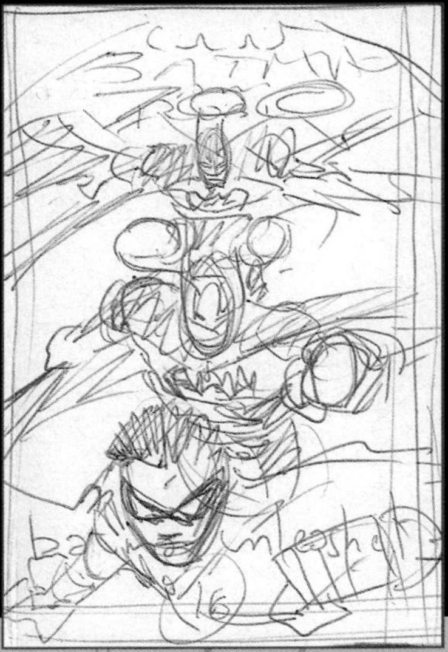

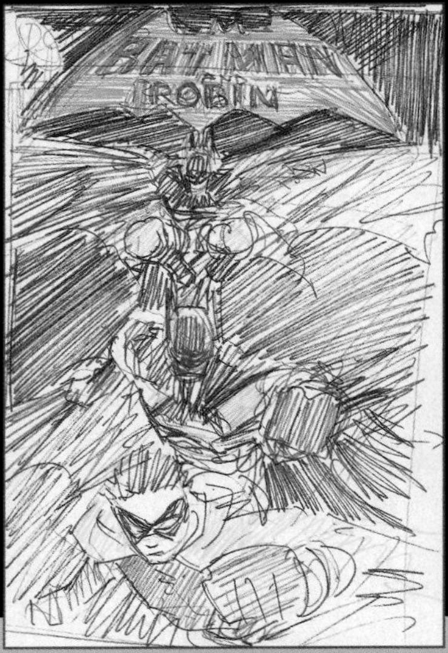
BATMAN
ROBIN

This was the first cover to feature our two Batmen — pinch-hitting Dick Grayson and the returned Bruce Wayne — together in action with Robin, and I'd imagined a kind of hierarchical "totem pole" stack of heroes with one above the other.

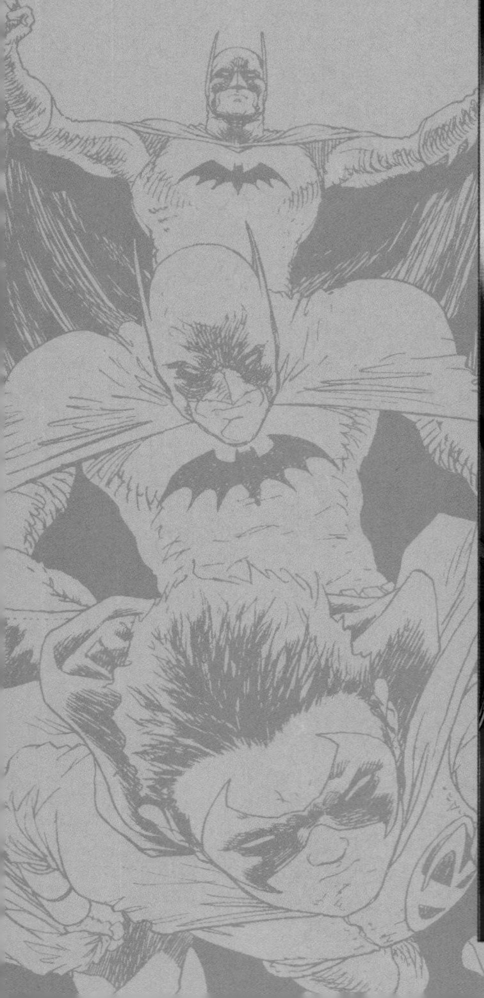

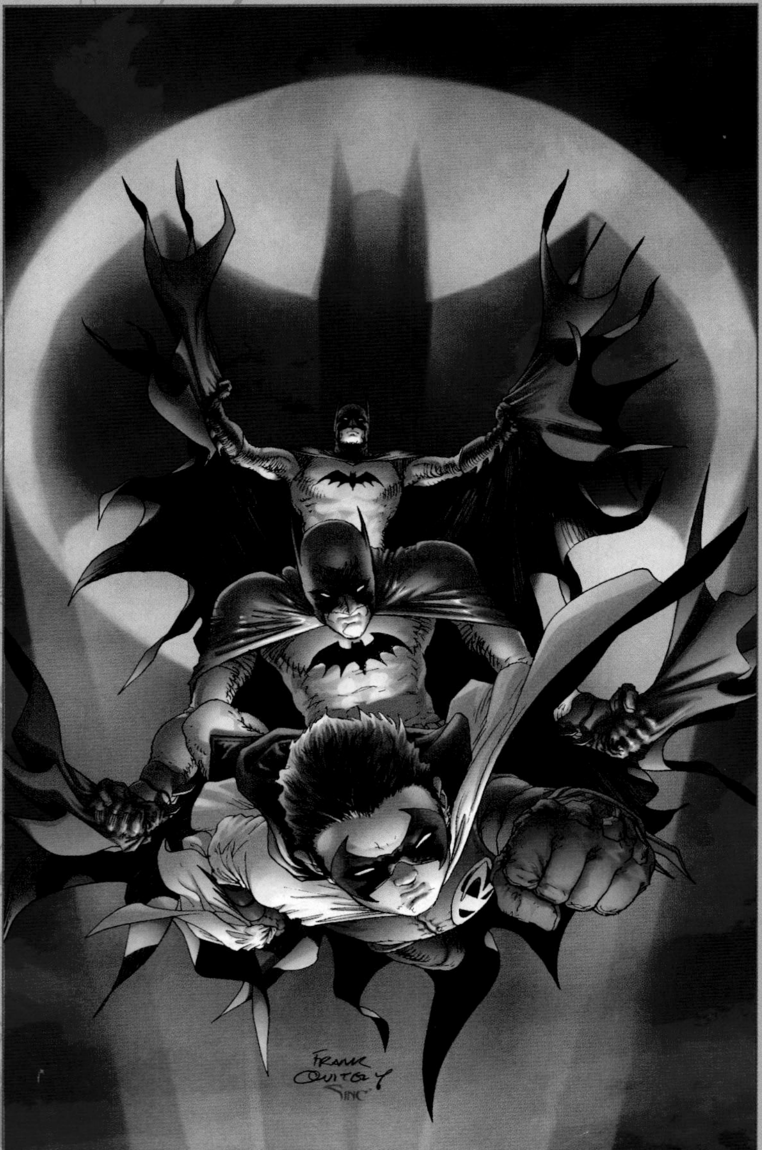
FRANK QUITELY

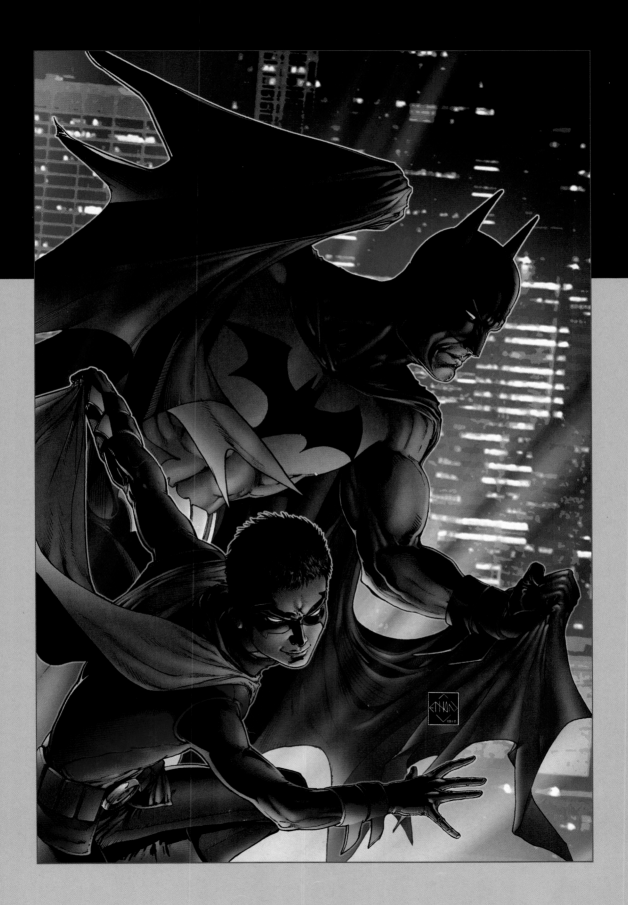

The Joker

Wreathed in Satanic imagery, it seemed only right that the sinister Doctor Hurt should suffer Lucifer's fate and experience the Fall from Heaven one more time — here in its most farcical form. I decided that the Joker's elaborately constructed and telegraphed multi-leveled assault on Hurt would end with one of the most basic of all jokes — the ol' banana peel gag — but when I read up on the origins of the banana pratfall I was surprised and delighted to learn that a particular variety of banana, known as a Big Mike, was considered the most effective prop, due to its special slipperiness and a tendency to rot quickly to a frictionless mush.

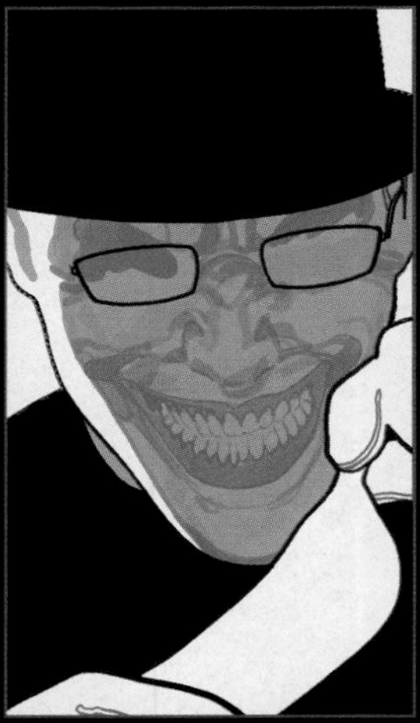

St. Michael was of course God's head enforcer and it was he who cast Lucifer out of Heaven. Ah, serendipity!

See also St. Thomas and burial alive.

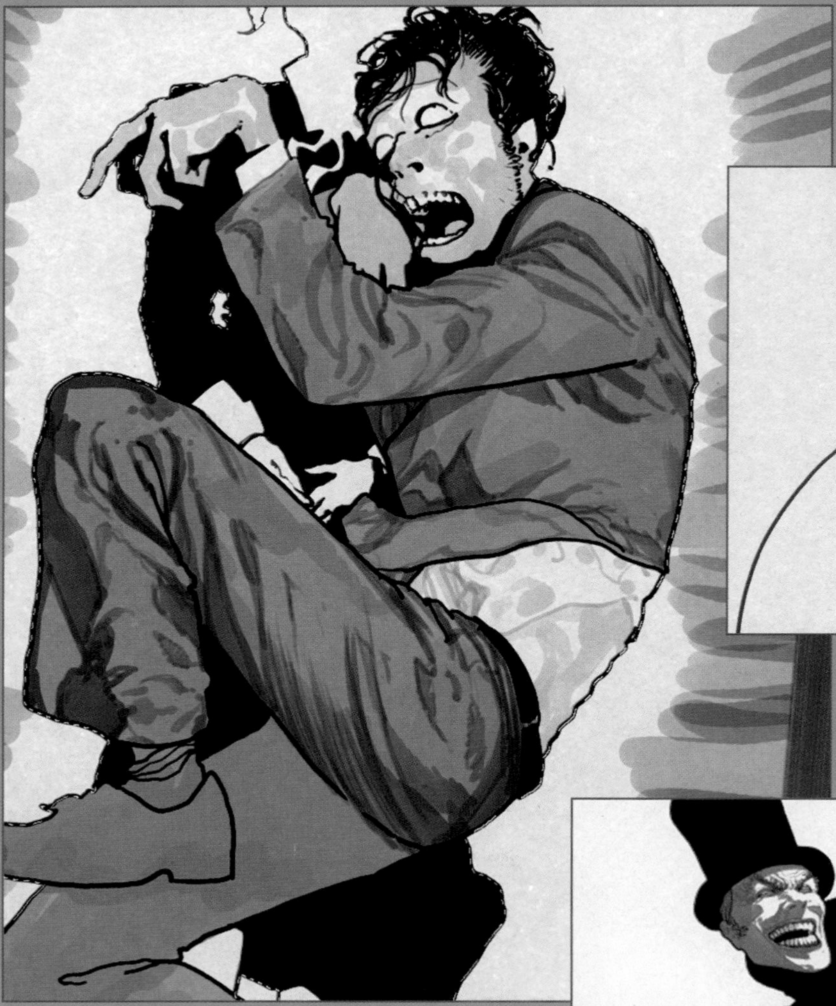

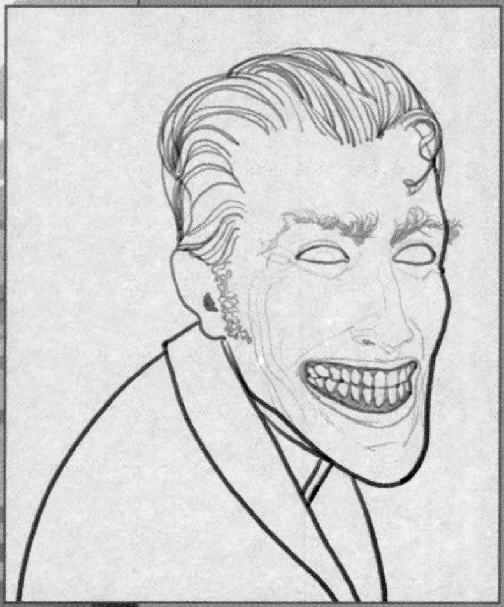

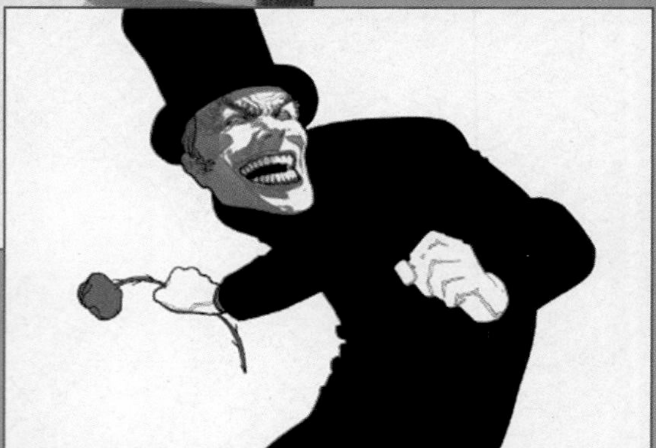

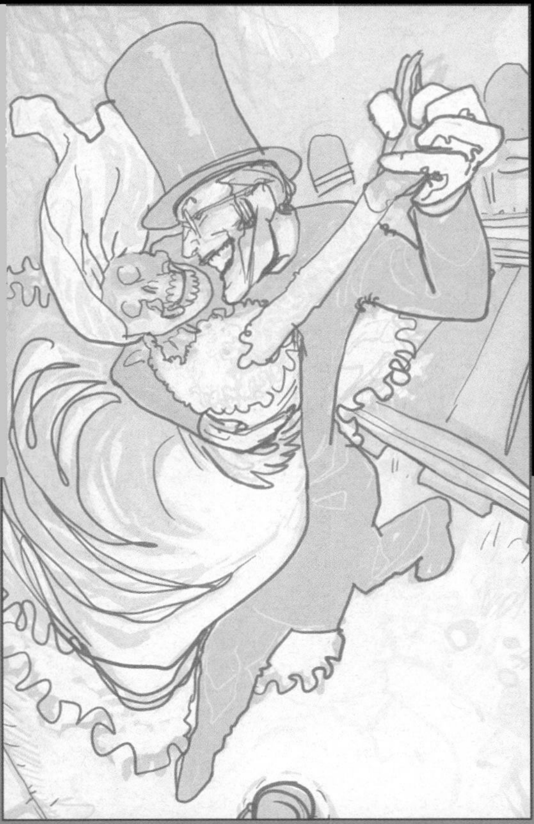

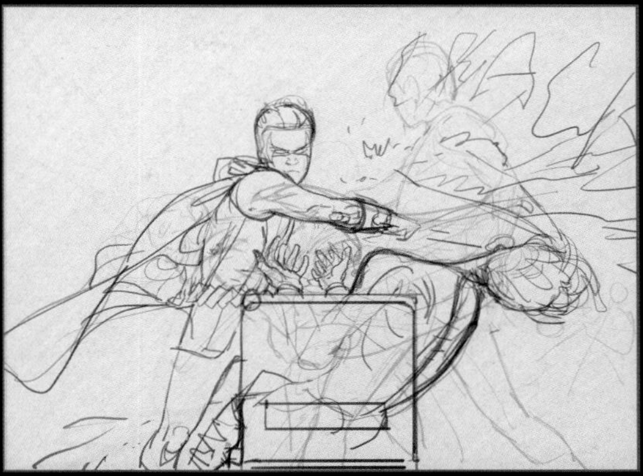

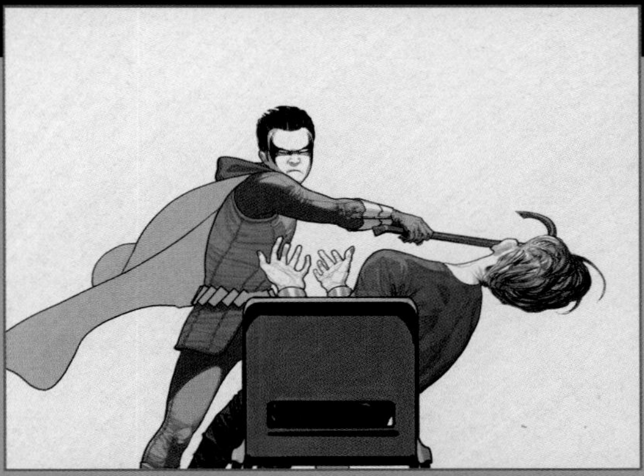

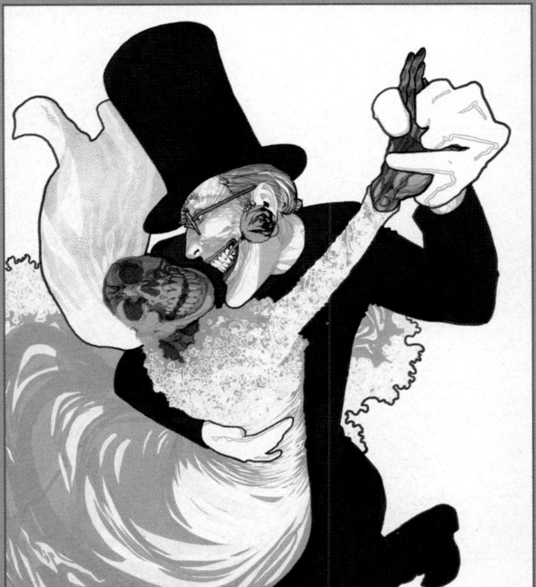

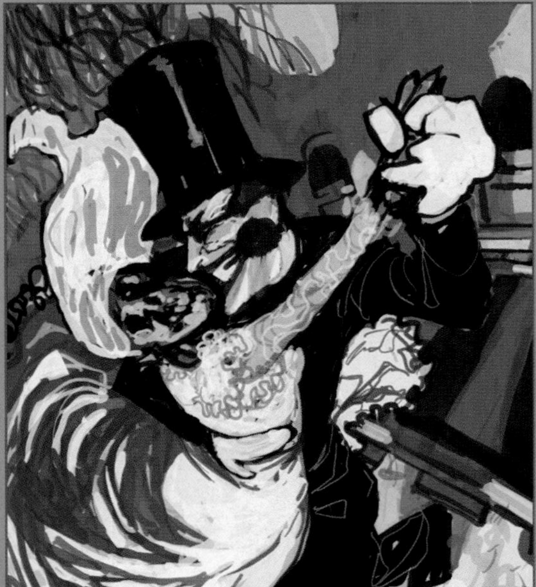

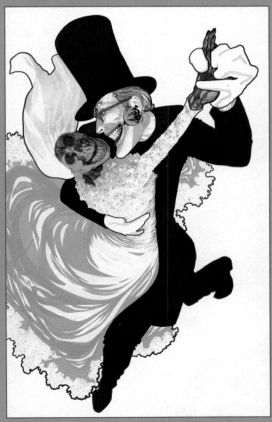

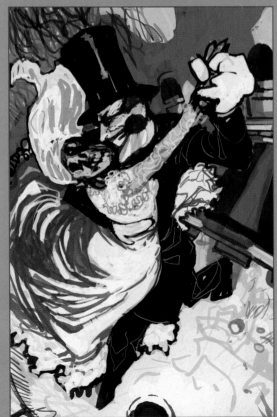

Professor Pyg

Like the Joker's elliptical, double-meaning dialogue, Professor Pyg's seemingly deranged rants are also stuffed with hidden allusions — in Pyg's case to a series of somewhat grotesque animal experiments that were conducted in the US at the mid-point of the 20th century and which inspired the self-styled Professor's horrific — and as yet unrevealed — origin story.

For those readers inclined to follow Pyg's schizophrenic snail trail to its grim source, the "Doctor Ha-Ha" that he refers to is both the Joker and behavioral scientist Harry Harlow, who conducted his infamous "wire mother/cloth mother" experiments on infant monkeys. "Doctor Johnny B. Damned," while it could as easily apply to Hurt, is also intended to suggest John B. Calhoun, whose Rockville barn rat population research makes fascinating (if uncomfortable) reading.

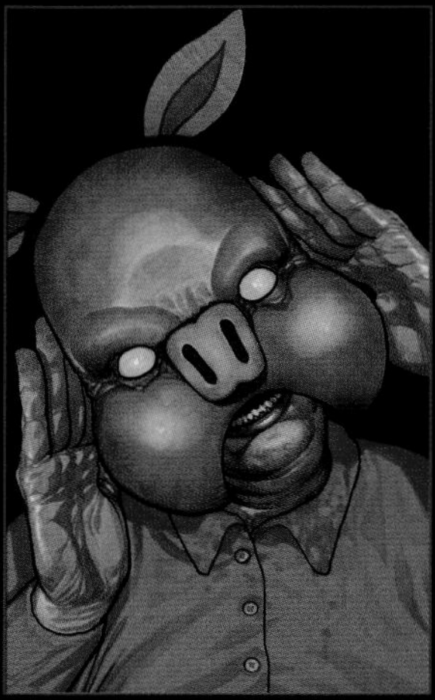

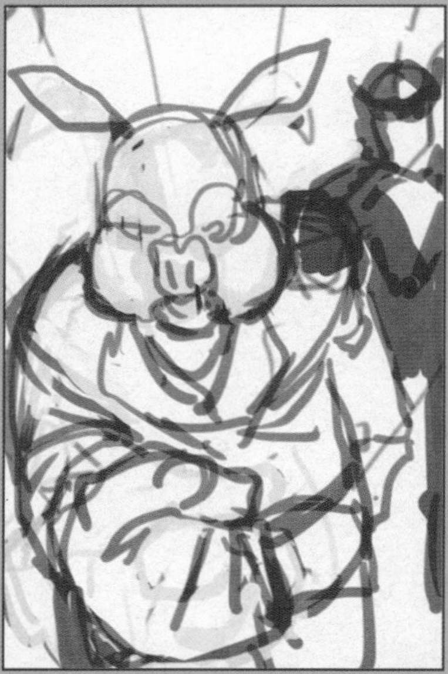

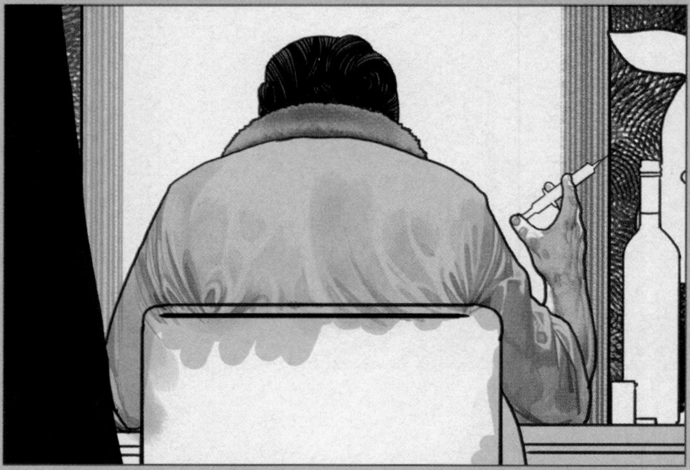

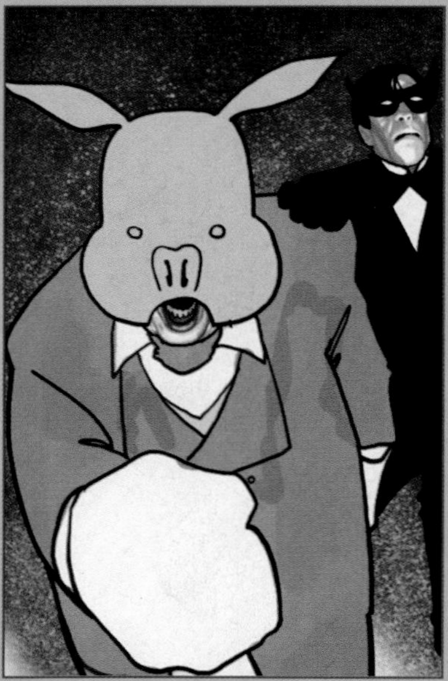

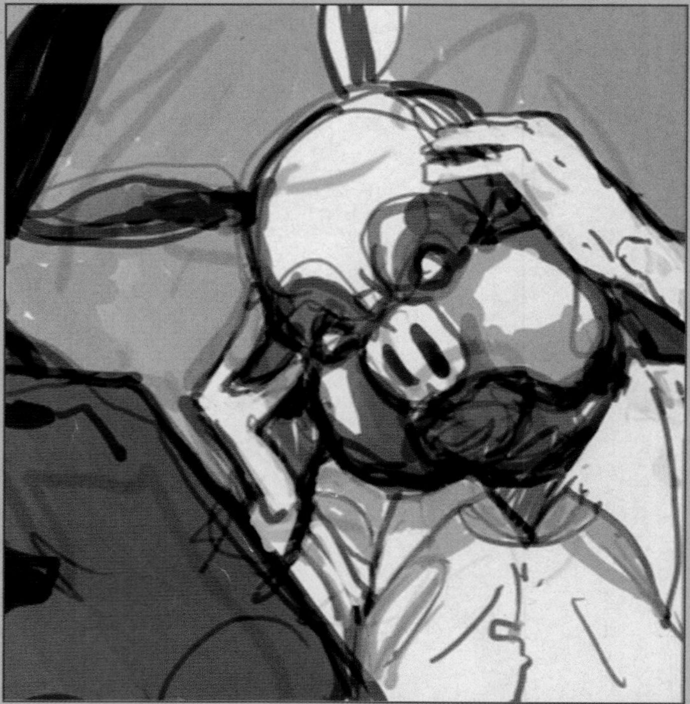

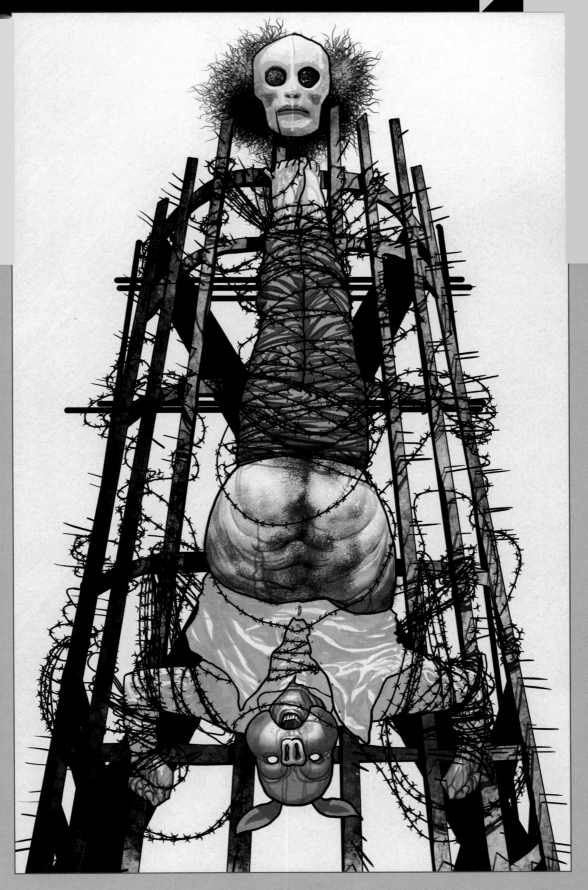

99 Fiends

With the exception of these characters, the villains in "Batman and Robin Must Die!" were returning faces: Doctor Hurt from "Batman R.I.P.," Professor Pyg from "Batman Reborn" and of course the perennial Joker.

The 99 Fiends were created as the enforcers for El Penitente (a.k.a. Doctor Hurt) and each was based on a different classical demon, with the majority of them deriving from the Goetia of the Lemegeton, a 17th century magical grimoire.

All 99 of the Fiends were carefully worked out, but in spite of my efforts I couldn't find a way to include them all on the page. Here, from the original script for BATMAN AND ROBIN #16, are a representative sample:

Glasyolabalas — a brutish man with a snarling dog on a leash and spiked collar.

Duke Agares is an older, wiry man with a crocodile skin coat and boots and a hawk on his arm.

President Buer is a big black guy with bows and arrows.

President Barbas has the lion as his totem and governs things mechanical, so maybe a little steampunk.

Duke Eligos, "a knight with a lance" — the homeless crustie demon version of Don Quixote.

Marquis Forneus is an outsize, hulking brute in green, with shaggy dyed-green hair and beard and filed teeth. The original demonic Forneus was described as a sea monster.

Duke Bune wears a necklace of three shrunken heads.

King Balam is a huge bear-like man wearing bear-like clothes, with double-pronged meat hooks that he grips in both fists and wields like Wolverine's claws. He and Forneus make a good pair of hulks.

Count Ronove is a big silent Native American bad man with a staff.

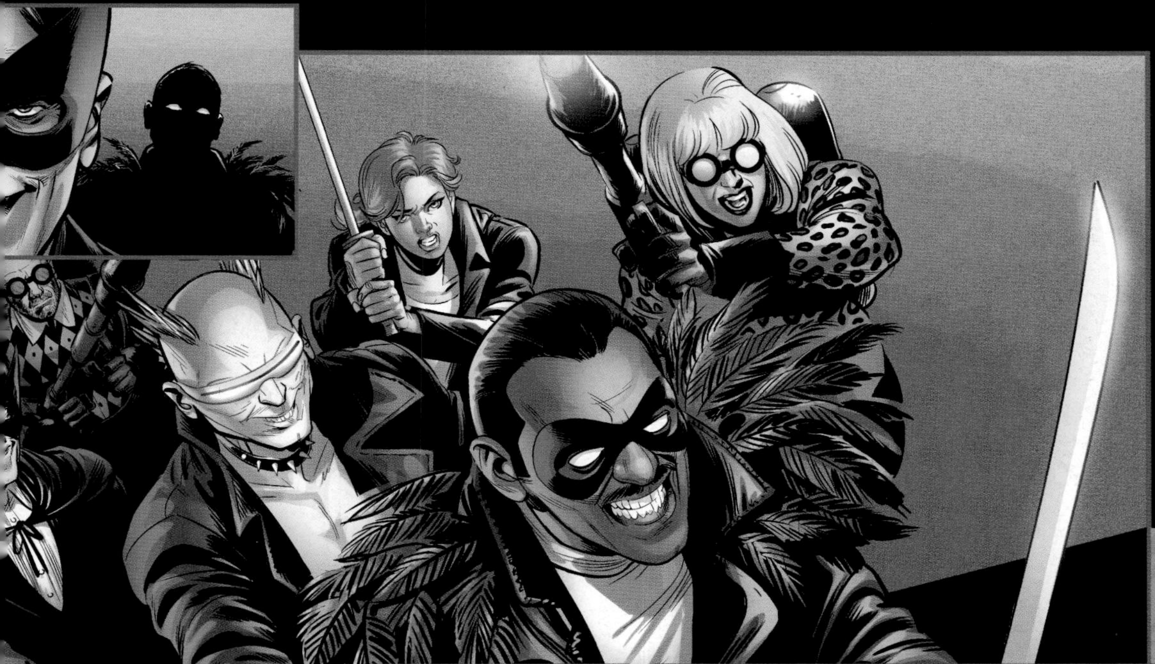

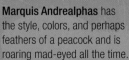

Marquis Leraje is a lithe, androgynous creature in green, with a bow and arrows like some evil Legolas.

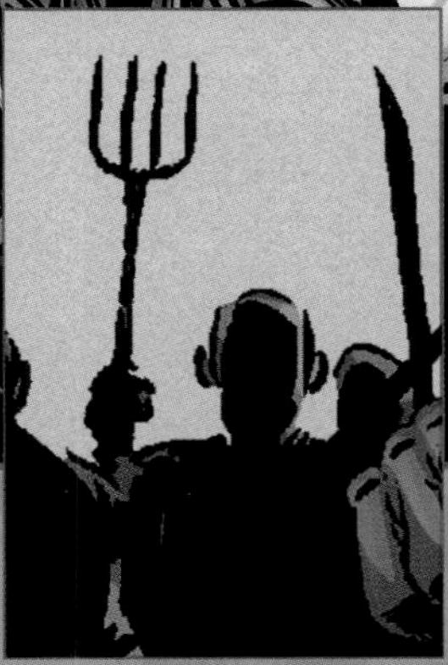

Sir Furcas, Knight of Hell, is another evil older man, hunched and sneaking, with a pitchfork as his weapon.

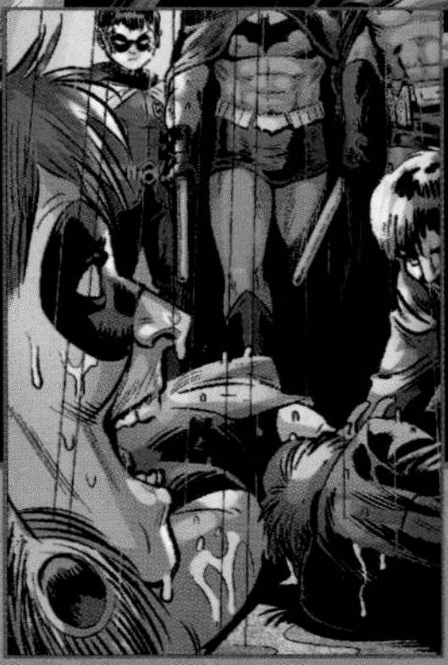

Marquis Andrealphas has the style, colors, and perhaps feathers of a peacock and is roaring mad-eyed all the time.

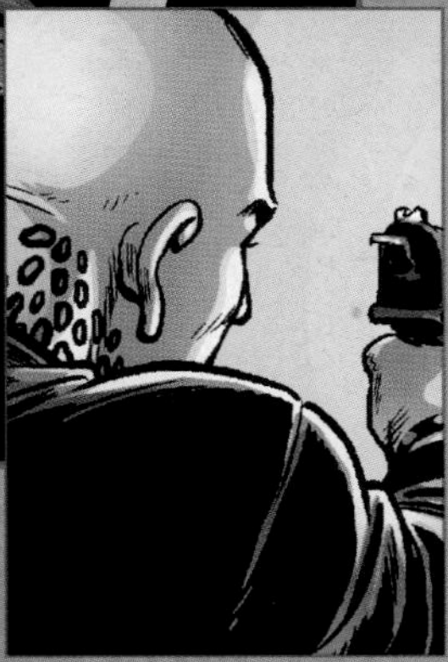

Prince Sitri, a beautiful man; so beautiful, in fact, that it's creepy, otherworldly. His cheekbones a little too high, too refined; his lips a little too pursed, becoming almost proboscis-like; his eyes hooded, like some awful aesthete looking down his nose at us. White skin and a powdered wig, like Adam Ant's Prince Charming beginning a transformation into an insect. His skin from the neck up to his jaw line is tattooed with leopard-like spots.

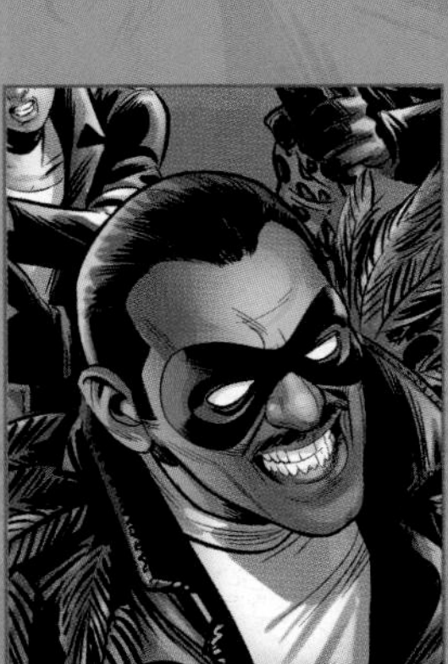

President Caim carries a sword and has "blackbird" clothes, characteristics or logos.

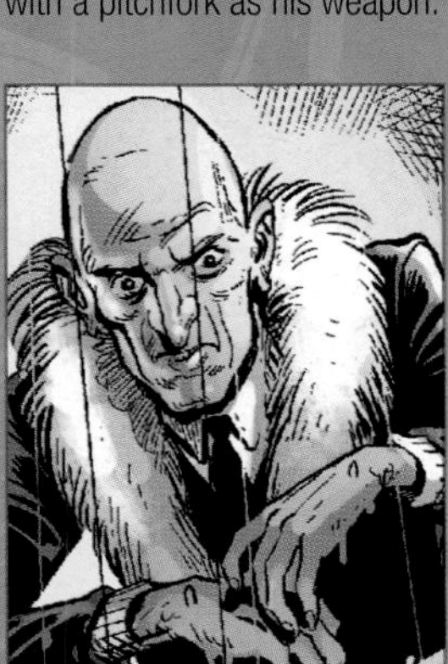

Duke Murmur is vulturous in aspect.

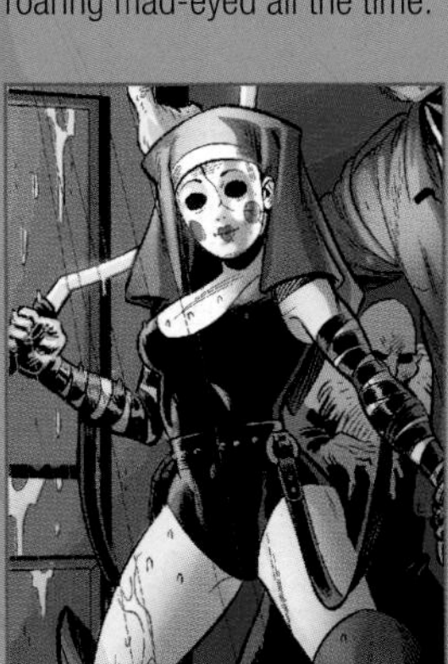

Duke Gremory is a fit woman wielding dual swords and wearing a nun-like outfit and a cracked doll-face mask of beauty.

BATMAN: THE RETURN

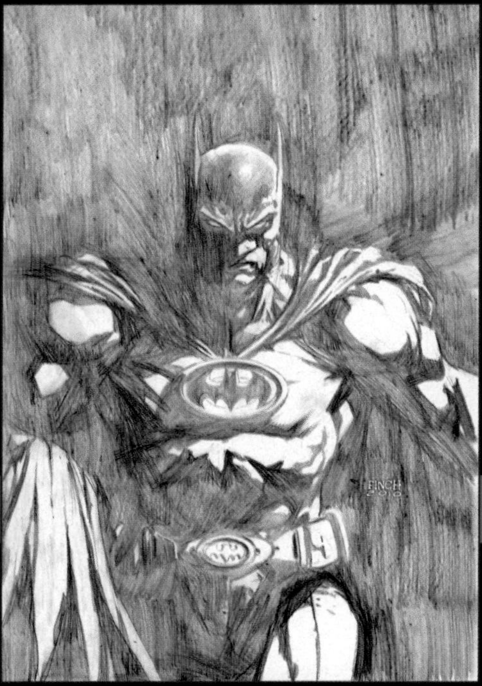

Following the supernatural, psycho-sci-fi of BATMAN: THE RETURN OF BRUCE WAYNE, which brought the original Caped Crusader back after over a year's absence, I wanted to change direction and tackle stories that were a little more international in scope, playing up the Bond-style gadgetry aspects of Batman's adventures. The high-tech Batman of THE RETURN, with his robots and jet-suits, was a nod in the direction of the future Batman from Alex Ross and Mark Waid's KINGDOM COME series.

I had no input in the cover art this time, leaving it to my collaborator David Finch to supply another of his iconic Batman images. Instead I sent David some thoughts on how we might revamp the details of the uniform and I include these below.

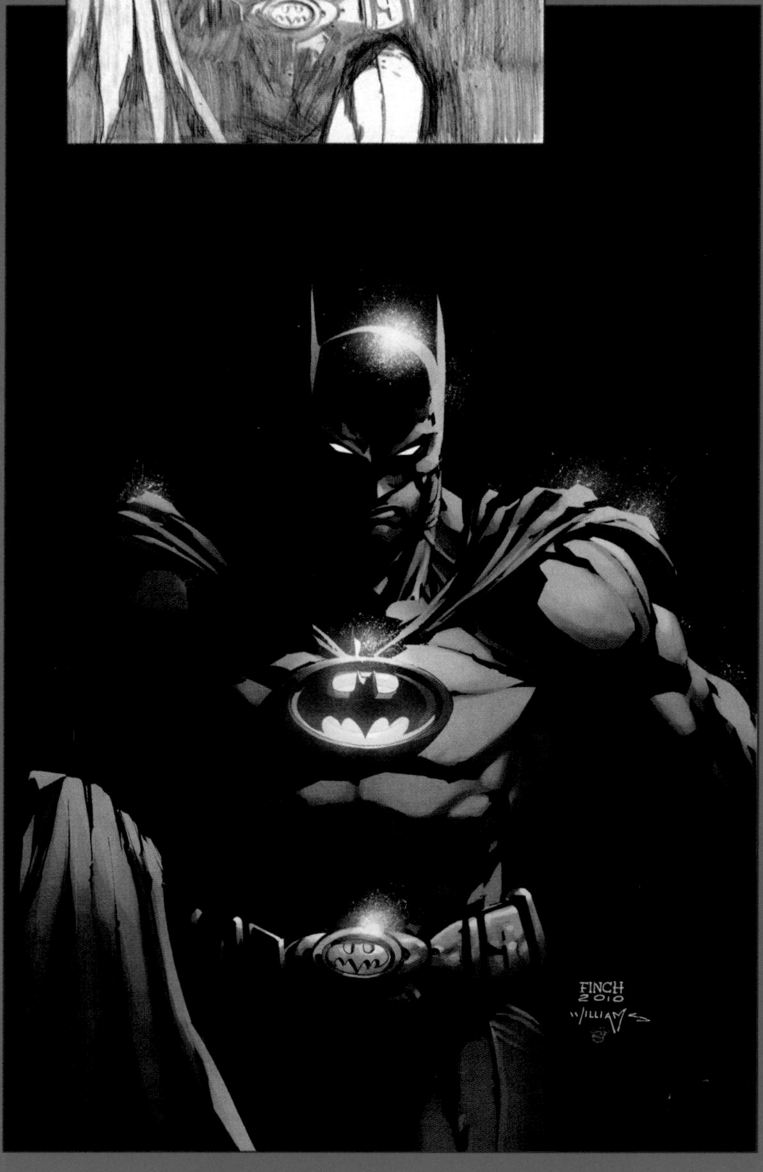
FINCH
2010

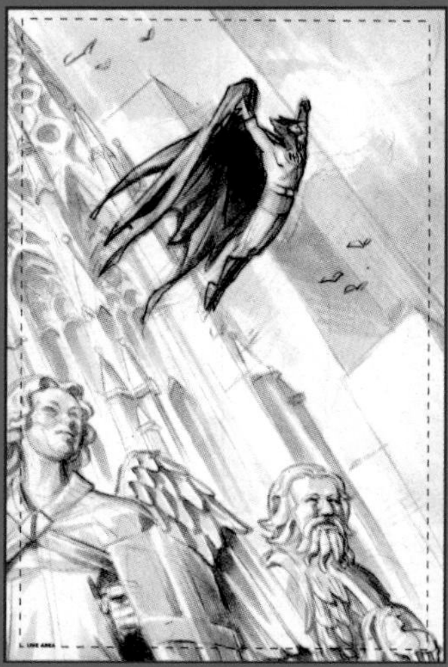

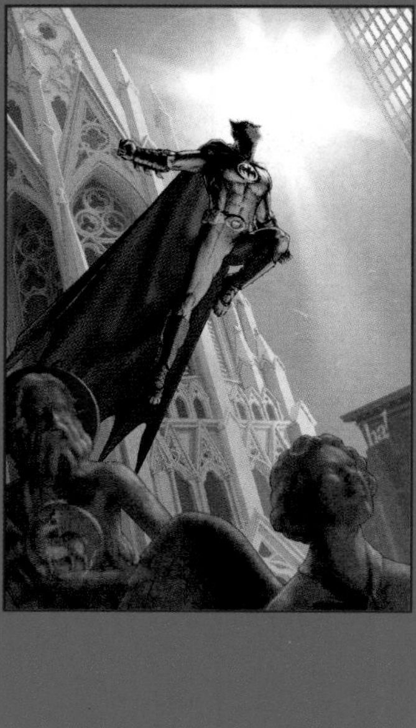

The Costume

As far as the Batman costume re-design goes, we need first of all to differentiate him from Dick Grayson — the current Batman — who will be continuing in his new role over in BATMAN AND ROBIN. Body shape comes into it — Bruce is generally depicted as more massive than the lithe and acrobatic Grayson, so the design can be constructed around his distinctive shape. It's easy to think the Batman costume is too "classic" to change much, but it's been tweaked on a feverish and consistent basis for 70 years, always retaining certain essential elements expressed through wildly different fabrics, decorations and drapery to achieve a fresh yet iconic look. Adam West's flimsy, hand-sewn nylon and George Clooney's outrageous disco armor are worlds apart visually and yet they are both clearly Batman.

With that in mind, here are a few thoughts to take into account or disregard:

General appearance

Today's audiences like a bit of authenticity, so the more "real" the costume looks — i.e., the more it seems like someone could actually put it together using the best available materials — the better. In *The Batman Handbook* Scott Beatty writes. "The costume is sewn from Nomex fabric, making it fireproof under even the hottest temperatures. More importantly the Batsuit is bulletproof, with Kevlar panels sewn into the shirt portion to protect Bruce's torso from ballistic projectiles, particularly in the area surrounding the bat-emblem." It also contains a mess of electronics, including a heating and cooling system and secure broadband communications.

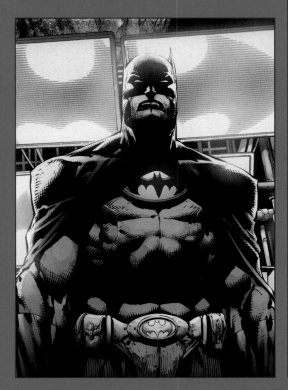

Utility belt

I tend to favor a chunky belt as more "mythic," in the sense that it looks like the girdles worn by Greek demigods and heroes. And it's good to work out exactly what he carries in those pouches, pods or cartridges. *The Batman Encyclopedia* has various takes on the contents, as does *The Batman Handbook*.

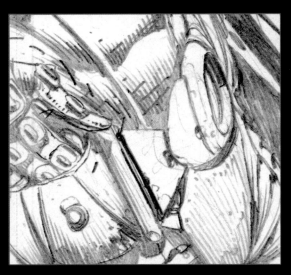

Shield

Should we bring back some version of the yellow shield and leave Grayson with the simple black bat chest emblem? Although comics fans traditionally dislike the shield, it has the virtue of having been part of one of the biggest marketing campaigns in history. Tim Burton's *Batman* burned that image of the black on yellow shield (which looks like a gaping toothy maw if you reverse figure and ground) into the cultural memory of nations.

The shield is also used in the early animated series episodes, and Batman wears it throughout Neal Adams's groundbreaking run and for about half of Frank Miller's THE DARK KNIGHT RETURNS so there's more to it than just its ties to the "goofy" *Batman* TV show. I thought it could light up to project a bat-signal onto a crime scene or dazzle an enemy. It could even be powered down to black or gray so that it camouflages itself when necessary.

Just in case this sounds like I'm making a case for the shield, I'll happily go along with whatever looks best in the final design. Ideas welcome.

Cape & cowl

Looking through the various versions of Batman, including the Bruce Timm animated stuff, I've noticed that he always looks especially cool when there are no highlights on his cape and cowl. So how about we try making a feature of a matte black cape and cowl combo with no reflected light — a pure silhouette that dissolves completely into the background shadows.

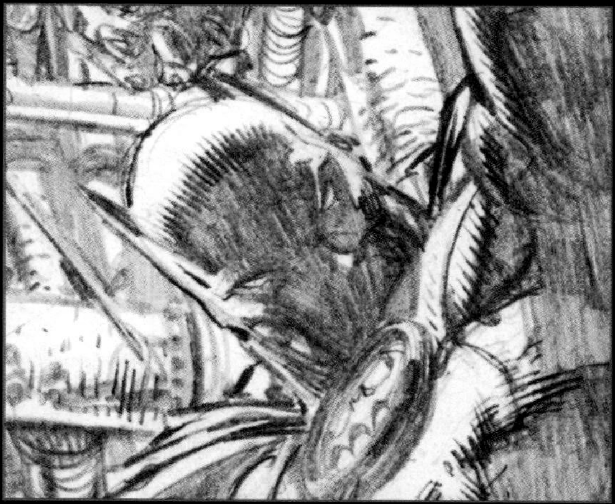

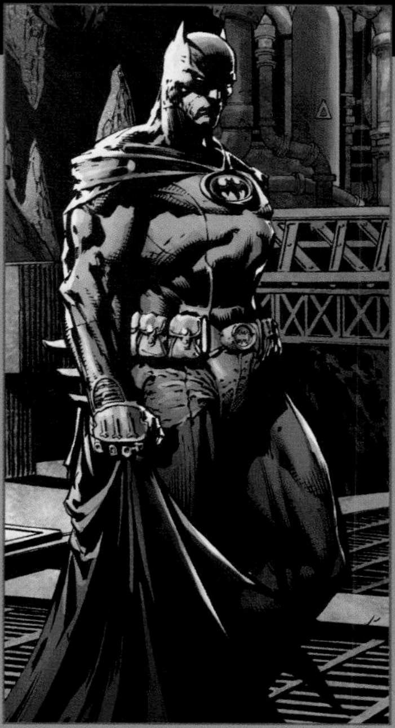

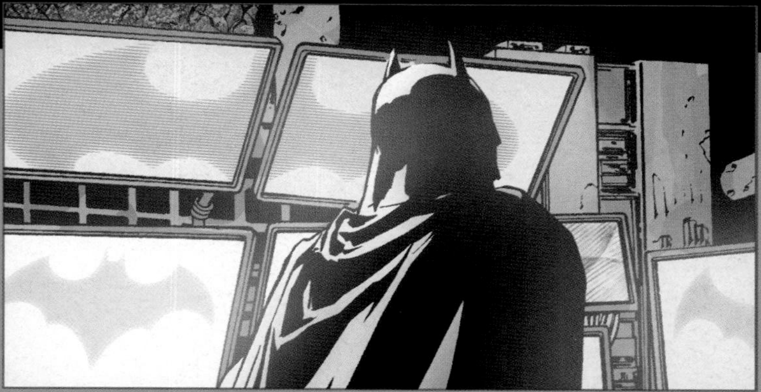

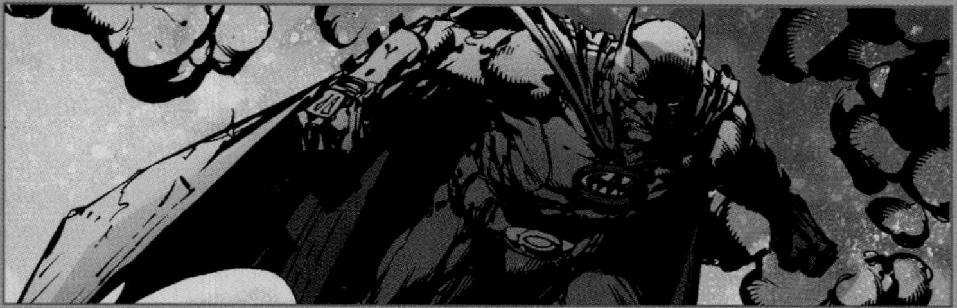

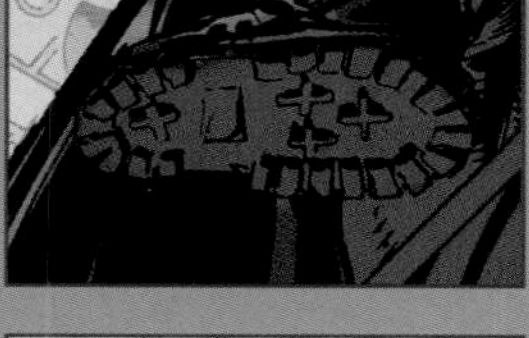

Boots

The rugged treads of the Frank Miller and Jim Lee versions look more bad-ass so have a look at some current and concept athletic shoe soles and find something cool and up-to-date or a little bit futuristic.

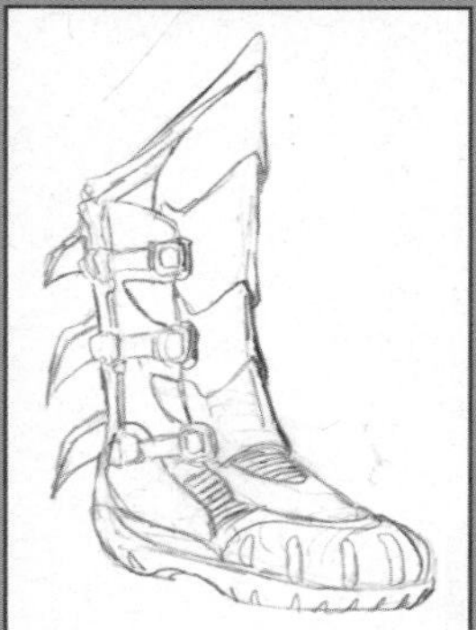

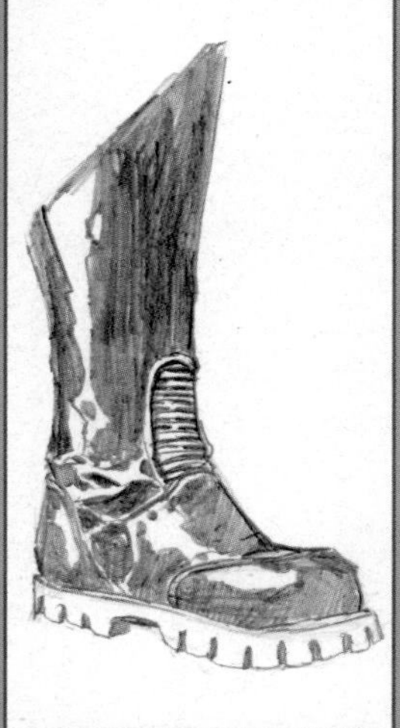

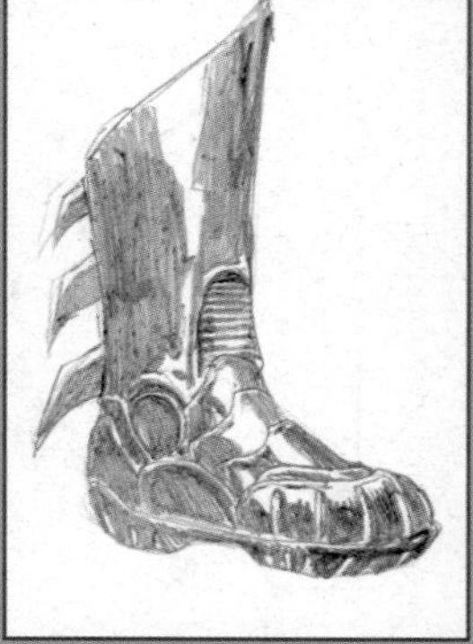

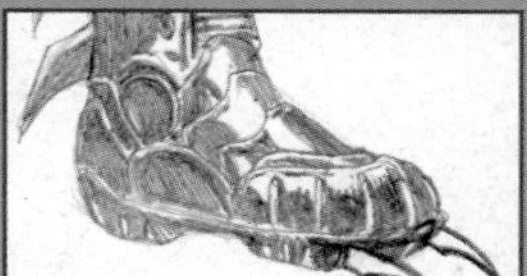

Gauntlets

As long as they still have the three bat-blades, I'm fine with it. Again, keep them real by checking out the latest in racing driver gloves or firefighter gloves and see if there are some interesting new designs that could inspire a bit of detail and modernity.

Ears

Long or short? Horns or vanes? Your call.

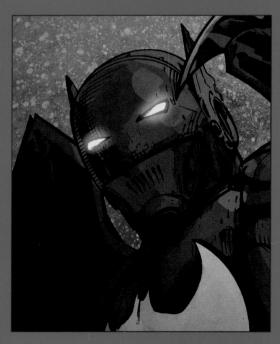

Basically, I imagine the new international sex god Bruce Wayne Bat-colossus to be a kind of "definitive" distillation of everything we like into one hardcore, modernized and coolly understated package. Batman's look stripped of frills and brought back to its basic essentials. We're looking for a costume that's convincing, functional, sexy and modern. Something that takes him back to his primal roots and adds your 21st century cool comics aesthetic.

Easy for me to say! Over to you, Mr. F!

— **Grant Morrison**
Scotland
February 2011

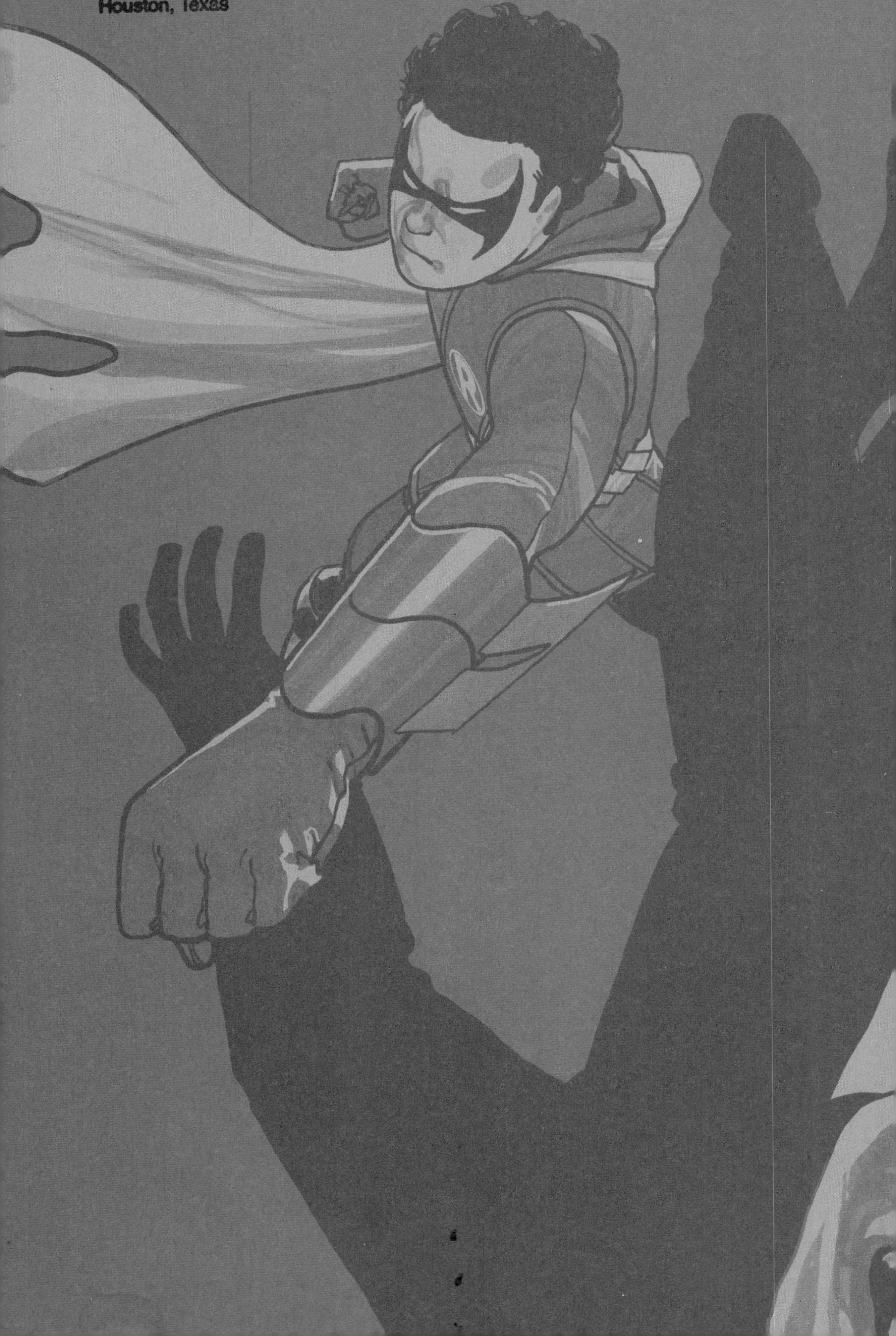